The Working Class in American History

A list of books in the series appears at the end of this volume.

TRADE UNIONS
AND
COMMUNITY

"Der Arbeit Siegeszug" (Labor's March to Victory), reproduced from *New Yorker Volkszeitung*, Dec. 22, 1889, courtesy of Tamiment Institute Library, New York University.

TRADE UNIONS AND COMMUNITY

The German Working Class in New York City, 1870–1900

DOROTHEE SCHNEIDER

UNIVERSITY OF ILLINOIS PRESS
Urbana and Chicago

Publication of this work has been supported by a grant from the Oliver M. Dickerson Fund. The fund was established by Mr. Dickerson (Ph.D., Illinois, 1906) to enable the University of Illinois Press to publish selected works in American history, designated by the executive committee of the Department of History.

This book is printed on acid-free paper.

An earlier version of chapter 4 was published in *Labor History*, 25 (Summer, 1985); used with permission.

Library of Congress Cataloging-in-Publication Data

Schneider, Dorothee, 1952–
    Trade unions and community : the German working class in New York City, 1870–1900 / Dorothee Schneider.
        p.   cm. — (The Working class in American history)
    Includes bibliographical references and index.
    ISBN 0-252-02057-X (alk. paper)
    1. Trade-unions—New York (N.Y.)—History. 2. German Americans—Employment—New York (N.Y.)—History. 3. Alien labor—New York (N.Y.)—History. 4. Community—New York (N.Y.)—History.
I. Title. II. Series.
HD6519.N5S36   1994
331.88'09747'1—dc20   93-24325
                                                                CIP

To Harry Liebersohn

Contents

Acknowledgments

This book started out as a dissertation for the University of Munich. With financial support from the German Academic Exchange Service most of the research was performed in New York City at the Tamiment Library of New York University and the New York Public Library. My thanks are therefore due to the staffs of these two libraries and to professors Hans Schmidt and Klaus Tenfelde for their helpful advice in this early stage of the work. Subsequently my work on the Samuel Gompers Papers provided many additional research opportunities and I am grateful for the critical insights into the history of the labor movement from my colleagues Peter Albert, Dolores Janiewski, Stuart Kaufman, and Grace Palladino. During a one-year stay at the National Museum of American History I had the opportunity to work with Cynthia Hoover and William Z. Steinway on the history of the Steinway family. As I moved to southern California and then to the University of Illinois, the criticism of colleagues continued to improve the manuscript in many ways. My thanks go to James Barrett, Hal Barron, Patricia Cooper, Tom Dublin, Eric Foner, Jackie Greenberg, John Jentz, John Laslett, Steve Ross, Rosemarie Scherman, Devra Weber, and Sean Wilentz.

Finally I owe a great deal to two historians who, for different reasons, always wanted to find out more about what became of the German working class. Herbert Gutman originally put me on the trail of the cigar makers and I benefited immensely from his persistent questioning of the standard myths of American labor history. Harry Liebersohn, who had originally crossed the Atlantic in the opposite direction to find out about the history of Germany, accompanied this project from the beginning. To have a fellow historian in the house meant that this project often provided more questions than answers. But his commitment also taught me that sometimes asking the right questions is more important than providing all the answers. In this sense I do hope that this book provides many new questions and some answers.

Introduction

The history of this study, like the history of the men and women it describes, has many beginnings. I grew up in post–World War II West Germany, in Heidelberg, a town known for its six-hundred-year-old university but also home to one of the largest concentrations of American troops in Europe. In this setting I, like many Germans of my generation, could not escape the confluence and conflict of German and American cultures. While, on the surface, Johann Sebastian Bach and Bob Dylan led an easy and peaceful coexistence, the simmering tensions between the friendly GIs and the many intellectuals of this university town never quite went away and were never explored. When I later began my studies at another small university town, I found few academics willing to probe into the relationship between Germany and America with a historical perspective and an interest in the reciprocity of these ties. German historians, political scientists, and literary scholars saw little reason to connect pre-1945 North American and German history, politics, and culture.

This lack of connection was not just the result of an oversight or of isolated thinking peculiar to German scholars. It was mirrored in a similarly narrow vision from the American perspective. As I found out when I entered graduate school in the United States in the mid-1970s, very little had been written in the previous twenty years about Germans in the United States or pre-1945 German-American relations. Germans had been the topic of a number of earlier, sometimes quite lengthy, studies such as Albert Faust's *The German Element in the United States* or more recent works by Carl Wittke.[1] Most of these studies, however scholarly, were celebratory as well and argued that above all Germans had contributed in fundamental ways to institutions that were central to American civic life such as the Constitution, the Revolution, or the Abolitionist movement.[2]

The perspective was almost entirely on events and personalities that were important from an American point of view; the analysis of German immigrants paid little attention to the peculiarities of their German backgrounds or their continuing differences. Beginning in the 1960s another spate of studies on German-Americans focused on a different theme in the relationship between the United States and Germany: conflicts and enmities, highlighted by the two world wars. Books on German-Americans in World War I or histories of German-Jewish refugees of the 1930s and, conversely, of the German-American *Bund* in the United States illuminated an important and problematic period in the relationship of the two countries.[3] But these studies rarely made the attempt to integrate the events of World War I and the Nazi period into the larger picture of German immigration or German-American relations in a general sense.

But what was most glaring to me as I started researching the history of the mass immigration of Germans to the United States was the absence of any comprehensive treatment of German immigration between the 1840s and World War I. With the exception of people from the British Isles, Germans were the largest group coming into the United States up to World War I, yet their story was essentially uncharted territory. With the arrival of community-focused social history in the 1970s this began to change, albeit slowly. Kathleen Conzen's study, *Immigrant Milwaukee,* and Alan Burstein's and Nora Faire's studies of Germans in Philadelphia and Pittsburgh respectively brought to light some of the contours of German immigrant communities in an urban environment. Conzen's study also highlighted the sheer diversity of institutional and cultural life among Germans in what was probably North America's most German city.[4] A number of urban and rural studies of German-American communities followed the seminal work of Conzen and others, stressing the diversity as well as certain distinct social characteristics of German immigrants in the mid-nineteenth century.[5] Some of the elements of diversity within the German immigrant community emerged clearly in these studies but they were almost wholly limited to differences that were demographically visible: Germans preferred certain occupations and neighborhoods over others, or they organized in ways that differed from those of other immigrants and native-born Americans.

Such answers did little to satisfy my original curiosity about the mutual influence of Germans in the United States and Americans on Germans. The culture and politics of German-Americans in particular seemed to develop much more dynamically than early community studies had indicated. As I began to focus my field of inquiry on these questions, a new generation of social historians, influenced by the seminal work of E. P. Thompson and Herbert Gutman, were beginning to publish and discuss similar questions about the convergence and divergence of immigrant cultures. I was fortunate to have Herbert Gutman as one of my teachers and to observe firsthand his attempts to delineate the emergence of the American working class in its broadest sense. Gutman wanted to describe the vastly complex process of class formation and class consciousness as it evolved throughout the nineteenth century on the American continent. In the case of North America, he contended, this process could only be understood in the context of the ethnic diversity which increasingly characterized North American society. The politics and culture of immigrant groups held particular interest for him; in order to understand the formation of the modern American working class one needed to study its origins among the immigrant working classes in the late nineteenth century.

By the mid-1980s numerous studies on non-English-speaking immigrants had appeared which had profited from Gutman's insights into the interactive nature of "foreign" and "American" cultures within the nineteenth-century working class in the United States. The first of these studies of immigrant communities dealt with Irish and Italian workers, but by the early 1990s their number had proliferated to include most ethnic groups and both large and minor industrializing cities and regions. These monographs have added considerable complexity to our knowledge of the formation of the American working class.[6]

While I benefited very much from the scholarship of historians who (like myself) work to combine the perspectives of working-class and immigrant history, I found that the case of German immigrants offered special problems. Most studies of Irish, Italian, or Slavic immigrants focus on people whose experience of immigration coincided with their entry into industrialized and urbanized society. The experiences of these immigrants in institutional politics were also limited, which is why institutional and organizational politics play a very minor role in most of the literature on them. For Germans the situation was quite different, however. In contrast to Irish, eastern European, and southern European immigrants, most Germans who migrated to America's large cities in the mid- to late nineteenth century were skilled workers with industrial experience; before the 1890s even the minority of unskilled workers had some familiarity with urban life in rapidly industrializing central Europe.[7] By and large late-nineteenth-century Germans migrated from one industrializing economy to another. This had consequences not only for their integration into the North American labor market but also for a political and cultural life in the New World which had no parallel in most other immigrant groups. Only one study, Bruce Levine's *The Spirit of 1848*, takes account of this special situation of German immigrants. Levine's main theme is the social and political impact of German immigrants on the antislavery debate in the Civil War era, and the book deals only with the very beginning of working-class politics in the industrial age.[8]

The particular situation of late-nineteenth-century German immigrants has only recently been taken into consideration by scholars— most of them German-based historians. The large-scale research and editorial projects directed by Dirk Hoerder (at the University of Bremen) and Hartmut Keil and John Jentz (at the University of Munich) have yielded useful information and insights which go beyond most research done on other immigrant groups. The work of these scholars has drawn attention to the primarily urban and industrial character of the German migration and has focused on the highly developed network of formal organizations among German immigrants and the political culture that flourished within it. This type of inquiry not only provides new insights about the shape of class formation and ethnic consciousness among German-Americans but also makes the meaning of politics a central part of its study.[9]

At the same time even the recent research on German-Americans usually remains within the self-imposed borders of ethnic history. The culture and politics described are the relatively insular ones of German-America only, and the researchers show how little survived beyond World War I. The following study will attempt to widen the field of inquiry to address an important but little-studied topic: the influence of German immigrant workers on the formation of the mainstream American labor movement. The German role in making an institution as "American" as the American Federation of Labor goes beyond the traditional perspectives of "ethnic" influence. It reaches into the world of centralized and bureaucratized institution-building which has long been considered an indigenous North American labor product (or at most a British export) with little connection to the supposedly more community-focused organizations of immigrants. This study will first give a portrait of the community and the local organizations of German immigrants as the soil on which the more bureaucratized and centralized structure of American labor grew in the late nineteenth century. By connecting the history of the community of workers with that of institutional labor I hope to overcome one of the more dissatisfying aspects of the "new" social history: its lack of connection to the "old" labor history, that is, the history of institutions and organizations of mainstream organized labor in the United States.[10]

In many ways the study of German working-class immigrants lends itself very well to this kind of connection. Germans played a core role in the early American Federation of Labor; certain leaders and certain organizational characteristics of AFL unionism were clearly influenced by traditions of organizing and politics that German immigrants had brought with them and adapted to the American political landscape. This connection may seem obvious, but it has been obscured by the desire of AFL leaders who, from the earliest beginnings of the federation, were devoted to projecting a solidly "American" identity. The desire to minimize the influence of immigrant political culture has also obscured the vision of historians of the AFL and has led to a view of the federation as an example of American exceptionalism par excellence. Using German immigrants as an example, this study will show how immigrants and their specific forms of organizing and political culture were at the core of the American Federation of Labor in its formative years.

I have chosen the largest American city—home to the largest community of German-speaking immigrants in the United States during the second half of the nineteenth century—as my main field of inquiry. As New Yorkers have always maintained (and many scholars have agreed), New York is neither typical for the history of North American political and social movements nor just a peculiar case. For the origin of working-class movements at least, nineteenth-century New York was the most important national center, from which much activism and many organizations came forth. An examination of labor politics in this city is therefore more than a case study for the origins of mainstream labor organization in industrial America. To trace the origins of the American Federation of Labor in one of the largest, most highly organized and politicized working-class communities in the country is to shed light on the social, political, and cultural origins of twentieth-century organized labor in the United States in general.

Because of its size and importance, New York has its own rich historiography, especially for the early and mid-nineteenth century.[11] For the second half of the nineteenth century the historiography is less rich, especially concerning the connection between immigrant communities and urban and labor politics.[12] Within this context the task of my study is twofold: to map out the history of one of the largest immigrant groups in late-nineteenth-century New

York City and to analyze the meaning and activities of labor politics for this community.

Within the historiography of the North American labor movement, this study attempts to fill in the notable gap between modern organized labor and one of the immigrant communities from which it came. In order to make it both comprehensive and comprehensible I have chosen to outline the general contours of the community in two introductory chapters first and then proceed to three case studies of trades in which German workers and organizers played a role in forming the early AFL—cigar makers, brewers, and bakers.

The first two chapters will survey the components of New York's German community—the overlapping structures of generations, classes, and neighborhoods that added up to its basic demographic matrix. The social order and political behavior among German New Yorkers was as much defined by their voluntary associations, to which so many of them belonged, as by their demographic origins. Chapter 2 will focus on a whole range of voluntary associations from religious denominations to trade unions to provide readers with a way to integrate the more in-depth analysis of the succeeding chapters into the general framework of the German community of the city.

The core of this study (sections two and three) will deal with the origins and development of three predominantly German-American unions in New York City and their community of workers. All three unions had their roots among German-American socialists, yet they all ended up as important members of the American Federation of Labor early on. Section two (chapters 3, 4, and 5) is devoted to the German-American cigar makers and their community during the 1870s and 1880s. It will outline how one of the strongest unions in the early American Federation of Labor, the Cigar Makers International Union (CMIU), emerged from a community of workers with few traditions and an unusually heterogeneous work force. The example of the German-American cigar makers will show that any preconceived notions of what "German" meant in the context of the Old or the New World are inadequate in describing this group of workers, who succeeded in forging solidarity out of a largely invented sense of craft tradition and shared history.

The history of the German cigar makers comes first not just because their union was one of the first of the modern American labor movement but also because this group of workers charted a path which, though hard to follow, would provide a standard of comparison for other unions in later years. The founder and first president of the American Federation of Labor, Samuel Gompers, grew up in New

York's German-American cigar makers' community, and for him and many of his colleagues affiliation with German-American workers led to the adoption of German-American traditions of organizing and politicizing workers. To show how the ideas of organizing and politics played themselves out in a larger arena of New York politics, chapter 5 will be followed by a brief chapter describing and analyzing the involvement of German-American labor in the Henry George campaign of 1886.

In many ways the mid-1880s gave German-American labor organizations their moments of highest visibility. As the succeeding chapters on the German brewery workers and the German bakers demonstrate, the late 1880s were a more difficult and more problematic period for German-American unions. The brewers and the bakers, whose national unions grew out of New York City, were stalwarts of the early American Federation of Labor, like the cigar makers. But in other respects these largely German-American unions have little in common, for in contrast to the cigar makers, both brewers and bakers were much beholden to their respective craft traditions, many of which survived under the peculiar circumstances of American capitalism in the Gilded Age. Traditional ideas of work and craft status proved to be remarkably enduring and important in the forging of a union movement which tried to prevail over conditions of rapid mechanization, industrialization, and pauperization. German socialist traditions, too, nurtured the struggle to organize New York's workers. The link with the craft unionism of other AFL unions and the socialism of German-American organizations put the cigar makers, brewers, and bakers at the crossroads of many struggles during the late 1880s and early 1890s. Ultimately it was the bureaucratic centralism common to both the socialists and the AFL which would provide continuity and a measure of success to both movements.

By the early twentieth century the relationship between German immigrant workers and the American labor movement had come full circle. While in the 1870s the cigar makers had been pioneers in building an American labor movement out of a heavily ethnic organization, by the 1890s the American Federation of Labor contained many other German-American unions representing diverse trades. This book describes the process which made "American" out of "German" forms of organization and politics. In doing so I also want to redefine the meaning of German ethnicity and Americanness. As it will turn out, each side of the equation is shaped by the other: the Germanness of some labor organizations will be affected by the nature of the immigrants' experience in the New World, while American labor turns out to be influenced by many characteristics of German political and organizational culture. In the conclusion, I will try to assess what such a dialectical relation implies for the history of main-stream labor in the United States. In this study, I try to understand the relationship between North American and German culture and politics and to go beyond contributionism toward the integrated view that this complex relationship deserves.

1

New York's German Immigrants: Parameters of a Community

Generations, Origins, Classes

Old-Timers

On June 9, 1850, Heinrich Engelhard Steinweg and his family landed in New York harbor. Together with hundreds of other German immigrants he had left central Europe about a week earlier on the steamer *Helene Slomann,* which had sailed from Bremen to the New World. As the Steinways this family would become known as one of the wealthiest immigrant dynasties in Gilded Age New York, but in 1850 little distinguished them from thousands of others who were landing in Castle Garden, New York's immigrant station.[1]

Heinrich Steinweg was a cabinetmaker who, at age fifty-three, had left behind a modest furniture and instrument-making business in his hometown of Seesen in Germany's Harz mountains. The Harz was a hardscrabble area in the small duchy of Braunschweig, where people tried to eke out a living in agriculture, mining, and various lumber-related trades. The Steinweg family had old roots in the area and for decades Heinrich Steinweg had continued the traditional settled life of a modest artisan trying to feed a large family in this mountainous region.[2] Nine children—three daughters and six sons—survived infancy. By the late 1840s his three oldest sons, Christian Friedrich Theodor (born in 1825), Carl (born in 1829), and Heinrich (born in 1830), could help their father as trained furniture makers and piano builders. By then the elder Steinweg probably belonged to the more prosperous segment of the working classes in the Harz, for he owned a house (part of which he rented out for cash) and was able to stay afloat as an independent cabinetmaker.[3] But Steinweg's chances for lasting prosperity were not good in mid-nineteenth-century Germany. Furniture making, his bread-and-butter trade, had become very competitive, with furniture manufactories replacing artisan

shops on the low end of the market (which was doubtless of importance in such relatively poor areas as the Harz). Making musical instruments for the homes of the middle class was a much more lucra-
tive and less competitive trade; but despite the fact that small square
pianos became the rage for the homes of even modest burghers by
the mid-nineteenth century, there was not enough of a market in a
small town such as Seesen to support a piano builder. Chances for
relocating or expanding the business into a better-off area or larger
town were limited for Steinweg, for as an illiterate craftsman with no
formal musical education, he had few opportunities to make the necessary business and social connections to the middle class. He would
always be regarded as a simple craftsman in the context of German
society. Only his eldest son, Theodor, was better educated and more
at ease with the middle classes (and with these advantages was able
to establish a successful piano-making business later in the city of
Braunschweig).[4]

Heinrich Steinweg's circumstances as a craftsman and head of a
family were not unusual for many artisans who came to the United
States in the 1840s and 1850s, even if he was a bit better off than most.
The fortunes of artisans, small shop owners, and farmers in the German states were precarious in the first half of the nineteenth century.
Periodic agricultural crises, a population explosion, and steadily wors-
ening underemployment and unemployment made the economic situation for the lower classes in Germany unsettled at best. For artisans in particular the abolition of the old guild rules brought a time
of great uncertainty and, in many trades, proletarianization for journeymen and small masters as well. While specialized artisans like the
Steinwegs were apparently suffering more from the uncertain economic and political climate than from economic destitution, tailors
and shoemakers were radicalized by the rapid pauperization of their
trades. In particular the journeymen in these trades became the politicized core of a movement to change the economic and political circumstances of their lives.[5]

The activism of journeymen took place within the remnants of
guild-type organizations for journeymen, so-called *Gesellenbruder-
schaften* (journeymen brotherhoods), that were rapidly transformed
from mutual aid groups to politicized groups of workers demanding
political change, freedom from oppressive regulation by the remaining masters' organizations and the state, and a better livelihood. These
demands were voiced often amid the latent economic crisis and political unrest of the 1840s. In 1848 the scattered protests erupted into
a full-scale political upheaval, carried out by dissatisfied students and

a restless urban middle class as well as journeymen. Each of these groups had distinct and sometimes opposing agendas and in the end they failed to bring about most of the changes they had sought.[6] The revolution did not establish a united Germany, a constitutional monarchy, or significantly improved civil rights for citizens of the different German states. Despite initial attempts at restoring guild legislation to protect master craftsmen, within a decade of 1848 most German states had done away with the last remaining guild privileges, while at the same time suppressing the nascent labor movement that had emerged from the journeymen brotherhoods in the Revolution of 1848. The seesaw course between ineffectual protection and liberalization of artisanal laws did not yield benefits for most journeymen artisans and small masters, while the backlash against their organization meant that their voice was lost in the political landscape of the restoration era of the 1850s and early 1860s.[7]

The events of 1848 and the years thereafter triggered an increase in the rate of emigration from Germany to the United States over the already growing numbers of the 1830s. As in the 1830s, most emigrants of the 1848 generation fled deteriorating economic conditions at home; many had been touched by, but few had been directly involved in, political activism in Germany. The emigrants reflected those trades that had suffered a decline in status and income in Germany but were not completely pauperized: tailors, shoemakers, and cabinetmakers (such as the Steinweg family) were numerous, while members of the building trades were more inclined to stay, since they were somewhat better off. Weavers or landless laborers, on the other hand, were usually too poor to have the means for overseas emigration. The impetus to leave was strongest in the densely populated areas of southern and southwestern Germany (Bavaria, Württemberg, Baden, and Hesse) as well as in some of the small provinces of central Germany (such as the Steinwegs' home, the duchy of Braunschweig). Although these were not considered the most backward areas of Germany, they had the largest relative overpopulation of journeymen and skilled workers and the most inefficient agricultural structure as well.[8]

The Steinwegs' family fortunes after the failed Revolution of 1848 were typical. The precarious stability Heinrich Steinweg had achieved as a craftsman was as threatened as ever during the period of political stagnation immediately following 1848. The economy languished—which for the Steinweg family meant that while factory production was not yet a serious threat, customers for handmade furniture were rare, and those who could afford musical instruments were even rarer.[9] Faced with such uncertain prospects, the Steinwegs arranged for their departure to North America, the preferred goal for those who could afford to emigrate overseas rather than to the industrializing cities of Europe. But this was not a hasty affair. In 1849 the elder Heinrich prepared the way cautiously, sending his second oldest son ahead of the rest of the family to judge conditions in New York. Apparently Carl reported back favorably, for a year later the other Steinwegs prepared to move too. They got the necessary permits from the authorities (except the military draft board, which apparently was not notified), sold their house, had their second youngest son Albert confirmed as a Lutheran, and booked passage on the steamer.[10]

The Steinwegs were able to pay for steamship tickets rather than for the slower and less comfortable trip by sail taken by most immigrants; in other respects, though, they differed little from other Germans arriving in unprecedented numbers during the decade between 1848 and 1858. In 1854 alone, over 176,000 German immigrants landed in Castle Garden. The figure did not reach such heights again until after the Civil War, but there were never fewer than 28,000 newcomers per year in the nine years between 1847 and 1856. The Forty-eighters, as they were soon called, swelled the ranks of Germans living in the city from 24,000 to over 95,000 within the 1850s (the overall population of the city increased by about 70 percent during the same time period). By 1855 over 15 percent of all inhabitants of New York City were German-born.[11] A disproportionate number of immigrants in the 1850s and 1860s came from the German southwest, although northerners, usually subsumed as "Prussians" (Saxons, Westphalians, and people from Schleswig-Holstein), and immigrants from the northern cities of Hamburg and Bremen were also quite numerous.[12]

Like the Steinwegs the majority of the newcomers were skilled workers and craftsmen who had come for a variety of reasons: social, economic, and political motives blended with a desire for escape from the confines of old-world society to adventure in the new. The minority of immigrants who came to escape political persecution tended to be middle class, and more urban in background. Even though they were a small group numerically, the political refugees added significant variety to the social and political makeup of the German immigrants. No longer were Germans just proletarian and rural folks. The political refugees added a peppering of teachers, academics, and other professionals, most of whom kept their political culture alive through a network of voluntary associations, journals, and other publications. In contrast to the Irish (the other large immigrant group of the 1840s), and also in contrast to earlier generations of Germans, the members of the Forty-eighter generation included a broad mix of backgrounds, social classes, and political interests. Heterogeneity would be a highly significant characteristic of the German-American community for decades to come.[13]

Nonetheless, some characteristics were common to almost all German newcomers. One was their tendency to live with families after their arrival. Germans did not always come with their own families; as in other immigrant groups, many single young men came too. But they tended to join families, either as relatives or acquaintances from the old country or as paying boarders. The Steinwegs were typical in this respect. During his first year in America, Carl Steinweg probably boarded with a German-American family rather than stay at a boardinghouse as did young men from other countries. Once Carl had scouted out the territory, the other Steinwegs came all at once as a family with the exception of Theodore, who remained in Germany for the better part of the next decade.[14] The family orientation of German New Yorkers furthered geographical and social stability, especially in comparison with other immigrants. Stanley Nadel has calculated that 80 percent of all German-American families with (New York–born) children who could be located in the 1880 census on the Lower East Side had lived in New York an average of sixteen years, which implied that many of them must have come during the 1850s or before, since the 1860s were not a time of large-scale immigration from Germany.[15] Germans, despite their large numbers and considerable social diversity, thus do not easily fit into the picture of high geographic mobility and, by implication, social instability. Their preference for family migration and family living, as well as their tendency to stay put in the metropolis, gave them a higher potential for community formation during the second half of the nineteenth century.

Demographic peculiarities contributed to the stability and family context of German immigrants. One of the most important ones was the fact that Germans already constituted a century-old community in the city by the time the Forty-eighters arrived. Germans had immigrated in appreciable numbers during the colonial era and the early decades of the Republic. Very little is known about these early immigrants, most of whom seem to have been merchants and craftsmen; they were numerous enough to support a German school, a German Lutheran Church (founded in 1748), and a German Reformed Church as well. In 1784 some of these early German New Yorkers founded the "German Society of the City of New York" in order to help incoming immigrants. The German community slowly became more visible in the city as the number of middle-class and artisan immigrants increased during the 1830s. At that point New York's first German neighborhood began to take shape in what was later to be called the Lower East Side. Property owners in this part of town were often German-Americans who had built brick row houses to live in or rent out. By the 1840s the numbered streets north of Houston Street were home to thousands of Germans.[16]

The Steinwegs, like other newcomers of the 1850s, rented a house in this area which soon became too small for their needs. As a German immigrant family they seem to have received a continuous flow of new arrivals from the old country who stayed with them until they got established in a job and a home. "We always have problems with taking somebody into the house, given the small size of the rooms here," wrote Charles Steinway (who anglicized his name soon after his arrival, as did his brothers and father) to his older brother Theodore in Germany. But the Steinways kept putting up guests, furthering the kind of informal networks of support among family and friends that were so important for German immigrants on their way to social and economic adjustment.[17] Such help kept a chain of immigrant generations alive and well acquainted with each other. In fact, family and interfamily association was probably also the major link that helped the newer immigrants gain an economic foothold in a labor market that was already extremely competitive for the kinds of trades most German immigrants represented.[18]

As far as their economic well-being was concerned, the Steinway family was rather fortunate. The brothers and their father rapidly established themselves in New York as artisan workers in its growing piano industry. Charles, his brother Henry, and their father earned between three and six dollars a week immediately working in different piano manufactories, most of them headed by German-born craftsmen. These were only middling wages, but the family could pool the income of its four male wage earners (the younger Steinways remained unmarried), who were lucky enough to find more or less continuous employment in a growing industry until they opened their own shop in 1853. Other workers of their generation met with less success. The majority of skilled craftsmen and workers fleeing the overcrowded labor markets of central Europe entered the urban economy of New York ill-equipped to compete in many of their traditional trades. Despite the expanding consumer markets of the New World, a flood of skilled immigrant workers, especially in such light consumer industries as garment making and shoemaking, competed fiercely with countless sweatshops offering lower prices and increasingly sub-divided work.[19] The Steinway brothers were well aware of these prob-lems. Some of their countrymen, they knew, had to use up all their cash reserves only to find a relatively poorly paid job. "I do not ad-vise you to come here," wrote Charles Steinway to his brother in See-sen, "if you are able to make an honest living with diligence and thrift. And I advise the same to everyone, whomever it may be."[20]

The Gilded Age Generation

German immigration was in a hiatus during the Civil War years of the early 1860s, but as soon as the war was over immigration re-sumed with renewed force and reached all-time highs during the 1880s and 1890s. As in preceding decades, the developments in Ger-many had a major influence over the course of emigration to the Unit-ed States. A few years after the end of the Civil War, the unification of Germany fundamentally changed the political and economic land-scape of central Europe. During a delayed but intensive "take-off" phase, the German economy industrialized rapidly during the 1870s and 1880s, sending a growing number of men and women from their rural homes into the city, where they worked in factories and small-er workshops. The living standards of many former rural and small-town dwellers did not improve when jobs became available in urban centers. On the contrary, they now often had to make do with cramped one-room apartments in industrial tenements. Food supplies, formerly supplemented by homegrown vegetables from the garden plot of part-time farmers, were high priced and anything more than a subsistence diet was out of reach for many workingmen. Because of the cramped spaces, insufficient nutrition, and bad sanitary con-ditions, the working-class families' health and quality of life in most industrial centers left much to be desired.[21]

These conditions once again spurred many Germans to try their luck overseas. The United States remained the most popular destina-tion, and New York was their largest point of arrival.[22] Even though most Germans landing in New York continued on to various desti-nations in the Midwest or Northeast, thousands stayed each year. The city's German-born population swelled by almost 50,000 between 1880 and 1890. The height in the increase of German-born New Yorkers was reached during the 1890s, when over 110,000 German New Yorkers were added to the city's inhabitants.[23] The surge in the number of German immigrants thus kept pace with the enormous population growth of the city in these decades. From 1870 up to World War I German-born New Yorkers were never less than 15 percent of the population and by the 1890s they had become the largest single immigrant group in New York City. Moreover, by that time second-generation Germans were probably more numerous than first-generation immigrants, and since the children of German immigrants and even their grandchildren tended to retain their affiliation with the community, German-Americans were a very large group within the increasingly heterogeneous quilt of people from all over the world in New York City.[24]

Internal differences played an important role in the way the German community saw itself. Generational difference was only one of the more obvious ways to define oneself in German New York. By the 1880s there was a clear consciousness of the divisions between the "Greys"—that is immigrants of the Forty-eighter era—and the "Greens," also called "Greenhorns," who had arrived more recently.[25] By the 1880s such near-universal terms of generational mistrust had acquired overtones of class consciousness, regional suspicions, and political conflict. German old-timers in New York mistrusted the newer generations just as, in Germany, southerners had traditionally mistrusted northerners (or "Prussians") and Catholics had mistrusted Protestants. By the 1880s, the "Grey" Forty-eighter generation had long shed its revolutionary image and now saw itself as a group of ambitious middle-class citizens in contrast to the newly arrived proletarians from industrializing Germany who challenged their beliefs in free enterprise and American economic freedom with the ideas of European socialism. Conflicts that had expressed themselves first in terms of generation became independent of the generational pattern and, as the German-American community became ever larger, its regional, class, and political divisions became more prominent.[26]

What were the parameters of change which shaped such conflicts in the 1880s and 1890s? Most visible in statistical terms was a shift in geographic origins among German newcomers to New York City. From the mid-1860s to the mid-1880s Germans from the traditional emigration areas of the southwest still predominated but gradually the northeastern provinces of Germany (East and West Prussia, Pomerania, and Mecklenburg) sent an increasing number of their superfluous rural labor force to New York. At the same time many immigrants who had at least temporarily lived and worked in urban industrial centers such as Berlin, Hamburg, or Leipzig continued to come. Among the urbanites were relatively many Jews, while the rural arrivals were now mostly Lutherans, a shift from the heavily Catholic migration that had taken place earlier.[27]

The increasing diversity in regional background among German immigrants contributed to the already considerable social stratification within German New York during the Gilded Age in a number of ways. As with other immigrant groups, the older generation of German New Yorkers tended to be more heavily middle class, and a few of them (including the Steinways) even formed a small upper class by the 1880s; newcomers tended to be more proletarian. Because of their background in the skilled trades and experience of working in urban or small-town environments, southerners and southwesterners tended to have an advantage over northern German immigrants from rural areas. On the other hand, immigrants from such urban areas as Berlin, Hamburg, or the Saxon and Rhineland industrial areas also came with industrial and commercial experience which was easily adaptable to New York. The meaning of regional identity among Germans in New York is difficult to gauge in more precise social and demographic terms. Stanley Nadel has demonstrated that a certain amount of geographic clustering took place in New York's Lower East Side and that immigrants from the large provinces (such as Bavaria or Prussia) tended to marry partners from a similar province even in the New World. I would argue, though, that regional origins, even if they were preserved to the extent that Nadel contends, were connected only indirectly to the subtle shades of class and status that governed the life of the community. Even though regional differences translated into shadings of class and occupation, they did not create marked divisions within the German working class. Regionalism was not one of the important features of German New York.[28]

Economic and occupational status, far more than regional affiliation, shaped the German community in New York City. Measured by these categories, the vast majority of German New Yorkers remained solidly rooted in the working class. But by the 1880s a considerable number of originally poor German immigrant families had already begun a precarious upward mobility and had achieved a certain degree of economic well-being. They had usually climbed to the lower rungs of the middle class in one of two ways: either they had found work as specialized and highly prized craftsmen in the "high-end" shops of their trade or they had opened businesses on their own. Skilled workers with good and steady wages could be found in such occupations as musical instrument or scientific instrument making, printing, or specialized metalwork. Workers who had not landed jobs in such relatively well-paying trades often tried to open a shop of their own. This was a precarious undertaking in a city where competition among small shopowners was always intense. The move upward into independent proprietorship could be followed swiftly by a renewed dependence on an employer when the business failed. Such was often the case in low-capital industries such as food retailing, garment manufacturing, or cigar making. German businesses dominated many of these industries up to the late 1880s. While their luck lasted, these small proprietors formed the solid basis for an increasingly prosperous business class of German New Yorkers.[29]

In a more stable position than the small businessmen was the small but growing class of German-American professionals in the city. Since the 1840s there had been German-American teachers, doctors, writers, lawyers, and pharmacists, who for the most part served the growing German community. By the 1880s this group, strengthened by some second-generation immigrants, had grown, and many German-American professionals by then dealt with non-Germans too. While not large numerically, the professionals together with the owners of small businesses formed the core of organizers and supporters for the rich cultural (especially musical) life of German New York.[30]

A last, almost invisible segment of the middle class consisted of immigrants with a middle- or upper-class background who, because of their lack of resources and skills, were forced into a proletarian existence in the New World. This was not new (some Forty-eighters had suffered similar downward mobility because of their lack of practical skills) or as rare as one might think among German immigrants. Just after the turn of the century, Alfred Kolb, an upper-level bureaucrat for the Prussian state government with a lawyer's education and a doctorate, spent a year in Chicago as a working-class immigrant and recorded his experiences. Kolb had no trouble getting aid from charitable organizations, fellow workers, and employers when he posed variously as a former reserve officer or as a university dropout from Germany down on his luck. There were apparently many like him who were forced to shelve their dreams and take on any menial job they could find.[31]

While the majority of Gilded Age German immigrants came from and continued to belong to the working class, and while many middle-class immigrants faced a precarious stability, an increasingly visible upper class of wealthy German-Americans cast the light of its success over German immigration. Almost all members of the Gilded Age German American upper class came from nouveau riche business families that had come to wealth within the past thirty or forty years. Most of them came from relatively humble origins, and almost none had been to a university in Europe, although a few had come with money to invest. They were prominent among import-export merchants, as well as in certain industries such as beer brewing, furniture making, and, of course, musical instrument making. The Steinways belonged to this class of immigrants by the 1880s, having come a long way within three decades from their modest beginnings as an artisan family in the New World. As the Steinway sons and daughters had started families of their own, they had grown to a veritable clan involving most male relatives closely in the family business, which had expanded enormously since its humble beginnings in 1853. By the turn of the century the Steinways were part of the social and economic upper class of New York City in general, not just leaders of its German segment.[32]

Not every wealthy German-American family had the prominence and visibility of the Steinways. Many of the so-called *Brauerfürsten* ("Brewery Princes"), for example, were important figures only within the confines of New York's German community, active only in its charitable causes and business circles. But the limited visibility to outsiders of most wealthy German-Americans does not diminish the importance of their existence for the mass of working-class Germans. The existence of a German-American group of upper-class capitalists, employers, and politicians was a reminder of the possibilities of the New World. German working-class immigrants also perceived that their hardships were linked to the behavior of the wealthy German-Americans who were often their employers, their elected politicians, and the editors of newspapers or directors of German charitable societies. These men on whose wisdom, generosity, and business acumen German working-class men and women had to rely to make a living, or to press their cause, were more often than not influenced not by any ethnic solidarity but by their class interests as businessmen or politicians. The well-to-do may have celebrated ethnic solidarity at their annual commemorations of the 1848 revolution or the German national spirit at the *Sedansfeier* (commemorating the German victory over France in 1871) but their decisions as Gilded Age entrepreneurs were dictated by their interests as businessmen, not by their sentiments for fellow Germans. As we will see in the subsequent chapters the question of ethnic solidarity and economic interest was a more difficult one for the German-American middle class; whereas for the working class, ethnic solidarity was clearly a must, usually coincident with economic interests to a degree. But before we focus on the circumstances of class conflict and ethnic solidarity among New York's German working class, its demographic parameters need further examination.

Family and Neighborhood among the German Working Class

Three coordinates fixed the German working class particularly clearly in the context of German New York and the working class of the city in general: family organization, neighborhood, and work. All three helped group the German immigrants as a class and ethnic group in specific ways. The meaning of "family" differed for members of the upper and working classes. By 1860, when they were prospering but not yet wealthy, the Steinways, for example, lived in a three-generation household which included the first-generation parents, one son, and his family. They were able to maintain a large enough residence to house all three generations comfortably. Such extended, multigenerational families were rare in the German working-class districts, if only because apartments were simply too small to house more than two generations. Usually children of working-class parents set up their own living quarters as soon as they were married. If there was extra space available in the small tenement apartments it was filled by boarders who, in a sense, were paying family members.[33]

Much of the setup of German working-class families in New York City can surely be explained by the extremely cramped conditions under which they lived. The most important German working-class neighborhood in the late nineteenth century was on the Lower East Side of Manhattan. In fact by the 1870s much of the Lower East Side was aptly named Kleindeutschland (called Dutchtown by English-speaking residents). It stretched from Division and Grand Street to Fourteenth Street in the north with the Bowery as its western border. Although generally a working-class district, Kleindeutschland was as diverse as its inhabitants, with the poorer immigrants living in the south and the better-off in the northwest of the area. Politically this part of the Lower East Side consisted of the Eighth, Tenth, Twelfth, and Fourteenth assembly districts. Even though to the visitor from uptown or elsewhere New York's Lower East Side presented a solid mass of working-class residents, with a clear preponderance of Germans during the 1870s and 1880s, people from many countries lived there. Within the neighborhood clear gradations as to the class background and aspirations of the inhabitants could be observed. Geographic segregation according to class and ethnicity did not work neatly. Instead geography integrated Germans of many backgrounds with working- and middle-class immigrants from other countries.[34]

The poorest and most crowded parts of Kleindeutschland could generally be found in the Eighth District. Here young Samuel Gompers's family found their first apartment after they arrived from London in 1863. Gompers's family was not German; they belonged to the small settlement of Dutch Jews in New York. Most of their members, however, settled in the German neighborhood and worked with Germans in various trades. At age thirteen, the future labor leader perceived his new environment with mixed feelings. On the one hand, the four small rooms the family rented "signified progress" compared to what the family had known in Europe (this was probably true for immigrants from urban Germany as well, many of whom had had only one-room apartments). On the other hand the house was opposite a slaughter house whose "penetrating and sickening odor" wafted through the neighborhood. The backyard looked out on a small brewery in which "conditions were dreadful."[35] Many of the tenements in the Eighth District were situated among workshops, factories, and other industrial enterprises, which provided thousands of readily accessible jobs for the inhabitants but also increased the already uncomfortable and unhygienic living conditions. Some of the blocks in the area contained tenements built continuously since the 1850s and were the most crowded in the entire Lower East Side. Most of the houses were small—twenty-five feet wide, with four to five floors and up to four apartments to a floor. Each apartment had a bit more than 200 square feet. Families of five to six people shared one apartment, consisting of a "parlor," one or two windowless chambers which served as bedrooms, and sometimes a kitchen. Most of the dwellings built before the Civil War had water only in the backyard (where an outhouse was also located). Newer buildings usually had water in the hallway. As a rule these tenements were dark, damp, and dirty. The rent varied according to the area and the exact position of the apartment in a house. The fifth-floor apartment of a rear house cost less than the first- or second-floor apartment on the front house, which would typically go for about eight to ten dollars a month in the 1880s.[36]

Just how crowded the tenements in the Eighth Assembly District were can be gleaned from looking at a typical block of tenement houses as it appears in the 1880 federal census. On Orchard Street between Broome and Delancey, ten houses lined each side of the narrow sidewalks. They gave shelter to 846 people in 176 households. None of the houses was more than five stories high (quite a few had four or even just two floors), but each contained an average of eight apartments and forty-two inhabitants. The ethnic composition of this part of Orchard Street was also fairly typical of the poorer segment of Kleindeutschland. Seventy percent of the people were born in Germany or were American-born children of German immigrants; the other inhabitants were almost exclusively Russian Jews, with a few Austrians, Swiss, and Irish also living on the block. By 1890 the neighborhood contained many more eastern European Jews, and by the turn of the century Orchard Street was the center of the eastern European Jewish settlement in the city. But in 1880 a wide variety of Germans still lived there, about one-third of them Jewish. The occupations of the Orchard Street dwellers were also quite varied: hucksters and law clerks, woodworkers and tailors, actors and cooks, with over sixty-five different occupations listed in all. The only common characteristic of all the jobs was their low pay.[37]

While the southern end of Kleindeutschland was home to the poorest and most recent immigrants, the central and northern parts offered a slightly greater diversity of accommodations and therefore inhabitants as well. Moving into one floor of a converted one-family house was the goal of many working-class families; others aimed for more spacious or just somewhat cleaner and airier living accommodations. The Gompers family fit a common pattern: they moved frequently within the Lower East Side in the 1860s and 1870s, forever looking for a larger, better-priced apartment or one that would be closer to work or to one's friends and countrymen.[38] By 1867, when young Sam got married to a fellow cigar worker, Sophia Julian (but lacked the resources to set up house with her), the Gompers family lived on First Street in the heart of the German district. The population density there was at least as high as it was further south, for most housing consisted of recently built tenements which were higher and deeper than the older houses. A typical "new" tenement built in the 1870s was about twice as wide as the old tenements and had about five to eight stories which housed up to forty-eight families. The size of the apartments and the rents varied little from those in older buildings further south; hygienic conditions were equally bad.[39]

The living conditions in the northeastern corner of the Seventeenth Ward were somewhat better than in the southern and eastern parts. Here brownstones could be found next to small tenements on side streets. On the very edge, around Second and First Avenue, the old flavor of the merchant bourgeoisie was still alive. By the 1880s most of the houses formerly inhabited by the city's better-off merchants were rented by the floor to small businesspeople and skilled workers for twelve to twenty dollars a month, while their owners had moved on to the more fashionable uptown addresses. This section of the Lower East Side had the highest concentration of American-born inhabitants, some of them English-speaking immigrants but also native New Yorkers from British backgrounds.[40]

Germans and other central European immigrants sought out the Lower East Side in the 1870s and 1880s because it offered ready access to a great variety of jobs and business opportunities. This was true for the Gompers family, too, for whom the close proximity of many cigar manufacturers proved indispensable. Solomon Gompers set up shop in the family's small apartment and started making cigars with Sam, his eldest child, for larger manufacturers in the neighborhood who also acted as wholesale agents.[41] But the area was by no means dominated by the cigar industry. Small workshops of every description could be found in the neighborhood—in basements, on the ground floor, in rear houses, and in the apartments themselves. The Fourteenth and Twelfth districts also offered employment in a number of larger factories such as iron works, timber and coal yards, furniture factories, and the Manhattan gas works. Large retail establishments ringed Fourteenth Street, which was the shopping street for the city's consumers of all classes. It offered jobs to sales clerks and messengers from the neighborhood. Numerous hotels and restaurants could be found on the Bowery and further east. They employed many German immigrants as cooks, servants, and waiters.[42]

Despite its diversity, the area impressed inhabitants and visitors with its predominantly German flavor. The character of the Lower East Side as a German-American neighborhood was greatly reinforced by the many German-American voluntary associations or *Vereine* and other German institutions that made their home there. The geographic center of the Verein culture—which formed the German-American community socially more than anything else—was in the Lower East Side. For young working-class men with political ambitions and interests (like Samuel Gompers) living on the Lower East Side meant growing up close to numerous neighborhood meeting places such as the Tenth Ward Hotel where Gompers and a number of German-American workers (who called themselves "the ten philosophers") met to discuss the theoretical questions raised by the labor movement in the 1870s. There were also the Germania and Concordia assembly rooms, the sites of numerous meetings for the emerging union movement. There was Cooper Union, Peter Cooper's academy for the working man, where Gompers attended lectures as a young man, to which he later returned as head of the AFL to lecture to the working class of the Lower East Side. Not every German-American institution in the Lower East Side had such obvious political ends, of course. The New York Turnverein (gymnastics society) as well as the Free German School and the German Polyclinic had their headquarters in the area; the Germania Savings Bank and the German Insurance Society were important businesses. Kleindeutschland attracted numerous visitors and suburban Germans because of its plethora of businesses catering to German tastes, such as German theaters and music halls, beer halls, and beer gardens where German-American families and clubs met for evenings of relaxation and drink. Countless small businesses catering to German tastes—bakeries, grocery stores, butcher shops, travel agencies, and pastry shops—served the many needs of a large immigrant community.[43]

The Lower East Side continued to be the major center for German-Americans until the turn of the century, despite the fact that an increasing number of them moved to other parts of Manhattan as well as to suburban areas. One of the primary new areas of settlement for Germans was Yorkville, an area in uptown Manhattan around Eighty-sixth Street. The Gompers family, too, moved there in the late 1880s. The population density was not yet as high uptown as in the downtown wards, and the quality of housing in the newly built tenements and brownstones was also usually better than farther south. At the same time, rents were higher in this part of town. In addition, by and large the Upper East Side (as it would later be called) offered fewer areas of employment to German working-class immigrants. Except for some newly constructed cigar factories and a few large breweries, there were few businesses. Workers with less than secure employment and unskilled workers were not easily inclined to move there in the nineteenth century. Only in the early twentieth century, with its improvement in public transportation, did the focus of German settlement shift to Yorkville.[44]

But while the center of German ethnic settlement and culture moved north toward the turn of the century, the focus of the Lower East Side's political culture never moved with the German immigrant population uptown. Instead it remained with the new generation of working-class immigrants who populated the Lower East Side, most of whom were not of German but of eastern European Jewish background. To a certain extent ethnicity and its cultural connotations were mobile. Germans took both with them as they moved to Yorkville. The underpinnings of class-conscious working men and women's culture, however, stayed with those who had to struggle in the cramped tenements of the Lower East Side, German or not. Neighborhood was defined within geographical as well as cultural and political coordinates. The Lower East Side, the old stronghold of the German working class, was unique; it signified a special territory in American as well as German-American working-class history.

Work and the Family Economy in German New York

When the young journalist and geographer Friedrich Ratzel visited New York from Germany in 1873 he was impressed with the activity in the city's commercial areas. On lower Broadway he noticed the "extraordinary amount of activity and bustle. On the wide sidewalks on both sides of the street the people without exception go by in a hurry. . . . One cannot help but notice a strong disposition towards energetic activity and youthful elasticity . . . making a living or buying goods seemed to be the passion of New Yorkers." On Broadway and its side streets he saw not only the ubiquitous businessmen in their suits but also "numerous wandering petty tradesmen, the bootblacks with their stereotyped call, the men walking around like kiosks, festooned with advertisements, those who shove leaflets into the hands of the passerby or even throw them by the bushel into the coaches, the boys who deliver newspapers from house to house." Even on side streets buying and selling were conducted in a semipublic atmosphere which differed markedly from that of European cities. "An abundance of ballyhoo" confronted Ratzel as he made his way past "the display of goods placed under canvas awnings that extend out over the sidewalk so that one often has to walk entirely between booths."[45]

As an explorer of the New World Ratzel was not interested in finding traces of the Old, and he therefore gave few specific observations on Germans in the midst of this marketplace. But immigrants of German origin were involved in large numbers in the many occupational and commercial pursuits of the city that Ratzel observed. There was practically no profession or occupation in late-nineteenth-century New York where Germans could not be found. Yet certain factors gave the community a distinct overall cast: German workers were largely skilled workers, and as a result certain skilled trades in the city assumed a German character. A brief look at the census statistics will underscore these points. Only about 2,600 of the 92,657 wage-earning Germans counted in the 1880 census worked as professionals or in "high white collar" occupations. At 2.5 percent this was still a higher percentage of professionals than for most other ethnic groups (e.g., the Irish). The proportion of professionals among second-generation Germans was, of course, much higher. Nevertheless significant occupational diversity existed mostly within the large category (about 40,000 people) classifiable as "low white collar" workers and small businessmen, and the 50,000 or so men and women who worked in blue-collar occupations. About 80 percent of the German-born blue-collar workers were skilled, while the rest were classified as laborers or unskilled by the census.[46] In order to analyze the meaning of these classifications for class and ethnic consciousness among German New Yorkers, we need to draw on specific examples from within the broad stratum of working-class Germans.

The high proportion of skilled workers and small businessmen gave the German-Americans' socioeconomic profile its distinctive features. Skilled German workers went in large numbers to the garment, woodworking, and food trades, which were important sectors in the metropolitan economy. New York City had relatively little heavy industry. Its economy rested on light manufacturing in thousands of smaller factories and workshops which produced a wide variety of consumer goods such as clothes and clothing accessories, furniture, toys, cigars, and shoes.[47] Within the skilled trades, Germans clearly dominated in some and were underrepresented in others. The reason for this lay in the patterns of emigration which, in turn, were influenced by the structural changes in the German economy in the course of the nineteenth century. While we will look in detail at these patterns in three trades in the later chapters of this study, they call for a few general observations which should be made at this point.

Food and food-related trades such as butchering, brewing, and cigar making were the fields in which German immigrants were probably the most prominent. This had been a traditional pattern at least since the 1840s, when German bakers, butchers, and grocers were already numerous in Manhattan. In the 1880s more than 10 percent of all wage-earning Germans worked in food-related trades. At that point well over 50 percent of all bakers, over 40 percent of the butchers, and over 80 percent of all brewers were German-born.[48]

The term "food industries" hides an enormous difference in internal structure, development, traditions, and status of the workers involved. Even though collectively these trades played a very large role in the growing metropolis, their dispersal throughout many neighborhoods and the variations in size and degree of mechanization make it difficult to see the workers in these industries, even if they were mostly German, as a collective group. The most German of the food industries, beer brewing, was also in some ways its most industrial and was therefore an oddity within the food trades. From the time Germans introduced lager beer brewing in the United States in the 1840s, the industry in New York (and everywhere else) was virtually in German hands. Even though it had started out as a craft, with most of the workers immigrant journeymen until the turn of the century, the industry had become a "high technology" trade by the 1880s. Unlike other food trades, beer brewing was relatively centralized, concentrated in increasingly mechanized beer factories in the northern part of Manhattan. Brewery workers therefore lived clustered around the breweries at the northern end of town, relatively isolated from the rest of the German-American community and separated from workers in other trades.[49]

The work setting of bakers and butchers was more varied; both had been heavily German occupations since the 1840s, and both were in a state of transition in the late nineteenth century. Having arrived as skilled journeymen in search of a better livelihood, butchers and bakers from Germany usually found work rather easily, though under conditions that varied very little from those they had left behind. As in Germany most of these workers toiled in small establishments for long hours and under incredibly harsh conditions. Toward the end of the century, though, an increasing share of bread baking and most of the slaughtering and meat packing was done by larger, quasi-factory establishments that also employed German workers. Their work environment had little to do with the artisan tradition from which many of the immigrants had come. Instead they resembled factory workers in most ways. They often worked in the industrial districts of Brooklyn or Manhattan and commuted to work from the German-American neighborhoods. In contrast, the employees of small bakeries and butchers both lived and worked not only on the Lower East Side but could be found far beyond the limits of Kleindeutschland all over town.[50]

More traditional in their setting and always closely involved with their neighborhood were the many German grocers who plied their trade in Kleindeutschland and in many other neighborhoods of the city. German grocers had dominated this trade since the 1850s, selling their wares on every block of the Lower East Side but also far away from the *Landsleute,* in Irish or "American" neighborhoods all over town. Grocers were, of course, rarely artisans and usually considered themselves to be members of the petite bourgeoisie rather than the working class. But their connections to working-class Germans were as close as that of any group of small businessmen, and the probability that they themselves might have to make a living as wage earners if their businesses failed was always high.[51] In a similar situation were the over 2,300 German-born managers and owners of bars and saloons who played an important role in working-class neighborhoods. Most of these publicans were former workers themselves (often brewers), and they provided crucial sympathy and support for their customers in time of need.[52] Related to the food trades in structural ways was the cigar industry. Cigar making occupied a field between the retail-oriented neighborhood trades and factory production. Skilled cigar makers had come to the United States from Germany since the 1840s and had established their own small businesses in Kleindeutschland. In 1880 the Lower East Side was still dotted by hundreds of small cigar shops. But by that time a few members of the first generation of immigrant cigar makers had founded large cigar factories in the German neighborhood to which much of the production had shifted by the 1880s. Thus the cigar trade stayed in close proximity to the German neighborhood, and cigar makers as a group were less widely dispersed throughout town than other trades.[53]

While Germans could be found in great numbers in many food industries, the largest employer of German workers was the New York garment industry, which employed 7.5 percent of all German wage earners, toiling away as tailors, seamstresses, pressers, button-hole makers, and so on. By the 1880s Germans had a forty-year history in the garment industry. Mechanization had only had a limited impact, and the German workers' skill was in demand, but subdivision and fierce competition had eroded wages badly. Only in the custom trade were the working conditions and wages reasonably good. Downward pressure on wages and workers' status was kept up by the large number of women who worked at finishing garments at home. Because of the relatively long tradition of Germans working in the trade, Germans were prominent as manufacturers and contractors in the industry. The subdivisions, the fierce competition, and the vulnerability of the garment industry to depressions made the situation of workers difficult and solidarity not easy to achieve. By the late 1880s, even though the number of German-born tailors and seamstresses was still growing, more immigrants from eastern Europe and Italy entered the business and the situation of German workers became less relevant to the German community at large.[54]

As in the cigar-making trade, the shops of the garment manufacturers were concentrated on Manhattan's Lower East Side, close to the tenements of the German working class. Interspersed with the garment-making lofts were old-fashioned tailors' shops and innumerable houses where garment workers made clothes in the "front parlor" of their tenement apartment. Garment-related businesses such as millinery, artificial flower making, embroidering, or button making were also numerous in the German neighborhoods. Much of the work in these trades was performed at home, often by German immigrant women.[55]

Like garment makers, Germans also had a tradition of dominating the city's shoemaking trade, but by the 1880s the number of German shoemakers had decreased as the industry moved from New York City primarily to New England. Although over 3,300 German-born shoemakers tried to eke out a living in their trade in 1880, overall their economic and political importance had greatly diminished within the German working class.[56]

In some ways most representative of the situation of skilled German workers in New York's metropolitan economy was the position of the almost 6,000 Germans who were woodworkers of one kind or another. The declining fortunes of craftsmen in the German cabinet-making trades had sent thousands of skilled woodworkers to the United States beginning in the 1840s. As skilled craftsmen they had hoped to find stable and remunerative employment in the expanding North American furniture industry. For the pre–Civil War decade this hope was often realized and a number of master woodworkers such as August Belter and Christian and Gustave Herter and musical instrument makers with a cabinetmaking background such as the Steinways established themselves as makers of high-class furniture, wooden interiors, and musical instruments. But for most artisans who had hoped to continue a life as craftsmen, independence was hard to come by in the post–Civil War decades. By 1880, when German immigrants had become dominant in all branches of New York's indoor woodworking trades, most of the furniture trade had become mechanized and oriented toward factory-style specialized production. Many thousands of skilled German-American cabinetmakers found work only as operators of furniture-making machinery which turned out cheap and simple furniture. Even though the factory owners preferred to hire skilled workers, especially when they were as abundant as in New York during the years of heavy German immigration, they were not dependent on their actual skills and did not have to pay them wages that reflected their qualifications. German craftsmen who had come to New York in the hope of maintaining the life of independent artisans had been overtaken by the mechanization and subdivision of labor in their field. The term *skilled workers* for many furniture workers as well as for skilled German-American artisans in many other fields signified little more than a type of consciousness and history, not a social position or economic security.[57]

If subdivision and separation of skills destroyed or undermined the attempts of skilled workers at cohesion based on traditional artisanal forms of competence, the position of semiskilled and unskilled workers among German immigrants was even more tenuous in the New World. *Skill* was a relative term; so-called unskilled workers often needed a complex array of abilities to master the intricacies of finding and keeping a job in the metropolitan economy. This was true for the thousands of working-class German immigrants who had to earn their livelihood as laborers, teamsters, peddlers, or door-to-door salesmen. Such workers were often from a great variety of backgrounds. They ranged from middle-class immigrants with no marketable skills to craftsmen fallen on hard times and rural immigrants with few connections in the United States. Although the unskilled were not a majority among the Germans, as they were in other immigrant groups, they were a significant group. Their cohesion and their sense of community were not helped by the tenuous economic position most of them had within New York's competitive and chaotic economy of the late nineteenth century. We know almost nothing about these Germans, who left few traces in the historical record.[58]

Not all German immigrant wage earners can be adequately described by keeping to such categories as skill, white-collar, or blue-collar work. Gender divisions, important among Germans as among all other immigrant groups, also influenced the overall makeup of the German working class. In some heavily German trades no women could be found, while others observed a sexual division of labor within certain "skill categories." However, statistical evidence for a close analysis of the role of German immigrant women in the labor force is hard to come by, since these women rarely show up in the census statistics. The published census does not specify the total number of German working women in New York City, and heavily female occupations show relatively few Germans working in them. In 1880, for example, only about 5,800 domestic servants, out of a total of 56,000, were German-born. This is a modest number compared to the 24,000 Irish domestics working in New York that year. Among 7,700 laundresses only 1,300 were German-born. For the garment trades, probably the largest employer of German immigrant women, no precise figures can be extrapolated, and even the census manuscript gives no clear information in the matter, since many German women seem to have done piecework in the garment trades on a seasonal basis and at home. German women also worked as cigar makers, milliners, and in a host of other trades, though probably not in very large numbers. Only in the cigar trade did they form a distinct group, together with Bohemian women; occasionally they became active and organized in special groups. In general though, German women workers were a group which rarely became visible within the framework of the male-dominated unions, the German labor papers, or the Vereine. This does not mean that German women were not important in providing their working-class families with economic and social stability; it just indicates that certain methods of analyzing and understanding working-class activity and organization are inadequate to sketching the role of women. In order to understand the role of female immigrants, we have to look not so much at individual workers and their status and position but at families, households, and their ways of organizing.[59]

Wages and the Family Economy

As skilled workers, new German arrivals often found work relatively quickly in the city's expanding light industries and retail establishments. But the hopes of many immigrants for a secure and well-paid position were usually not fulfilled. In fact, in many cases skilled workers earned less on a daily basis than unskilled laborers, although the latter usually worked fewer days a year and often in more hazardous jobs. Even in occupations which were basically structured the same way they had been in the Old World, such as baking or tailoring, intense competition had forced wages down and had lengthened the hours of work. A cigar maker, for example, who was employed as a buncher in a factory often made no more than six or seven dollars a week, a cabinetmaker who worked in a chair or desk factory often made even less. A dock laborer, on the other hand, could expect to make about eight dollars a week in times of full employment. Moreover, with the seasonal and cyclical fluctuations in industrial employment, the yearly earnings of skilled German workers in the 1880s were often below the minimum needed to support a small family ($600–$800). This was in part because German immigrants usually were paid less than skilled workers of Anglo-Irish descent, since Germans often lacked the "know how," English-language skills, and funds to move to better-paying sectors of their industry or other parts of the country. Relatively few Germans found a way out of the sweatshops into more specialized "high-end" workshops such as the Steinway piano factory, where pay was better and work more stable. Few working men could therefore hope to earn enough money on a yearly basis (about $650) to feed even a small family adequately.[60]

Because wages even for skilled individuals were low, German immigrants tried to rely on more than one way of making money in order to make ends meet. When the Steinway family settled in New York in the early 1850s its members did not earn what we could call family wages, despite the skills of Heinrich Engelhardt and his sons. But because none of the younger Steinways had a family to feed yet, the male wage earners could pool their wages to maintain the household in which the elder Mrs. Steinway and two of her daughters did the housework. A family with younger children would have been very hard pressed to make ends meet in that situation. The Gompers family was a case in point. The pressure was strong on such working-class families to cut short their children's schooling and send them to work as early as possible. Only one of the six children of Solomon

Gompers was of working age, fourteen-year-old Sam, and even at the price of cutting short his formal education, young Sam did not increase his family's earnings by very much with his meager apprentice wages.[61] Thus sons and daughters of German immigrants were sent to work regularly after the age of fourteen and were expected to contribute something to the common till until they moved out of the house when they got married.[62] As for young married couples, the search for additional income began anew as soon as children arrived, requiring mothers to stay at home. Young Samuel Gompers, who became a father at eighteen (almost as soon as he reached the zenith of his earning power as a cigar maker) and whose family rapidly increased to six children, remembered how difficult it was to feed a family adequately on his wages. His wife "prepared soup out of water, pepper and flour" and the family was dependent on help from relatives or co-workers in times of need.[63] If the help of children was not possible because they were too small or already out of the house, the wage-earning power of women was crucial to German working-class families. German immigrant women tried to avoid wage labor outside the home. Taking in boarders, sewing, taking in wash, or making cigars were ways of earning additional dollars while officially retaining the status of housewife.[64]

Despite a variety of strategies aimed at increasing family earnings, at least half of all German households in New York City seemed to have only one wage earner. Between 5 percent and 10 percent of these families were headed by women. It was almost impossible for women with small children to earn a sufficient livelihood.[65] The same was true for families with five or more small children and for those with a disabled or unemployed head of household. Germans, like other working-class families, were very vulnerable to poverty, especially in times of economic depression. During the depression of the mid-1870s, 1,400 German families applied to the German Society for relief each month, receiving an average of about $1.70 a week. Those unable to manage on their own were sent to the poorhouse on Wards Island, where Germans represented the majority of inmates in some years. No wonder that German-born New Yorkers also had the highest rate of suicides of any ethnic group in the late-nineteenth-century city. Family cohesion, the skill of individual workers, and their effort to provide for themselves and their kind did not shelter them from poverty or depression.[66]

The short portrait painted here of the German working class can only highlight the complexities and many-layeredness of these immigrants' circumstances. They were embedded in a large community of immigrants from German-speaking countries which had stretched over at least three generations already by the 1880s. The layers of history were supplemented by the layers of class and neighborhood, occupation and family. These layers multiplied the complexities of community identity even within the German working class; there seemed to be few common denominators for a broad class or ethnic solidarity. The fact that such complexity existed should not throw us off altogether, though. Demographic analysis alone does not provide a sufficient answer to the basis for this solidarity. If we wish to understand how the German immigrant population saw itself, its goals, and its status, we will have to turn to its institutional form of self-expression: the voluntary associations.

2

Politics and Culture of German New York: The World of the *Vereine*

For Germans, as for so many other immigrant groups, the succession of generations and the stability of families were the most constant factors that defined their lives. In addition, the neighborhood provided the stage for the community life of German-Americans, and work formed the basis for individual families' economic wellbeing. But the true matrix of German-American culture and politics was the highly stratified and differentiated network of voluntary organizations which flourished among German-Americans, more than other immigrant communities. *Vereine,* as the voluntary associations were called, gave shape to an immigrant group that was divided by its internally diverse cultural heritage, its many generations, its heterogeneous neighborhoods and its emerging classes. If non-Germans identified Germans by their language and place of origin, German New Yorkers identified one another as belonging to a certain organized group within the community. Organized by class, religion, political preference, occupation, or region of origin in Germany, the Vereine presented German immigrants with a myriad of possible self-identifying moments. The multiplicity of Vereine cast a fine net of stratification over the German immigrant community. Despite their differences, which closely reflected the heterogeneity of this immigrant group, the Vereine as a structuring moment provided an overarching unity for Kleindeutschland.

Why were the Vereine such crucial elements for the German-American community—much more so than, by contrast, for Irish or Italian immigrants? The answer lies in part in the German origins of the *Vereinswesen* during the nineteenth century and in part in the American conditions that widened the scope and importance of these organizations. The origins of the Vereine in central Europe arose in the time of the first flowering of bourgeois culture in the late eighteenth century; as the traditional society of estates decayed, to be replaced by an industrializing society in central Europe, the Vereine flourished and expanded. During the nineteenth century, Germany especially took on the character of an industrial, urban society with a mobile labor force, in which the regional, ecclesiastical, and even familial bonds of the old order were no longer the defining forces. As we have discussed in the previous chapter, the possibilities for response to these challenges varied, with calls for political change, migration, and emigration heading the list. By and large though, the response to change was class-specific, and the class that most actively confronted the changed conditions and tried to transform them for their benefit was the bourgeoisie. Voluntary associations, including the nucleus of political parties, educational circles, and charitable groups, were the organizations that formulated the bourgeoisie's response to the social and political changes taking place in central Europe.[1]

Especially in the period after the 1848 revolution the Vereine began to play a key role in the political arena at large, widening their scope to include journeymen and workers as well as the middle classes. By the late 1840s Vereine no longer just represented the opinions and preferences of the bourgeoisie at large (in contrast to the nobility and the church) but also the increasingly diverse interests within middle and working classes: *Arbeitervereine* (working men's associations) were founded in which the working class organized for politics and leisure, and *Bürgervereine* united various parts of the increasingly stratified bourgeoisie, some of them quite revolutionary, others interested in maintaining the status quo.[2]

Out of the voluntary associations of the 1848 decade grew a system of permanent political parties, a labor movement, and a system of mutual benefit societies which put its stamp on the social structure of late-nineteenth-century Germany. These Vereine were structures independent of the state and often organized in conscious opposition to its authority or to benevolence from above. Persistent state efforts to regulate or suppress part of the Vereine's activities or to outlaw some organizations altogether were mostly unsuccessful.[3] In short, the political culture of late-nineteenth-century Germany became rooted in the dense network of Vereine, which spanned virtually all classes, regions, and political beliefs by the time of German unification in 1871. With German political structure only slowly changing away from an authoritarian monarchical system, the political parties and the labor movement, both built on the basis of voluntary associations, were the most obvious expressions of new class interests in a modern industrial society.[4]

The United States during the second half of the nineteenth century was a society quite different from that of Germany. Relatively unencumbered by a traditional social order, it had become the bourgeois,
capitalist society par excellence. Mobile, heterogeneous, and growing,
its working and middle classes had, from the beginning, organized
themselves into groups by class, cultural interest, occupation, geographic origin, and political beliefs. In some ways American society
was more fundamentally structured by voluntary organization than
was German society, but the political impetus behind the entire German Vereinswesen was missing from the American groupings. Rather than pushing against an authoritarian state for the emancipation
and legal equalization of all citizens, American organizations could
be found on both sides of the fence: defending the established order
or pushing for a new one, organizing for regional or for national interests, relying on the separation of the races or fighting against it.
Political parties, churches, clubs, associations, and unions had been
integral to the American order since prerevolutionary times, while in
Germany the rise of voluntary associations that opposed an authoritarian aristocratic state signified a new bourgeois society in the nineteenth century.

German immigrants in the United States found themselves in a
peculiar situation. Vereine seemed more necessary than ever in a society that provided no ready-made avenues for social organization and
cultural and political expression, yet the ultimate effect and direction
of the Vereine were often diffuse and uncertain to their members. To
the historian some structures and directions are more clearly visible.
At first sight though, the number and range of German-American voluntary associations were daunting. At times it looked as if every German-born New Yorker belonged to a voluntary association of some
type. Much more comprehensive in their constituents and programs
than in Germany, Vereine spanned the entire spectrum of classes, regional origins, cultural and political interests, and religious denominations in the United States. Some, like conservative church organizations, represented the old corporatist order; others, more in the
tradition of German Vereine, worked for political and social change.
But most Vereine in the New World had no definite political world-
view. They provided German immigrants of all ages, classes, provinces, religions, and occupations a chance to develop an identity not
just as German-Americans but also as members of an increasingly
stratified immigrant community.[5] In fact, the Vereine reflected the
changing internal character of German-American society more accu-
rately than occupational or geographical stratification and distribu-

tion did. Germans thus organized themselves by their generational affiliation as immigrants (into groups dominated by "greys" and those started by "greens," for example); or they emphasized regional origins, religion, or occupational status in their organizational choice. Out of this pattern of organizational affiliation according to demographic criteria grew different layers of cultural ideals and political preferences. In the end, the Vereine would provide a rich soil for the often clashing views of German-Americans of different classes, whose presumed ethnic solidarity dissolved amid the conflicts of interest between the better-off and the poor, between the upwardly mobile and the working class.

Ultimately, it turned out that the basis for organizing was not so much ethnic identity, which had originally constituted a fundamental impetus for getting together, but class or occupational interests, which, in theory at least, Germans shared with others of different ethnic backgrounds. In the end Vereine were not the best organizations to represent the German immigrants' competing and diverse interests in many arenas. Organizations with a more open structure, designed to reach out to people of many backgrounds, would come to play the dominant role for German working-class immigrants during the last decade of the nineteenth century. Trade unions, mainstream political parties, and the immigrant and working-class press would take up where the Vereine were forced to leave off as the German-American community grew and became better integrated into the economy and society of the city and the country at large. The new generation of organizations took many of their lessons from the successes and mistakes of the Vereine, but they gradually grew beyond the *Vereinswelt*. Thus, the United States, a paradise for free organizing in the eyes of many German emigrants, would absorb and finally dissolve the Vereine as organizations that made German-American society distinctive.

Churches, Religious Denominations, and the Old Order

In some ways unique among the Vereine in German New York were those organizations which, though deeply rooted in the German community's free organizational life, did not represent the ideals of an enlightened and free society of individuals that were at the center of the *Vereinsleben* in Germany during much of the nineteenth century. Some of them were, in fact, defenders of the European old order, and to some extent rejected the society of free individuals on which North America was founded. German-American churches and reli-

gious denominations were the most prominent of the three groups
with a corporate ideology. Their situation was paradoxical: their members came from a Germany in which denominational affiliation was
not a matter of free choice and where churches were closely supervised by the state. They arrived in a United States in which religious
affiliation was certainly voluntary and churches had developed largely separate from the political structures of the state. This had led to
the flowering of a heterogeneous network of religious organizations,
many of which were highly decentralized and independent from each
other in financial and doctrinal matters. In contrast, the immigrant
German denominations in the New World retained somewhat greater uniformity and less social stratification than the English-speaking
communities that surrounded them.[6]

Among New York's German immigrants, the largest religious denomination and the one which organized all classes of immigrants
most comprehensively was the Catholic church. Estimates of the number of active German-born Catholics in the city around 1880 vary
widely, from 28,000 to 70,000, but to judge from the size of the elev-
en German Catholic parishes in New York City, probably no more
than 30,000 Germans were regular churchgoers. This may have had
to do partly with the difficulties of obtaining German-speaking priests
and adequate funding, or with the lack of general support from the
hierarchy, which throughout the nineteenth century remained dominated by Irish immigrants and their descendants, a source of constant
friction for the Germans.[7]

New York's German Catholics supported a large network of organizations and publications, most of them devotional. Certain groups,
such as the St. Vincent's Society, were not strictly local in character
but part of a growing network of national organizations for German-
speaking Catholics in the United States. Beyond offering spiritual
guidance, a place of worship, and charity, the Catholic church attempted to organize its members into a whole network of Vereine
which paralleled the nonreligious singing, shooting, and mutual aid
associations which made up the bulk of the German-American Vereinsleben. The Catholic church in Germany had traditionally rejected the emancipatory ideals of the Forty-eighters (and later the republican labor movement in the Old as well as the New World). The
church and its representatives also objected to Catholics taking part
in the Turner movement (the widely popular gymnastics clubs with
a tinge of self-help ideology), the labor movement, and the well-attended Masonic lodges. Alternative Vereine under the tutelage of the
church, such as *Schützenvereine* and mutual aid associations, were pro-

vided for church members who did not want to be cut off from these kinds of organized sociability and mutual help.[8]

The attempt at building an alternative culture to counteract the emancipatory tendencies of German-American associational life was not very successful in New York City. From the 1840s on, when local Catholic church authorities and the Catholic press had taken a position hostile to the revolution of 1848, through the 1850s and 1860s, when the Catholic hierarchy emerged as hostile to the demands of organized labor and the abolitionist cause, the Catholic church stood on the other side of many issues that united the German working class. This continued into the 1880s and 1890s with Catholic opposition to the Knights of Labor and the Henry George campaign. Too conservative to fit into the political culture of working-class German-America and organizationally too weak in a church apparatus dominated by the Irish, New York's German Catholics failed to bind substantial numbers of nominally Catholic immigrants to the church, especially among laboring people.[9] German Catholicism in New York never had the strength of its counterparts in Chicago and Milwaukee. The Catholic church's lack of power in New York's German-American community exemplifies the declining influence of organizations that had determined the traditional social order in Germany: the extended family, the village, and the church overseen by the state. Even though the Catholic church tried to make the transition to the different social order of industrial North America, its activism did not attract German immigrants in New York.

Lutheranism, the next largest denomination among Germans in New York and considered "the most distinctively German church organization in the City," had a similar fate.[10] A largely German-American denomination with over twenty churches in Manhattan during the late nineteenth century, it included mostly better-off citizens of the middle classes. Lutherans, less centralized in their organization and less able to retain loyalty in Europe, made much less of an attempt to bind their adherents to the church through a comprehensive network of social organizations than did the Catholics. An immigrant hostel and a downtown parochial school were the only institutions that seem to have served a working-class clientele. Unlike the Catholic church's controversial stances, Lutherans had almost no visibility within the political culture of German New York. This is hardly surprising given the fact that Protestant workers in Germany were largely disaffected from the church, whose paternalistic ideology tended to make them ready recruits for the socialist movement.[11]

In 1880 the vast majority of Greater New York's 85,000 Jews were of German origin. Since the late eighteenth century Jews in Germany had gradually been "emancipated"—that is, their special legal status was dissolved and they were integrated into the political and economic life of the German states as full-fledged citizens. This gradual integration, which was not complete until the 1870s, brought about some degree of state regulation of internal Jewish religious and community life, yet governmental oversight never reached the degree of regulation that the Catholic and Protestant churches were subject to. German Jews remained organized in an independent, decentralized, yet comprehensive way which was comparable to the organization of most denominations in the United States.[12] Therefore, they had few problems fitting into the structure of the Vereine in New York as representatives of a new order rather than of the old corporate society.

German Jews were organizationally much more visible than German Protestants in the city. Synagogues and Jewish voluntary associations could be found in every neighborhood and for every group of people or cause. Unfortunately, very little has been written about the extent of New York's German Jewish religious organization in the late nineteenth century. The six large German-speaking synagogues listed in late-nineteenth-century New York guidebooks served a mainly upper-class clientele, but there were countless others, many of them in working-class districts, serving the local communities of German Jews who lived interspersed with Gentile immigrants from central Europe. Apart from synagogues, most German Jewish organizations lacked a religious character; rather, they organized Jewish immigrants from Germany for mutual benefit and help as well as cultural purposes. Influential benevolent groups such as the United Hebrew Charities, the Hebrew Free School (with over 3,100 students in the late 1870s), and the Hebrew Benevolent and Orphan Asylum were well known all over town. Even though in terms of their structure and interests they could rarely be distinguished from non-Jewish German Vereine, their very existence as separate organizations reflected the fact that legal and political equality of German Jews had not brought about social assimilation in the Old World nor had it meant the total integration of Jewish immigrants from Germany into the organizations of the Gentile majority of German New Yorkers.[13]

Churches and denominational organizations on the whole were no match for the appeal of secular Vereine among German-Americans. Membership in churches and synagogues would be part of the life of many immigrants but for only a few did it define their place in the community. For most Germans, their sense of belonging was not determined by religion but by cultural forces that had separated from the church-centered form of social organization characteristic of the old order. Unlike immigrants from more traditional agrarian societies, working-class Germans, with the partial exception of Catholics, came to New York as people whose past was already formed by a secular culture within which organized religion occupied only a small niche.

Generations and Classes within the Vereinswelt

As the church-based organizations did not prove attractive to most German New Yorkers, what bound them to the Vereinswelt? Between the late 1840s and the 1880s the Vereine of German New York grew rapidly in tandem with the German community at large, reflecting its many allegiances and affiliations. The threads of generation, class, and, to some extent, regionalism ran strong through the hundreds of clubs and associations that existed in late-nineteenth-century German New York. For the immigrants the plethora of choices meant that they could make a social identity for themselves by associating with men and women from the same home province, or the same new neighborhood in New York City, by singing, by joining a shooting club, a mutual benefit society, or a lodge, or by becoming politically active.

Among the most popular organizations from the 1850s through the late nineteenth century were the so-called *Landsmannschaften* which organized Germans by regions of origin. The Landsmannschaften were devoted to mutual benefit and to socializing as well. By the 1870s a number of them had united to form umbrella groups consisting of north Germans (Plattdeutsche), southwest Germans, and so on. These societies, which could be very large indeed, were most visible among German New Yorkers as organizers of a multitude of festivities, fairs, and picnics which they held for members and for the general public. The yearly festivities of the north German, Bavarian, and southwest German fair associations were very popular, drawing over 100,000 people each in the 1870s. But other than their popularity, very little is known about the activities of these organizations. It is clear, however, that despite the regional flavor of these groups, they were no harbingers of regionalism in any political sense within the German community of New York.[14]

Mutual benefit societies that took the form of lodges and fraternal associations were also popular among Germans. Some of them had evolved since the 1840s as Masonic lodges such as the Freiheitssöhne (Sons of Liberty) or the Order of Harugari. Others were more informal and based on neighborhood, occupational, or kinship ties. In fact the lines between trade-based mutual benefit societies, lodges, and labor organizations were often fluid before the Civil War.[15]

Rivaling the Landsmannschaften and mutual benefit societies in

size and popularity were the innumerable sports, singing, and shooting societies which continued to flourish in German New York during the 1880s and 1890s. In contrast to earlier decades, when the singers and Turners kept up the spiritual legacy of the 1848 revolution in
parades, songs, and other commemorations, by the 1870s most of
these organizations had lost their political profile. What did differ-
entiate them was the increasingly stratified membership. Gone were
the days in the 1840s when the German Society or the Liederkranz
united German immigrants with modest means with wealthy citizens;
by the last quarter of the nineteenth century class divisions between
the mass of singing societies and cultural groups which served the
petite bourgeoisie and working class and the small group that harbored the upper crust were obvious. In the Gilded Age the Deutsche
Gesellschaft was the organization of the German-American upper
crust.[16] Other groups such as the Liederkranz, the Harmonie Club, or
the New Yorker Turnverein had become mostly upper-middle class
by the 1880s. Many clubs and literary societies had also become ha-
vens for upwardly mobile middle-class citizens by the 1880s, as had
professional and business groups such as the German-American Pharmacists Association, the German Teachers Association, or the German-
American Physicians. They often represented a clientele that mingled
socially with the German-American upper class in clubs such as the
Liederkranz or the German Society.[17]

None of these groups for the upper and upper-middle class had
an overt political purpose or program. But in general they represented a nationalist membership (they were America boosters as well
as admirers of the newly formed German empire), which was also
paternalistic (toward poorer fellow immigrants). A common conservative front against the demands of more militant working-class immigrants also brought together those wealthy Germans who headed businesses, especially in heavily German-American industries,
and who organized in German-American business associations, such
as the United States Brewers Association or the Tobacco Merchants
Association.

On the other side of the spectrum there were groups that were obviously and consciously working class. For them class stratification
in organizations implied proletarian class consciousness as well. Most
of these organizations had members who were relatively new immigrants for whom the older generation of singers and gymnasts had
become too middle class and too conservative in their politics. They
put new life into old organizations such as the Sozialistischer Turnverein or started new groups such as the Arbeiter Männerchor in the

spirit of what they saw as a revival of the progressive traditions of the Forty-eighters and, later, the continuation of a flourishing Social Democratic culture in Germany. The existence of these socialist Vereine, however, did little to alter the fundamentally apolitical character of the Vereinswelt. While they provided an alternative to a politicized minority of singers and Turners, they could not recover the general spirit of revolutionary enthusiasm that had been important to the Vereine of an earlier generation.[18]

But by and large, even though the leisure-oriented and mutual benefit associations of the Gilded Age stratified the German-American community according to socioeconomic class, few associations adopted a class-conscious agenda. Indeed, in contrast to the Forty-eighter generation, the vast majority of Vereine representing German-Americans during the Gilded Age were apolitical in almost all respects. Only on a few occasions, such as to protest against temperance or blue laws or at the time of the Franco-Prussian War in 1871, did these organizations show a degree of public involvement in politics that made them visible to a wider public. In general, most of the Vereine with their focus on entertainment and Gemütlichkeit gave only muted expression to the political stratification of the German community that developed with increasing clarity at the same time. The Vereinswelt had begun to split off political activism into a subgroup of political Vereine, largely segregated from the rest of the social and cultural groups of German New York by the post–Civil War decade.

The Political Vereine: From the Forty-eighters to the Socialist Labor Party

From the perspective of the vast range of the Vereinswelt the world of the political Vereine looked like a small satellite trying to break loose into an orbit of its own but overwhelmed by its organizational and social ties to the largely nonpolitical groups. But from the perspective of the political Vereine, the world of German-American organizations looked different indeed. Leaders and rank and file of the many political groups that populated German New York throughout the second half of the nineteenth century saw themselves as a vanguard whose organizations aimed at reorganizing the community as a whole—its culture, its political perspective, and its economic power structure. The fact that they were small in numbers did not disturb them; the size of their vision was what mattered to them. The small-mindedness of the countless unpolitical Vereine was a constant irritant to these political groups. Taking a large perspective was more important than size of membership, and it was the political perspective that would determine their weight within the community.

The political Vereine had a tradition in German New York which was at least as old as that of other Vereine. During the 1840s a number of trade unions and other political groups of German-Americans suffused German New York with the political spirit of 1848. In fact most descriptions of German-American associational life in the 1840s give the impression that the Vereinsleben was consumed by political discussion and activism.[19] Hermann Kriege, an exiled revolutionary of the pre-1848 era, was among the first to start such a Forty-eighter organization, the Social Reform Association, initially a branch of the secret European revolutionary group Bund der Gerechten (League of the Just). Kriege also edited a short-lived paper, the *Volkstribun*. Initially a close associate of Marx, Kriege became mostly active on behalf of land reform by the late 1840s and also cooperated with the nascent labor movement in New York City in the 1850s. But the Social Reformers were no group of mere theoreticians; their *Gesangverein* entertained at picnics and other festivities which drew a large number of visitors, and their *Arbeiter Halle* drew crowds of beer-drinkers and workers for meetings.[20]

Kriege's Social Reformers were also the early hosts to another German political activist, Wilhelm Weitling, who started an early communist organization, the Befreiungsbund (League of Liberation) in 1846. Weitling left to fight in the Revolution of 1848 but returned to New York a year later to edit his newspaper, *Republik der Arbeiter,* in which he supported the organization of labor, the founding of an economic exchange association for workers, and various other utopian schemes. Weitling was one of the driving forces behind the creation of a central organization for German workers in the early 1850s. He also founded a workers' colony in Communia, Iowa. Another radical exile, Wilhelm Weydemeyer, played an important role amidst the world of the political Vereine in the early 1850s, when he sought to promote Marx's ideas of class struggle in his Proletarierbund (League of Proletarians). The group was mostly successful for its cooperation with the radical German-American labor unions who joined together to form the American Workers League in 1853.[21]

The political groups, together with the nascent union movement, played a distinct role within the Vereinswelt, but their general thrust was similar to that of many Vereine with no official political program, such as the Turners and some singing societies. Joined in parades and demonstrations, they all upheld a common allegiance to the emancipatory, anti-aristocratic ideals of the 1848 revolution in Europe. In the

New World they translated their ideals into support for artisan republicanism and labor activism in general. When the labor movement went into a temporary decline after the mid-1850s, abolitionism provided the cement which united much of the Vereinswelt behind a common political goal in German New York and other German-American communities throughout the country.[22]

The split between the world of political activism and the more purely social activism of most Gilded Age Vereine began to emerge after the Civil War. Few of the prewar political groups survived; in fact, only one, the Commmunistenbund, founded in the mid-1850s by a group of radical Forty-eighters led by Friedrich Adolf Sorge, is known to have survived the Civil War. This organization was sought out by a new group of German immigrants who arrived in New York enthusiastic about the ideas of the German socialist writer and organizer Ferdinand Lassalle. In the wake of a revival among German labor organizations in general (see below), they started the General German Workingmen's Association (an exact namesake of the Lassallean organization in Germany) in 1865. Members of the old Communist Club joined, and the entire organization became a member of the First International as Section 1 in 1869. The section carried much of the burden of keeping the International alive during the final four years when it was headquartered in New York.[23]

While the socialists of the 1860s and early 1870s may have played a significant role within the First International, their position within the politics of the United States or New York City was insignificant. They did not constitute a party (nor did they claim to) nor did they represent a movement (as they wanted to). In reality their status was close to that of a political Verein, separated from the rest of the Vereinswelt by their focus on political theorizing. Section 1 was a group into which German immigrant socialists drifted, which made little effort to appeal to non-Germans or people who were not already converted to the cause of Marxian socialism. Much of its attention was focused on European events such as the Franco-Prussian War and the Paris Commune in 1871. In its political sectarianism and ethnic isolation Section 1 embodied some of the most narrow-minded aspects of a German-American *Vereinskultur*: the need to reassert one's identity by staying as close as possible to familiar ways of of thinking and organizing.[24] At the same time, the socialists were isolated from the majority of the Vereine by their exclusion of a broader social agenda in favor of political activism.

Beginning in the early 1870s, the German-American socialists made some efforts to overcome this double isolation from German-American Vereine on the one hand and the broader North American labor movement on the other. At first the attempts to connect to the English-speaking labor movement looked unpromising as an alliance with the National Labor Union came to nothing when the latter organization dissolved in 1870, and efforts to bind English-speaking radicals to the party's creed with a so-called American Section of the International failed, too.

But efforts to organize a larger number of their own German compatriots for their cause bore some fruit. Thus Section 1 members became active in trade unions which they started or revived, especially in the building trades and in furniture making. On the neighborhood level the German socialists also scored some success by organizing a so-called Tenth Ward Council which became active in 1873, the first year of a massive depression. Soup kitchens and cooperative shops were organized by the council and it staged demonstrations where people demanded public works projects.

The highly visible activism of the organized socialists among working-class New Yorkers ended in 1874 when a demonstration for unemployment relief in Tompkins Square on the Lower East Side was broken up violently by the police.[25] Hostility by the authorities and the hardships of the depression once again reduced the small band of immigrant socialists in the International Workingmen's Association to a dismal 635 members; its rival, the (Lassallean) Social Democratic party, could muster 1500 members nationwide in 1875. A year later they joined forces with a third group to form the Socialistic (later Socialist) Labor party (SLP).[26]

Over the next decade the SLP would continue the struggle to become a permanent political force for the city's working class at large, breaking out of its ethnic isolation, and to create a larger network of social and cultural organizations for its members as an alternative to the depoliticized Vereine. By and large the first part of the struggle was unsuccessful. Continued disagreement over ideological questions that had little relevance to the American situation hampered the party and prevented it from reaching out to non-Germans. The influx of working-class immigrants who were familiar with and sympathetic to socialism did not help the SLP either. Rather than providing it with a widening and more diverse membership base, the new immigrants isolated the party even more. Not only were newcomers caught up in German ideological squabbles, few of them could even vote, which proved to be a crucial disadvantage to the party at election time. In local elections the party rarely gained over 1,000 votes citywide. Even in the heavily German wards of the Lower East Side, voter turnout for the socialists rarely exceeded 800 in the 1880s even though the Socialist Labor party received verbal support from a number of important German-American trade unions.[27]

Measured against other political parties in electoral results or other forms of citywide influence, the Socialists were a failure in New York City, even within the German community. But in fact the SLP hardly resembled political parties of the era: it did not form lobbying groups, covet the powerful, or mount national campaigns, nor was it in any other way involved in the American political system until the mid-1880s. Instead, the Socialists continued to perform many of the functions of a political Verein. In fact, by the late 1870s, the Socialists had managed to overcome some of the gaps that had separated them from the Vereinswelt by forming politicized Vereine devoted to social, cultural, and charitable activities such as the singing and Turner societies mentioned earlier. Socialism had become a movement in German New York which did not just include the party itself but encompassed numerous enterprises designed to educate, entertain, and help its members. From the Socialist Publishing Association (printing the works of Marx and Lassalle in cheap editions) to the *Sozialistische Liedertafel,* to Justus Schwab's saloon, Socialists were given a social, cultural, and political home in this political subculture of the German Vereinswelt. It provided their members with a sense of belonging that extended far beyond electoral politics. While this may have eased the pain of leaving the old country behind for many, it did not provide an entrée into the world of American political institutions. On the contrary, up to a certain point it prevented the socialist movement from growing within the American political arena.[28]

German Voters and Mainstream Parties

The Socialist Labor party through most of the 1870s and 1880s remained a Verein in the narrow sense, offering Germans little chance to become part of the wider arena of American politics, especially electoral politics. The mainstream political parties, on the other hand, did show at least sporadic interest in German voters between the 1850s and the 1880s. But neither the Democrats nor the Republicans did much to organize the German immigrant community in a lasting way.

Since the mid-1850s an increasing number of German immigrants had become eligible to vote. On a national level the increasing participation of German immigrants in North American politics during the 1850s and 1860s almost paralleled the rise of the Republican party, which the vast majority of Germans supported.[29] But New York

City's Germans did not fit into this general pattern. In the city the Democratic party ruled almost unchallenged and was especially dominant in the immigrant wards from the 1840s on. Within the Democrats, native (English-speaking) and Irish politicians had firmly established their dominance, which left Germans (as relative latecomers to the electoral scene) on the sidelines. Only occasional challengers, at first from the Whigs and later from dissident factions within the Democratic party, made the Germans an important voting block and induced the majority faction—Tammany Hall—to share occasional spoils with German voters in order to retain their loyalty.

Some of the mayoral contests of the 1850s, 1860s, and 1870s illustrate how at times German voters were able to form temporary coalitions with other groups to unseat entrenched Tammany forces. Between 1857 and 1860, for example, Germans were important backers of Fernando Wood for mayor, a candidate of the so-called Mozart Hall (minority) Democrats. Wood, a well-known antitemperance advocate who appealed to Germans, was elected in 1857 but lost in a subsequent attempt. A minority coalition consisting of anti-Tammany forces among the German business-class and working-class voters also took advantage of the political disarray in the wake of the New York City draft riots in 1863 and the Tweed scandal of the early 1870s. Both times second-generation German-Americans, Godfrey Gunther in 1863 and William Havemeyer in 1872, were elected mayor, only to be unseated by Tammany candidates in the next election.[30] Despite these challenges, Tammany was able to marshal the loyalty of a considerable number of German voters when it needed to, especially among the newer German immigrants of the city's working-class wards, even though German immigrants were always much more ambivalent in their loyalty to Tammany than the Irish. After the Civil War Germans lent their support to candidates of the so-called County Democrats or of other coalitions of anti-Tammany forces within the Democratic party. Thus the Tenth Assembly District voted for Democratic reform candidates around the so-called Tilden faction in the late 1870s; and when that group weakened around 1880, the district's German-American electorate flocked to Grover Cleveland, first as a gubernatorial candidate (1882), and later as a presidential candidate (1884, 1888, 1894). In mayoral elections the Tenth also consistently supported Democratic candidates who were running against Tammany stalwarts such as Mayor Grace.[31]

Republicans meanwhile tried in vain to translate their popularity with German voters elsewhere into electoral successes in the city, although they did better among Germans than among most other im-

migrants. New York's Republican leaders were temperance supporters whose sympathies for the immigrant working class did not run
deep. Closely aligned with a Republican state government in the
1850s, they alienated working-class New Yorkers by introducing a
much hated "Metropolitan Police" in the city. After a police riot in
which a German immigrant was killed in 1857, the Republican party's appeal was badly damaged in the city's German wards, despite
the support of some prominent Forty-eighters for the party and its
abolitionist ideals.[32] After the Civil War the Republican vote in the
German areas of the city would always be higher than in other working-class areas of New York, but only in the mayoral election of 1880
and the election for State Assembly in 1879 did the voters of the working-class Tenth Ward give the majority to a Republican.[33]

The political factionalization of New York politics was, of course,
a reflection of the heterogeneous nature of the city's population in
general and the German community in particular. It is important to
remember, though, that while on the part of the established political
parties there was a growing concern with German voters in the most
general sense, candidacies and campaigns were engineered without
the knowledge or participation of the vast majority of German voters and did little to draw the German voters into the political process. A class of political leaders within the German community had
emerged by the 1870s and continued to be active throughout the rest
of the century, but for most of the 1870s and 1880s, this small group
of wealthy businessmen (William Steinway and Oswald Ottendorfer
among them) represented above all the interest of their peers—immigrant businessmen and professionals—not those of the German-
American working class. So-called citizens clubs of German-Americans (organized by assembly district) were convened at election time
to give endorsements to whatever candidate the German-American
elite (usually active within the reform Democrats) had chosen, but this
amounted to mere window dressing and left the mass of German-
American voters out of any meaningful political participation.[34]

German-American voters were not the only ones reduced to ap-
plauding or voting on command. Before the 1880s neither the Republican party nor the various wings of the Democrats had organized
their voters consistently and year-round. It was not until the late 1880s
that the Tammany machine began to create a large number of neighborhood political clubs whose activities went beyond "fixing" elections and providing ad hoc services just before election time. Only in
the 1890s did Tammany and reform Democrats begin to build an all-
encompassing political culture around a permanent clubhouse and

various year-round political activities in addition to organizing the neighborhood at election time. In other words, mainstream political parties in New York City did little to structure the communities of voters they relied on in any comprehensive sense. Tammany may have provided jobs to some immigrant voters and made some business-men prosperous, but it did not superimpose a culture on the various constituencies. By the late 1880s when the Democrats took on some of the characteristics of the neighborhood Vereine, they became root-ed in German America on a continuing basis. The catalyst for this transformation would be the election campaign of 1886 with Henry George as a mayoral candidate and the organizers of this transfor-mation would be among the German working-class organizations that were most successful at maintaining a close connection of political and social involvement among members: German-American trade unions.[35]

Fusing the Verein and Working-Class Politics: German-American Trade Unions

If the mainstream political parties lacked roots in the German-American community and if, on the other hand, the Socialist Labor party functioned as a Verein despite its claims to be a political party, trade unions were in part unabashed about their character as Vereine. Unions saw themselves increasingly as centers of a political move-ment that reached far beyond the boundaries of their trades. Labor unions and union-related institutions (newspapers, mutual benefit and leisure organizations) were part of the Vereinswelt and in many ways their structure and focus addressed the needs of German im-migrant workers better than any other type of organization. Commu-nity based, they organized those who shared work and often the tra-ditions that came with it. Even though their concerns were practical and closely related to the everyday life of immigrants, they also pro-vided a larger perspective on their members' place within American society at large. Their peculiar strength within the American socio-economic system derived from their ability to bridge the gap between past experience and new realities for the German working class. Ger-man-American trade unions of the 1870s and 1880s also tried to fuse both German and American traditions of political organizing and class consciousness and would continue to draw on both. The successful connection between German traditions and the demands of the Amer-ican political scene would determine to what extent unions could make the voice of German-American workers heard in New York City.

For centuries, trade organizations had defined the political and social traditions of German workers. Medieval artisans belonged to guilds which never entirely disappeared and instead, with government support, evolved into modern trade associations. As late as the turn into the twentieth century, most skilled trades in Germany were organized into guild-type organizations (*Innungen*) headed by master craftsmen who monopolized the training of apprentices and determined which ones would be promoted to journeyman. The system was skillfully integrated into the industrializing economy of late-nineteenth-century Germany. Large factories would employ master artisans who would then oversee the "education" of apprentices and journeymen, in effect training a work force that was young and unskilled to become skilled workers with artisanal knowledge in an industrial setting. A three-tier hierarchy of masters, journeymen, and apprentices thus determined the structure of German labor organizations in factories and small shops throughout the nineteenth century.[36]

Continued adherence to the artisanal order had important consequences for the political direction of the labor movement in Germany. For as long as the *Innung* system persisted, the old corporate order would shape the perspective of some workers. Many journeymen favored a return to a society of estates in which craftsmen through the corporate power of the guilds would be guaranteed a livelihood and a respected place in society. Despite their revolutionary role, activists who participated in the 1848 movements on behalf of artisans often represented this fundamentally conservative view. In the years after the failed revolution these groups became the nucleus of a conservative labor movement focused around cooperative schemes and Christian unionism. The conservative potential among German workers in the old country remained alive through these alternatives to the large socialist-inspired union movement.

The vast majority of workers' organizations in late-nineteenth-century Germany were, however, dominated by the Social Democratic party and were thoroughly industrial in their orientation, if not always revolutionary in their outlook. They also looked back to the Forty-eighter movements, mostly in journeymen brotherhoods belonging to the revolutionary avant-garde of the era. Demanding just wages for all workers and political participation in a democratic state, these groups, though originally far from unified, formed the core of a politicized socialist labor movement which first emerged in the mid-1860s in Germany. The socialist trade-union movement, though dominant throughout the late nineteenth century, was plagued by conflict with the Social Democratic party, which at times hampered its growth and hindered its consolidation. By about 1880, though, the free unions, as the socialist labor organizations were called, were clearly the dominant force in the labor movement of the new German Empire and exerted a powerful influence by example on similar movements overseas.[37]

The role of German trade unions in New York City was in some ways closely connected to their ambiguous role in the Old World, but also to the course of the English-speaking labor movement in the United States from the 1840s on. Heavily German trades had well-known unions by the late 1840s: tailors, bakers, and cabinetmakers were organized into unions which were active on behalf of their trades as well as in general political campaigns. Connected in their program with the more radical workers' organizations of 1848 but also with the republican workingmen's movements of the 1840s, German unions advocated better wages and improved working conditions for German-American skilled workers as well as a broader political program of land reform and producers' cooperatives. Their activism culminated in a citywide spate of strikes in 1850 and, in subsequent years, focused on the shorter workday, higher wages, and the need for relief for the unemployed. To increase their effectiveness the German unions formed the Centralkommission der Vereinigten Gewerbe von New York (Central Commission of United Trades of New York) in early 1850; within six months it had united 4,500 members in many trades. The German workers' organizations cooperated closely with the English-speaking workingmen's associations as part of a general protest movement which reverberated through the city during the early 1850s.[38]

The depression of 1857 destroyed most of the labor movement among German-Americans (and English-speaking workers), although some German unions survived with greatly reduced agendas. This meant, for example, that the German workers' organizations tried above all to preserve the economic status of their members in the skilled trades, and that they could do little beyond it except to provide some financial aid in emergencies. On the other hand such a conservative agenda could very well coexist with a politically radical program (muted though as it would be during a depression). At any rate, the unions that continued to exist during the 1850s and early 1860s (including the tailors, cigar makers, printers, and furniture makers) did so mostly as mutual benefit societies. Some of them lost their character as unions entirely and turned into fraternal societies. The conservative core of many unions became very obvious in these lean times but, at the same time, their conservatism helped the unions stay afloat.[39]

Beginning in the mid-1860s the German-American labor movement revived, and with it—cautiously—a more politicized agenda began to emerge. A number of German unions from the blacksmiths to the upholsterers met regularly again, and in 1864 they founded a new umbrella organization which, in reference to New York's English-speaking Workingmen's Union (which served a similar purpose), eventually named itself Arbeiter Union.[40] The Arbeiter Union at first kept a low political profile, professing not a socialist but a social reformist creed. It supported higher wages and consumers' cooperatives.[41] In fact, seven of the most active unions in the Arbeiter Union started a weekly (later daily) newspaper in 1868 as a cooperative enterprise. This paper, also called *Arbeiter Union*, flourished for two years before it broke up amid disunity among the German workers over the Franco-Prussian War.[42] While it lasted, however, the organization reached out to workers all over the city in ways unseen since the early 1850s: it facilitated improved contacts between the English-speaking and the German labor movements in the city by helping to organize part of the eight-hour movement, the early closing movement for clerks, and a campaign for higher hourly wages in 1871–72. The unions around the Arbeiter Union also cooperated with the socialists in the First International for the first time. Some union heads were members of the IWA, others (such as young Samuel Gompers himself) were merely sympathizers who attended occasional meetings.[43] These unions became the stalwarts of a lively eight-hour movement which culminated in an eight-hour strike during the spring of 1872.

By the early 1870s the German-American unions had shown considerable effectiveness, resilience, and potential for growth within the German-American working class in the city. They were successful in binding a heterogeneous group of immigrants to a program of trade solidarity, economic betterment, and mutual help. But the limited nature of their program and outlook also at times became apparent: they tended to be protective of their own rather than expansive, seeking allies only when times got tough. They had just recently made the connection to the more politically oriented socialists and there were still relatively few institutional contacts to workers of other ethnic and language backgrounds. But perhaps most important: only a minority of German immigrant workers were members of a union in the early 1870s—semiskilled workers were rarely unionized and the unskilled were outside organized labor. It would take a firmer and more expansive type of association to reach a majority of German-American workers in order to organize the community in a lasting way.

But the modest achievements of the German unions were almost entirely destroyed by the onset of a depression in 1873. New York's German working class was hit particularly hard because the 1870s were also a decade of strong, continuing immigration from Germany. New arrivals clogged the labor market and depressed wages in many of the skilled trades that were traditionally the preserve of Germans. In many "German" occupations, wages declined by 20 to 25 percent during the mid-1870s.[44] For the labor organizations of German America, mere survival was difficult at a time when many of their members were going hungry. The German-American labor movement weathered this period more successfully than it did the 1850s depression. Once again, most of the unions retreated from political activism into benefit activities. Groups such as the furniture workers, who remained politically active, relied on the solidarity of the ethnic community rather than the help of the American labor movement at large.[45] Where it survived, unionism in New York City retained a strongly ethnic and parochial flavor during these years. The cigar makers were one of the few heavily German unions who resisted this trend toward ethnic unionism, but they, too, had a difficult time attracting and maintaining a membership that was in any way representative of this cosmopolitan trade.[46]

But the barren years of the mid-1870s also contained the seeds of a more expansive labor movement which eventually could reach men and women beyond the confines of German-American craft unions. As we shall see, new alliances and indeed a new brand of unionism grew out of the cigar makers' union and its great strike of 1877. The cigar makers also became leading members of a new umbrella organization of German unions, the Vereinigte Deutsche Gewerkschaften (Amalgamated German Trade Unions), which survived well into the 1880s, when it was gradually superseded by the multi-ethnic Central Labor Union. The readiness to start cooperatives among skilled workers (usually doomed during this period of economic hardship) was irrepressible in the 1870s and pointed to a desire to create economic alternatives built on the structure of the trade unions.[47]

Reaching Out in New Ways: The New Yorker Volkszeitung *and the German-American Press*

One cooperative venture, begun in late 1877, turned out to be the most successful and long-lived enterprise of the German-American labor movement, reaching an unprecedented number of working-class German immigrants. The *New Yorker Volkszeitung* was a German socialist daily whose lively coverage of New York's labor scene and close involvement in union-organizing efforts made it an organ of vital importance to the German-American community at large. German socialists and trade unionists had published a number of weekly and even daily papers in earlier years, such as the *Arbeiter Union, Arbeiter Zeitung, Neue Arbeiter Zeitung,* and eventually *Der Social Democrat,* but the *New Yorker Volkszeitung* proved to be far more successful than these weeklies.[48] The paper, a daily from its inception until its demise in 1932, started out on a shoestring budget, with an initial print run of 5,500 copies, but it soon sold about 10,000 copies each day. During the height of its influence in the 1890s, it sold over 20,000 copies daily.

One of the reasons for its success was that the editors were a group of German-speaking socialists who had little sympathy with the more sectarian politics of the SLP, even though they were members of it. The first chief editor was Alexander Jonas (1878–89), the German-born son of a Berlin book-dealer. His short-term successor, Sergius Shevitch, was a Russian by birth and cut a dashing figure in New York socialist circles.[49] Hermann Schlueter, editor from 1891 to 1919, became also the first historian and analyst of the German socialist and labor movement in the United States. These editors made sure that the linguistic standards remained high but also that the paper contained a mix of general reporting, cultural items, and news and commentary about the labor movement in the United States and Europe. The *Volkszeitung* thus appealed to an audience far beyond the hard-core members of the socialist labor movement in the city.[50]

The political influence of the paper increased in the early 1880s, when internecine fighting between socialists, unionists, and the Knights of Labor began to break out in the Central Labor Union with increasing frequency. While the editors remained stalwart socialists (and often hostile to the Knights of Labor), they retained their independent judgment and often criticized the SLP. The paper's most important mission, as the editors saw it, was to show that socialism was compatible with support for the practical side of the trade union movement in the New World.[51]

Because of the openness and effective reporting of the *Volkszeitung,* the German labor movement in New York lost some of its parochial character and became decidedly less Eurocentric in its political interests. Within the community the organized working class also had in the *Volkszeitung* a consistent and well-publicized voice to oppose the increasingly shrill anti-labor bias of the rival middle-class paper, the *New Yorker Staats Zeitung* which, under the editorship of Oswald Ottendorfer, claimed leadership over the entire German immigrant community. The *Volkszeitung* thus not only gave a voice to the German working class of the city, it also became one of the earliest effective advocates of expanding the scope of German-American labor beyond the boundaries of the German working class in New York. As a means to hold the community together and expand its visibility the *New Yorker Volkszeitung* was perhaps the most effective community institution among working-class Germans in the late nineteenth century.

In the end the lean 1870s left a dual legacy for German-American labor organizations. They had shown that German-American workers had the experience and resources to maintain organizations even in difficult times. But the price of continuity was retreat to one's own ethnic group and isolation from other parts of the labor movement. At the same time the expansion of the German Vereine into the larger working class was foreshadowed by the emergence of the *New Yorker Volkszeitung* and the Vereinigte Deutsche Gewerkschaften, two institutions that would reach far beyond the traditional definitions of the Vereinswelt. The German labor movement in New York City would enter the 1880s with the possibility of bridges built by these two organizations. During that decade, the liveliest and most fateful for organized labor in the late nineteenth century, the German working class would have to find a way to emancipate itself from the constricting influences of the ethnic Vereine, while at the same time retaining the experience and strength it could draw from the community in which the Vereine had been built. Its solutions would go far in determining the general shape of the American working-class movement.

From the inward-looking organization of the churches to the expansive activism of the trade unions, the Vereine of German America offered a wide spectrum of opportunities. All of them provided a social "home" to the immigrants who joined, a sheltered place and a vantage point from which to explore or just learn to live with the new country. The approach the Vereine took varied widely and determined their influence within the German community and their importance for their members as well. The mutual benefit associations and the many singing and gymnastics societies capitalized on the cultural and social bonds their members brought from the Old World without showing much interest in the New World around them. Their role would change little over the decades to come and their importance would decline greatly as the English-speaking world became more important to German immigrants. Churches and organizations of businessmen and professionals were more ambiguous in their role, professing to care mostly for the maintenance of ethnic cultural and social bonds but also providing a way to assimilate into more main-stream American society through business contacts or relations with multi-ethnic church institutions. On the other end of the spectrum were the political parties which nominally professed to have an interest in German immigrants as a world unto themselves, but whose main purpose was actually to bind immigrants into mainstream political culture.

Unions and the labor movement had an in-between position in this scheme. To their working-class immigrant constituents they were of vital importance as places to socialize and enjoy familiar ties. But most of their members also had to rely on labor organizations to make successful contact with the non-German-speaking world for them; as manual workers they were confronted with English-speaking bosses, politicians, and competitors without the means to negotiate to their best advantage alone. It became crucial for German-American labor organizations to open up their world to the English-speaking majority of workers in order to organize together, coordinate, or just understand what was going on. This was a tall order, especially for working-class immigrants who had fewer economic resources than more upwardly mobile German-Americans. But only by filling it could German labor organizations hope to survive at all, even if that ultimately meant giving up an important part of their collective ethnic identity.

3

New York's Cigar Makers and Their Trade: The American Cigar Industry in Historical Perspective

Cigar making was not one of the better-known trades in late-nineteenth- and early-twentieth-century New York. The industry had neither the aura of history that embellished the city's old-time crafts such as shipbuilding nor the prestige of the luxury crafts that supplied expensive furnishings for the wealthy. Cigar makers also lacked the intellectual and political tradition associated with the city's printers and garment makers. Its lack of folklore as well as prestige is surprising in light of the fact that, after the garment industry, the cigar trade was the city's second largest employer during the late nineteenth century. Over 14,000 men and women (2.7 percent of the total work force) earned their livelihood in the cigar industry in 1880.[1] Sheer numbers and the wish to rescue them from historical oblivion are not, however, what put the cigar makers in a prominent place in any study of the German working class. Throughout the United States the cigar trade was always a heavily German occupation during the nineteenth century, especially in New York, the center of cigar manufacturing in the country. In such a large community of workers, differentiation among generations, classes of cigar makers, and regional origins loomed rather large and would find expression in various forms of self-organization. Cigar makers were always prominent organizers, not just in their own trade but in the union movement at large; the following chapters will explore some of the reasons why this was so. In the course of our analysis we will also be able to uncover some of the most important sources of the political culture of mainstream American unionism that originated in the cigar makers' community. In other words, if the German cigar makers in New York were in their diversity and size representative of the *German* community as a whole, their organizations were also at the core of the *American* labor movement at large. In a unique way the cigar makers and their organizations linked immigrant culture to the politics of American labor.

The First Decades

Few industries of the modern age have such international origins as cigar making. Because their manufacture is closely related to tobacco cultivation (mainly in the Spanish colonies of the New World), cigars were soon made in the harbor cities of Cuba, Spain, England, and the European continent. By the late eighteenth century, European trading centers such as London, Amsterdam, Hamburg, and Bremen had the largest cigar-making industries outside Havana. The work force in the young industry was equally international in character. Spaniards, Mestizos, Blacks, and Chinese worked next to each other in Cuba. British, Dutch, Scandinavian, German, and western European Jewish workers rolled cigars in European cities. Cigar makers were a small, well-paid, and all-male group of international workers before the 1830s. Despite a lack of traditional roots in the craft system of pre-industrial Europe, they were carving out a respected and seemingly secure niche in the early-nineteenth-century western economy.[2]

Industrialization had a profound effect on the small industry, however. Germany, not otherwise in the early forefront of industrial development, saw an expansion of cigar making between the late eighteenth and the mid-nineteenth century from the coastal cities of Hamburg and Bremen to numerous provincial centers. In the hinterlands German cigar factories started out as profitable sources of income for local princes, who either owned the cigar manufactories or licensed them, extracting heavy fees and taxes.[3] By about 1860 there were established cigar industries in the port cities of Hamburg and Bremen, and also in Berlin, Breslau, and in rural areas of Baden, Bavaria, Westphalia, and Saxony.

As the industry expanded, its workers came from ever more varied backgrounds. A relatively young trade, cigar making had never been subject to guild rules in Germany, which even in the nineteenth century often restricted access to other crafts and prohibited those marginal to the social order from becoming full-fledged members of a trade. Cigar making, by contrast, was an open trade, and many workers who had trouble entering a more regulated craft found work in this newly expanding industry. Especially in urban areas, many of the full-time cigar makers were Jews, while others were farmers or their children who could no longer make a living off the land. Farmers and—by the 1840s—their wives and children were especially attracted to the cigar manufactories in villages and small-town Germany, where they could work either seasonally or year-round while still holding on to their land, farming it part-time.[4]

With the increasingly sharp division of the German cigar industry into rural and urban manufactories came a differentiation in production and a clear separation of the workers into different classes. Urban industries, especially in Hamburg and Bremen but also in Berlin, began to specialize in "high-end" cigars, that is, expensive brands made by hand from high-grade tobacco. The workers in these industries had a relatively secure livelihood, at least up to the 1860s. Their craft demanded considerable skill, and although there was no formal, fixed training period, a young apprentice needed years to become proficient at the craft. Since the demand for skilled workers increased steadily but the supply of cigar makers grew slowly, German cigar workers were in a relatively favorable position when it came to securing good wages and working conditions during the first half of the nineteenth century.[5]

By the 1850s though the market share of the high-end manufactories was shrinking as rural industries supplied an ever larger number of smokers with cheaper and medium-grade cigars. The workers in these industries were trained less extensively and paid much less. Many of them were only offered seasonal employment. Because of these conditions, the trade became increasingly dominated by women who had no choice but to accept this type of employment close to home.[6] Women and children had traditionally worked as helpers to cigar makers in the urban industry of north Germany, but the feminization of the rural cigar industry set off a wave of discontent starting in the 1850s, when male cigar makers in the high-end shops started their first cigar makers' unions, in order to preserve—or introduce—a formal craft status to their trade. Against the backdrop of the political upheaval of the 1848 revolution, the German Cigar Workers Association (Assoziation der Zigarrenarbeiter Deutschlands) was founded in the same year, making the cigar makers (together with the printers) among the first trades in Germany to form a national labor organization. Despite the craft's heterogeneity, the members of the association presented themselves as a group of skilled male workers whose interests focused on winning higher wages, shorter hours, and a closed-shop system. The group's demands for exclusion of female cigar workers and a strict apprenticeship system were also important; these were not just attempts to reverse the trend toward cheaper, semiskilled labor but were also aimed at introducing an unprecedented "traditionality" and exclusiveness to the trade. Few, if any, of the union's demands were ever realized in negotiations with manufacturers, but the union was popular, counting over 1,000 members by 1850.[7] The association kept intact the ideological ties to the old order which the labor movement, especially in the skilled trades, maintained in Germany during the Revolution of 1848. It is ironic that the cigar makers were in the vanguard of this movement toward the craft principles of the traditional order, when in fact there was very little tradition in the trade; if there had been a true guild or organization of masters, it would have probably stifled the vigorous organization of workers in the first place.

Pseudotraditionalism was not the only side to the organization of cigar makers in the 1840s and 1850s. As part of the politicized movement of skilled workers and journeymen, the Cigar Workers Association aligned itself, after much discussion and dissent among members, with the most radical wing of the Forty-eighter revolutionaries, the "Arbeiterverbrüderung." We know very little about the result of this alliance, but it showed that even though the organized cigar makers were conservative when it came to preserving what they considered their interests, they were a politicized group with little stake in the old political order. But it should also not surprise us that after the failure of the 1848 movement and its repression by the state authorities in the early 1850s, the cigar makers' movement remained alive only within local mutual benefit societies. This sort of retreat was typical for the labor movement in Germany during the 1850s and 1860s.[8]

Rather than accommodate themselves to a continuing loss in status, wages, and security in the old country, thousands of cigar makers went to the New World in the 1850s. The steady exodus swelled to a stream when in 1863 the United States government introduced import duties on cigars so that it was no longer economically feasible to import cheaper and medium-priced cigars from overseas. As a consequence European cigar manufacturers cut back their production greatly, reserving only their high-end brands for export. Widespread unemployment and declining wages destroyed the livelihood of British cigar makers, many of whom borrowed money and emigrated to America. Dutch workers (including Samuel Gompers's father, who lived in London at the time) did the same.[9] German cigar makers suffered most from the North American tariff as almost the entire German industry became geared toward the low-end domestic market. The well-paid workers in the urban centers were the first to lose their livelihood, whereas the impoverished workers of rural areas were employed in ever larger numbers.[10]

These changes in the German cigar industry led to a revival of union activity among German cigar makers beginning in the 1860s. Local cigar makers' groups helped found the Lassallean General German Cigar Workers' Association in 1865. The group was probably among the most successful labor organizations in Germany during the late 1860s and early 1870s with about 10,000 members in 1869. Like its predecessor in the late 1840s it tried to improve wages and working conditions in the industry. Yet the spread of low-paid female labor, the ruralization of the industry, and the general deterioration of wages could not be halted. Once again this was partly because of the two-faced nature of the organization, which was a vigorous part of the socialist labor movement, yet opposed female labor and thus attracted an exclusively male, mostly urban membership.[11]

While in Germany thousands of cigar makers struggled to organize and earn a livelihood, thousands more left home to follow the shift of the industry to the United States. As an internationally mobile proletariat, they were attracted by the relative ease with which one could earn a living at the trade in the United States before the late 1860s; after that time they were forced to move to North America in order to earn any livelihood at all. Their search for stable work led many German cigar makers to the already heavily German cities of the Midwest—Cincinnati, Cleveland, Chicago, Milwaukee, and St. Louis. New York, which was rapidly fortifying its status as the North American cigar industry's capital, attracted even more Germans. Over 2,800 cigar makers lived there by 1870; their number increased to over 3,500 by 1880.[12]

The United States cigar industry was even younger than the industry in central Europe. The domestic tobacco industries of Pennsylvania and Connecticut had, since colonial times, manufactured mostly pipe and chewing tobacco, while stogies and cheap cigars for local consumption were made on a small scale by local farm families at home. By 1850 a small urban cigar industry had established itself in North America with European and Caribbean immigrant cigar makers who manufactured higher grades of cigars.[13]

Caribbean ("Spanish") workers would remain a small but significant group of cigar workers in the United States, although their branch of the industry soon became quite separate.[14] The early American cigar industry was relatively small, but growing fast from the early 1850s on as demand increased due to more Europeanized tastes in urban America. Wages were good for most immigrants, and the future seemed secure from the intrusion of machines.

Because of these attractions, the budding New York cigar industry began, during the 1850s, to look more and more like an extension of the German cigar industry. The majority of employers as well as workers seem to have been German. The practice of the trade was, if anything, even more craftlike than in central Europe. The city's cigar industry was dominated by small shops with fewer than three workers. Cigar manufacturer Edward Hall remembered seeing only about a dozen small manufacturers with more employees during this early period. Even "large" manufacturers rarely employed more than twenty workers.[15] The scale of production was therefore quite modest even in the larger factories, which were usually situated in lofts, warehouses, and other rented spaces. Some employers joined their workers and rolled cigars with them, as did David Hirsch, in whose shop young Samuel Gompers made his first acquaintance with the labor movement. In Edward Hall's factory on the Lower East Side the owner himself did not make cigars, but he sorted the wrapper leaves and the finished cigars, which he then sold in his own store. Hall's firm was typical of the early cigar factories in selling its products directly to private customers in its own store or to saloonkeepers and peddlers. Some cigar makers also worked at home on contract for larger manufacturers.[16]

Thus the line between the workers and employers was not rigid. Compared to many German factories and the New York industry in later years, the cigar makers' community was relatively homogeneous. Virtually all cigar makers were adult males with similar skills and economic status. Because of shared work and status, ethnic divisions among the workers themselves were not critical, even though cigar makers were immigrants from many countries and cultures. Just as they had hoped, New York's newly arrived cigar makers, up to the early 1870s, seemed to have a prized skill and an honored position as craftsmen secure from competition.[17]

A number of developments during the Civil War decade dramatically disturbed this tranquil situation and once again altered the balance of positive and negative factors for immigrants from central Europe. The introduction of import duties by the United States government in 1863 meant that the small domestic cigar industry in urban areas of the Northeast and Midwest was the first to benefit from the sudden closing off of overseas imports. With relatively little capital the owners of cigar-making establishments were able to expand their workshops by employing cigar makers emigrating from Europe.[18]

The years between 1865 and 1873 were boom times for the New York cigar industry. The number of shops in general—most of them owned by German immigrants of an earlier generation—increased dramatically. Manufactories with five or more workers, the first real cigar factories, grew with striking rapidity. Large shops, some of them with a dozen workers, others with one hundred or more, began to emerge. The growth of the New York industry also brought about a hierarchization and an increased growth of large firms.[19]

The character of the work, on the other hand, hardly changed at all. Subdivision of labor remained rudimentary, with female workers doing the auxiliary preparatory tasks while skilled male workers made the cigar bunches by hand, cut the wrapper leaves, and wrapped the bunches. There was little child labor in New York factories at the time. Samuel Gompers fondly remembered his work as a cigar maker in the cigar factories of New York City during the late 1860s: "I loved the freedom of that work, for I had earned the mind freedom that accompanied skill as a craftsman."[20] Political discussion, singing, and reading (one of the workers would be paid by his colleagues to read aloud while the others worked) were part of young Gompers's working life.[21]

Most of the workers with whom Samuel Gompers shared the bench in the 1860s were members of the first generation of immigrant cigar workers, having arrived between 1850 and 1868 or so. They shared a craft consciousness and work culture which, though not rooted in premodern European tradition, was strong and extended to organizing and political activity as well. In New York cigar makers had organized since the early 1850s, later than in other American cities and not in a very prominent way.[22] It seems that the membership of the early union was limited to workers in a few shops and that it made no attempt to organize large numbers of workers.[23] Most of the German craftsmen with whom the young Samuel Gompers shared the cigar maker's bench in New York City were members of the cigar makers' union, but at that point the political culture of German workers was centered on the socialist movement (represented by such organizations as the Workingmen's party and the First International).[24] As Gompers reminds us vividly in his memoirs, many of the members of the International had a considerable influence not just on him but eventually reaching out beyond the socialist circles of fellow immigrants, and thus on the nascent American labor movement at large. Calling themselves the "Ten Philosophers," he and his friends met once a week to discuss the writings of Marx, Lassalle, and other early socialists. Gompers later remembered with pride how much he had benefited from such instruction on and off the job by the members of a politicized generation of old-timers. "We dreamed together and thrashed out our dreams to see what might be of practical value. From this little group came the purpose and the initiative that finally resulted in the present American labor movement."[25] Gompers's memories may have been tinged with nostalgia and his description of his fellow workers may give the wrong impression when the majority of workers in the industry were far from prominent politically, but it is nonetheless remarkable that such a strongly politicized shop culture flourished in the cigar shops of New York City. The lack of pre-industrial traditions, which would have locked the perspectives of the cigar makers into the old order, and the relative heterogeneity of the work force explain some of the German cultural origins of this trade. Its New York roots were laid in an era of security and prosperity which gave the first generation of workers time for cultural adjustment. As skilled craftsmen embedded in an organizational network of *Vereine*, a quiescent union, and a small activist socialist movement, cigar makers were in a comfortable position where they could safely use their time "philosophizing."

Change and Depression

Two events brought to an end the age of craftsmanship for New York cigar makers and the relative isolation of the Germans within the trade in particular: the introduction of the cigar-making mold and the panic of 1873. Each by itself would have been enough to change the trade profoundly. When technological and organizational change coincided with one of the most severe depressions of the nineteenth century, the impact was redoubled. Almost no cigar maker could escape the difficulties and hardship that the 1870s brought to the industry.

The introduction of cigar molds from Germany in 1868 had an immediate impact on the entire New York cigar industry. The making of the "fillers" (the tobacco body of the cigar), which was the most difficult part of the cigar-making process, was drastically simplified through the use of molds. Cigar makers no longer had to roll the tobacco filler into an even, round shape by hand before wrapping it with the binder. Instead, the filler was only roughly rolled by hand and then pressed into a cigar-shaped mold. Cigars shaped by such molds were a little uneven and therefore of lower quality, but it no longer took years to train to make them. Semiskilled workers could learn how to make cigars with a mold within a few weeks, and after a short while their output was about twice that of hand workers. With the introduction of the mold, specialized, well-paid craftsmen lost their monopoly in the industry. Although manufacturers would retain some of their skilled workers to make the more expensive grades of cigars, most cigar production in New York soon shifted to the lower-grade mold cigars for which workers were paid much less. While, at least initially, most of the mold workers were still skilled male immigrants who had now been demoted in status and pay, a new group of workers also began to intrude into this male realm. For the first time, women were employed as cigar makers, as were young teenagers and immigrants with no previous experience in the industry.[26]

The shops in which many new workers found employment also bore little resemblance to the craft shops of the 1860s. Work in these larger manufactories was usually strictly subdivided, and the workers performed their specialized tasks in five different departments. Bookers, the lowest paid workers in the shops (usually girls and old workers), prepared the leaves by bending and moistening them. "Strippers" (also usually girls and women) then took out the ribs while "bunchbreakers" prepared the filler tobacco. Cigar makers— also called "rollers" in this system—pressed the filler and wrapped it with the wrapper leaf. Packers (always male workers) then sorted the cigars according to size and color and packed them into boxes.[27]

Despite the considerable gain in productivity through the use of the mold and the intense division of labor in large factories, during the first years after the introduction of the mold the rapidly expanding markets for New York's cigars seemed to provide a place for everybody in the industry, from the workers in the large factory to the independent craftsmen. Between 1868 and 1873 New York's cigar production increased by almost 500 percent. Over 1,550 shops were licensed to make cigars in Manhattan alone during the latter year. There was plenty of work for the many immigrant cigar makers entering the city, even if newcomers rarely enjoyed the craft status, the adequate wages, and the shop camaraderie of Gompers and his friends of the 1860s. Smaller craft shops coexisted alongside large factories and independent cigar makers; cigar makers working on contract also had a niche in the market. In the early 1870s rapid growth mitigated the potentially devastating effects that the introduction of the mold would have later on.[28]

The Panic of 1873 and the onset of the depression soon changed the state of the industry. Although the production and sale of New York cigars decreased only during 1874 and afterwards slowly grew, the mid-1870s brought unemployment and drastically falling wages for the cigar makers. Low-priced cigars (like alcohol) were a depression commodity, a cheap thrill for men of all ages with little spending money. New York's industry used the depression as an opportunity to specialize in the manufacture of low-grade cigars. In the competition for this segment of the market, the larger manufacturers who employed semiskilled workers had obvious advantages over smaller shops in which productivity was lower and wages were slightly higher. Many of the smaller employers were forced into bankruptcy during the depression. The dismissed workers either tried to eke out a living on their own—the number of licensed shops increased during the 1870s—or they joined the large number of workers in search of employment. This cycle of bankruptcies, unemployment, and competition led to severe wage cuts, especially for those forced into semiskilled jobs. Mold-workers earned no more than about $6.00 a week by 1877, 25 percent less than five years before. [29]

The surplus of workers and the depressed wages favored the establishment of a new branch of the industry: tenement manufacture. Beginning in 1873 a few (mostly larger) New York manufacturers had begun renting whole tenements whose apartments they then sublet to cigar makers and their families. The renters were obliged to work for their landlords by making cigars at home. At the end of every week these tenement workers delivered the finished cigars to the "office"—usually a ground floor apartment—where the cigars were bought by the boss at a fixed price. At the same time a family would pick up next week's load of tobacco, which it had to store, sort, and strip in the apartment. The price paid per thousand cigars was far below what was paid to factory workers who did not have to prepare the tobacco themselves. During the mid-1870s manufacturers paid $4.50 per thousand cigars to tenement workers (a practiced adult could roll about 1,200 cigars per week). If the market was slack, little or no tobacco was supplied and the tenement bosses refused to "buy" cigars from their workers. Rent, on the other hand, always had to be paid in cash and in advance; the rent for a small tenement apartment amounted to about a week's wages per month.[30]

Profits in the tenement industry (which supplied only the cheapest grades of cigars) were high, especially during the depression. By 1877 tenement workers numbered between 3,000 and 5,000, roughly a third of all cigar makers in New York City. In fact, tenement cigar making was probably the fastest-growing branch of the industry as a whole during the 1870s.[31] Tenement cigar making had little to do with the craft shop production that had dominated the New York industry just a few years earlier. Almost overnight, it seemed to observers, cigar making had become associated with the most degraded working and living conditions of the industrial age.

New York's Cigar Makers in the Industrial Age

The spectacular growth of the tenement industry during the depression was made possible by the influx of a new generation of central European cigar makers into the United States. Most of the newcomers had left the cigar makers' benches of German cities because there, too, a general pauperization of the trade was taking place as more and more of the work shifted to the rural industry, which paid starvation wages. In the traditional urban centers, in which skilled male workers had been well paid, this trend led to factory closings, and cigar makers were forced to work in their homes on contract for the manufacturer, an arrangement that resembled New York's tenement system.[32] In search of their lost status and security, the largely urban newcomers were joined by some workers from rural areas and unskilled Germans who were hoping to earn a living by rolling cigars. These social backgrounds were much more heterogeneous than those of the first generation of cigar makers. The skilled craftsman from Hamburg, the semiskilled former peasant from Baden, and the young Jewish immigrant from Westphalia or the Rhineland came from different worlds. Cigar making meant different things to them and their ultimate aspirations might be quite different from each other, even though the reality of unemployment and low wages was the same for all.

If the work force in New York's cigar factories presented a socially much more heterogeneous picture in 1880 than it had a decade earlier, the trade was also losing some of its polyglot makeup and becoming dominated by two national groups of workers: Germans and Bohemians. Over a quarter (25.5 percent) of all cigar makers living in New York City in 1880 were German-born, but an even larger percentage, about 35 percent, came from Austria-Hungary, of whom the overwhelming majority were Bohemians. Because of their size and their complex relationship to each other in the labor movement, these groups deserve to be portrayed in some detail as they appeared around 1880.[33]

German cigar makers, in some ways, were a cross section of German immigrants to New York. They came as (or lived with) families; they settled mostly but not exclusively in the tenements of the Lower East Side; they had been neither the poorest nor the best-off workers before emigration. In other ways, however, the immigrant cigar makers were different from the rest of German America. For one thing, the percentage of Baden cigar makers—traditionally among the poorest in Germany—was no higher than the percentage of immigrants from Baden in general to New York, while cigar makers from Saxony, Prussia, and Hamburg were slightly overrepresented.[34] The latter were heavily urban regions in which cigar makers had suffered the greatest decline in status and pay during the 1870s. A significant proportion of German immigrant cigar makers of the 1870s consisted of men who had hoped to escape a further deterioration of their status by emigrating.

While many of the immigrant cigar makers were young single men hoping for a better future, a considerable percentage came with families. In the New World these men hoped to earn a "family wage," that is, enough to feed their wives and children. The newly established German practice of having women work in the industry was, for the time being, not transplanted to the United States. Only twenty-three German-American women were found among a sample of 421 German or German-American cigar makers from the 1880 manuscript census. Certainly many women listed as "keeping house" helped their husbands make cigars (if the men worked at home), but the reluctance to say so also suggests the desire to follow the ideal of exclusively male breadwinners.[35]

Given the precariously low wages of most cigar makers and their traditional reluctance to send their wives to work, German immigrant cigar makers had to follow a variety of strategies to make ends meet. If the family had three or more children, as was often the case among German immigrants, the father and at least one of the children went to work in the cigar industry. Mothers were always "keeping house" in such families, and daughters worked at cigar making in only a few cases.[36] In the late 1880s such families had become relatively rare though, as most workers were much younger. This new generation was faced with a different situation when it came to earning a living in the trade. Partly because they were, on average, still young, many cigar makers were childless or had only one or two children. Low wages and a very high child mortality rate in the cigar-making districts, and perhaps the practice of contraception, made large families with six or more children (such as Gompers's) a relative rarity. Only as heads of small families could young cigar makers maintain their role as sole breadwinners and hope for a better future for their children outside the industry.[37]

Children of German immigrant cigar makers frequently left the trade if they had a chance. Only the oldest children in large families— those with the fewest choices—worked at the same trade as their father or were forced to roll cigars in support of their widowed mother. Younger siblings and the offspring in smaller families almost invariably turned to trades in which pay was higher and upward mobility more likely than in the cigar trade. By 1900 the number of German-Americans in the New York cigar industry had drastically declined. Only middle-aged and older Germans remained at the cigar maker's bench. Workers who had a choice left it behind.[38]

Although Germans and their American-born children remained the most activist and visible group among the cigar makers in the 1870s and 1880s, Bohemians became more numerous and turned out to be valuable allies in the struggle to organize the trade. Compared to Germans, Bohemian cigar makers in the United States belonged to a very recent group of immigrants. Only a few Bohemians had worked in the American cigar industry before the Civil War, since it was difficult for administrative and legal reasons to emigrate from Austria-Hungary before the 1850s. From the 1850s to the 1880s this partly industrial but mostly rural part of the Habsburg empire sent its emigrants to rural areas of the American Midwest and West. But some craftsmen were also part of the exodus, among them the first Bohemian cigar makers who found their way to New York City.[39] These men came from small towns in which, under government auspices, a rural cigar and tobacco industry had sprung up by the 1840s. Earlier than in Germany, the Austro-Hungarian industry employed women and children as semiskilled workers. The makeup of its work force, low wages, and seasonal employment patterns closely resembled the conditions of the southwest German industry about twenty years later. The early Bohemian arrivals fit right into New York's cigar industry without at first forming a distinct ethnic community in the 1850s and 1860s.[40]

The first generation of Bohemian cigar makers was followed by a much larger group of newcomers who came to New York after the Austro-Prussian War of 1866. These immigrants did not come as cigar makers, but had been farmers and craftsmen in the old country, although they were probably familiar with the cigar industry in their old homeland. Socially and culturally isolated and without financial resources, Bohemians had a hard time making a living, particularly during the depression of the 1870s, the peak years of Bohemian immigration to New York. The only Bohemian immigrants who had preceded them in the city and could therefore help in any way were the cigar makers. Many of these relatively established compatriots taught the newcomers how to roll cigars and helped them find jobs in the growing cigar industry of New York City.[41]

By the 1870s the Bohemian cigar makers had become a sizable group within the New York trade. As poor newcomers who, in contrast to the Germans, had little traditional connection to the cigar industry, the Bohemians never made "high-end" Spanish-style cigars and rarely owned their own shops or worked independently. None of the larger factories with ten or more workers was owned by a Bohemian in 1880. Instead most of them found work in the newest branches of the industry, the large factories and tenements (both usually owned by German immigrants) in which they worked as semi-skilled mold workers. Contemporary observers even regarded tenement manufacturing as an exclusively Bohemian industry—a false impression, since German families could be found among the tenement cigar makers as well. Compared to other immigrant workers, though, Bohemians remained an isolated proletariat and continued to be employed in the lowest-paid ranks of the trade throughout the 1870s.[42]

The concentration of Bohemians in certain branches of the cigar industry fortified their socio-cultural isolation. As a younger and economically more isolated group of workers than German cigar makers, they had to fit their own lives even more tightly into the preformed grid of industrial work. They remained socially distant from German and other immigrant workers, sharing with them the cigar maker's bench but rarely a roof: the tenements on the extreme eastern rim of the German quarter housed the Bohemian workers in isolation from Germans.[43]

Like Germans and other immigrants, New York's Bohemians usually lived in nuclear families. But in contrast to the Germans, Bohemians put the entire family to work making cigars, especially but not exclusively among tenement cigar makers. In the tenements husband and wife rolled cigars together and often enough a lodger helped too, while children pitched in as strippers and bookers.[44] Even single workers tried to find family settings as lodgers or lived together in order to work as a group, replicating family labor this way. Unlike some German cigar makers no Bohemian cigar makers lived in boardinghouses. As befitted such a recent group of immigrants, Bohemians also tended to be younger (65 percent were under 33) and more often female (36 percent of all Bohemian cigar makers) than German cigar makers.[45] In sharp contrast to the Germans, Bohemians seem to have brought the practice of having women work as cigar makers with them from the old country and adapted it to New World conditions, rather than shunning it as the Germans tried to do. Cigar making continued to be to an important occupation for Bohemian women, who worked not just within the family in tenements but also in factories all over town as strippers and rollers. Later, during the 1880s,

they were the first to challenge notions of male skill when they began to work as packers. During the 1870s Bohemian women also
formed their own mutual benefit societies—separate from those of
men.[46] Over time the important economic role of Bohemian women
and their organizational experience would gradually evolve into an
increased political presence in the New York City labor movement.

While Bohemian women slowly found ways to transform their role
from a barely audible group of ill-paid workers into a position of economic stability and organizational visibility, the children of Bohemian workers remained largely invisible. Because of the extreme poverty of most Bohemian cigar-making families during the 1870s and
1880s, children, if they were old enough (six years and older), almost
always had to help their parents. But since most of them were still
very young, this did not necessarily determine their future occupation. As it turned out, the children of Bohemian immigrants left the
trade as rapidly as their parents had entered it. By the 1890s, when
the second generation had reached adulthood, the number of Bohemian cigar makers in the city fell precipitously. Freed from the most
dire economic pressures by the late 1880s, second-generation Bohemians were quick to show that they had little stake in the industry.
Although they may have helped their parents earlier, they, like children of other industrial workers (and unlike the children of many older German craftsmen), easily changed occupations when better opportunities beckoned.[47]

New York's cigar industry and its workers emerged from the turmoil of the 1870s as a trade and community vastly different from the
one that Samuel Gompers had entered as a youngster in the 1860s.
Producing over 595 million cigars in 1880, the industry had become
more than just an important factor in the overall economy of the city;
it represented a very diverse work force and a large spectrum of production methods, factory size and forms of distribution. The work
force itself had changed dramatically too, and now, just as in the German community at large, one could distinguish workers of different
regional origins, generations and classes. But it turned out that class
and generational differences began to diminish in importance as
working conditions in the industry became more uniform (i.e., more
uniformly industrial) and regardless of skill, background, or expectations workers were proletarianized. This had twofold consequences for the organization of the community: on the one hand the pressure to organize against the deterioration of wages and working
conditions was strong as all workers were affected by it; on the other
hand the persistence of regional, generational, and status differences

made unified organizing difficult. How could workers effectively organize all of their shop colleagues if they could not understand each other for lack of a common language? Beyond the problems of communication, the basis for a common language of culture and politics was elusive for the thousands of men and women at work in the city's cigar industry. By the mid-1870s it looked as if the turmoil in the industry, and the struggle to feed themselves and their families, had left the cigar makers, formerly a well-organized group, without much of a voice in determining their future or the future of the immigrant working class in New York.

New York's Cigar Makers' Organizations

Most of the changes that the depression and the introduction of the cigar mold enforced on the city's cigar workers were borne in silence, and most of the adjustments were made privately by families and individuals alike. But some of the new conditions were challenged by the workers through organizations embedded in the German-American network of Vereine. At first only a few cigar makers attempted to protest against the direction the trade was taking and to give the newer generation of semiskilled factory workers a forum to air their grievances. As the following pages will show, the 1870s and early 1880s thus saw a transformation in the organization of the cigar makers from a relatively small group of craft workers to a union trying to organize workers of many backgrounds.

The overwhelming problem for any organization trying to unite the cigar workers in the 1870s was the poverty of its constituents. A second, strategic problem immediately arose—the perennial dilemma of unions and other trade organizations: what direction should be taken to ameliorate the situation? Should the cigar makers try to resurrect the age of craftsmanship and fight for the privileges that artisanal cigar makers like Samuel Gompers had had? Or should they try to be part of the dynamic of change and work for a uniformly higher wage system within the conditions of semiskilled factory labor? The dilemma had been faced in different ways by workers' organizations in Germany during the 1840s and 1850s as well as in the United States. But the cigar makers' problem was exacerbated by the recent changes in the work force and industry, which left many layers of workers with different ideas about their status and their future while still in the same dismal circumstances.

Most workers opted for organizations that demanded little or no political involvement: mutual aid associations with a distinctly ethnic character were popular in the 1870s for economic security and social fellowship. These associations, especially the Bohemian ones, were barely visible to outsiders within the organized working class. They did not claim to offer any vision of the future and had no intention of building coalitions with workers from other ethnic backgrounds.

With such a limited program, the mutual benefit associations rarely competed head on with the two locals of the Cigar Makers' International Union (one English- and one German-speaking) which had existed in New York at least since the Civil War. The union had a difficult time staying afloat amid the turmoil of the late 1860s and early 1870s, a situation that grew worse during the depression. In the early 1870s the German local (No. 15 of the CMIU) was very small and the English one (No. 10) also included a few Germans and other old-timers of the trade of British, Dutch, or Scandinavian background. Gompers himself was a member of this local, as were most of the friends of his youth. No Bohemians were members of the CMIU in New York. Nevertheless the Cigar Makers' International Union was the only truly multinational organization of cigar makers in the city, encompassing the older generation of central and western European workers. It was therefore understandable that this union held a rather dim view of the changes in the industry and its work force and took a resolutely conservative stand in regard to membership qualifications and work rules. The union excluded most female workers and bunchbreakers, and tolerated no tenement workers. No wonder it made no effort to reach out to Bohemians or even to the newer generation of German workers. These exclusive craft practices probably helped the union survive since those workers who were members were usually among the better-off who could afford to pay regular membership fees and maintain a rudimentary benefit program. Outside its small circle of artisan members the CMIU was not a force either nationally or locally in the union movement; it had only about 2,000 members nationwide by 1874 and just a few hundred in New York City.[48]

For those cigar makers who favored a more activist stand on behalf of the industrial work force, who wanted to be part of the dynamic of change in the industry, and who wanted to raise their voice to demand their share in the new order that emerged, the political activism of the socialists offered the only alternative. The Tenth Ward organizations in which cigar makers like the Hungarian-born, German-speaking Adolph Strasser and the Hamburg socialist George Winter were active specifically demanded the abolition of tenement labor and assumed leadership in a few cigar makers' strikes. In fact, members and sympathizers of the First International, the Socialist party, and its successor, the Working Men's party, were probably among the most vocal groups on behalf of the cigar makers. But despite the collective weight that the socialists could lend to some of the cigar makers' causes, they were not particularly interested in the day-to-day hardships of the cigar makers or any other specific trade. Firmly rooted in the German socialist tradition, they were primarily concerned with criticizing and changing the basic economic order of North American capitalism, not in applying what they considered short-term solutions by organizing workers of one trade for higher wages and better shop conditions. We have already mentioned that the extent of the socialists' influence was also limited by a lack of contacts outside the German-American community.[49]

In 1873, on the eve of the depression, a small band of socialist cigar makers tried to overcome the ethnic isolation to which the cooperation with the socialists confined them and to form an interethnic organization on a trade basis without the limiting vision of the craft unionists. The group started a union called the United Cigar Makers (Vereinigte Cigarren Macher von Nord Amerika) in order to unite "all men and women workers in the industry, regardless of their national origins in order to fight the ever mightier capitalists and to defend the workers' interests."[50] This politicized but well-focused activist approach soon bore fruit. As Adolph Strasser, the secretary of the new organization, reported in his first annual report: "Right away, a German and a Bohemian section were formed, linked to a central body. (An English section was also formed but disbanded soon afterwards) . . . A life insurance fund was started which has already proven a blessing for some members. All membership dues were used for organizing and the officers did not get one cent for their labors."[51] Undaunted by the devastating effect of the depression on the industry, the United Cigar Makers embarked on a number of ambitious projects during their first year. They initiated a campaign against tenement cigar making, criticizing public officials for their complacency in this matter and trying to organize tenement workers. Typical for other labor organizations in the decade, the group also supported the establishment of cooperative shops, one of which flourished for three years during the depression.[52]

This activism helped to make the immigrant cigar makers' concerns much more visible within the hard-pressed fledgling New York labor movement of the mid-1870s. Although the United Cigar Makers was explicitly billed as a trade, not an ethnic, organization (English-speaking Samuel Gompers was a member), German-speaking immigrants clearly predominated. The political program of the group, with its critique of capitalism, bore a striking resemblance to the program of its German sister union, the General German Tobacco Workers' Association. But the group's basic organizing strategies proved most successful among Bohemian factory workers. The United Cigar Makers helped them during a number of strikes in 1874 by forming shop committees, holding meetings, and providing financial support to needy strikers. Although many Bohemians left the union again after a lost strike in the depth of the depression of 1874–75, this first encounter with a union proved important during the next major conflict two years later. Moreover, the cooperative shop and a sickness fund under union auspices continued to tie some Bohemian workers to the labor movement.[53]

Despite its relatively sophisticated organizing methods at a difficult time in the trade, the group only had between seven and eight hundred members in good standing in 1874, less than a tenth of the cigar workers in the city. This was by no means a bad record for a time of great hardship in the trade, but, typically for many unions in largely immigrant occupations, the appeal of the organization to English-speaking workers remained limited. This fact may not seem important in a trade in which English speakers were a shrinking minority. It made it difficult, however, for the United Cigar Makers (and for other German-American unions) to reach beyond the confines of the ethnic ghetto to forge links with what remained of the English-speaking labor movement in the city.[54] This must have been a bitter experience for the multilingual leaders of the United Cigar Makers. By 1875 a deepening depression as well as feelings of acute political and economic powerlessness had spread among the organized cigar makers of the city. A reorganization of the union seemed necessary in order to realize the goal of reaching out beyond the confines of the German-American Vereinswesen.

The only way to break out of the ethnic and localized isolation of the cigar makers in the 1870s was to link up with some sort of multiethnic national movement. The socialists, who had repeatedly tried to build up just such a movement, had succeeded on neither front by the mid-1870s. Before the founding of the Socialist Labor party they remained badly split internally and largely confined in membership to German-Americans in large urban areas. On the other side of the spectrum was the small remaining band of men in the CMIU, who, though more mixed in their ethnic composition, remained at least outwardly committed to strict craft unionism. The weak position of both partners made the unlikely marriage look more enticing. It nevertheless took some debating over the perceived ideological differences of both groups and energetic mediation from Gompers and his friend Adolph Strasser, who were members of both organizations, to bring about an agreement.[55] In November of 1875 the United Cigar Makers became an official affiliate of the CMIU and renamed itself CMIU Local 144 of New York City. The young Samuel Gompers was elected president, and stalwarts of the United Cigar Makers continued to serve as leaders of the new local.[56]

The new organization was a remarkable attempt to bring together some very different traditions in the budding American labor movement. The new local fused beliefs and principles of the politicized German-American socialists with the more pragmatic goals of craft organizations. Its theoretical principles, especially, bore the stamp of central European socialism, and its political activism was also closely associated with the First International. On the other hand ethnic isolation, from which the German socialists were unable to free themselves, was rejected in favor of a strict "Americanization" policy within its own ranks. The union's benefit policies also reflected some of the conservative financial strategies often associated with British craft unionism. By fusing these traditions into a workable pragmatic model, the cigar makers' organization demonstrated that while ethnic divisions might still dominate within the social community of workers, their political organizations were able to overcome them, at least in principle.

For the next two years, Local 144 slowly gained members and influence. The new union local immediately became important for the national leadership of the CMIU in a number of ways. On the political and organizational level, the constitution of the local (passed shortly before the merger) indicated the direction which the future of the CMIU would take. It contained a mixture of socialist principles as advocated by the Workingmen's party and the German socialists and the more pragmatic goals of many German-American as well as British unions—both already well-represented by the United Cigar Makers. The introduction to the constitution opened with the following passages:

> The constant attacks and acts of repression by capitalists as well as the recognition of the position of the working class make it necessary for all workers to unite with their fellow workmen in order to better their lot and to attain an existence commensurate with human dignity. It will be the main objective of this organization to improve the lot of the worst-paid. To this end, we, the members of the organization will be standing one for all and all for one.

The experience of the working classes has proven that single trade unions cannot put up sufficient resistance to the united capitalists. Therefore it will always be the goal of this organization to unite the workers in a uniform central association.

The dependency of the workers' very existence on the capitalists is the basis of servitude in every form. Therefore the workers of New York City are striving to work in cooperatives rather than as wage laborers so that each of them can secure the fruits of his own labor.[57]

A lengthy description of the generous benefit program followed this political introduction. It promised health and unemployment benefits to every member who had paid the ten cents weekly membership dues for at least one year.[58] The union also paid strike benefits, but this support was tied to a very restrictive system of official endorsements and prescribed arbitration efforts. The benefit system was administered by a centralized, paid leadership, including the president of the local, its secretary, and other officers who received a generous sixty cents an hour for their efforts. Such a tight organizational structure combined with strike benefits was reminiscent of craft unionism. Nevertheless Local 144 stuck to its socialist origins by opening its doors to all male and female cigar makers regardless of skill or type of work. While the constitution thus expressed a fusion of two different parts of the labor movement, the interests of craft workers could not always be reconciled with socialist principles. The tension between these two groups was built into the constitution and would find expression in a number of conflicts in the future.

What were the consequences of this development for the community of cigar makers in New York City? Did it have any wider significance for the labor movement during the mid-1870s? At first the new beginning seemed auspicious. During a time of hardship and retrenchment for the American labor movement, the cigar makers' organization offered a way to combine trade solidarity, encompassing many ethnic groups, with the close connections to a heavily ethnic local membership base whose views on politics and the contours of the labor movement were unified. The cigar makers combined institutional stability and a very generous and organized benefit system with the old socialist principles of openness and mass organizing.

But it soon became apparent that two difficulties virtually nullified these advantages for most cigar makers. For one, the new local was too expensive for workers in a trade whose wages had badly eroded during the depression. This became particularly clear when, after one year, the union raised its weekly dues to twenty-five cents in order to remain solvent. Many members dropped out at this point.[59] Local 144 became de facto restricted to cigar makers who had stable

employment and earned relatively good wages—craftsmen, not tenement workers or rollers. Thus the restrictions of the CMIU were preserved under only slightly altered circumstances. A second, far more
important decision which would limit the union's appeal to many
potential members was made soon after the merger. The leadership
of the New York union, in its attempt to break out of ethnic unionism, decided that New York's Local 144 was to become an "American local," that is, English-speaking. The German-speaking Local 90
and Local 15, the small English-speaking local, were forced to merge
into Local 144. Union officers had to be English speakers, and members had to know at least some English to be able to follow the pro-
cedures. This was a decided turn away from the central European
origins of the local and excluded Bohemian workers almost completely.[60] This move was almost certainly instigated and promoted by the
two most influential leaders of the new local, Samuel Gompers (the
newly elected president) and Adolph Strasser, who had no ethnic
"home" among New York's many immigrant groups. Both spoke German and had elected to affiliate themselves mostly with German-
American trade unionists in the early 1870s, but were easily able to
switch their allegiance to an English-speaking labor movement. Other leaders of the local were German-Americans who were bilingual.[61]

The CMIU warmly received the move toward craft unionism and
English-speaking organization. Strasser was elected president and
editor of the union's paper, the *Cigar Makers' Official Journal*, in 1877.[62]
The opinions of the leaders of Local 144 thereafter received much attention on the pages of the *Journal*. Gompers and Strasser, for example, frequently voiced demands for reorganization of the entire union
along the lines of Local 144 and for stricter fiscal controls of the
union's benefit funds.[63]

But on the local level the tactics of de-ethnicization and a return
to implicit (if not politically formulated) craft unionism had little effect. The local communities of cigar makers in New York City and
elsewhere resisted the implementation of such ideas. In New York
some members of the old locals refused to merge into Local 144. It
seems that many former members dropped their affiliation rather than
pay the high dues and join the "American" organization. Women,
Bohemians, and tenement workers—formerly groups from which
members of the United Cigar Makers sought recruits—were no longer among the members. Separated from the vast majority of this potential constituency by rules and structure, the prospects for Local 144
did not look very good. In 1877 it had no more than two hundred
members in all of New York City, many fewer than in 1874.

The strategy of the cigar makers' organizations may have resulted in a certain internal stability and the badly needed financial solvency during the depression, but the obviously limiting nature of the reforms proved no model for labor organizations in the city. In 1877 the CMIU Local 144, which had wanted to both provide some financial stability for its members and protect all cigar makers regardless of status, background, or income, seemed to have lost the struggle on both fronts.[64] The union had tried to confront a dilemma common to all union organizations in industrializing America at a particularly difficult time: whether to assume the conservative face of organized labor and preserve the artisan status of its members—a stance adopted by German unions as well, as we have seen—or to reach out and be an active part in the industrialization of the trade, again a position taken by many German socialists in the union movement both in Germany and the United States. Both directions and the ambivalence they would foster were part of the German labor movement's continuing characteristics. But in the United States the attempt to balance the two conflicting positions was further complicated by the close links of the German-American unions to the Vereine. Strength and cohesion for German-American unions came from their close connection to other German-American or predominantly German institutions and groups. But this was also a source of isolation and sectarianism, as we have seen in dealing with the socialists and some other German unions, especially in times of economic hardship.

The leaders of New York's cigar makers' union wanted to overcome all these problems at once: they wanted to preserve at least some economic stability for their members through a benefit program, while reaching out to all workers in the trade and overcoming the isolation of any particular ethnic group. But the workers were not ready for such a radical step. German and Bohemian workers literally each spoke their own language, and they had different occupational, political, or cultural traditions which had to be integrated into a union to make it attractive to these workers. An America without ties to their specific cultures of origin meant little to them, and they were not to be Americanized by organizational fiat. The strategy of the United Cigar Makers, with Gompers and Strasser at the helm, might look visionary in retrospect, but in the 1870s it served only to weaken the already shaky community foundation of the union. In their zealous attempt to free the cigar makers' union from the organizational and social limitations of a German-American Verein, they had severed the ties to one of New York's liveliest communities of politically active workers, without replacing them with anything as viable. The attempt to replace the ethnic community of a largely German trade with a centralized organizational structure backfired badly. It left the majority of cigar workers outside the union and effectively without much of a voice in trade matters. It also rendered the union an organization without much of a social base. There was no community of "American" workers that could replace what the Germans and Bohemians could provide. It would take an explosive event to bring about a merger of the potential for activism among the ethnic communities behind the workers and the "American" labor union's interests.

4

The Great Strike of 1877

The CMIU was not the only trade organization which had failed in its efforts to unite workers behind its cause by the mid-1870s. The few other unions that weathered the depression had similar experiences. In the summer of 1877 though, the general despair and powerlessness of the labor movement was suddenly swept away by the great railroad strikes which shook the Midwest and many cities on the East Coast. The strike involved thousands of workers in the Pittsburgh and St. Louis areas in particular, but since the workers at the New York Central struck, New York was also affected. The level of excitement was considerable among the city's working class. The newspapers, echoing the fears of the middle class, expected a mass strike during the last week of July.[1] But New York's workers acted differently from their counterparts in the industrial Midwest. They were divided in their reaction to the mass walkout of the railroad workers. Some workers were cautious in their support for the strikers. A number of socialists, on the other hand, organized a mass meeting in support of the striking workers at Tompkins Square (where a similar protest gathering had ended in demonstrators being beaten up by the police three years earlier). Most of the organizers of the meeting were German-American, with a few cigar makers among them. After speeches by some of New York's most prominent socialists and a minor scuffle with the police, the meeting disbanded peacefully.[2] But some trade unions, Local 144 among them, dissociated themselves from the socialists and held a gathering of their own at the big hall of the Cooper Institute not far from Tompkins Square. At the indoor meeting the twenty-seven-year-old Gompers expressed solidarity with the railroad workers. The newspapers reported that "Mr. Gompers thought the workers had a right to strike for their bread and their families." But even at the time the July 27 meeting took place, it had already become clear that the railroad strike was not going to catch on in the city, for no group had called for a sympathy strike.[3] Organized labor, it seemed, was not ready to mount a major protest in conjunction with their brethren elsewhere.

On the surface, New York seemed calm by August 1877. But in the cigar makers' neighborhoods and on the shop floors of the cigar factories, a sullen quiet masked the dissatisfaction of thousands of German and Bohemian cigar workers who were in their fourth season of wage cuts and had endured long periods of idleness each winter since 1873. Still, when the one hundred workers of DeBary's cigar factory walked out in the middle of August to protest a 20 percent pay cut, nobody expected that this would spark a mass strike with political overtones similar to the great railroad strikes. Two weeks later the workers at Stachelberg's cigar factory also struck, this time for higher wages. Unlike DeBary's, many of Stachelberg's workers belonged to the union, which may have contributed to their winning a pay raise after holding out for nine weeks. Their colleagues at DeBary's had their reductions repealed after a similarly extended walkout.[4] While these strikes were still in full swing, workers in three other factories left their workbenches to demand higher wages. By mid-September they were joined by a stream of mostly Bohemian tenement workers. This was a unique development: tenement workers had almost never gone on strike before. With the number of striking tenement workers increasing daily, the strike had reached major dimensions by the first week of October, involving workers in at least twenty-five different firms.[5]

Up to this point there had been almost no contact between the strikers and the CMIU. With the exception of Stachelberg's workers, the strikers were not union members and although the union had previously led strikes of nonunionized cigar makers successfully, the policies of Local 144 discouraged such actions. Members could only strike at a select number of shops at a time so that fellow unionists still working could adequately support all those on strike. Officially the union only sanctioned strikes if its financial situation permitted full support of all striking union members.[6] The mass walkout in the fall of 1877 contradicted these guidelines. The local's coffers held $4,000, a large sum of money for the 250 union members but not enough to feed the thousands of strikers for more than a few days. In the eyes of the CMIU the unorganized and seemingly inarticulate tenement workers had little to offer to the union. Gompers complained: "We union men saw our hard won achievements likely to vanish because of this reckless precipitate action without the consultation of our union."[7]

By mid-October, however, the union realized that the cigar makers' strike was becoming a mass movement which called for a reconsideration of Local 144's tactics. Previous attempts to stabilize union membership and insulate the union from the worst effects of the depression had cut Local 144 off from the majority of cigar makers who worked in factories and tenements. The sudden mass strike, however, presented the small union with the chance to gain a long-sought leadership role not only among a few craft-workers but among the great mass of cigar makers in factories and tenements. It was a risky proposition to be sure, but Adolph Strasser, who had just been elected president of the CMIU, was quick to seize on the potential of the situation and discarded the union's restrictive rules governing strikes in an editorial in the union's official paper, the *Cigar Makers' Official Journal:* "Strikes are not always a loss to the strikers, as capitalists say, but on the other hand they are always a gain, if not in money they are in principle, for every strike, however feeble, educates people to demand their rights. Strikes on a small scale often fail in the special object they strike for, but strikes on a large scale are always successful." Accompanying Strasser's statement was a call to New York's cigar makers to send delegates to a meeting to be held in the middle of the month.[8]

Workers responded immediately to this rallying cry, and on October 14, five thousand cigar makers convened in Germania Assembly Hall "organized under the auspices of union 144," as the *New York Times* reported. While the union was the initiator of the meeting, it remained very much in the background as an organization. The community of workers, it seemed, were in charge of their own future unencumbered by union rules and a pre-existing leadership.

Unlike previous events connected to the strike, this gathering received extensive press coverage. "The meeting was full of enthusiasm and some of the speaking in relation to capital and labor was very spirited and a part rose to the point of genuine eloquence," remarked the conservative *New York Herald*. Local 144 activists Henry van der Porten and Daniel Harris headed the assembly. President Strasser spoke to the strikers in German; Samuel Gompers (already an impressive speaker) spoke in English; the editor of the Bohemian-American socialist paper *Delnicky Listy* gave a Czech speech as did Marie Hausler, a striker from the large Kerbs and Spiess factory. Hausler caught the fancy of all journalists since she was, in the words of one reporter, "a rather comely and decidedly intelligent woman, thirty to thirty-five years of age." After the speeches, the cigar makers (following a suggestion from Local 144 members) selected an executive committee. This group was appointed to conduct the daily business of the strike. It consisted of Strasser as president, Hausler as vice president and ten other members, some of them also members of Local 144. This executive committee headed the Cigar Makers' Central Organization, as the strikers' organization officially named itself.[9]

The central organization looked very much like the structure pursued by Local 144 for organizing the shops of the city before. There were none of the traditional ethnic subdivisions or groupings according to specific skills (i.e., strippers, rollers, bunchmakers, etc.)—a remarkable fact, since the vast majority of the strikers were Bohemians and Germans whose ethnic ties were of primary importance to them and who spoke little if any English. Instead, small shops, tenements, and factories alike were represented by one or more shop stewards who had been elected by their co-workers. The shop stewards had to report daily to the executive committee and were responsible for picketing and discipline among the strikers. The executive committee had to decide on settlement offers from manufacturers and mediated in conflicts among the strikers. In effect, the central organization had thus become a comprehensive union, representing virtually all workers in New York's cigar factories. Whereas the CMIU's leaders had formerly been unable or unwilling to integrate the lowest-paid tenement workers, bunchmakers, or strippers into their union, they now had no qualms about uniting them into a large-scale organization. Despite their structural similarities and overlapping leadership, the Cigar Makers' Central Organization was not officially linked to the CMIU. The union's regulars were, of course, heavily represented in the strikers' organization, but they rarely identified themselves as union men. Moreover, the international union did not pressure the strikers to become union members, although many cigar makers nevertheless joined Local 144 during the walkout. Strike government by the central organization and the CMIU involved two separate institutions.[10]

During the first week of the strike the delegates and the executive committee worked to keep track of the extent of the strike and to get the striking workers to elect delegates. On October 14, when the organization had its first meeting, it counted 2,500 strikers at about twenty-five factories. The next day the number of strikers swelled to at least 5,000 in more than thirty factories. By October 17 more than 8,000 cigar makers had walked out of more than fifty shops. This number increased more slowly during the following days. But by the end of October the strikers numbered approximately 10,000 and at least sixty factories were affected by the walkout.[11]

The central organization's second task was to establish a unified scale of wage demands for the strikers. This proved to be difficult since workers in the cigar industry were generally paid by the piece and wages varied depending on the grade of tobacco and the cigar. In most factories and tenement houses the strikers demanded a raise of $1.00 per thousand cigars and a minimum wage of $6.00 per thousand for all cigar makers. Bunchmakers asked for raises of 25 to 50 cents per thousand. The central committee also asked employers to include all classes of workers in their settlement offers, to rehire all old hands, and to recognize the union as the legitimate representative of all cigar makers. These demands became universal throughout the city, and the central organization accepted no compromises on them.[12] In many shops cigar makers also wanted to improve their lot in more specific ways. The workers at the Wrangler and Hahn factory, for example, wanted to have an obnoxious foreman dismissed; elsewhere cigar makers wanted to regain the right to make free cigars for themselves. Other workers wanted the right to talk and sing during work, which had been forbidden by some manufacturers.[13] Tenement workers were eager to improve their living conditions. They asked not only for higher wages but also, as the *Cigar Makers' Official Journal* noted, "the rent to be lowered, the houses to be cleaned and whitewashed, light on the floors."[14] Altogether, the strikers' agenda reflected the basic dichotomy characteristic of the cigar makers' status and self-image. Many of the workers continued to see themselves as a group of craftsmen who demanded a just price for their work and had a right to socialize in traditional ways during their working hours. At the same time the quest for the universal wage base reflected the uniformity of the industrial work environment for the majority of the strikers who were semiskilled factory workers. The emphasis of the strikers' organization on uniform wages and working conditions revealed a rather strict shop floor orientation and a turning away from issues of ethnicity that had been so important for the cigar makers' union before.

While the workers had organized their strike and had unified their demands within a week, the manufacturers' response initially showed confusion and disunity. A few firms yielded completely to the workers during the first week of the strike. Others offered increases of 50 cents as a compromise (which the strikers rejected). The willingness of manufacturers to meet the cigar makers' demands declined when, after the first days of the strike, the central organization had formulated its goals and workers became more adamant, insisting on a $1.00 increase. At that point a *New York Herald* reporter found the manufacturers "unwilling to state what action should be taken,—they thought the strike would soon be over."[15] The manufacturers' lack of coordination reflected the fact that their mutual relationships had long been dominated "by a spirit of jealousy and rivalry," as the *United States Tobacco Journal* remarked.[16] Owners of medium-sized shops felt threatened by the more efficient large manufacturers, who in turn fought the big tenement bosses. But in the fall of 1877 over fifty firms of all sizes suddenly and unexpectedly faced unified opposition from their workers, whose actions were directed against all large and many small manufacturers, and not against individual firms.

The disunity of manufacturers stood in sharp contrast to the continuing efficiency of the Cigar Makers' Central Organization. At first, most of the organization's time was taken up by setting up a system of financial support for the strikers. Two days after the big gathering on October 14, the executive committee appointed a group to raise funds for indigent strikers.[17] Originally, the cigar makers had planned to follow Local 144's strike support system, which called for a self-imposed 10 percent tax on those cigar makers who were still working.[18] However, with the majority of the city's cigar makers on strike, this method of fund-raising could only produce meager results. The executive committee instead sent out a call for support to the German and Bohemian community in the city, to cigar makers and trade unionists all over the country, and to their sister organizations in Europe.[19] The plea for aid stimulated an immediate and overwhelming response. The central organization collected $5,800 in October, and November's and December's aid sometimes reached $500 a day. Contributions continued to flow in until the end of March 1878, often accompanied by letters or telegrams of support ("Hold forth—sending money every week!"). Altogether the central organization received over $38,000 between October 15, 1877, and March 30, 1878.[20] This financial support reflected the keen interest of labor organizations, especially German-American unions, all over the country in the cigar makers' struggle.

While the mailed contributions were important, local efforts revealed more specifically which segments of the organized working class of the city and which parts of the German community in particular supported the cigar makers. Special fund-raising events generated many of the contributions. The central organization staged benefit concerts and theater performances and in December strikers sold homemade gifts and cigars at a Christmas fair. "Every city should get an entertainment for the strikers," urged the *Labor Standard,* and in fact all over the country workers' organizations staged "entertainments" to raise money. Union supporters held balls and other activities in Detroit, Philadelphia, and Cincinnati; the proceedings from these and many more concerts and socials all over the country flowed into the cigar makers' treasury.[21] The list of individual contributors, which was meticulously kept by the strikers, reveals which groups strongly supported the cigar makers. Three constituencies contributed the most substantial sums. Individual cigar makers made a large number of collections among their friends and neighbors, most of whom were German and Bohemian immigrants like themselves. Locals of the Cigar Makers' International Union also sent generous contributions from all over the country. But the support lent by mutual aid organizations, especially Bohemian groups, was even more impressive. The financial report of the central organization listed over ten different "Bohemian sickness societies" whose repeated contributions were never under $100.00 at any one time.[22] In late November these societies pledged their collective savings of over $50,000 in support of the strikers should it become necessary (the offer was not taken up). Although the Bohemian immigrant community was still relatively young and most of its members were very poor, it provided substantial support for the strikers. This was the first (and last) time Bohemians in New York became prominently involved in the city's working-class politics.[23]

The many German-American benevolent associations, on the other hand, were mostly absent from the list of donors. Only socialist groups such as the German branch of the Workingmen's party did make contributions. Some support also came from individual Germans who organized in the Lower East Side's Seventeenth Ward to donate money, free housing, and foodstuffs. But these efforts hardly reflected their size and the relative wealth of the German-American community in the city, with its vast network of benevolent societies. Most of New York's German-American organizations remained aloof. Such a distance between most of the Vereinswelt and the striking workers illustrates the emerging dichotomy between a few overtly political Vereine such as the Arbeiter Liedertafel and the increasingly depoliticized rest of organized German New York.[24] Indifference to the politically charged issues of working-class protest also suggests a gradually rising conservatism among the German middle classes which would contribute to intra-ethnic class conflicts among German-Americans in later years and which would force German-American unions to look for support outside their ethnic group even more vigorously.

The relief committee's distribution of aid among the strikers was as efficient and as imaginative as its fund-raising efforts. Instead of handing out cash, the committee set up a relief store which began to distribute food to the strikers on October 23. The daily ration for each family was one loaf of bread and one pound of meat; cabbage, potatoes, and coffee were distributed in weekly rations. In addition each family received $1.00 per week for incidentals, while single workers were paid $1.00 per day for food and lodging. The relief program of the central organization, an instant success with the strikers, also won many admirers among the newspaper reporters. After the first week it opened two more stores on the Lower East Side. But the lines of strikers patiently waiting to have their empty baskets filled hardly diminished. Over ten thousand strikers and their families depended on the central organization's food every week, yet the relief program functioned smoothly throughout the strike. "It was a sight for the philanthropist, a text for the preacher, a lesson to Dives, a suggestion for the bosses," wrote one journalist admiringly about the food stores.[25] Like the leaders of the CMIU, the strikers concentrated first and foremost on gaining financial support and running a comprehensive relief program. Through their successful fund-raising efforts, the strikers were now hoping to gain what Gompers and Strasser had worked to achieve for the union: a minimum of economic and financial security for all workers, putting them into a stronger position when pressing any political demands.

While the central organization concentrated on its relief program, the manufacturers made attempts to form an organization of their own to counter the strikers. After two informal meetings, the National Cigar Manufacturers Association was officially founded on October 23. The thirty-six members of the association were mostly proprietors of large factories in New York with twenty or more employees. The group represented most major manufacturers in town, although a few big firms and the majority of smaller manufacturers involved in the strike stayed away from the organization.[26] The association aimed above all at unifying all cigar manufacturers against the strikers. "We hereby affirm our declared determination not to yield to the unjust demands of our late workmen or to reinstate them in our employment while members of the Cigar Makers Union," read the first bulletin of the group. The manufacturers also used the association to defend their wage policies and the institution of tenement manufacturing.[27]

Most of the small manufacturers disagreed with the policies of the Cigar Manufacturers Association. Few of their workers had walked out. Instead, employers and employees jointly sympathized with the strikers. They disliked the large manufacturers, especially the tenement manufacturers, for systematically undercutting prices by using cheap labor. The strikers, on the other hand, were seen as neighbors, *Landsleute,* and friends from the workplace. A feeling for the workers' problems was not foreign to the small operators, for many of them were former factory workers. Thus, an organization of small manufacturers founded on October 21, the National Cigar Manufacturers and Storekeepers Association, had the explicit purpose of aiding strikers with favorable publicity and money.[28]

With the different factions of the strikers clarified, the strike reached a new phase at the end of October. Most of the manufacturers who had earlier indicated their readiness to compromise had withdrawn their offers by then. Firms that had already reached an agreement recalled their wage hikes, and their workers went on strike a second time. At this point some cigar manufacturers also began to talk about introducing strikebreakers. The workers were not particularly impressed by such threats until rumors spread that manufacturers had sent to the West Coast for Chinese cigar makers to act as scabs. This news created "considerable excitement among the strikers," the papers noted. In the end, no Chinese came to New York to roll cigars, as the manufacturers were reluctant to pay the transportation costs.[29]

Another reserve army was more readily at hand: young women. The manufacturers' campaign to train them for cigar making began in early November. The factory of Kerbs and Spiess was the first to hire young women—first for a two-week training period, and then as regular mold workers for $3.00 to $3.50 a week. Some of them had worked as dry goods saleswomen or seamstresses before and were indeed new to the trade; but many were Bohemian and German women who had previously worked as cigar strippers and now had the opportunity to become regular cigar makers. In order to win favorable publicity the manufacturers called their effort "a blessing in disguise, as it affords employment to women." They pasted labels on every cigar box proclaiming: "These cigars were made by American girls educated since the strike."[30] But the drive to recruit and train unskilled women as cigar makers was not successful. Their cigars were of inferior quality, since the manufacturers were unwilling to invest the time and money to train the women properly. Most of them were therefore dismissed after a few weeks.[31]

The failed attempts to train young women as strikebreakers induced few of the strikers to go back to work, and by mid-November the central organization counted only 665 strikebreakers; but with winter coming and no end of the strike in sight by late November, the need to secure housing and financial support for their families forced a growing number of men and women to go back to their jobs. Edward A. Smith, head of the Manufacturers Association, was even able to start an entirely new factory with low-wage workers. In the middle of December the employers claimed that five thousand cigar makers were back at their benches, although the central organization denied these claims.[32] The growing number of strikebreakers markedly increased tensions between the workers, and violence flared up between the hitherto peaceful strikers, strikebreakers, and police. On their way to work, scabs were greeted with jeers, rotten eggs, and cabbage heads. Some strikers were arrested and the police also began to put pickets in jail.[33]

In early November, the manufacturers had strained the solidarity of the strikers even more by evicting tenement workers from their homes. Rumors and threats about such plans had begun circulating at the end of October. When another month's rent fell due at the end of October, the manufacturers applied to the courts for permission to eject the strikers. The first eviction of tenement families for nonpayment of rent occurred on November 5, an event "which wrought the strikers almost into a state of frenzy," as one newspaper reported.[34] By mid-November the evictions were proceeding apace; on single days in November and December more than seventy-five families were turned out. Altogether the courts had granted 1,300 eviction warrants by December, and by Christmas entire tenement complexes were vacant.[35]

To combat the evictions and their demoralizing effects on the strikers, the central organization set up a housing committee headed by a woman cigar maker. It tried to stop evictions by making rent payments for the strikers to the tenement owners. The central organization hired a lawyer to fight other eviction notices.[36] Despite some successes, the housing committee still had to find shelter for the 1,500 families that were in fact evicted. Its efforts were remarkably successful. By the end of December it had furnished over 1,000 evicted tenement families with new apartments.[37] To underscore the strength and solidarity of the strikers, the housing committee organized makeshift parades for evicted families, escorting them to their new homes "accompanied by a band of music, flags flying, dancing, crackers firing and further indications of a Fourth of July jubilee."[38] Nevertheless the evictions strained the physical resources of the central organization, and the striking workers were demoralized by the sight of new families, willing to work for the old wages, moving into the abandoned tenement houses a few weeks after the evicted strikers had left. Clearly, the misery of the evicted tenement

workers revealed that the resources of the workers and their supporters were insufficient to counter the pressure from an increasingly
united group of manufacturers.[39]

At the beginning of December, the strikers were losing the will to
hold out; the central organization needed more than dollars and
speeches to keep the workers from drifting back to their old employers. Hence it began to think of other ways to put the strikers back to
work. In mid-November, the sympathetic *New York Sun* had urged the
strikers to open their own cigar factories "as a constructive measure
to undercut the bosses' resistance."[40]

The executive committee saw no way to put this suggestion into
practice. Yet the idea of cooperatives, which had a tradition within
the German as well as the American trade union movement, had
many followers among New York's cigar makers. In 1874 a group of
New York Bohemian cigar makers had started a cooperative after losing a strike. The small shop flourished until 1877 despite the recession. But the leaders of Local 144 were critical of cooperatives, probably sharing the feeling of many Marxian socialists that they were an
intolerable compromise with the evils of capitalism. German socialists (and their German-American brethren) especially believed that
for workers to go into business for themselves would only detract
from what had to be the ultimate goal: complete control of the means
of production.[41] It was therefore not only "a bombshell in the enemy's
camp," as the *Labor Standard* noted, but also a surprise to many strikers, when Adolph Strasser announced on December 6 that the central organization had made arrangements to buy Mathias M. Smith's
shop on Vesey Street and that the strikers were going to operate their
own shop there right away.[42]

The takeover of the shop was celebrated on the next day with music and a parade whose participants carried banners proclaiming:
"No more Tenement Houses for Cigar Makers!" "United We Stand,
Divided We Fall!" "Down with Monopoly!" Adolph Strasser and the
executive committee marched in the front of the parade; women and
girls accompanied the men on the sidewalk. Smith played the role
of benefactor to the workers and was duly celebrated for his progressive act—as a result of which he was expelled by the Manufacturers Association.[43]

The shop began operations the next day with about 150 workers
who had been selected by delegates of the central organization from
striking shops all over the city. Samuel Gompers acted as foreman.
Initially, the shop was a success. A considerable demand for cigars
had built up during the strike, and soon the workers' factory was

turning out over 500,000 cigars a week; their "Strikers Miniatura" (with a portrait of Strasser and Hausler on the label) was a particularly successful brand. The union-shop workers received wages only slightly above the prestrike average: the rollers earned from $7.50 to $10.00 per week. Within the shop, the hierarchy remained traditional, with the strippers earning the least and the packers the most. Male and female cigar makers received the same wages. Foreman Gompers made $12.00 a week.[44] The central organization deducted 25 percent of the weekly wages from union-shop workers in order to pay off the $4,000 needed to acquire the factory from Smith. The union would only gain complete control of the operation after it had finished paying for the factory. The arrangement specified that Smith remained the sole wholesale merchant even after the union took over.[45]

Despite the opening of the shop, the psychological and economic climate among the strikers deteriorated rapidly after mid-December. Only two firms had yielded to the strikers in the preceding months, and no other negotiations seemed to be in the offing. Worn out by months of hardship, the strikers vented their sense of desperation through increasing violence against scabs. Pickets left their posts in front of the factory to return to their benches inside, and even some prominent members of the central organization went back to work.[46] On December 14 the National Manufacturers Association announced that the strike had ended. For the central organization and the thousands of strikers still holding out, this was, of course, not the case. But one crucial ally to the strikers' cause, the newspapers, took the manufacturers' statement at face value and virtually stopped reporting on the walkout.[47] As a result we know very little about the last month of the strike. Thousands of cigar makers held out until the end of January: the relief system was still functioning and, because of the seasonal low in sales, the manufacturers were not eager to hire back all their old workers. Those that did go back sometimes had their old wages cut even further and had to sign declarations severing their ties to any cigar makers' union. Only 1,150 of the remaining strikers convened on January 24 to discuss the future of the walkout. A slight majority of 612 workers voted to return to work.[48]

The vote ended the strike. Most workers who had held out to the end could not find work during the following weeks. Over 1,000 of them depended on the central organization for material support, and the executive committee handed out cash payments to over 900 families until March 1878.[49] Meanwhile, the central organization tried to work out a financial report of the strike before officially dissolving. This proved to be an unexpectedly difficult task, since the debt incurred proved to be much larger than expected. By mid-March the debt had grown to $8,000. This piece of news provoked a heated discussion among the CMIU and a number of mutual aid associations over how to divide the responsibility for it.[50] In the end the debt was mostly paid by the CMIU. But the financial problems also prevented the realization of a plan promoted by Local 144. Strasser and his colleagues did not want to abandon an organization which had actually realized their ambition of representing all types of workers in the trade. The executive committee of the Cigar Makers' Central Organization announced plans to transform itself into a new union at the end of January. But the debt problem made it postpone the transformation week after week, and in the end the plan failed.[51] Although the strike had served as a crucial factor in forging the central organization, it had also been an emergency with unique conditions. Under less pressured circumstances the Cigar Makers' Central Organization was not able to maintain sufficient strength and unity to shape the diverse cigar makers into a single community.

The significance of the great cigar makers' strike for the development of the cigar makers' union lies in the fact that the strike was "the most formidable and skillfully managed labor revolt ever inaugurated in this country" (as the cigar manufacturers said)—and also in the fact that the workers were defeated in the end.[52] The defeat of the strikers came about as a result of the impoverished status of the workers, for economic depression and technological change had wiped out the craftsman status they had enjoyed in the early decades of the industry. The rapid pauperization that went along with this loss of status had so severely eroded the cigar makers' means of support that their ability to survive a protracted labor struggle was very limited. Some factors peculiar to the New York cigar industry aggravated the workers' situation. In the late 1870s the majority of New York's cigar makers were semiskilled workers, recent immigrants from Germany and Bohemia who had little opportunity to assimilate or experience the limited shop culture and few traditions of the North American cigar trade. The social isolation of the newer workers was heightened by the differences in language and culture which separated Germans from Bohemians, old-timers from newcomers. Each immigrant group had a strong ethic of neighborliness and ethnic solidarity, with definite political undertones. Still, the Cigar Makers' Central Organization had been able to make use of the existing network of organized working-class support to overcome the economic vulnerability and political impotence of the cigar makers. By drawing support from all ethnic groups, yet subordinating their interests to its strategy, the central organization briefly transcended the isolation and the particularism of the cigar makers.

The principles of supra-ethnic organization, centralized administration, and economic strength had been espoused by CMIU Local 144 for some time before the strike. But during the depression years the union's attempts at reorganizing had been largely unsuccessful. In the central organization the leaders of the international union could realize their plans for a comprehensive mass organization along the lines of class *and* ethnicity. The strike turned into a catalyst, bringing together the organizers of the union and the Bohemian and German immigrants. The leaders of Local 144 proved to be skilled organizers, and the rank and file of the strikers accepted the organizational structure laid out for them by Strasser and his colleagues with few important modifications. Gone was the CMIU's policy of "American unionism" which implied rejection of the strong ethnic flavor within the cigar makers' community. The central organization became an open structure which had a place for all workers in the cigar trade. Tenement cigar makers were on an equal footing with skilled shop workers, and women figured prominently in the strike's administration. The central organization essentially proved to be a highly successful model of an industrial trade union, fusing together the elements of tightly organized economic trade unionism represented by Local 144 and immigrant activism as shown by the enthusiastic support among organized and unorganized groups within the immigrant community.

The leaders of Local 144 were clearly aware that the central organization exemplified many of their ideas for a successful cigar makers' union. But despite Strasser's efforts to transform the temporary organization of strikers into a permanent union, the coalition of unionists and activist immigrant workers fell apart after the strike was over. The immediate legacy of the 1877 experience for the CMIU leaders was the hope that, given certain changes in the economic situation of most workers, such a coalition could be achieved again and form the basis of a large cigar makers' union. The aspirations of the CMIU leaders were largely realized during the years after 1878, as the 1880s brought a somewhat improved situation in the cigar trade as well as a greater degree of assimilation on the part of the cigar makers into the world of the American factory. Although the increased participation of German and Bohemian immigrants in the CMIU was welcomed, it also forced the leadership of Local 144 to modify its structure and political priorities to accommodate the interests of the newcomers. Ethnic groupings were no longer banned after 1881, women became a large constituency within the New York union, and a minority even favored admitting tenement workers in the early 1880s.

But the defeat of 1877 also meant that Gompers and his friends grew more skeptical than ever about the inclusion of large numbers of poor and unassimilated workers in their union. The CMIU leadership favored the admission of assimilated and better-off workers, but at the same time it hardened its stance against tenement workers and did little to organize lower-paid factory operatives and poor workers nationwide. One of the CMIU's most important conclusions from the lost strike was that financial security and economic stability had to take precedence over all other concerns in building a stable trade union. As the history of the CMIU after 1878 showed, Gompers and Strasser fared well with their program of high dues and financial stability. As the wages of many cigar makers improved, thousands joined the CMIU during the early 1880s. But the union's growth did not end the challenges posed by socialist members from within and low-income workers from without. For the next half-century, the CMIU, like so many other American trade unions, was continually pushed to open its ranks to a wider constituency, while the leadership tried to pull together the union members to overcome economic insecurity and political factionalism. The need to balance between these opposing forces would often threaten the unity of the CMIU, but it also made the union a dynamic force in the North American labor movement.

5

Cigar Makers and Trade Unions: Politics and the Community

The 1880s brought a multitude of changes to New York's cigar industry and its workers. An accelerating reorganization of production and the introduction of new manufacturing technology shifted the trade so far away from its craft origins that by 1890 this former handicraft began to resemble a mechanized industry. Craft shops had given way to large factories built for the purpose and tenement and home production had almost entirely ceased to exist in the city. For the cigar workers this reorganization affirmed the proletarianization that had been going on since the late 1860s. While craftsmen and their consciousness had still been important influences among the community of workers in the 1870s, by the late 1880s semiskilled factory workers dominated. The domination of factory workers in the industry also meant that social and cultural differences among the workers began to give way as cigar makers from different backgrounds mingled on the shop floor of factories. As a result, the importance of ethnic subdivisions and organization in the trade gradually faded. Ethnicity remained important as an identifying moment for workers in their free time, but as members of unions cigar makers were less segregated by ethnicity and became divided along political lines.

The industrialization of the cigar-making work force and its consequences for social and political organization was not a unique event in New York during the 1880s. It had parallels in many other urban industries such as printing, furniture making, beer brewing, and others. There too the industry was fundamentally restructured, with large factories rather than small or medium-sized workshops dominating production by the late 1880s, and machinery determining the pace and shape of the work. Like cigar makers, in the 1880s workers in many other trades were confronted with new urgency by problems resulting from deskilling and loss of control over the production process.

In order to cope with such changes, new forms of organization were imperative for workers in many urban industries. Out of the need to tackle these and other tasks, a new generation of regional and national labor organizations grew in the late 1880s, and the cigar makers played an important role in some of them. Ethnicity was no longer the most important rallying point for these organizations. Instead they defined themselves by a political program and ideology. Labor conflict among workers thus increasingly turned into an ideological quarrel by the mid-1880s and could no longer be defined in terms of outright ethnic hostility (although many political differences were rooted in the diverse historical experiences of union members from different ethnic groups). Regional and national organizations were often deeply shaken by such conflicts during the 1880s and 1890s, especially in New York City; the cigar makers' organizations more often than not were at the center of such troubles, for they were among the most influential labor organizations and they embodied ethnic and political diversity within their own ranks in an exemplary way. The discord among the cigar makers not only resulted in a period of dual unionism (from 1882 to 1886) but also brought about a major confrontation between the two national labor bodies of the time, the Knights of Labor and the emerging American Federation of Labor. More than ever before, the cigar makers' development therefore has to be seen as emblematic of the union movement at large in the 1880s.

As the cigar makers became a powerful—if split—national union movement with close involvement in the labor and political struggles of the decade, the local ethnic communities that had created the union in New York City and elsewhere receded in importance. Labor organizations like the CMIU continued to be led by German speakers, but this mattered less and less. Direct action on the local level, involving members of the German-American community, continued to be a factor in the union's organizing tactics, but national coordination of campaigns and regional and national alliances with other labor groups as well as a selective entry into electoral politics became more important tools for unions during the 1880s. Other ethnically rooted unions too were learning the same lessons during the 1880s and, among the more established immigrant groups, we see a general fading of ethnic community in the determination of union policy. The price for these weakening bonds with ethnic groups was union alienation from its members, only sometimes overcome through labor-oriented political organizing. It is in this context that the Henry George campaign in New York City will be discussed in the next chapter. The campaign was a prime example for the attempt to organize a large and diverse constituency fused along the lines of class and ethnicity. But ultimately third-party politics proved no alternative to maintaining class and ethnic solidarity within a union. Only apart from electoral politics could unions provide a sense of security and solidarity which crossed ethnic lines.

The Development of the New York Cigar Industry after the Great Strike

The two years before and after the strike of 1877 were probably the low points in the nineteenth-century New York cigar industry. With its pressure for low wages and low-cost products, the depression had favored the less technologically and organizationally sophisticated branches of cigar making such as tenement manufacturing. There was no incentive for the introduction of new technologies or a more rational organization of production. With a return to more prosperous times beginning in the summer of 1879, the situation changed fundamentally for the New York industry.[1]

While the expansion of New York's cigar production meant more stable employment for many cigar makers, the labor market for workers in the trade expanded only modestly. The number of factories, for example, remained fairly constant during the years of biggest production increases (until 1884). The same holds true for the number of workers overall; although there are no reliable statistics, plausible estimates indicate that the work force probably reached its maximum strength in 1881, when some 20,000 cigar makers were employed in New York City, and then leveled off despite the increasing output of cigars. Productivity per worker rather than the hiring of new hands accounted for the industry's ongoing expansion during the mid-1880s.[2]

The most important goal of this second phase of restructuring of the New York cigar industry was higher productivity as a result of a reorganization of the industry in general, combined with a gradual process of mechanization. In the push to increase production and productivity of individual workers, factories were organized according to the "scientific" principles of the day. Large new factories were built, many of them on new land uptown, specifically to accommodate cigar manufacturing. The factory of Brown and Earle, which opened in 1881, was typical of a new generation of "mammoth factories," as they were called by business boosters. Its building had five floors (including a basement), with each floor devoted to one step in the cigar-making process. In the basement, a modern heating system served the sweating department in which the tobacco leaves were prepared (it also heated the rest of the building). The ground floor had offices, exhibition rooms, and storage space for boxes, labels and cigars; on the first floor workers stripped cigar leaves; on the second floor bunchmakers prepared the fillers and rollers, and wrapped the cigar bunches in their wrapper leaves; on the top floor the packers, who needed good light for their work, sorted the cigars; alongside, in a separate department, "Spanish" workers made high-quality cigars by hand.[3] Factories such as this one were far removed from the dank and dirty tenements where families made cigars in small groups. Industry boosters, aware of the bad image of a trade associated with tenement manufacturing, praised the new shops as examples of progress and modernity which also guaranteed a more uniform and hygienic product. "Only what offers the most hygienic conditions, the best materials and the most pleasant architectural features is good enough for the cigar manufacturers these days; the inner workings of such factories has become a true science," wrote the *United States Tobacco Journal.*[4]

Factories like the new Brown and Earle shop permitted an intensified drive toward mechanization from the mid-1880s on. Bunching machines appeared in many of the larger firms by 1885 and suction tables for rollers were widespread by the 1890s. Like many early machines, these contraptions were not adequate replacements for the skills of workers, but the devices served a political purpose for the manufacturers: they accelerated the feminization of the industry—women were acceptable as machine operators, even if they had previously been banned from the regular jobs. Machines also intimidated workers who feared a loss of their jobs and could be cowed into wage and other concessions.[5]

Large modern manufacturing establishments such as Brown and Earle's did not become the norm for the New York industry during the late nineteenth century, but they did employ an ever larger percentage of workers in the trade during the 1880s and thus helped change the structure of the industry and the work force in fundamental ways. During the strike of 1877, just three manufacturers employed more than 500 workers. By 1881 their number had doubled, and by 1888 Manhattan had twelve factories of this size.[6] Smaller shops had a difficult time competing with the more efficient, better capitalized giants, although their low level of mechanization and modest capital needs permitted small cigar factories to hold their own to a remarkable extent. Nevertheless two branches of the industry began to decline, in part because of competition from big firms. One was the manufacture of expensive "Spanish" cigars, which were produced entirely by hand without molds. Although there had always been just a few Spanish shops in Manhattan (compared to Florida) they represented an old, prestigious, and stable branch of the industry. Beginning with the closing in 1878 of New York's largest Spanish shop, Ybor y Martínez, the Spanish manufacturers gradually moved to Florida.[7] A less dramatic event was the decline of tenement manufacture. The better quality control and much greater efficiency of large factories (combined with the improving economy) gradually undercut the financial advantage that tenement manufacturers had during the depression. One by one, the manufacturers of the cheapest brands of cigars moved to the rural districts of Pennsylvania during the latter half of the 1880s.[8]

The changes in the cigar industry in metropolitan New York City were not untypical of change in other trades of the city. As the mass market manufacturing of ready-made goods expanded, industries with large space and capital needs concentrated their production sites in large factories, and often this required a move out of New York City with its high real estate prices. Firms that remained in the city often declined in relative importance and lost out to those in other industrial areas. Few observers would have noticed a decline in New York's industrial base in general as early as 1890, and many industries such as printing and garment making still had decades of expansion to look forward to. But the decline of some key trades such as furniture making, brewing, or the tobacco industry was noted by observers. New York City could not be a national powerhouse for all industries; its limits as an industrial center were already evident in the late nineteenth century.

The Cigar Makers in a Changing Industry

For the cigar makers the move toward factory production accelerated the pace of change that had started in the 1870s and brought new forms of dislocation. The emergence of large-scale factories with their increasing subdivision brought about a decline in craft status for workers, whose workplace bore little resemblance to the craft shop Samuel Gompers had entered in the 1860s. Skilled workers in factories like Liechtenstein Brothers and Bondy found work adequate to their skills only in the small departments that were specializing in the manufacture of high-grade cigars. All other workers were hired as semiskilled hands, only performing a particular task. Craft consciousness was by no means dying out, but it was increasingly confined to an older generation of workers who stayed in small shops or earned their wages in the "Spanish department" of large factories. This separation of the small groups of skilled workers from the large number of factory hands—already in evidence in the 1877 strike—underlay some of the political divisions of the union split in 1882.

The dominance of factory workers was connected to a shift in the ethnic and gender composition of the work force and it also found a geographic expression as communities of workers moved to other parts of town. The percentage of German-American workers seems to have declined after about 1881. As in the garment industry, Germans (and other northwest Europeans) were to be found disproportionately in skilled and supervisory jobs. Even though the Germans were among the first to leave the trade as the second generation came of age during the 1880s, this impression is blurred by the arrival of new immigrant cigar makers from Germany in the early 1880s. These newcomers did not reverse the movement of Germans out of the trade but they had a political impact on the workers' community and the union which made them visible beyond their numbers. Many of the newcomers had been active Social Democrats in Germany who were forced to emigrate after the antisocialist law under Bismarck (1878–90). In political experiences and perspectives these workers were in many ways quite different from the older generation of immigrants from the late 1860s and early 1870s. The differing interests and visions of the old and the new Germans would play an important role in the shaping of the labor movement among the cigar workers and other trades during the 1880s.[9]

By and large Bohemians were replacing the German workers in many semiskilled jobs in large factories. The situation of these workers improved during the 1880s as they moved out of the tenements into large factories, where they became integrated into a multi-ethnic work force. Not only did their economic situation improve somewhat but their potential for labor organization outside their own ethnic group also increased dramatically. But since cigar making remained a one-generation occupation for the Bohemian workers, their participation in the politics of the cigar makers' union had limited impact in the long run.[10]

Most of the new entrants to the trade in the 1880s were eastern European Jews. Jewish immigrants from Poland and Hungary could already be found in the trade in the 1870s, and some of the many "German" Jews in the trade at that time were really Yiddish-speaking immigrants from German-occupied Poland.[11] But a much larger number of eastern European Jews had come in 1882–83 fleeing from the first wave of pogroms in Russia. These newcomers found work in the cigar industry for the same reason they drifted into garment making: some of them (especially those from Hungary) had previous experience in the tobacco industries of their homelands, but for the majority the jobs as cigar makers were attractive because the industry was open to them and required little entry-level skill. Cigar manufacturers, some of them active in Jewish charitable organizations, others more openly eager to preserve a pool of low-paid labor, started "apprenticeship" programs to teach the new arrivals cigar making. They would declare confidently "that by such means hundreds of forlorn and destitute but deserving people can be made useful members of society."[12] The more established cigar workers were less sanguine about the charitable aspects of the program. They appealed to the aid committee for Russian Jews not to have Jewish immigrants used as strikebreakers.[13]

No sudden and massive attempt at displacement of workers through eastern Europeans took place over the next few years, but gradually the newcomers would change the social profile of the cigar makers' community fundamentally and challenge workers' organizations in new ways. The most decisive difference between eastern European Jews and previous newcomers was that a higher percentage of women from eastern European Jewish families worked as cigar makers in factories and tenements. In fact the feminization of the work was largely synonymous with the move of Jewish women into the trade in great numbers in the second half of the 1880s. About 50 percent of the work force in New York's cigar factories was female by 1888 in the estimation of union officials and manufacturers alike. Unlike in the case of previous generations of immigrants, eastern European Jewish women did not just work in factories as "strippers" for a short while before marriage, or in cooperation with their husbands in tenements; they now entered the factories to stay, married or not, and even in tenements they worked on their own at times.[14]

The cigar makers' organizations, especially the officials of the international union, viewed these changes as detrimental to their position. To them, the entry of yet another new group of immigrants into the industry was not the continuation of a tradition but an obstacle to the improvement of the unionists' position. "Yes, they have driven the American workingmen from the trade altogether," declared Local 144 president Daniel Harris before the House Committee on Immigration, adding, "they work for a price Americans could not work for." He blamed not only the failed strike of 1877 but also more recent conflicts on these "cheap, half-civilized Slavs." Other unionists seconded Harris, explaining that recent eastern European immigrants had caused "all the trouble within the cigarmakers' organizations" as well.[15] The cigar makers' organizations also blamed a resurgence of tenement work, observed between 1886 and the late 1880s, on the arrival of new cheap labor from eastern Europe.[16] In general, the negative response of the unions to the arrival of this new class of workers demonstrated their inability to come to grips with the changing nature of the work force. The political infighting of the mid-1880s, which involved the new arrivals only peripherally, took up all the energies of the leaders of a split cigar makers' union and it left them unable to attend to the increasing importance of this group. Unlike in 1877 no explosive action forced the CMIU to pay attention to the plight of the newcomers; their entry was less dramatic and their actions less spectacular. But ultimately the inability of the union to integrate them contributed to its decline in New York City during the late 1880s.

As the ethnic composition of the work force changed so did the neighborhoods in which cigar makers had traditionally lived. Since the cigar industry relocated from the southern tip of Manhattan to cheaper land uptown starting in the late 1870s, many cigar makers were confronted with the choice between a long commute from the Lower East Side and a move uptown. Most workers in large cigar factories, seem to have followed their employers uptown to Yorkville, the neighborhood around Eighty-sixth Street, which was fast becoming a new Kleindeutschland. Bohemians, too, joined the exodus, settling on the eastern and southern margins of Yorkville in tenements larger and somewhat more comfortable than the ones they had left behind. The Bohemian exodus from the Lower East Side was so complete that by the mid-1890s hardly a Bohemian remained there.[17] But poorer Germans and eastern European Jews stayed on the Lower East Side. If they were factory workers they became commuters, separate from their place of work; only if they found employment in the small shops which remained in the Lower East Side did they retain their connection to a neighborhood industry.

The Organized Community: Cigar Makers and Their Unions in the Early 1880s

If the potential for unionization in the cigar industry improved in many ways during the 1880s, the actual organizing efforts of the CMIU were sluggish for a long time in the early 1880s. This was hardly the fault of the workers themselves, who vigorously organized as soon as the depression began to subside in the spring of 1879. At that point thousands of workers in many New York industries went on strike for higher wages, in a movement that was in some ways reminiscent of the 1877 strike. The demands for better wages were certainly similar but in other ways the movement developed in different directions. For one, the strike wave remained a truly decentralized workers' movement, in which each shop's delegates presented the specific demands of their shopmates to their boss. Only occasionally were there meetings to discuss the progress of strikes among delegates from different shops; also in contrast to 1877, business was flourishing (bosses had plenty of orders and low reserves), and therefore most workers were able to win wage hikes almost immediately.[18]

In all this flurry of activity which lasted (with minor interruptions) until the spring of 1881, the cigar makers' union played almost no role. The CMIU locals in New York City hardly capitalized on the gains in wages and potential for new recruits; in fact, membership in Local 144 barely increased at first; by the end of 1880 the local had only 336 members in good standing.[19] The leadership of the CMIU only shifted its cautious stance in early 1881, when it launched an unusually vigorous organizing campaign. "The movement of the cigarmakers seems to become more lively, which is certainly desirable," commented the *New Yorker Volkszeitung* approvingly.[20] Up to 180 new members per week were recruited for the union during the early months of the campaign.[21] The primary recruiting ground for the union this time around was not the traditional German-American group of craftsmen but Bohemian factory workers. Members of Local 144 held organizing meetings in Czech, published the union's constitution in that language, and even introduced a Czech page into the CMOJ. The recruitment among Bohemian workers was so successful that the Bohemian benevolent organizations protested that their members were being snatched away by the union, a protest the union's leaders proudly took as a sign of their success.[22] By October of 1882 the Bohemians had become an important and large enough group that Local 144 relaxed its anti-ethnic stand on unions and allowed a separate Bohemian local (No. 141) to be chartered by the international union.[23]

The CMIU remained slow to open its ranks to new members apparently because it wanted to do so on its own terms. Bohemians were welcome, even recognized as an ethnic subgroup, but only if they conformed to the basic premises of the union: fiscal conservatism and craft protection. As factory workers with some experience Bohemians were now seen as able to comprehend and support the goals of the international union. But tenement workers, many Bohemians still among them, were unsuitable candidates for union membership. With the exception of a short period during the strike of 1877, no tenement workers had ever been admitted to the union.[24]

The ramifications of the CMIU's membership strategy became evident as the union, with the help of a number of other labor organizations such as the Amalgamated Trades and Labor Union, got increasingly involved in an effort to end tenement cigar making in the late 1870s and early 1880s. This movement would focus the energies of the cigar makers' leaders for the first time on the institutions of the federal, state, and local governments and called on them as representatives of the workers to regulate the cigar industry. "This government is based on the principles of liberty and commonwealth of the people and it has to make laws in such a way that they conform to these principles," is the way Samuel Gompers formulated his appeal to the state as the ultimate arbiter in labor relations.[25] In their campaign, the CMIU leaders concentrated on petitioning and personally lobbying such people as the commissioner of the Internal Revenue, the members of the U.S. Senate finance committee, the New York City health commissioner, the mayor of New York City and the New York State Assembly.[26] The systematic lobbying effort (which included support for a Republican party candidate for State Assembly who was sympathetic to the anti-tenement campaign) was accompanied by a series of articles describing life and work in the cigar tenements in detail, published in the *New Yorker Volkszeitung* and written by Gompers himself. These and other articles were written to appeal to the health and welfare concerns of the city's reform-minded middle class.[27] The cigar makers themselves were left out of the crusade, which took the union's leaders to the halls of power more frequently than to the beer halls of the Lower East Side.[28] At first it looked as if this new approach was going to be successful. Five months after Gompers's articles appeared, the New York State Assembly approved a bill to ban cigar making in any kind of living quarters. When the state Senate was supposed to vote on it a few weeks later, however, the manufacturers saw to it that the passage of the bill was stymied by the machinations of the senate Speaker.[29]

The failure of the bill on the state level brought the efforts of the CMIU to a temporary halt in 1881. Although in the long run the union's leaders were ready to continue their fight with the same tactics, in the short run their failure to bring about legislative change showed the limits of power that even such a politically active and well-organized union as the CMIU faced in dealing with entrenched

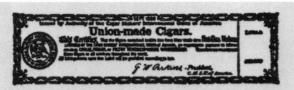

The picture on the other side
REPRESENTS A

TENEMENT HOUSE CIGAR FACTORY.

BEWARE OF CIGARS MADE IN THOSE FILTHY PLACES.

· THEY BREED DISEASE ·

The above Blue Label of the

C.M.I.U. OF A.

*on a box containing cigars
is the only safe-guard
against
Tenement House Product.*

Anti-tenement label of the Cigar Makers' International Union; reprinted from *Labor History*.

machine politicians. As in later efforts at legislative reform spearhead-
ed by the labor movement in the Progressive Era, the lobbying of
politicians, organizing of information campaigns, and involvement of
middle-class citizens showed that cross-class involvement was crucial at gaining the passage of labor legislation. But the lobbying strategies of organized labor often came at the expense of community involvement of the workers themselves. As in later campaigns for
reform legislation, such as the regulation of bakeshops or the passage
of child labor and workmen's compensation laws in New York, such
regulations would, in the end, benefit organized and unorganized
workers. But the lack of involvement of the workers themselves and
the predominance of paid labor functionaries and middle-class reformers in the lobbying campaigns could limit the reforms' impact,
and leave workers in the most marginal areas of the industry excluded
from the reach of organized labor.[30]

The temporary end of the anti-tenement campaign set off a crisis
within the cigar makers' union. At its core was the increasing hostility of a group of German-American and Czech socialists who were
opposed to the cautious political and organizational tactics of the
CMIU. The German socialists within the cigar makers' union had first
raised their voice in 1878 when the *Arbeiter-Stimme*, the official organ
of the Socialist Labor party, published a series of articles assessing the
outcome of the great strike. It accused the CMIU leadership of doing
nothing to further the cause of the workers and of being insufficient-
ly rigorous socialists. "We are suffering," wrote the newspaper, "from
too many American socialists who are practical philosophers and who
have copied all kinds of hair-splitting ideas from the ruling band of
robbers."[31] Later the same year, when Strasser endorsed the election
of Republican assemblyman Edward Grosse, the *New Yorker Volkszeitung* accused the union of selling out to the Democrats.[32]

In the late spring of 1880 the opposition became more organized
when a group of German-speaking cigar makers organized a German
section. At first they remained within Local 144, but they called themselves "Amerikanischer Cigarren und Tabak-Arbeiter Verein" (American Cigar and Tobacco Workers Association). The CMIU threw out
the members of the new organization, but this failed to stop its
growth. By the fall, the new group had eight hundred members in
New York; a year later it had five subsections, including German and
Bohemian groups. In 1882 a tenement workers' association joined the
organization as a sixth subsection. With nearly a thousand members
and vigorous support from the Socialist Labor party, the association
was even able to edit its own newspaper.[33] It was obvious that the

new union had successfully organized a constituency alienated by the CMIU's politics. In contradiction to its name, the union was dominated by German-speakers, most of them recent, politicized immigrants. Like the socialist unions in Germany, the association considered itself to be a political trade union working in close cooperation with the Socialist Labor party, which, it argued, was the only real agent of change in the political arena. The new union's activism was limited mostly to verbal and political support of strikes, and—in contrast to the CMIU—it tried to work for change in the industry by organizing tenement workers.[34]

While the rival union grew in 1881, the CMIU leadership was most disturbed by continuing criticism from the ranks of Local 144 members. During a series of mass meetings on tenement reform during February of 1882, socialist cigar makers who had remained in Local 144 accused Strasser, Gompers, and others of forsaking the principle of class solidarity in their campaign against tenement labor. "They denounced us in the most abusive terms," wrote Gompers later, but he in turn also "had a few pet names for them," accusing his critics of being immigrant novices in politics. The polemics continued throughout the spring, making it clear that the "greenhorns" and "utopians" who opposed the leadership were a sizable constituency even within Local 144.[35]

An unusual atmosphere of tension therefore surrounded the regular biennial election of officers for Local 144, scheduled for March of 1882. For each of the four offices up for election—president, vice president, treasurer, and secretary—two opposing factions had their slate of candidates. The German socialist press openly called on its readers to cast their votes in order to "protest the dictatorial system of the union."[36] The result of the vote was a shock for the established leadership: a majority for three of the four socialist candidates.[37] The CMIU leaders disputed the outcome of the election and retroactively disqualified the socialist candidate for the presidency of the local.[38] "Such a colossal electoral fraud will raise doubts among many union members whether it is at all possible to achieve what we want with this strategy" was one of the socialists' comments. After a personal confrontation of the two factions which ended in a shouting match, no more direct confrontations took place, but the wrangling behind the scenes continued, mostly over the local's treasury and its membership records.[39] The dissidents were quick in building up a new organization from scratch which culminated in the official "declaration of independence" of the dissidents on July 16, 1882, in which they adopted a new name, the Cigar Makers' Progressive Union (CMPU).[40]

The struggle of the CMIU for survival and the ethnocultural divisions among the cigar makers had masked the different and opposing political opinions within the union. But the economic boom and the industrialization of the trade which resulted in the rapid growth of the union had the opposite effect. With more economic maneuvering, a heightened political visibility had made the potential for factionalism much stronger. The early 1880s therefore replaced economic instability by political factionalism as a primary source of friction among the organized cigar makers.

Dual Unionism and the Cigar Makers

The two unions, which existed side by side with each other for the next four years, represented different segments in the cigar makers' community. The CMPU or progressives (joined by the American Cigar and Tobacco Workers Association in August of 1882) consisted mainly of Germans or Bohemians who retained a strong connection to the German and Bohemian communities, especially to the German socialists in New York and Chicago. The CMIU became the union of the more assimilated workers, Germans and Bohemians alike. The available evidence on the membership of the CMPU shows that three out of five district groups making up the New York CMPU were German-speaking; one was Czech-speaking; and only one was English-speaking. The names of new members published in 1885 and 1886 showed that even after the CMPU had been established for several years, about 70 percent of all new members had unmistakably German surnames, while less than 10 percent had English or Anglicized names. Native English speakers were so rare in the union that even speeches made in English were usually delivered by German-Americans. None of the CMPU's leaders was a native English speaker.[41]

The different constituencies of the unions were also reflected in the different emphasis on national organization. The CMIU, placing little emphasis on the specific needs of local ethnic communities within the union, followed Gompers's and Strasser's path toward a centralized national union, seeking political effectiveness on a national level.[42] Between 1881 and 1886 the CMIU gradually widened its national network of unions and stabilized its financial and political situation by broadening the membership base throughout the country. It therefore shifted its entire organizational and political emphasis away from New York and finally even moved its headquarters to Buffalo in 1886. Membership had already reached over 13,000 in the international union by 1883 (from 3,800 two years before), and the number of locals grew dramatically, especially between 1883 and 1885 (from 162 to 203).[43] In New York, membership in the international union remained weak among employees of the big factories.[44]

These years also saw the first concerted effort by the CMIU leaders to build a national labor movement through the Federation of Trades and Labor Unions (FOTLU), founded in 1882. During its four years of existence FOTLU, which was transformed into the American Federation of Labor in 1886, embodied the national ambitions of the CMIU leadership. FOTLU was expressly organized as a lobbying organization of trade unions to fight for better wages and working conditions by influencing legislators and the judiciary, the kind of political approach the CMIU had always espoused. Gompers and Strasser thus created a network of support for their union by founding a national organization based on its political principles.[45]

The progressive union, on the other hand, though it quickly spread beyond New York City, retained its local character, with national cooperation between locals remaining loose.[46] On the local level the union was quite successful from the start. This had to do with the sense of practicality that its organizers showed. Progressives were keenly aware that practical benefits were important for potential union members. The union kept the comprehensive benefit program which had made the CMIU attractive to many workers, but lowered the fees slightly. This gave the CMPU an edge in attracting the lower-paid workers in large factories and tenements in New York. Soon the progressives had members in all the larger New York firms, and they held a majority among workers in the three largest shops, Kerbs and Spiess, Straiton and Storm, and Liechtenstein Brothers.[47]

What set the two unions fundamentally apart was not just their social or even their organizational profile but their different political agendas. "Independent political action was inevitable," proclaimed the new union early on and this meant for the progressive unionists that the struggle for radical political change was at the center of its concerns.[48] Like trade unions in Germany, the CMPU saw itself as a political organization whose constituents happened to belong to the same trade but whose goals were identical with wage workers in general and whose organizing and political campaigns would always happen in close connection with a wider socialist movement. The constitution of the CMPU reflected this approach to trade unionism, from which the CMIU had distanced itself long ago.

> In all cultured nations of the world the workers try to organize in order to resist the united capitalists whose force grows every year. . . . the

struggle against the capitalists cannot be conducted in the economic field alone, or it would not be successful in the long run. The workers have to gain power in the legislature as a class, because the ruling classes in the legislature annihilate any political freedoms of the working class. Our motto is: only working men in the legislature. They know how people suffer and they know where to start in their efforts to secure for the working man the full fruit of his labors.[49]

With electoral politics playing such a central role in the union's creed, a close organizational affiliation with the Socialist Labor party was taken for granted. Apparently many members of the progressive union were also in the SLP. One of its leading members, Vincent Woytisek, ran for alderman on a combined CLU/SLP ticket in 1882.[50]

In other ways, too, the union was closely affiliated with the German-American socialist movement. "Educational presentations to foment class consciousness" were announced as early as July 1882, and to underline the union's desire to educate members further in the ways of socialism, the union's journal *Progress* frequently printed articles on socialism. At the union's *Stiftungsfest* (founding celebration), which was held in December 1882, various socialist singing societies gave special guest performances. On other occasions too these groups showed up for entertainment, underlining a cultural as well as a political affinity between German-American socialists in general and the progressive union in particular.[51] In fact, the close affiliation with the SLP and socialist culture in the city underlined the continued ethnic dimension which defined the progressive union. A political disagreement had precipitated the split of the unions, but the division of the community could not solely be summarized in political terms. With its strong roots in central European socialism and its close affiliation with German radical unions in New York, the "Germanic" character of the progressive union was much more pronounced than in the CMIU, which had largely succeeded in relegating ethnicity and culture to the outskirts of the organizational and political framework of the international union by the 1880s.

The ethnic character of the union was not something the CMPU liked to be reminded of. It defensively stated that its many "green" members had brought a superior class consciousness with them from Europe. But in actively searching for political allies within the New York labor movement the limits of the progressives' reach soon became evident. Amid a resurgence of the labor movement in general in the early 1880s, it seemed like an auspicious time to build a citywide organization of labor, based on common political denominators and transcending ethnic rivalries. The progressives, together with other German socialist unions such as the furniture workers, were ardent supporters of the emerging Central Labor Union from its beginning in 1881, and in subsequent years tried to push the new umbrella organization into a more decidedly prosocialist direction. But as it turned out, these attempts were not very successful. With over two hundred delegates representing 20,000 members of the working class in the city (among them Local 144 and other members of the Cigar Makers' International Union) the Central Labor Union of New York City had many constituents and its leaders tried to steer a cautious course, advocating political action on behalf of the entire working class without committing itself to a specific ideological program. Attempts to enter the political arena in the elections of 1882 and 1883, partly because of pressure from the CMPU and other socialist unions, ended in a disastrous showing at the polls and increased strife within the CLU.[52] Instead of serving as a vehicle of political activism and a power base for the progressive cigar makers and other socialist unions, the Central Labor Union became the forum of bitter fights between the rival cigar makers' unions and other labor groups that were split along political lines in the early 1880s. To the disappointment of the progressive cigar makers and other (mostly German-American) socialist unions, the CLU, though growing in members, barely stuck together through 1884 and 1885 and could not be expected to serve as a cohesive structure that would put the entire New York labor movement on a more radical political footing. For the most part, the CMPU's alliances remained limited to a core of German-American socialist organizations, a group that remained narrow in focus politically and ethnically.[53]

In their search for political consensus the activists in the Cigar Makers' Progressive Union could not find a powerful ally in the Central Labor Union. Instead they turned to the remaining national umbrella group which held that promise, the Knights of Labor. The attraction of the Knights was obvious on a national level for the progressive cigar makers and their fledgling organization. The Knights were nationally feared by employers for their loyalty to each other and their effectiveness in staging boycotts and large-scale walkouts. Their "White Label" and its aggressive use in enforcing union demands had made this group an attractive ally in the struggle for better wages and hours. But even though nationally German socialists and Knights worked together well in some cities, in New York the ideological affinities and ethnic bonds were not strong between the socialist cigar makers and the local leaders of the Knights of Labor. In New York City, few German-Americans belonged to the Knights of Labor. Indeed the Knights were perceived as an organization of the Irish, or at least of the English-speaking working class, by German workers. Especially the leaders of New York's largest district assembly, D.A. 49, were known for their antisocialist and anti–craft union bias. They also were still secretive at a time when nationwide the Knights of Labor were conducting their affairs more openly, like other trade unions. Possibly because of such mixed feelings about the politically uneven alliance and in order to conform with the policies of D.A. 49, the leaders of the CMPU in New York voted to join the Knights of Labor in secret in 1882. Many progressive cigar makers therefore were not particularly aware that collectively they were to consider themselves Knights of Labor from now on, even if they had not become members individually. The only open sign of this new and potentially powerful alliance was the official adoption of the Knight's "White Label" by the CMPU in 1883. Only gradually would the importance of this step for cigar workers in New York City emerge over the following years. As it stood, though, joining the Knights was already a decision on the part of the progressives' leaders that marked a turning away from their community of origin (German-Americans and Bohemians) and even its fundamental political principles of socialist trade unionism.[54]

Dual Unionism and the Cigar Manufacturers

While the cigar workers struggled but failed to find a unified voice between 1881 and 1886, the cigar manufacturers were more successful in organizing. Transcending their common ethnic ties with their workers and seeing themselves as businessmen and manufacturers first, the united employers would pose a decisive challenge to the divided workers by the mid-1880s. It was ultimately the manufacturers' attempt to break the the cigar makers' unions that demonstrated to the progressive union the problems of dual unionism that would prompt them to give up their independence in favor of uniting with the international union. The cigar makers' unification also precipitated a singular moment of unity within the entire New York labor movement that culminated in the most formidable political challenge by organized labor in the nineteenth-century city—the Henry George campaign of 1886.

Up to about 1880 the New York manufacturers were as heterogeneous a group as their workers. Mostly of German origin, they ranged from owners of large and well-organized factories to master crafts-men with a few journeymen employees and slumlords who had turned a tenement into a cigar factory. Because of their different busi-ness perspectives and interests, the manufacturers were usually un-able to meet the workers with a united front even during large-scale confrontations such as the 1877 strike. By the 1880s, however, the po-tential for unified action greatly increased, for a small group of large manufacturers began to dominate the structure of New York's cigar industry. Economic interest rather than traditional bonds of common culture or ethnicity bound together these factory owners. Recogniz-ing the need to meet the challenges of the two labor organizations, some of the largest New York firms revived an organization that had already played a role during the 1877 strike but had largely vanished from public view in the years afterward, the National Cigar Manu-facturers Association (NCMA).[55] Founded in 1881, it had about four-teen members in New York City by 1883, each of whom employed over two hundred workers. By the standards of the cigar industry this made it the representative of the very largest firms. During the next decade, the NCMA (which was New York centered) turned the Amer-ican cigar industry into one of the first urban industries to organize and sustain systematic lobbying efforts. It also grew to be a formida-ble adversary of the cigar makers' unions.[56]

Two events in particular served as tests of power for organized manufacturers and organized labor: the CMIU's renewed campaign against tenement labor and the manufacturers' attempt to introduce uniform labor regulations and wages in all large New York cigar fac-tories. From the international union's point of view the anti-tenement crusade of 1883–84 was more or less a repetition of the earlier anti-tenement campaign, except that Strasser and Gompers even more than before focused their energies entirely on gaining support in the New York state legislature for a new law against tenement labor. They sought almost no community involvement.[57] Even if the CMIU lead-ers wasted no time with mass meetings and concentrated on the cor-ridors of power, when it came to pressuring politicians they found their match in the organized manufacturers. Although the cigar bosses lost the first round when a law prohibiting cigar manufacturing in New York City tenements was passed by both houses of the New York legislature in March of 1883, the NCMA successfully pursued an ap-peal in the courts which proved effective even against the CMIU's efforts to pass a second law. At that point, in the fall of 1884, the CMIU was running out of money and political support and had to give up its legislative fight against tenement cigar making. The manufactur-

ers, aided by the courts, came out victorious.[58] In the next few years
the importance of the tenement system would diminish for economic reasons that had little to do with union activity.[59]

If the manufacturers had successfully challenged at least part of
the organized cigar makers' community on the issue of tenement labor, a more difficult test of the employers' unity occurred in 1883 and
1885 when the NCMA tried to put labor relations in the industry on
a new footing by introducing a uniform set of work rules and a uniform wage scale for all workers in member firms. The most important part of the new rules, which the NCMA members secretly agreed
to in 1883, stipulated that any disagreements between a member firm
and its workers had to be submitted to an NCMA arbitration board
whose decision the firm and the workers were obliged to follow. If
the workers refused to go along with the panel's ruling, their employer was assured the full support of all the other NCMA members. The
creation of such an arbitration board gave a new shape to labor relations in the New York cigar industry, making a dispute within any
one NCMA firm a matter of concern to the workers and employers
in all the other twenty-odd firms. Through the use of the board the
manufacturers were attempting to exercise collective control over each
other, the industry, and its unions in New York.[60]

Since the agreement on labor relations within the manufacturers'
association was not made public at the time, the cigar makers were
quite surprised when it was put into force for the first time during a
strike at Ottenberg's cigar factory in July of 1883. The dispute at this
factory, about 80 percent of whose workers belonged to the progressive union (the rest were members of the CMIU), began over a new
pay system introduced unilaterally by the owners. At first all workers protested in unison, but only the CMPU members went on strike
and refused to budge when the arbitration panel's decision in the
matter was only partially in favor of the workers. Confusion reigned
when, in accordance with their rules, all NCMA firms locked out their
workers, for reasons few cigar makers understood. All of a sudden
the organized cigar makers saw themselves confronted with unprecedented unity among their bosses. This would have challenged the
cohesiveness and organizing power of any labor organization, but for
the quarreling cigar makers it came at an especially difficult moment.[61]

For the manufacturers, however, the decision to call a lockout
turned out not to be the show of strength they had counted on. Although fourteen member factories officially closed down on July 18,
three continued to let their tenement workers make cigars; others allowed their packers to keep working until all supplies ran out, since

the lockout fell in the middle of the busy season.[62] Under considerable market pressure and faced with the well-organized support of the locked-out workers by their respective unions, the manufacturers felt compelled to negotiate for a compromise with the CMPU which ended the lockout on terms favorable neither to the union nor to the manufacturers.[63]

Even though the confrontation of 1883 had ended in a stalemate, the existence of two rival unions and the economic depression in 1884 made a renewed conflict between workers and manufacturers likely during the next year. This time the progressive union, relying on its new alliance with the Knights of Labor, took the initiative and struck for higher wages at the firm of Straiton and Storm (which was not a member of the National Cigar Manufacturers Association). The strike had disappointing results for the cigar makers. Although the Knights placed Straiton and Storm's cigars on their boycott lists nationwide, they did nothing further to support the strikers or to promote the boycott; Straiton and Storm, on the other hand, kept most of its workers and eventually agreed to hire members of the international union. Community support for the strikers could not overcome the combined resistance of the manufacturer, the availability of the international union, and a bad labor market.[64]

To many members this loss signaled a failure of the CMPU to build up a power base and convinced them to give up their quest for independence and join the CMIU again. Relations between the two groups had become more relaxed on the shop floor level, where by and large there were few conflicts. More and more members of the rival organizations showed up at each other's social events where they "amused themselves well and set aside their differences."[65] In the fall of 1885, after a series of meetings between the CMIU and the CMPU in New York City, an agreement was worked out and endorsed by the majority of members in both unions. In return for unconditional reinstatement of CMPU members in the CMIU the progressives had to give up any further claims to autonomy or special status. The majority of members of the CMPU locals in Philadelphia, Chicago, and Boston accepted this agreement and joined the international union as separate locals in the fall of 1885. In New York City, however, only a minority of progressive members endorsed the merger plan. This led to a split of the progressives in the city; the minority became Local 10 of the CMIU, while the majority remained outside and formed the core of the remaining CMPU, which continued to exist in a number of other American cities as well.[66]

Even though the conflict at Straiton and Storm did not involve the

NCMA, its outcome was welcome news for the cigar manufacturers, who were able to lower wages without encountering serious resistance from the unions. By 1885–86 manufacturers were attempting to reduce production costs even more by introducing mechanical labor-saving devices such as bunchmaking machines and by shifting the work force almost exclusively to semiskilled (often female) labor. In conjunction with this restructuring of the work force, employers also secretly agreed to a unified list of wages which was to apply to all workers in NCMA shops. After much deliberation, the list was published in January of 1886 in the middle of the slack season. The agreement revealed that the lowest wages paid to workers in each category were now to become the standard for the entire industry in the city, so that none of the NCMA shops could bid against another by paying better wages. For the vast majority of workers the new list of wages resulted in a considerable pay cut.[67]

The announcement of this unprecedented measure caused considerable confusion among the cigar makers. It seems that nobody on the workers' side was prepared for such a radical step by the employers. Busy wrangling over political and tactical questions, the two unions had not prepared themselves for a massive labor conflict which involved almost all major employers in the city's cigar industry. Both the CMPU and the CMIU therefore reacted cautiously at first. They discussed the matter for a few days and decided to strike in one shop each.[68] For the manufacturers this sufficed as a pretext to lock out all six thousand workers in NCMA member shops.

The workers—unionists and nonunionists alike—fell back on the same organizing strategies as in the 1877 strike: mass walkouts, spontaneous shop meetings, and support from the community. The tenement workers, whose wages were included in the agreement, were the first and most resolute group to act, although only a small minority of them were unionized. They met in their houses and immediately organized a Tenement House Union which coordinated a comprehensive strike by tenement workers. Soon the CMPU joined the tenement workers and began to call numerous meetings to strengthen the solidarity and persistence of the workers. Contributions were collected, and all locked-out workers, even those not belonging to a union, were supported financially by the progressives. The CMIU also came out in support of the strikers, but it was able to rely almost exclusively on its well-endowed accounts to support union members and nonmembers alike.[69]

In many ways the outpouring of community support for the cigar makers in 1886 was reminiscent of the 1877 strike, but significant differences influenced the outcome of the new conflict. For one thing, the lockout of 1886 showed how support from the German-American community was now to be found in middle-class and working-class homes alike. While in the earlier conflict most of the German supporters were immediate neighbors and came from a similarly poor background, now the list of supporters showed many businessmen as well as the usual working-class organizations and individuals. From the "big lot of wool fabric" sent by one business to the more immediately useful "40 pounds of meat" sent by another, the locked-out workers received support from businesses. "Most of the businessmen used to be workers themselves, but found out they couldn't feed themselves," as the *New Yorker Volkszeitung* almost apologetically explained.[70] The more established character of the labor movement was also evident when mass meetings were no longer held in the beer halls of the Lower East Side but in the assembly rooms and theaters of Yorkville, where many German immigrants had come to live. In contrast to 1877, Bohemian businesses such as groceries and bars were also now among the financial supporters of the locked-out workers. It now seemed that financial support was not just provided to help workers in distress but to demonstrate that the German-American and Bohemian communities could afford to be generous.[71]

In the midst of this wave of solidarity the quarrels between the CMIU and the CMPU seemed insignificant. On the shop level both unions had been forced to unite in their struggle against the employers. But the leadership of the two unions was far from practicing the solidarity of their constituents. During the second week of the lockout it became known that the NCMA had been in touch with the progressives in order to agree on a wage compromise. Despite sharp attacks from the international union and other labor groups, negotiations were concluded after two weeks when the manufacturers and the CMPU reached an agreement. The new wage scales were almost uniformly higher than those announced by the NCMA, and they concentrated the pay cuts among the most skilled groups of cigar makers, usually members of the CMIU.[72] The contract also contained a closed-shop clause for the CMPU. In turn, the trade union was obliged to fill all jobs with union men and to provide the Knights' label for all cigars manufactured by NCMA shops. A mass meeting of CMPU members approved this contract on February 11, 1886.[73]

With this move the CMPU leadership was making a desperate attempt to shore up its position by securing a large number of shops for its workers. But the acceptance of the manufacturers' contract proved politically disastrous for the progressive union. Even though most New York City labor organizations had kept out of the cigar makers' conflict before, former allies of the progressives—the socialist unions, the *New Yorker Volkszeitung*, the cigar packers' union, and even the SLP—voiced strong objections to this agreement.[74] The verbal and financial support that had been so strong during the lockout evaporated within a few weeks. In its desperation to keep afloat as an independent union, the CMPU had stepped outside its circle of support and made a pact with the manufacturers against other unions.

Only one part of organized labor should have been pleased by the outcome, the Knights of Labor. But instead of strengthening the alliance between the CMPU and the Knights, the pact only brought to the fore the many problems of this alliance. The new agreement awarded the Knights' label to all NCMA cigars and implicitly made the Knights, represented by the CMPU, the organization of all workers in NCMA shops. The relationship of trade unions and trade assemblies of the Knights had been the source of conflict in other trades too, and it was about to erupt on a national level (between the Knights and the AFL) in the summer of 1886. In the cigar makers' case a power struggle between the District Assembly 49 leaders and the CMPU erupted in April of that year. The leaders of District Assembly 49 ordered all CMPU members to take out individual membership in the Knights and finally it ordered the progressive union to disband altogether in the summer of 1886.[75] The CMPU tried to ignore this order, but the manufacturers—eager to retain the Knights' label on their cigars and to have the use of mechanized bunch-making machines sanctioned by the Knights—began to force their workers to follow the prescription of District Assembly 49.[76] In early August of 1886, as the tensions between the Knights and the progressive union reached their height, the manufacturers, irritated and confused over the CMPU's refusal to give in to the demands of the Knights, tried to solve their problems with one bold stroke: they locked out all workers who did not individually belong to the Knights of Labor.[77] Once again, five thousand workers in seventeen factories were without work. This action by the manufacturers exposed the lack of community support for the Knights. Despite a massive effort to recruit cigar workers from outside the city, only about one thousand of them were willing to return to the benches as members of the Knights' district assembly. Many potential strikebreakers were intimidated by the hostile picket lines of the trade unions in front of the factories and therefore much of the New York industry was paralyzed by confusion and conflict for about a week.[78] Since the factories were in the middle of the high season, however, neither manufacturers nor workers were interested in prolonging the conflict, and it seemed that with the exception of the Knights, all groups concerned were interested in a quick settlement. At that point the only labor group that held out a promise of unity and concerted action was the CMIU, which had only been marginally involved in the local conflicts between the manufacturers and the Knights during the past six months.[79] Although the CMIU had lost to the CMPU in the shops of the manufacturers' association in February, it had done well in the city's other establishments and retained a growing following there. Sensing a chance to enlarge its membership by coming to the rescue of the weakened progressive union, the international union offered help in early August. The organization was ready to support the CMPU financially and politically in its struggle against the Knights, as Strasser had made clear to the socialist cigar makers. Money was collected and a unification committee began talks about a possible merger between both organizations. Other New York labor unions and the Central Labor Union enthusiastically supported these negotiations.[80]

The stage was thus set when the leadership of the CMPU asked its member locals whether they would be willing to merge into the CMIU. The New York local of the progressives was the first group to decide on this question. On August 12, its 2,823 members voted unanimously to become part of the CMIU and dissolve as an independent union. A few weeks later the members of the CMIU locals in turn decided to accept the progressives back into their fold. In September the progressives of New York City were officially chartered as Cigar Makers Progressive International Union No. 90 by CMIU president Strasser.[81]

The National Cigar Manufacturers Association reacted quickly to the planned unification. Many manufacturers feared the reunification of the workers into one union: "for heavens sake, don't unite with the Internationals," one manufacturer exclaimed to his workmen in July.[82] Anxious to avoid a conflict with the much-strengthened CMIU, the manufacturers abandoned their alliance with the Knights literally overnight and opened their factories regardless of union membership on August 12. Within a few days all Manhattan cigar factories were working full shifts again. The six-month-old conflict was resolved and the industry was peaceful for the rest of the year.[83]

The Cigar Makers after 1886

The resolution of the conflict between the New York cigar makers' organizations signaled the end of the progressive union nationwide.

The unification conference which led to the merger of the New York progressives also made possible the merger of all other CMPU locals into the international union. Although the merger did not eliminate all rival organizations—the Knights of Labor continued to organize cigar makers—the CMIU had now become the sole national organization of cigar makers in the United States.[84]

Though the organizational cohesion of the cigar makers increased considerably from 1886, internally the union reflected its diverse constituencies. Well into the 1890s the socialist trade unionists who had joined the CMIU as separate "progressive" locals mounted campaigns opposing several union policies and at some points tried to depose the leadership. In turn the progressive locals, notably Local 90, came close to being expelled for various infractions several times.[85] This opposition within the CMIU found its large-scale equivalent in the opposition of socialist unions to the leadership of the American Federation of Labor, which would result in the (temporary) removal of Samuel Gompers from the AFL presidency in 1893. But within the CMIU the socialists, though distinct, were never able to mount an effective alternative program, have their representatives elected to leadership positions in the unions, or influence the agenda of the union in a lasting way.

The diminishing importance of the socialists was not just caused by their own ineffectiveness and the implacable opposition of the CMIU's leadership. It was the membership of the international union at large that showed an increasingly conservative face when it came to union reform or taking up risky programs. In the late 1880s, for example, Strasser and Gompers tried to have the union adopt an out-of-work benefit and to accept the introduction of bunch-making machines. Both measures were resoundingly defeated, though the out-of-work benefit was adopted in 1889. The union locals also turned down an attempt to reinject a political theme onto the preamble of the constitution.[86]

The increasingly conservative cast of the union was in part the result of its membership strategy. After the mid-1880s the CMIU tried to attract workers in rural areas and small towns who were more "American" (that is, more conservative) than the workers who could be found in the multi-ethnic cities. Indeed, even the merger with the largely urban CMPU did not reverse the diminishing importance of the union in urban areas in the long run. Even though union membership increased between 1885 and 1889, many formerly large urban locals (some of them former CMPU locals) lost up to two-thirds of their members between 1887 and 1889. New York's Local 90, the former progressive union, went from 2,500 members to about 800 in that time period. Local 144 lost even more members.[87] The shift in membership was not just the result of selective organizing on the part of the union, it was also caused by the large-scale move of the cigar industry away from urban centers in the late nineteenth and early twentieth century. Even though New York City manufacturers tried to match the emerging rural industries by recruiting among new immigrants from eastern Europe, Italy, and Puerto Rico, their success was limited in the long run. Only a minority of cigar workers were members of the union in New York City at the turn of the century, but the costs of doing business for cigar manufacturers remained high enough to make most larger firms abandon their urban factories for more rural and cheaper locations in Pennsylvania, New Jersey, and the southern states.[88]

Despite the changes in the industry, the CMIU changed its program and its recruitment tactics very little. No modifications in the union's system of organization were made to attract low-paid rural workers. On the contrary, in many locals large numbers of workers were explicitly excluded because they worked with machines or in teams with machine workers. In urban areas no efforts were made during the nineteenth century to encourage Yiddish- or Spanish-speaking immigrants to join. In the past, the CMIU had, over time, been forced to change its rules and political emphasis somewhat to make room for the newcomers in the industry. But by the 1890s no pressure would move the union leadership to change its framework of fiscal conservatism and political caution. Instead, the CMIU was now on the road to becoming a true craft union, content with organizing only a part of the work force in the nation's cigar factories.[89] Politically the CMIU (in unison with the growing American Federation of Labor) continued to push for legislative reform concerning the shorter workday and tried to lobby to maintain existing tax regulations concerning tobacco products. Otherwise, the international union largely refrained from involvement in political campaigns of the labor movement. Although dissidents were tolerated, none of the socialists who continued to raise their voices during the biennial meetings ever found majority support for their actions within the CMIU.[90]

The sudden end of the conflict between the cigar makers had repercussions throughout the labor movement in New York City. The progressive cigar makers gave up their quest for a separate, politically radical union because they lacked a sufficient organizational, financial, and political base for successful action. Neither the diverse

union movement of the city nor the increasingly divided Knights of
Labor were able to provide the needed political base. Even though,
compared to earlier decades, the labor movement was politically more
sophisticated and economically more stable, the need for cohesive
organization also increased enormously as the battle against manufacturers with unprecedented economic resources and political influence shaped up all over the country. By the mid-1880s no amount of
community organizing and revolutionary spirit could offset the need
for a well-filled treasury and a well-coordinated national leadership
in a large labor organization. These were the realities that the progressive cigar makers faced, a distasteful but unavoidable development for the enemies of Gompers and his increasingly conservative
brand of unionism.

Even though the failed example of the cigar makers did not end
political splits within unions and destructive dual unionism, it inaugurated a moment of unity within the Central Labor Union in the
spring and summer of 1886. The spring witnessed the culmination of
the largest eight-hour movement the country had ever seen. Even
though it was only partially successful in New York City, it provided
the Central Labor Union with a much-needed focus and gave organizational experience to this large federation.[91] The election campaign
for Henry George in the summer and fall of the same year similarly
provided a crucial uplift for organized labor in the city. The cigar
makers were enthusiastic supporters of George, as were most craft
unions and socialists. As we shall see below, the Henry George campaign was the culmination of the quest for political community during the 1880s.[92]

Few trades were as successful and prominent in their organizing
efforts as the cigar makers during the last three decades of the nineteenth century. But in many ways the rise of the cigar makers and
their organizations from a humble Verein with definite ethnic overtones to a large bureaucratic craft union is exemplary for much of the
development of American labor in the nineteenth and early twentieth century; it foreshadowed the development of a large cohort of AFL
craft unions.

Because of their peculiar European history, the cigar makers were
never deeply rooted in a cohesive craft culture; cigar making was a
young and open trade in Europe which welcomed workers from a
variety of backgrounds. In the United States the trade continued to
attract an unusually heterogeneous work force whose stake in the traditions of craft production was tenuous or nonexistent. Heterogeneity of the work force and a recent craft history turned out to be large

advantages for the formation of unions of North American cigar makers, since the need to start an organization with a forward-looking political program tailored to this dynamic trade was not lost on these workers, at least in the 1870s and early 1880s.

But as the first generation of cigar makers became more established, craft consciousness and a desire to preserve the recently achieved status of well-paid craft workers intermingled with ideas of Americanization and made it difficult for more recent newcomers—Bohemians and many Germans—to link forces with more established workers. The CMIU's Local 144 was born out of the need to fuse the experience and status of old-timers with the energy and numbers of the newcomers. For a while the CMIU in New York succeeded in bridging the gaps of generations, culture, and economic status. Gompers and his friends saw clearly the need for cohesion in the organizational and political realm rather than reliance on ethnocultural bonds as the basis for union organization.

But political consensus remained elusive in the early 1880s; the cigar makers exemplified the problems which intensified during the mid-1880s as the differences between various parts of the labor movement became particularly glaring and destructive. Old-timers and newcomers had opposing interests, socialists were lined up against more pragmatic unionists, semiskilled workers and skilled cigar makers had opposing goals. The dissident Cigar Makers Progressive Union tried to unite a large segment of those dissatisfied with the Cigar Makers' International Union and formulated an alternative political agenda. But the CMPU succeeded even less than the CMIU in creating a community of workers based on political creed. Instead they relied heavily on the ethnic and political bonds of German-American socialism. Such a limiting alliance proved to be an ineffective alternative labor organization in a trade which was becoming increasingly uniform and in which workers of all backgrounds were confronted with the same exploitative conditions. Alliances with national labor organizations such as the Knights of Labor or even regional ones like the Central Labor Union were also of limited value for the specific needs of the cigar makers.

In the end, the German-American socialists, in many ways the union's most committed members, lost out to the international union. The victory of the CMIU was not based on the authoritarianism or financial power of their leaders, but on the cigar makers' perceived needs for stability and financial security. In the daily struggle with economic uncertainty and political confusion, the CMIU's strategy of financial conservatism and political caution was appealing to more and more workers who, by the mid-1880s, tended to be no longer so alienated from the "American" unionism of Samuel Gompers and Adolph Strasser. This tendency was, in part, certainly due to the greater degree of assimilation among German and Bohemian workers. It also showed the workers' awareness that in order to fight the increasingly united manufacturers, one united national organization was preferable to a multiplicity of more community-based efforts.

The reunification and sustained growth which the CMIU was ultimately able to achieve in the late 1880s came at a price, however. Within the tight structure of the organization, many dissenting voices were stifled and change came slowly as it seemed to carry too high a price for many members. As the cigar industry continued to change and new immigrants arrived to take their places at the workbenches of cigar factories, the union was losing its connection to the changing community base of workers, especially in the New York metropolitan area. By the 1890s the Cigar Makers' International Union had become inflexible, bureaucratic, and interested in maintaining the status quo. The conservative consensus and the craft orientation which the union would have for the coming decades made it a solid example of what AFL unionism would stand for by the early twentieth century.

The search for community gave way to a much more pragmatic program to organize workers according to the most easily reached common ground, trade interest in the narrow sense. This new political unionism was not initially a bureaucratic movement, however. Its founders hoped to create a new sense of community based on class consciousness. The campaign of Henry George for mayor of New York City in 1886 was such an attempt at creating a community with a lasting effect on the political landscape of American workers' organizations. The following chapter will illuminate this campaign and its attempt to link the concerns of German-Americans and other immigrant groups among workers with a common political agenda which was largely class-based. The strengths and weaknesses of the coalition and the campaign will highlight many of the problems unions faced during the 1880s.

6

Working-Class Politics and the Henry George Campaign of 1886

The struggle to overcome ethnic and cultural divisions in favor of class-based political unity took many forms in late-nineteenth-century America. It was fought out within unions, as in the cigar makers' case, but sometimes the struggle for political unity took place on a broader regional or national level. At times the attempt to forge a broad political movement out of a diverse working-class constituency was successful enough to attract national attention and raise the specter of a viable labor party nationwide. Such was the case with the New York City mayoral campaign of Henry George in 1886. This election campaign was the culmination of efforts to build a working-class political movement in North America's most diverse city. It was a pioneering effort to overcome many of the ethnic and political divisions within the North American working class. On the following pages we will discuss the organization of the campaign and the events that led up to it with a particular focus on the interplay between German- and English-speaking labor organizations. The replacement of ethnic loyalties by class-based politics will also be viewed from a different angle by contrasting the labor activism of German- and English-speaking groups on behalf of Henry George with the involvement of the city's German-American middle class during the campaign. Such an analysis will serve as a way to focus on the general question of ethnicity and politics once again before we discuss the problems of the late 1880s in terms of the brewers' and bakers' unions.[1]

The Henry George campaign would not have happened without the Central Labor Union of New York City, the country's largest regional labor organization in the mid-1880s. The CLU united over 120 independent unions and Knights of Labor local assemblies representing around 40,000 workers in mid-1886.[2] From its beginnings in early 1882 the CLU understood itself as an umbrella organization of all unions in the city and as the spearhead of political activism on behalf of the working class in New York. Even though by the mid-1880s the Central Labor Union was the largest and one of the most long-lived umbrella organizations of labor in the country, its diverse constituency perpetually pulled the organization in many different directions at once. By 1886 it had only been in existence for four years but had already survived a number of political crises which would define its perspective during the 1886 campaign and thereafter in important ways.

The Central Labor Union of New York City was founded in 1882 after a mass meeting organized by the Irish Land League. Speeches tied the cause of land reform to the cause of Irish freedom and—as New York followers saw it—to the cause of working-class politics in general.[3] The adherents of land reform (mostly Anglo-Irish workers who were organized in the Knights of Labor) were joined—despite some misgivings—by some heavily German-American socialist unions such as the furniture makers and the progressive cigar makers.[4] A third group in the CLU, unique to New York in many ways, were the socialists within the Knights of Labor, usually not German-speaking, who were members of the Excelsior Labor Club, a mixed assembly of trades. These Knights were not typical of the national KOL organization, but they would play an important role in the Knights' largest New York-based group, District Assembly 49.[5] Together with the German socialists, with whom they had an uneasy alliance, they formed the political core of the Central Labor Union.[6]

The new organization enthusiastically entered electoral politics and within months of its founding had formed a committee to work out more detailed plans to start an "independent labor party to unite all labor elements."[7] In a joint effort with the Socialist Labor party, the progressive cigar maker Vincent Woytisek and another CLU member were put forth as the CLU's candidates for alderman in the municipal election of 1882. Neither gained more than 850 votes. A similar attempt in 1883 was no more successful.[8] This poor showing kept the CLU from entering the electoral arena again in the following years. Instead the resources of the organization were devoted to organizing campaigns among workers ripe for unionization and the support of labor boycotts.[9]

The involvement in unionizing campaigns helped the CLU members gain organizational and political experience, but it also brought to the fore the diverse political and ethnic forces represented in the organization. As the number of unions increased, many trades were represented by more than one union with different ethnic constituencies. Conflicts were inevitable under such circumstances among such highly subdivided trades as the bakers, but also in other industries.[10] The dual unionism that went along with such infighting usually involved one group aligned with the Knights of Labor and another aligned with the independent labor organizations—often German socialists.[11] Some socialists who had been among the founders of the original organization resigned from the CLU over such conflicts; others such as P. J. McGuire, head of the carpenters' union, exclaimed in disgust that "the meetings of the CLU have become stomping grounds of politicians and selfish men."[12] Within a few years of its founding little of the political energy and unity that had characterized the early CLU survived. *John Swinton's Paper* stated sadly that "the Central Labor Union has reached a crisis in its history."[13]

Not until the beginnings of the eight-hour campaign in the early fall of 1885 was the momentum among the unions in the city for concerted action starting to revive. But while elsewhere central labor bodies took a crucial role in organizing the movement for an eight-hour workday, the New York CLU, wracked by conflict around the competing cigar makers' unions, only got sporadically involved in the months preceding May 1, 1886. For the most part, the eight-hour movement in the city was a decentralized affair, carried on to a large extent by some of the more politicized German-American trade unions: the clothing cutters, the cigar makers, and the German printers in the German-American Typographia. These unions were the only ones which won the eight-hour day, at least temporarily, while a few others, namely the furniture makers, achieved the nine-hour day. But the vast majority of workers—organized and unorganized—saw no lasting change in their work hours.[14] Nationally, the failure of the eight-hour movement of the mid-1880s was at least in part caused by the Haymarket bombing in Chicago. In the words of Samuel Gompers, "the effect of that bomb was that it not only killed the policemen, but it killed the eight hour movement for that year."[15] But locally, the failure of the movement in the city was also rooted in the disunity of the labor movement, as reflected in the Central Labor Union. During the first half of 1886 New York City was an unlikely place for a strong union movement to revive.

If the national eight-hour movement had failed to ignite a citywide activism in New York, a much more local conflict in the summer of 1886 proved to be the catalyst that brought the constituents of the CLU together across ethnic and craft lines in unprecedented numbers. In a lengthy struggle the German waiters' union and a German musicians' union, the Carl Sahm Club, had won the union shop at Theiss's beer garden, one of the largest in the city. The owner had been forced to give in to the union's demands in the spring of 1886, after a boycott against the establishment had been waged with much enthusiasm and support from the CLU and its member unions. As part of the settlement Theiss had agreed to pay the boycotters $1,000.[16] As soon as the settlement was finalized, Theiss went to court, suing the union for extortion. On July 2, a judge sentenced the five leading members of the German waiters' union to prison terms ranging from six to eighteen months.[17]

The Theiss case, even though it involved chiefly German unionists, created outrage far beyond the German unions who had most actively supported the waiters and their boycott against Theiss. In a mass meeting organized by the CLU on July 7, speakers representing a broad spectrum of the city's labor movement appeared, from the socialist Sergius Shevitch to the reformer Edward King and the Knights of Labor unionist James Archibald. Henry George, at the time known mostly as a land reform theorist, sent a letter of support. Most speakers saw the Theiss decision as ominous for the liberty of the entire labor movement in the state and urged the CLU to become once again directly involved in the electoral politics of the city.[18] In a regular meeting four days later, the Central Labor Union passed a resolution which endorsed this call for political action.[19]

Against this background over four hundred representatives of labor organizations (many of them not part of the Central Labor Union) met in early August to discuss labor's participation in the upcoming mayoral contest. Speakers representing different parts of the labor movement, among them German socialists but also many Knights, linked the current movement to the activism of the German socialists in Europe and the Free Ireland movement.[20] While the fissures of the past had not healed—the election over who was to chair the meeting was openly contested—and while a few unions were opposed to political activism, most of the enthusiastic delegates endorsed the suggestion of James Archibald to ask Henry George to be their candidate for mayor in the fall election.[21]

George was officially nominated in late August by a meeting of hundreds of labor representatives.[22] In a shrewd move that assured an early start of the campaign, George refused to accept the nomination until at least 30,000 votes had been pledged by prospective voters.[23] Neighborhood organizers immediately set to work gathering the signatures needed. Meanwhile, an election platform was discussed by the informal convention that met weekly, with about one hundred unions represented.[24] Labor Day in early September brought an impressive demonstration of the George forces and, for the first time, caused an echo in the city's middle-class press.[25] By mid-September it was clear that the campaign was going to take off. "The work of forming campaign clubs in the Assembly Districts of the city is well-advanced and it is proposed to have organizations in every election district. Trade Unions and Knights of Labor have sunk their differences of opinion and are working hand in hand," wrote *John Swinton's Paper.*[26] On September 24, in a large meeting of the delegates for the George campaign, Henry George accepted the nomination as mayoral candidate of the Central Labor Union when over 34,000 signatures were presented to him.[27]

What were the resources of organized labor in the city for such a campaign, and particularly what role did the German labor movement play in it? German socialists and their unions turned out to be the most articulate group of George supporters. They had demonstrated their militance and cohesion in the eight-hour movement and had always been in support of independent political action.[28] In their desire to support unified action, German-American unionists even prevailed upon the Socialist Labor party itself to join the active promoters of Henry George, forsaking its own electoral ambitions for the season.[29] But it was as organizers in the German-American neighborhoods that German unionists were most important. Most of the Lower East Side was organized by German-Americans; the furniture workers and the German cigar makers were particularly active in registering new voters and calling for their support of George.[30] Registration for citizenship and voting was important for German immigrants, since many of them, while politically active, had been unable to vote in the past. Eighty-five percent of the more than 2,000 new citizens who were registered in the early part of the campaign were Germans, the *New Yorker Staats-Zeitung* estimated, and 3,000 more prospective voters had declared their intention of taking out citizenship papers by late September. The campaign organizers of the Lower East Side also made special attempts to register first-time eastern European Jewish voters.[31] The large presence of German-American supporters was visible in the grand parade of Henry George supporters on October 30 through the working-class areas of the Lower East Side of Manhattan. From the German carpenters to the German-American tailors, bakers, cigar makers, brewers, printers, painters, and upholsterers stretched a two-hour parade of supporters who marched by their candidate in pouring rain. Henry George election clubs, which had been formed in virtually every assembly district of Manhattan, also sent large delegations from the German-American parts of the city.[32]

But if the presence and activism of German-American unionists was one of the vital underpinnings of the George campaign, Germans were rarely prominent among the leaders of the organization. The most visible early spokesmen of the campaign, John Morrison and James Archibald, were both prominent representatives of the Knights of Labor (although they belonged to opposing camps). The permanent committee for the election campaign also consisted almost entirely of Knights of Labor, with only a few Germans among them.[33]

German influence was also nearly imperceptible in the platform and the general political program of the campaign. Written by George himself, the platform mentioned traditional CLU demands: public works, the abolition of prison and tenement labor, and better health and sanitation laws; but its focus was the single tax for which George had become famous.[34] This preoccupation, long condemned by Marx himself as retrograde thinking, made the German socialists uneasy. But in recognition of the momentum of the campaign, even the SLP leadership decided that support for Henry George was more important than ideological purity. The substance of the George campaign was practical socialism; theoretical considerations could be overlooked for the moment.[35]

If the German labor movement played a prominent role in the campaign in some ways but was curiously absent in others, this was rarely pointed out by the George supporters themselves. To the New York labor movement, the universality of George's appeal was the most important characteristic of the campaign. The unity created by his candidacy superseded all previous subdivisions and made a powerful political movement possible. In countless articles, papers such as the *New Yorker Volkszeitung, John Swinton's Paper,* and the campaign publication *The Leader* stressed the universality of George's support among the working classes of the city and avoided any mention of the ethnic origins or previous political affiliations of various supporting groups. It was the class character rather than the ethnic tinge of the campaign that was important to its organizers.[36]

An analysis of the organizing and voting patterns among Germans in the election confirms the impression that the campaign marked the turn away from ethnic- toward class-dominated politics within the German-American community. By the middle of September the middle-class press began to report on the George candidacy in tones of worry and alarm: "The appearance of a labor candidate for mayor has put the vote counters in desperate straits: how many votes can George get and from whom will he take them away?"[37] asked the *New Yorker Staats-Zeitung* in a worried tone. For this self-proclaimed representative of an enlightened upwardly mobile class of (German) immigrants, the challenge of the George campaign was a particularly painful reminder of the strong presence of a recalcitrant German-American labor movement in the city—the black sheep in the family of successful German immigrants. The paper editorialized ponderously:

> The mayoral election has raised such unusual questions of principle that an intelligent judgment places higher demands on the voters' thinking than is generally the case in similar situations. It is therefore natural that those elements of the citizenry which are accustomed to independent political action will play a leading if not decisive role. We strongly hope that the German citizens whose independence in politics is usually attributed to their capacity for independent political thinking will also maintain their reputation this time. They should not let themselves be won over by a cheerleading campaign (led, unfortunately, for the most part by Germans) to a nonsensical and dangerous political experiment.[38]

The appearance of Henry George's strong and widely supported labor candidacy was particularly worrisome to upper-class Germans, for it came at a time when their influence within the Democratic and Republican parties was not well established. In addition, the organizations of both parties were in considerable disarray in the city.[39]

By the first week of October when the first constituent groups of the County Democrats and Tammany met to discuss nominating a candidate for mayor, the George campaign had received nearly undivided attention for over a month. Moreover, even as the parties met, no consensus candidate seemed to emerge.[40] It came as a welcome surprise when finally, on October 11, three weeks before the election, Tammany Hall nominated Abram Hewitt as its mayoral contender. Unlike previous Tammany candidates, Hewitt was a reform Democrat of relatively impeccable credentials and he quickly got the backing of the other factions of the Democratic party.[41] When Hewitt accepted the nomination on October 14, the *Staats-Zeitung* wrote confidently "the mayoral candidacy of Mr. Hewitt rises completely above the level of a party or factional candidacy."[42] This was indeed the case in the sense that Hewitt's candidacy would probably not have occurred if it had not been for the challenge from George. United behind a reform candidate, the various wings of the Democrats hoped to woo potential George adherents while keeping the traditional Tammany and reform Democrats in line. The only spoilers in this strategy were the Republicans who insisted on nominating a reformer of their own, the young Theodore Roosevelt. While his candidacy was a long shot, mainstream election watchers such as the *Staats-Zeitung* worried that the three-way race would make the campaign even more winnable for George.[43]

Though the candidacy of George was a strong challenge, the votes counted on November 2 gave a clear plurality to Abram Hewitt, with over 90,000 votes. With 67,000 votes George outflanked Roosevelt, who received only 40,000.[44] It is likely that the count was tampered with, but contemporary critics of the Tammany machine seem to have accepted George's defeat.[45] As staunchly working class as the George campaign had represented itself to be, voting returns indicate that a large percentage of New York's working class had not voted for him. An analysis of the vote by assembly district shows that the poorest of the Irish and Anglo-Irish working class had continued to vote the Tammany ticket. It is also likely that Catholic working-class voters heeded the opposition of the archbishop of New York and his clerics to Henry George.[46] German working-class voters seem to have been among the stalwarts of the George campaign to the end. But despite the registration efforts that preceded the election, many German immigrants continued to be disenfranchised, since they were too recently arrived to qualify for citizenship. Among older generations of Germans, on the other hand, citizenship and integration into the political process could mean integration into a political culture that muddied class issues behind a populist rhetoric and localist issues. Even if they constituted a considerable block of voters in the George campaign, German New Yorkers in general were far from being a unified block of voters, dispersed as they were throughout the economic and class structure of the city.[47]

The election campaign of Henry George, while clearly based on class solidarity, thus failed to make good on its promise of uniting the working-class electorate. Cultural and generational divisions continued to separate working-class New Yorkers. At the same time the voting patterns of the George campaign also show how political divisions within the working-class electorate were becoming an important factor, sometimes superseding ethnocultural factors. Tammany adherents, for example, did not vote this ticket just out of ignorance or tradition, but also because Tammany rule held the promise of jobs and a certain stability in the lives of poor immigrants. In many ways, the voting and alliances of the mid-1880s reflect a transitional phase of political realignment of working-class voters from the "old immigrant groups" and their ethnic bonds to new political alliances. The George campaign was an attempt to accelerate this trend and translate it into a powerful statement of political unity and potential power among the working class. But the promise of class solidarity over ethnic particularism went further than the organizations and constituencies of the labor movement were able to realize in 1886. Strict ethnic loyalties declined and their replacement by shifting political alliances continued, even if they were partly built on older ethnic patterns as well.

After their November defeat, the member organizations of the Central Labor Union were split on what to do next. A number of unions—most of them heavily German—asked to make the George movement into a permanent political organization in the winter of 1887. But the majority of CLU unions were more cautious and tried to avoid the entire debate over the revival of the "political question."[48] Those in favor of continued independent activism prevailed at first. Joined by the United German Trades, these CLU unions began to build a regular political party, the United Labor party, in order to enter the upcoming state and municipal elections with Henry George as their leading candidate. But serious dissent soon broke out around the party platform. George's stalwarts and the leader himself insisted on a strict single tax program, which was undigestible to the socialists in the new party. In a preemptive move the United Labor party therefore threw out all socialists from its convention in August of 1887.[49] The embittered socialists hastily mounted an alternative effort, calling themselves the Progressive Labor party and uniting most of the city's German socialist unions behind their banner. In the end, neither campaign rallied a wide array of labor organizations—the CLU tried to enforce a strict policy of neutrality at its sessions—and both campaigns failed miserably at the polls.[50]

No labor candidates were fielded in the years to come as the labor movement in New York City tried to come to grips with the changing political geography of the post–Henry George era. Realignments took place on many levels, within unions (as we will see in the following chapter), but also within political parties and most notably within the Central Labor Union. The first groups to benefit from the politically fluid situation after the George campaign were the established political parties, most notably the Democrats. They took their cue from the organizers of the George campaign and induced a number of prominent unionists and CLU leaders to become members of the Democratic party. These newly minted Democrats never gained much influence within the established political coalitions of the city; nevertheless the ensuing debate in the CLU over the political affiliation of some of its members tore across ethnic and union lines, eventually causing a split in the Central Labor Union itself in the summer of 1889.[51] The situation was especially confusing for the German unions because none of their leading members were directly recruited by the major parties and their traditional connection with the Socialist Labor party was sorely tested as the SLP drifted between a sectarian and anti-union leadership in 1888 and 1889 and after 1891 and a more pro-union faction which was in power from 1889 to 1890.[52]

The ascendancy of the American Federation of Labor and the decline of the Knights of Labor did little to lessen the political confusion in which the New York labor movement found itself in the late 1880s. Despite energetic attempts by some CLU leaders to stay out of any conflict involving these two organizations, things came to a head in early 1889 over the discontinuance of the brewery boycott, and many of the more activist unions split off from the CLU to form the Central Labor Federation.[53] In December 1890, Samuel Gompers and the executive committee of the AFL turned down the Central Labor Federation's request for a charter, objecting to the membership of the Socialist Labor party in the CLF as an independent body with voting rights. Gompers's refusal split New York's unions yet again; some of them then decided to join still a third organization, the New York Federation of Labor, chartered by the AFL. This second split had the most serious repercussions for those German-American unions such as the bakers, the brewers, and some cigar makers, who had hoped to gain from an alliance with the AFL while maintaining their political affiliation with the SLP. They were now forced to choose sides and either renounce their socialist political affiliation or make do without their newly won allies within the federation.[54] Such a choice had disastrous consequences, especially for unions whose membership base and political cohesion were still weak. Some unions split; others lost most of their membership or deposed their leaders in sudden coups. It was a most difficult position to be in in the early 1890s as the specter of a lengthy depression began to loom over the labor movement once again.

The George campaign of 1886 was a powerful moment of unity in the history of working-class politics during the late nineteenth century. But in the long run, the George campaign was less a defining event for future similar campaigns than a signal for the transitions about to take place within the working-class politics of the city. The shift from ethnic craft to class-based industrywide organization had started long before Henry George was put on the ballot. The cigar makers had been the pioneers in this respect, and it would continue among parts of the New York working class for the next decades. At the same time the late 1880s did not spell the end of ethnic unionism. Ethnic unions continued to be founded, and they played an important role in their communities. Their larger significance diminished, however. They no longer defined most of the political discourse in American labor, and were increasingly seen as outsiders by the most powerful wings of the labor movement nationally. Newer unions, whose members, for various reasons, were still organized into a homogeneous network of ethnic crafts, would find it difficult to join forces with the older unions which were well on the way toward a transethnic political unity in the late 1880s. Two proletarianized groups, the bakers and the brewers, will illustrate the meaning of ethnic unionism in the changed context of the mid- and late 1880s, a world of class organizations which increasingly transcended ethnicity.

7

New York's Brewery Workers
and Their Union

Even casual observers of nineteenth-century New York could not miss
the importance of the beer-brewing industry in the city. Imposing
buildings of the numerous breweries dotted Manhattan and the surrounding communities with their turreted brewhouses, tall chimneys,
and massive icehouses. In a city that did not have much heavy industry and whose most prominent industrial buildings (apart from
gas tanks and sugar refineries) were anonymous factory lofts where
workers such as the cigar makers toiled in obscurity, the breweries
stood out as monuments to Gilded Age capitalism and to the glories
of barley brews. Many of the city's breweries, moreover, were ringed
by shady beer gardens where customers could indulge on the spot
in a European ambience, furnishing their own picnics and tasting their
favorite brand fresh from the barrel. The glories of beer making and
beer drinking were also celebrated in the city's countless saloons, from
the humble backroom tavern with few decorations to the large beer
halls of the Lower East Side. Beer was a social drink, always present
at large gatherings of nineteenth-century New Yorkers, from large
festivities such as the *Volksfeste* of the German Vereine to the parades
and assemblies of working-class New York. Like other food crafts
(such as baking) beer making and beer drinking were part of the culture of German-speaking immigrants. But beer was also part of New
York working-class life in general, and this fact was emphasized by
the systematic image building of the brewery owners of New York.
At a time when the forces of prohibition were gaining even in notoriously wet New York City, the brewers took great pains to raise the
profile of their industry as an ancient and noble craft embodying hon-
orable traditions, something that was grounded in history, even pa-
triotism. In a certain sense, no trade or craft was imbued with so much
political meaning as brewing in turn-of-the-century New York City.[1]

The brewers emphasized this affinity for tradition by retelling the history of the craft and its deep roots in European and, more recently, American culture. In contrast to cigar making, brewing was indeed an ancient craft. "Modern" lager beer brewing techniques dated back to the mid-seventeenth century, when the king of Bavaria determined that no barley could be used for brewing during the summer (harvest) months in order to secure a supply of food grains. In addition the Bavarian ruler adopted the *Reinheitsgebot* (purity regulation) limiting the ingredients of beer to barley, yeast, and water. As a result, beer could only be made during the winter and spring and had to be stored for summer and fall use. Particularly careful methods of manufacture and long-term storage at even temperature were necessary preconditions to produce the long-fermented, lightly carbonated lager beer.[2]

Not just German rulers took an interest in the brewing craft in medieval and modern Europe. Since Roman times, most European beer makers had been subject to special regulations, taxes, and licensing requirements by the local authorities. This had a twofold effect on the industry. For one, it limited the power of guilds in the craft. In fact the trade was never autonomous the way other trades, such as baking and a host of others, had become by the thirteenth century in most cities. Brewers were always dependent on the authorities from whom they had to get licenses, and they could be undercut by such corporate entities as the princely estates or church authorities such as a monastery which could operate their own breweries under any conditions they wished. Brewmasters lacked the autonomy which their colleagues such as the butchers or bakers had (at least in theory), and their journeymen in the trade were never organized under an all-encompassing guild system in all localities. Instead, workers could find themselves directly dependent on the feudal authorities and their brewmasters could be subservient to the local rulers as well.[3]

Because of the way the highly profitable brewing trade caught the attention of the territorial authorities it also developed in a more centralized fashion, at least in some areas. From the eighteenth century a tax system in the kingdom of Bavaria favored larger, more efficient businesses over smaller operations, and from the early nineteenth century on larger businesses were thus in a position to take advantage of certain technological innovations. Thus Austrian and Bavarian brewers from Vienna and Munich introduced the thermometer and saccharometer from the leading innovators in beer making during the early nineteenth century, the British brewers. These small but technologically important measures were followed by the introduction of steam engines for heating and transportation in breweries by the 1840s. By the 1860s the breweries in large cities of central Europe and Great Britain were industrialized and ready to supply an ever-increasing urban working class with their brews.[4]

The marriage of traditional beer-brewing techniques and modern industrial technology and business organization was not without its problems. The vast majority of central European breweries continued to be small operations in villages and small towns of the countryside. In Bavaria, where one brewery existed for every 769 inhabitants as late as 1875, the difference between the small local operations and the ever-growing giant breweries of Munich and Nuremberg was particularly striking.[5] Slowly but surely the existence of the small businesses became threatened by the expansion of the large beer factories. Even among the journeymen the gap in wages and working conditions between large urban breweries and small rural establishments began to widen; those workers who had a choice tried to leave the lesser establishments in favor of better-paying situations in the New or the Old World.[6]

Beer making in the New World had been part of the North American economy since colonial days. But New York's brewing industry in the late nineteenth century had little in common with these historic predecessors. In fact, most brewery owners in the Gilded Age city had not set foot in the New World before the mid-nineteenth century, nor was the kind of beer they were making available in the city before the 1840s. Before that time, during the first two centuries of European settlement in North America, makeshift brewing operations were set up mostly in the backyards of inns and taverns where heavy, English-style dark beers and ales were made for local customers. The lighter, more effervescent lager beer became a popular drink after a German immigrant to Philadelphia introduced the method of lager beer brewing in the early 1840s. In rapid succession hundreds of new lager beer breweries were started all over the country by German immigrants who came between the late 1840s and the Civil War. New York, Philadelphia, Cincinnati, Milwaukee, Chicago, and St. Louis became centers of a national brewing industry built by German immigrants.[7]

The establishment of New York's first lager beer breweries took place shortly after the completion in 1842 of the Croton reservoir and an aqueduct which drew water for the metropolis from the Catskill mountains. The plentiful supply of very good water helped the city's nascent lager beer industry, which grew rapidly from just a few breweries to over fifty in 1868.[8] By 1880 Manhattan had fifty-seven breweries with a combined output of over 1.5 million barrels a year. Brooklyn also housed a large brewing industry with an output of over 1.1 million barrels a year from thirty-eight breweries. Almost 80 percent of these breweries made lager beer by 1880, while only twenty breweries made the old-style English ale and porter.[9]

If the central European brew won over American customers because of its fresher taste (due to more carbonation) and lower alcohol content, the manufacture of such an appealing drink took much care, experience, and, almost from the beginning, capital to invest in an increasingly sophisticated technology. Previously, beer making had consisted of four steps which remained basically unchanged in North American breweries: malting, making the wort, fermenting, and storing. By 1880 machines had become important in all these phases of production. In the malthouse (often an enterprise entirely separate from the brewery), forced air was mechanically circulated around the barley in order to clean the grain, which was then mixed (mechanically) with water and pumped into steeping vats for fermentation. The resulting malt was dried in a kiln—again with forced air. In the brewhouse the malt was cut with steel blades and boiled in water. In a cost-cutting break with central European traditions, the mash was then mixed with cheap unmalted grains (corn, rice) which had been boiled separately and filtered through a sieve.[10] The clarified liquid—the so-called wort—was pumped mechanically into the pear-shaped brew kettles, where it was slowly boiled with hops as flavoring for about two and a half hours. Up to the mid-nineteenth century the large copper kettles had been hung directly over a wood fire; in later decades breweries switched to coal and to more indirect heating methods with steam and water. After the boiling process, the remaining particles were filtered out of the fluid, which was then pumped into large vats where it fermented with the occasional additions of yeast at 45° F for two days. Once the primary fermentation was over, the new beer was pumped into barrels where it would be stored (*lagern*) for a minimum of three months at cool, stable temperatures.[11]

Mechanical aids such as steam engines, pumps, and elevators played an important part in the brewing process, but the fermentation and storing of beer was not as easily controlled by mechanical implements. Thermometers and saccharometers measured temperature and sugar content in the fermenting vats, but they did little to control the crucial and lengthy "lagering" process. In the extremes of the North American climate it was difficult to create the evenly cool and humid environment which was necessary for proper storage and fermentation, especially during the summer months. Like their European counterparts, New York brewers therefore dug deep cellars into the rocky hills of Manhattan and constructed large icehouses in the flatter parts of Brooklyn. This type of natural cool storage was expensive and limited the expansion of storage (and therefore production) capacity, until artificial refrigeration was introduced after 1879.[12]

With all these machinery and building needs, New York's brewing industry was one of the most capital intensive of the city. In contrast to the many craft trades and sweated industries such as garment making, cigar making, or baking, the capital investments of brewing were very high—second only to those of gasworks in the census statistics of 1880. The introduction of refrigeration made the manufacture of beer even more capital intensive by the end of that decade. The number of breweries which could flourish in this "high tech" environment was quite limited. Small backyard breweries, with an output of seven hundred barrels, which had dominated in the early years, had trouble staying alive after the Civil War, but even harder hit were middling breweries which produced between 3,500 and 50,000 barrels a year. Too large to be merely backyard businesses which could do with a few workers and storage vats, middling producers had too little capital to invest in expensive machinery. Only those who had expanded beyond their neighborhood and produced over 50,000 barrels (and up to 500,000) could hope to participate in the beer-brewing boom that characterized the New York market after the Civil War.[13]

The marriage of traditional methods of brewing and modern machinery, of a venerable self-image and an industrial business climate, was visible to all New Yorkers in the architecture of the breweries of Manhattan, the Bronx, Brooklyn, and Staten Island. The breweries pictured here illustrate this two-faced nature of the business very well. Even such a small brewery as Joseph Fallert's in Brooklyn emphasized the elements of solidity and historicity in its simple architectural style. Behind the relatively simple exterior lay a complex arrangement of facilities built to meet the needs of a small urban brewery. The site was dominated by the three-story brewhouse and the four-story icehouse. These buildings had to be of massive construction. In the brewhouse the upper stories held the malt containers and the water kettles. Underneath were the mashing vats, while the brew kettles could be found on the ground floor. After brewing, the liquor was pumped into the icehouse, where ice was stored on the well-insulated top floor. The fermentation vats were positioned underneath the ice on the third floor, while the storage barrels were put on the two lower floors. A

Joseph Fallert's lager beer brewery, Brooklyn, 1888. From *Western Brewer*, Jan. 1888.

well-planned ventilation system helped to maintain even temperatures throughout the icehouse. The picture of Fallert's business also shows a number of lower buildings which served as storage areas for raw materials. All entrances had high doors for horse-drawn carriages. The office was the only building resembling normal commercial buildings in size and proportions.[14]

Philip Ebeling's brewery, a larger and more modern establishment than that of Fallert, was typical of most of New York's larger breweries in the late nineteenth century. The buildings had the same function and were placed in roughly the same sequence as those at Fallert's, with the brewhouse and the icehouse next to each other; the number of stories in each building also corresponded to the different steps in beer making. In this large brewery, however, the function of the buildings was hidden behind an elaborate Renaissance facade. Ventilation ducts were made into towers, while elaborate gables and imposing entrances underscored the impression that brewers were engaged in a noble business. At the same time the interior was equipped with the most advanced technology of the industry.[15]

Philipp and William Ebeling's ale and lager beer brewery, Morrisania, 1888.
From *Western Brewer*, Jan. 1888.

The Brewery Workers of New York

In the highly visible brewing industry of nineteenth-century America one group was almost entirely hidden from public view—the brewery workers. They labored under conditions which in many ways had changed little since pre-industrial times and which did not differ in substance from the terrible conditions of their brethren in the more anonymous sweated trades (especially the bakers). "We brewery workers have already reached the lowest level of social existence," wrote a brewery worker in 1881. "We are told that work ennobles, but in the breweries it debases him and makes him dumb."[16] Other observers confirmed the impression that brewery workers were living and working under inhuman conditions. Modern technology had done nothing to lighten the load or lessen the dangers associated with the brewer's tasks.[17] In the paradigm of image and reality, of tradition and modernity, which characterized the brewing industry the workers were considered to be subject to a traditional order. While presiding over one of the most technologically advanced industries of the city, the brewery owners of New York maintained a system of labor relations that was resolutely pre-industrial and was adapted only when necessary to the practices of the industrial workplace. Their approach, as we will see, rendered the workers dependent and disposable at the same time.

Whether the business was small or large, the work in a nineteenth-century brewery was still physically arduous. Materials had to be transported, barrels had to be rolled, maintenance work on vats, barrels, heating implements, and storage facilities had to be performed, and in smaller breweries fluids had to be stirred and ingredients mixed in by hand. The extreme climatic changes within the different departments of a brewery made the work even harder. Workers continually went back and forth between the cold icehouse, the humid, cool storage rooms, the warm mashing room, and the hot brewhouse—changes which contributed to the frequent occupational diseases of brewers (rheumatism, tuberculosis, and bronchial infections). The hard physical nature of the work also meant that the trade employed few workers under eighteen years of age and that almost no one could work for more than twenty years at it. Brewers older than forty-five were very rare.[18]

Other industrial workers in late-nineteenth-century America labored under similarly taxing physical conditions (sugar house workers, for example), but none worked the brewers' long hours. Regular daytime work began between six and seven o'clock in the morning in low season or as early as two in the morning in high season. With a one-hour lunch break, work lasted until six o'clock at night. Often there were overtime hours up to nine o'clock at night, but without overtime wage rates. Fifteen- to eighteen-hour workdays were common in the industry. All brewery workers also worked on Sunday mornings for five to six hours.[19] Such hours, virtually unknown outside the city's sweated industries (such as baking), were part of the traditional brewers' lot in central Europe. There the brewers workday had once been determined by the yearly cycle of the brewing process, which usually meant that most brewing was done in the winter and spring because of the prohibition of brewing during the summer. As the prohibition against summer brewing fell and the periods of storage grew shorter, the summer season became one of the most intense work periods of the year, while business was somewhat slower in the fall and winter. This reverse rhythm, with its ever-intensifying workload, became even more pronounced in North America, where few rules and regulations governed the work of brewers.

Despite all technical innovations, parts of the brewing process re-

Table 1. New York's German Brewery Workers

	New York City		Brooklyn	
	Total	German	Total	German
1870	686	492 (71.7%)	196	129 (65.8%)
1880	1,689	1,243 (73.6%)	501	365 (72.8%)

Source: Ninth and Tenth Census of the United States, Census of Population.

tained their European craft character as late as the 1880s. Before artificial refrigeration and without biologically controlled raw materials
(such as pure yeast, introduced in the late 1880s), the "feel" of the
brewmasters and their journeymen in controlling the brewing and
fermentation process was an indispensable skill, which had usually
been acquired in an European apprenticeship. While apprenticeship
was necessary, it was also a lengthy process which New York brewery owners did not invest in. They preferred to hire skilled immigrant
brewers "fresh off the boat"; as a result, the city's lager beer brewers
were almost all immigrants from Germany or German-speaking central Europe. Few Americans or even American-born sons of Germans
could be found in New York's lager beer breweries. Ale and porter
brewers were mostly of English or Irish origin.

The vast majority of immigrant brewers in late-nineteenth-century New York were not just Germans but had emigrated specifically
from Germany's southern states. According to a selective census sample from the 1880 manuscript census, almost 40 percent of all German brewery workers in New York were born in Bavaria, and 30 percent more came from other southern states (Württemberg and
Baden).[20] The closing of innumerable small breweries in the rural
south of Germany, losers in the competition with the more mechanized beer factories in urban areas, drove workers overseas. They
came to the New World in search of stable work in their craft and in
order to maintain and advance their standard of living and, if possible, their standing as craftsmen—in this they resembled the cigar
makers and the overwhelming majority of skilled German immigrants. After all, had not their predecessors, the immigrant craftsmen
of the 1840s and 1850s, become the bosses in many New York City

factories? Had not most of the brewery princes of the Gilded Age started out as journeymen?[21]

Brewery workers rarely expressed their aspirations in any form that has become part of the historical record. Even more than in other trades, we have to turn to census data in order to learn how brewers and their families tried to accommodate themselves to the big city. Most startling is the extent to which these workers were confined to an almost exclusively German environment dominated by their place of work. Single workers, who represented a considerable proportion of the industry's manpower (103 out of 244 German-born brewery workers in the census sample were single), lived overwhelmingly in boardinghouses affiliated with their brewery, which were run either by their foreman or somebody close to him. In a traditional German pattern preserved from the Middle Ages, these journeymen were assigned to their accommodations and could not change employment and accommodations independently from each other. The European *Herbergszwang* (forced lodging system), traditional for all apprentices and most journeymen in skilled trades, was thus preserved for the brewery workers of New York.[22] In New York, as in the Old World, the *Brauerherberge* was an instrument in the hands of employers to control their workers' behavior. It kept brewery workers isolated from other working-class New Yorkers and largely prevented any social assimilation. But the *Brauerherberge* was also a place were the journeymen brewers could talk to each other, and even organize to some extent. Unlike other workers, especially in the many small sweatshops, who had difficulties getting in touch with each other, shop floor solidarity was not hard to build among workers who spent their working days and their nights together under the same roof.

Brewery workers who had families of their own lived in remarkably similar circumstances. One hundred and nine of 141 brewery workers' families in our 1880 census sample lived in the same house with other brewers or workers in closely related trades (maltsers, coopers). Especially those who lived near the large breweries of the Upper East Side of Manhattan shared their houses almost exclusively with workers in brewery-related trades. As a rule, the apartment houses in which they lived belonged to the brewery owner, who was their employer, and the tenement was managed by somebody close to him (possibly the brewmaster or a relative); and only employees of the same brewer could rent apartments there. Such controlled housing arrangements for all employees of the same business were very rare in Manhattan, though the tenement cigar workers found themselves subject to somewhat similar controls.[23] In other respects, too, brewery workers' families showed a highly uniform pattern of organization: the wife stayed at home with the children, while the husband worked. No other family members (grandparents, adult children, or cousins) lived with the family. Unlike most working-class families in the metropolitan area, brewery workers' families usually had to rely on one wage earner alone. Few had even boarders, and it is unlikely that wives of brewers earned money on the side in any other way. The uniformity of these arrangements was related to the narrow age range of the workers and their families. Brewery workers were overwhelmingly between nineteen and forty-five years of age; if married, they were no younger than twenty-five or so. The median age of brewery workers in our sample was twenty-nine years (twenty-five for single, thirty-four for married workers); few had children of working age. The decision to maintain a traditional one-wage-earner family was therefore not voluntary or deliberate. It was also a function of the children's age, the relative isolation of women from places of employment (notably the garment-making shops of the Lower East Side), and, most of all, the long and irregular absences of the father from home.[24]

The fact that most brewery workers' families had one wage earner only was, of course, also based on the premise that brewers earned sufficient wages to feed the family. A journeyman brewer earned between eleven and fourteen dollars a week (about five dollars were deducted for food and lodging for single workers); foremen received about twenty dollars, and the brewmasters considerably more than that. From the time the industry expanded during the 1870s and 1880s, skilled workers could usually count on year-round employment; only semiskilled workers such as those working in the bottling department or another specialized segment of the trade were laid off for up to six months during the winter season.[25] These were relatively good wages, but they would not last a lifetime. Brewery workers could rarely stay in their job more than two decades, and men in their forties usually had to switch to less arduous jobs (in the bottling department of a brewery, for example) which also paid less, or they had to find a different occupation altogether. It was a precarious position to be in, since most brewery workers had little education and had damaged their physical health while working in the brewhouse. In that situation many of them tried their luck as saloonkeepers, while others fell back on their children for support. No wonder that most brewery workers, overwhelmed by their workload and family responsibilities, had little time to devote to organizing or becoming active in any German-American or labor organizations.

The opportunities that lured the journeymen brewers to the New World—for example, upward mobility to a position as foreman or brewmaster or even to ownership of a brewery—had become largely unattainable by the 1880s. The capital-intensive nature of the industry made the prospect of starting one's own business an unrealistic one. For brewery workers, unlike workers in most other metropolitan trades, the idea of becoming independent producers or even co-owners of a cooperative enterprise was not a powerful dream which would shape their political identity.[26] Even upward mobility within a brewery was a precarious hope. Few of the existing breweries still offered skilled workers the chance to rise to the position of foreman or brewmaster. Usually they had only one brewmaster (commonly called by the German title *Vormann* in the industry) who supervised the foremen (called *Vorderburschen*) who headed the crews in different departments. In small breweries the brewery owners doubled as brewmasters and supervised the technical as well as the commercial side of their operations.[27] Traditionally the brewmaster was a very experienced and highly skilled worker who had risen through the ranks. But in the 1870s, many brewery owners began to place their sons or other close relatives in these jobs, so that this traditional route of upward mobility for journeymen brewers was almost completely closed by the 1880s. In other words, brewery workers were part of an industrial workplace that allowed little room for a rise to economic independence.[28]

Of all the trades discussed in this study, the brewery workers came closest to constituting a traditional *Gemeinschaft* or community in the New World. Their origins in the craft traditions of central Europe, their living arrangements, and their work hours meant that there was little the brewery workers did not share or at least know about each other. But in an industrial New World environment, this relatively small and tight-knit community lacked what might have made it a true *Gemeinschaft* in the pre-industrial sense: consensual control and a mutual sense of obligation to community norms by all members. Brewery workers were not asked whether they wanted to live together, their employers forced them to; they were tightly controlled by their employers both on and off the job. The brewery owners, on the other hand, incurred virtually no obligation to their workers, as they might have in a pre-industrial setting. Unlike in pre-industrial Europe, there was no obligation to provide for workers in their old age or in sickness (through formal or informal arrangements) nor was there an attempt to keep workers employed throughout the year. Characteristically brewery owners in New York liked to think of themselves and their workers as a big family, with themselves as the ever watchful fathers who could turn into stern disciplinarians or magnanimous benefactors as they saw fit.

Under these circumstances any type of autonomous workers' organization was as necessary as it was difficult to achieve. Traditions were no help for the brewery workers. Unlike the cigar makers, many of whom brought with them a familiarity with the union movement, the German brewing trade was almost entirely unorganized until the mid-1880s. The only groups in existence during much of the nineteenth century were mutual aid associations which were tolerated by the employers and showed few political ambitions. Close supervision of workers by employers and the isolation of workers from any political activity, especially in the southern German provinces from which most New York brewery workers came, made this class of workers among the least politicized in late-nineteenth-century industrialized Germany.[29]

In New York City the situation was not very different. Any type of organized activity of workers usually took place at the instigation and under the watchful eyes of the employers. There were New Year's celebrations, summer picnics, and dances organized by the employers themselves, who would show up at these festivities to be duly feted by their employees.[30] Mutual benefit societies, which flourished in many German-American trades before unions were founded, were started and controlled by employers in the breweries. Rather than fostering mutual aid and community development, these groups were charities and therefore had virtually no effect on the self-organization of workers.[31]

On the few occasions when the brewery workers did try to break out of the confines of their forced community, the consequences were disastrous. When an attempt was made to start an independent union in Brooklyn's large Schaefer brewery during a strike in 1872, the reaction of the employers was prompt—dismissal and citywide blacklisting of the purported strike leaders. Such measures quickly broke the resistance of the workers. Attempts to organize brewers within the Knights of Labor during the 1870s also had little success. Longer than most trades—up to 1881—New York's brewery workers had no labor organization of their own; the political activism which swept the city's labor movement during the late 1870s did not reach them.[32] The tight-knit community of brewery workers in New York City and

Brooklyn were imprisoned in their tradition with little space for voluntary association. In this sense the brewers were far removed from the world of the Vereine and would have a difficult time organizing as trade unionists.

The First Union of Brewery Workers in New York City

The ideal of craft harmony and a docile work force in the brewery industry was shattered one January morning in 1881 when four brewery workers were killed in a fiery accident while varnishing a barrel in Peter Doelger's brewery in Manhattan. Such maintenance tasks were a routine part of the brewers' work. In this case a group of four workers had been ordered by the foreman of the brewery to crawl into the dark barrel to varnish it from the inside with an alcohol-shellac mix, which was highly flammable and left the workers gasping for breath. A stable lantern was used to light the interior of the barrel and it was this semi-open flame which ignited the alcohol fumes and led to the explosion on January 6. The brewers working inside the barrel could not be saved in time by the one man who was standing guard outside, since only a small opening existed through which he could pull out his colleagues. Within hours the four men, all of them immigrants from Germany and experienced journeymen brewers, died of their injuries.[33]

The accident attracted the attention of the press, and a grand jury investigation took place about a month later to look into the causes of the incident. Its findings shed light on the working and production conditions in New York's breweries and made them known to a wider public for the first time. In lengthy hearings the grand jury interviewed the wives of the dead workers, their colleagues, the foreman, and even Peter Doelger, the owner of the brewery, as well as a number of other brewery owners and technical experts. From the interviews with wives and co-workers it became clear that the brewery workers were well aware of the dangers of the varnishing work and did not like performing it. One of those who had been killed had often told his wife "that he dreaded to crawl inside the storage barrels for varnishing and that he expected to not come home one day." Other witnesses also underlined the danger of this work and the frequency of accidents which could have been avoided through special security measures such as safer lamps, larger openings of the barrels, less-crowded working space, and less-pressured working conditions.[34]

The grand jury found that such elementary safety precautions had not been taken, and that the working conditions and lines of author-

Brew and kettle room in George Ehret's Hell Gate Brewery, Manhattan, 1880s.
From George Ehret, *Twenty-Five Years of Brewing* (New York, 1891).

ity at the brewery were not conducive to maintaining safe working
conditions in the first place. On the morning of the accident the foreman of the brewery, Peter Buckel, was not even present but resting
at home with a bout of rheumatism. There was nobody who was in
charge in the absence of Buckel (who, even when he was present, was
known as an intemperate, abusive overseer). The owner of the brewery was, as a rule, not informed at all about the day-to-day work at
his firm.[35]

The cause of the accident lay not in the individual carelessness of
the workers (as the journal of the United States Brewers Association,
an organization of owners, had proclaimed) nor in the individual failure of Peter Doelger (as the labor press surmised), but in the shifting
structure of work and responsibility in a mechanized brewery. Much
of the work in the brewery remained inherently dangerous with or
without machinery. Traditionally the owner or brewmaster who supervised the work had made sure that such dangerous jobs as varnishing were done under his supervision and with the appropriate
safety precautions. But by the 1880s many Manhattan breweries had
grown too large and complex for the owner or even the brewmaster

to supervise the work personally. Work crews were given general instructions, spurred to do their job quickly, and otherwise left to their own devices. No clear responsibilities or chains of command were established to take the place of the old hierarchies, which were insufficient in the large beer factories. In the end, the grand jury did not indict anyone in the matter, but admonished all parties involved to follow their own safety rules more carefully.[36]

As unsatisfactory as this result was for the brewery workers themselves, the investigation had a lasting impact on labor relations in the industry. In January and February of 1881, immediately after the accident, the *New Yorker Volkszeitung* published a series of letters from brewery workers in which the difficult working conditions in the city's breweries were described in some detail. For the first time the brewery workers themselves raised their voices to describe their work and the dismal conditions under which they made their livelihood. The circumstances at Doelger's were no exception, asserted the letter writers: "Things aren't much better in other breweries, prison discipline rules almost everywhere."[37] Fourteen- to sixteen-hour workdays were standard, workers were verbally abused as a matter of course, and often enough they were beaten as well by their foremen. Besides, brewmasters were "almost always drunk." The obligation to live in the brewers' hostel reminded the journeymen of indentured servitude.[38] "It is impossible to sink deeper, to be more exploited than we are," concluded one of them. A colleague agreed, but ended on a more hopeful note: "One is almost tempted to believe that these people have lost all interest in themselves, have no love for their families. But I haven't given up hope and I am confidently looking forward to the unification of the brewery workers and the resulting improvement of their truly sad lot." Other brewery workers agreed with the call for a united journeymen brewers organization. "These evils can only be eradicated through a union," wrote one of them.[39]

The desire for action on behalf of the brewery workers came at a time when the New York labor movement was at the beginning of one of its most active phases in the nineteenth century. As discussed in earlier chapters, prosperity had finally returned to most trades after the long depression of the 1870s. Many trades were either starting unions or solidifying their organizations by fighting for higher wages and shorter hours. This activism gave rise to the Central Labor Union in the city and created the Federation of Trade and Labor Unions on a national level. When over three hundred brewery workers showed up on the afternoon of March 6 at Wendel's Assembly Rooms on the Lower East Side, it was not just their individual desire for action that motivated them to start a union but also a resurgence of the labor movement that carried this group into the middle of labor activity during the next year.[40]

Characteristic of the type of support that came from organized labor for the inexperienced brewers was the fact that the introductory speech at the initial brewery workers' meeting was made by socialist and trade union activist George Block, not a brewer but a sometime pocketbook maker, with no connection to the brewery workers' trade.[41] But Block knew how to organize workers. With his help a seven-member executive committee was elected by the audience. The committee proposed to form a "Union of Journeymen Brewers" (Union der Brauer Gehülfen). Without any further delay about 120 workers immediately paid the initiation fee, set at 50 cents, and became members. A week later another sixty workers joined the union after a similar meeting.[42] Membership of the new union grew steadily and by the end of its first month the union had about 250 members from all over Manhattan. At the end of March, brewery workers in Brooklyn and the Bronx organized subsections of the union in their areas, and at the end of April they were joined by the Staten Island brewers and the brewers of the New Jersey suburbs, who formed sections 4 and 5 of the Journeymen Brewers Union.[43] The membership figures continued to climb for the ensuing months, although the labor press no longer published exact figures.

The young union differed in some important ways from other trade unions in the city, providing a good illustration of the special problems faced by a labor organization whose members had been without a voice for so long and who remained within a tight network of employer control. Most notable was the anonymity of its leadership, which lay in the hands of the seven-man executive committee, whose members were almost never named by the labor or any other trade press. The executive committee coordinated the affairs of the six sections. Within the local sections the union's shop groups were clearly the most important entities, with shop stewards representing the interests of the organized brewery workers in each brewery. The union's shop floor orientation clearly reflected the fact that these workers were tied to their specific place of employment much more than most other trades and that workers changed their employer less frequently than those in other industries. In many ways the union thus contrasted sharply with others in the city, such as the cigar makers and the carpenters, which had leaders who were well known in labor circles and among employers too. The immature organization had to capitalize on its strength—the close contact of the brewery workers with each other in each brewery—while for leadership they relied on labor activists from outside the trade such as George Block and preferred to keep a low profile, fearful of employer sanctions.

From its structure and the way it had been organized, the brewery workers' union was not immediately visible as a German-American group or even a typically ethnic organization. But in its membership and its de facto admission criteria it remained very much tied to traditional German and German-American craft unionism. Nominally the organization was open to all brewery workers in New York who had paid the initiation fee, but in fact membership in the group was limited to skilled German-American workers in lager beer breweries. Meetings and discussions were always conducted in German. Semiskilled or non-German-speaking men who worked in the brewing trade as bottlers or helpers or those who were workers in the ale and porter breweries (mostly Anglo-Irish workers) were not part of this first brewery workers' movement in New York.[44]

Unlike other German-American unions such as the cigar makers and the bakers, the brewery workers' union did not have a discernible political program from its inception. But the outline of the workers' demands soon began to emerge as the brewery princes started resisting the union's organizing efforts. In late March of 1881 union members in the breweries of Ringler, Ruppert, and Schaefer were summarily dismissed. In a sign of the considerable solidarity the German-American workers had with each other regardless of union membership, all other workers in these breweries went on strike with their union colleagues and joined their demands for the right to organize freely. Supported by other trade unions, the union called for a consumer boycott of the three brands. A list of acceptable brands and the names of places where such beer was served were published and the German-American Vereine in the city (whose members were known to be avid beer drinkers) promised to patronize only establishments where nonboycotted beer was sold. This was the first time a beer boycott had been organized, and before this campaign was fully effective, the three brewery owners ordered a delegation of workers to appear before them; after some discussion, the owners solemnly affirmed the right of their workers to organize in a published declaration. Within three days the dismissed workers were reinstated and work resumed in all breweries. The trade union had passed its first test, winning its key demand—the right to organize.[45]

With this most basic demand won, some workers began to ask for closed-shop rules in their breweries. In the late spring the journeymen brewers at Liebmann and Sons, Brooklyn's largest brewery, succeeded in gaining this demand. The union seemed well on its way to become a powerful player in the city's brewing industry.[46]

Meanwhile the brewery owners grew increasingly wary of the new organization and its tactics. The employers had long realized, though, the need for an organization of their own that would express their interests in a unified fashion. The United States Brewers Association (founded in 1862) was one of the earliest national employer groups and it soon grew to encompass brewery owners from all over the United States with headquarters in New York City and a monthly journal, the *American Brewer*. Only the owners of the largest New York breweries were members in the USBA, but a local affiliate formally founded in the summer of 1881, which called itself the United Lager Beer Brewers of Greater New York, encompassed virtually all lager beer brewers of the city and Brooklyn.[47] Through the local organization and the USBA's journal, the brewery owners made it look as if they had nothing against any organization of workers, that in fact they welcomed such a group and were ready to talk over problems with it at any time. Indeed, during the spring of 1881, the brewery owners tried to defuse any rebelliousness on the part of their workers by showing a constant willingness to talk to them and to attend to the individual complaints and needs of the journeymen. They probably hoped that the new organization would turn into something akin to a European journeymen's association, in which workers would continue to see themselves as part of a world of craft solidarity in which the interests of journeymen and masters could harmonize.

But at the same time the brewery owners also seemed to be aware that chances were diminishing for such a conservative view of labor relations to take root among their workers. Other unions had long rejected this model of organization, and socialists had had some success in proclaiming the irreconcilable nature of class interests as their basic tenet of labor organization. The *American Brewer* wrote characteristically that the trade union would draw the workers, "normally a jolly and honest tribe," into the forbidden territory of socialist agitation. "A red menace" was what the paper called the union. New York's brewery bosses, not ready for any substantial changes in the way they ran their businesses, gradually tried to control the union movement more forcefully. Union members continued to be fired but, more subtly, foremen began to discourage workers from joining the organization. At the same time the brewery owners contemplated better control of their work force through the introduction of logbooks (*Gesellenbücher*) for all journeymen brewers. Such books had to be carried by journeymen in Germany as a record of their qualifications as well as their past employment and behavior. If the brewery owners had seriously wanted to introduce this traditional way of keeping the status and reputation of their journeymen in check, it would have meant a radical change in the relatively freewheeling employment system in North America, from which the bosses also profited, and nothing much came of the idea in the end. It did suggest, though, how completely European models structured their thinking.[48]

The Strike for the Twelve-Hour Day and the Defeat of the Union

Workers, too, were of two minds about the meaning and the future of the union. It would take time for this split to emerge because the leadership of the union took great pains to present itself as the head of a fast-growing, united body of workers who were solidly behind their new organization, as short strikes had shown during the spring. But rather than wait and build up the strength of the organization and its finances slowly, as other unions had done in a similarly early phase of their organization, the leaders of the brewery workers' union decided very quickly that the time had come for radical action. In June of 1881, the union leaders decided on an all-out effort to win shorter hours. It seems that this decision was made without much discussion with the rank and file or even with the shop stewards of the city's breweries; at least no such discussions were recorded. Instead, at a routine meeting of union shop stewards on June 1, the shop delegates were handed a leaflet by the executive committee which stated laconically: "The union of brewery workers has decided unanimously to ask all brewery owners of New York, Williamsburgh, Morrisania, Union Hill, Staten Island and Newark to limit the hours of work (including mealtimes) to twelve from June 7th on and that work should cease entirely on Sundays." To underline the seriousness of their intentions, the leaflet also stated "that we have decided to insist on this demand and to cease work in those breweries (where the employers do not accede) which is what we owe to those brewery owners who are willing to grant our wish."[49] The shop stewards were instructed to relay this news to their bosses and make them sign a declaration promising the twelve-hour workday and the cessation of all Sunday work. The signed declaration (or the refusal to sign) was to be reported on June 7 to the executive committee of the union, which would start an immediate walkout and boycott all recalcitrant brewery owners.[50]

Workers and bosses must have been almost equally surprised by these demands and the radical way in which the union leadership was ready to fight for them. By and large the workers seemed to heed the directives of the executive, while the brewery owners were hostile to the union's demands, especially to the cessation of Sunday work. After a compromise was reached on this point, fourteen breweries in the greater New York area were ready to work under the union's conditions. In all other firms over 1,200 organized brewery workers went on strike on June 7.[51]

Despite the fact that the brewery workers were only recently organized and had little in the way of financial reserves, the workers had some power over the bosses. As skilled workers in an expanding industry manufacturing highly perishable goods, brewery workers clearly had an advantage over workers in the garment or cigar industry when it came to striking. Most breweries needed them badly during the busy summer months. Especially smaller firms which had limited reserves in their small storage facilities saw their summer sales dwindle, as most beer brewing came to a halt during the second week of June. Strikebreakers were rare, and there seemed to be tight discipline on the striking brewers.[52]

But at the same time the union had to reckon with the United Lager Beer Brewers of Greater New York, a well-organized group of bosses who wielded impressive power now that they had decided to act collectively. Starting in early July, these brewery owners met regularly to reinforce their bargaining position toward the workers and to keep an eye on each other as well. No brewery owner in New York and vicinity dared to negotiate openly with the union after the United Lager Beer Brewers had decided on a policy of no compromise.[53]

With the brewery owners closing their ranks, it became doubly important for the union to secure the solidarity of all workers in the city's breweries. This task was difficult because many workers in the city's breweries were not organized at all: beer drivers, maltsers, firemen, and unskilled helpers had not yet been part of the union movement. Most of the strikebreakers came from the latter categories of members during the early days of the conflict. But even many of the organized workers were unsure of how to behave; brewery workers were inexperienced in union matters—this was true for their colleagues in Germany as well—and for most, it was probably the first strike they had ever taken part in.[54] Although the union's demands had widespread support among all the workers, the inexperienced rank and file was generally not prepared for such a massive action and easily thrown off by offers of compromise from the brewery owners. Submissiveness and faith in the employers' goodwill were deeply ingrained in these workers, who came from a world of paternalistic labor relations. Promises of shorter hours or modified working conditions from their employers made the strikers' front crumble rapidly after the first two weeks of the walkout.[55]

The organization of a beer-drinker boycott in support of the workers also ran into difficulties. After all, the union was asking for nothing less than total abstinence from beer drinking during the summer months, since the few "union breweries" were small and little beer from other cities reached New York during the early 1880s. The union tried a number of tactics to publicize its cause and drum up support for the boycott. A parade was organized in which over one thousand striking brewery workers marched through the city accompanied by flags and music; saloonkeepers offered free union beer to thirsty strikers, a baker helped with donations of bread and brewery workers' wives loudly expressed their scorn about "scabs" (that is, those who were seen drinking nonunion beer) to the neighborhood. Some groups also began to send financial contributions to the brewery workers' union. Such payments were gratefully accepted but not solicited at any time by the strikers. More important than the material support of the strikers was the political solidarity of labor organizations in the city. About 120 unions, cultural groups, and mutual aid societies— most of them German-American—vowed to support the struggle of the brewery workers by abstaining from beer entirely.[56] The union also attempted to win the solidarity of saloonkeepers, holding special meetings to induce them to switch from their customary brands to "union beer." Since the union breweries were small, and saloonkeepers were often in debt to their regular suppliers, it was difficult for most bar owners to switch brands. About 120 saloons in the city— again most of them owned by German-Americans—had union beer on tap, not a particularly impressive number considering that Manhattan alone had over one thousand saloons.[57]

While these shows of solidarity affirmed the rights of the long-isolated brewery workers within New York's working-class organizations, they did little to help resolve the walkout. The United Lager Beer Brewers' position remained unchanged. With no solution of the conflict in sight, the union began to lose its hold on the workers by the end of June. More and more brewery workers chose to go back to work, fearing a permanent loss of their jobs and their homes. Strikers who lived in brewery-owned houses had to move out, and the police began to arrest picketers for disorderly conduct. At the beginning of July the brewery owners declared that all their businesses were working at full capacity, and the union, by maintaining that six hundred men were still on strike, tacitly admitted that at least half of its members had returned to work.[58]

On July 5, 1881, the brewery workers' union was forced to admit defeat and declare the strike over. Those workers who held out until the end were blacklisted and now had to rely on financial support from the union. But the Union of Journeymen Brewers had no financial reserves; few brewery workers were willing to continue their support for an organization which had proven largely powerless to protect their interests. They therefore began to leave the union in droves. After a few months the union had ceased to exist. Despite the attempts of some to continue the organization as a secret trade union, no regular organization of journeymen brewers took the place of the vanquished union for four years.[59]

With no union protecting the journeymen brewers' interests, the old working conditions returned soon after the strike was over: in the fall of 1881 fourteen- to sixteen-hour workdays and six hours of work on Sundays were again the rule in New York City's breweries. These conditions would not change during the following years. While almost all of the more industrial trades in the city had some kind of unionization by 1885, and while wages and working conditions improved in many occupations, New York's German brewery workers made no discernible progress.[60]

How was it possible that the brewery workers' movement had broken down so quickly and showed no sign of recovery for the next four years? The most immediate explanation lies in the fact that the young and inexperienced organization of the brewery workers had taken on too much too suddenly. In challenging one of the best-organized and wealthiest industries of the city any union would have had a problem, but for the brewery workers with their scant financial and organizational resources an all-out strike was just too much. On another level, though, the conflict also sheds light on the limiting effects of ethnic cohesion and ethnically based community in the organization of labor. Especially in comparison with the cigar makers, the brewery workers' failures show in an exemplary way that traditions could cut two ways among the German working class of the city. While for the cigar makers a sense of pre-industrial tradition was weak and knowledge of a constantly changing work force was part of their identity, the brewery workers' sense of tradition meant a resistance to change by employers and workers. Experiences of organizing or exposure to the nascent labor organizations of Germany were not part of the brewery workers' history. The links to the emancipatory influence of labor organizing in Europe, which were so important for the cigar makers, were therefore not a force for the brewery workers. In other words: the isolation of the brewery workers from the rest of the German community was not a recent phenomenon but a characteristic with a long history which made it doubly difficult to mount an effective campaign against the united employers with the help of other workers.

While at the outset the brewery workers and their employers seem to epitomize Germanness in New York City, this group actually formed only a very small and isolated segment of German New York. The product of their labor linked them closely to the working-class neighborhoods of the city, but their actual contacts to German-American workers in other trades was very limited. Ultimately it was the brewery bosses that profited from the close connection of beer with German-American life through their domination of the neighborhood distribution and sale of beer. At the same time the brewery owners were able to organize cohesively as a class of employers well beyond the local and ethnic realm. Along with the steel and railroad barons who would exert national influence within their far-flung enterprises, the brewery princes were among the most cohesively organized groups of employers in the late nineteenth century. They organized their workers according to their needs and maintained similar working and living conditions throughout their industry nationwide.

Hierarchical thinking, isolation in one's ethnic and occupational community, and a tradition of paternalist relations between employers and journeymen made it difficult for an industrial union culture to take root. By 1881 there were ways to create a union with outside support from other parts of the New York labor movement, and that support was surely crucial in putting the union on its feet in the first place. But the New York labor movement, in itself not very strong yet, could not make up for what the community of workers lacked: political experience, class solidarity with other workers, and an ability to reach out beyond the ethnic borders of the German-American community.

8

The New Organization of Brewery Workers: Ethnic and Industrial Unionism

After the lockout of 1881 New York's German brewery workers had no official organization at all for three years. A number of faithful unionists continued to stay in touch with each other, but refrained from organizing their co-workers; journeymen brewers were once again limited to their informal associations in the boardinghouse or at work. Organized togetherness retreated into a few Vereine such as the Gambrinus shooting club and the sickness fund which the United States Brewers Association had started for brewery workers after the strike. These groups were entirely unpolitical in nature and would have no connection to any future union efforts. Six months after the lost strike, it looked as if the brewery workers' union had never existed. In letters to the *New Yorker Volkszeitung*, a few brewery workers occasionally revealed that all the abuses and exploitative practices of earlier years remained frequent in the city's breweries. Workers still had to work up to fifteen hours a day, and were beaten and cheated of their wages. They remained beholden to their foremen and boardinghouse keepers and many could not hope to have a family life or provide a future for their children.[1]

While it looked as if time had stood still for the brewery workers and their organization, both the brewing industry and the organized labor movement underwent momentous change during the period between 1881 and 1885. The industry faced some difficult issues which had little to do with organized labor. The most important development was the slowing growth of an industry that had been used to almost automatic expansion in the decades preceding 1880. The second half of the 1880s and the 1890s were characterized by the signs of a maturing market: slower growth, increased productivity, growing domination by a few large brewers.[2] This is not to say that New York's brewers in particular suddenly found themselves in a recession. On the contrary, production continued to increase; but despite the generally healthy state of the brewing trade in New York, the city's breweries seemed to lose their status as a national center of the brewing industry from the mid-1880s on. The percentage of all U.S. beer brewed in the city decreased from 22 percent in 1880 to 16 percent in 1900. Productivity growth also lagged behind the national average, which grew almost fourfold per brewery between 1880 and 1900; in New York City an average brewery made only two and a half times as much beer in 1900 as it had twenty years earlier—probably because the total number of licensed breweries held relatively steady in the city, while it declined in the nation. All these factors underlined the conservative marketing strategy which New York City's brewers followed. Only a few made attempts to market their products elsewhere, and only one brewery owner, George Ehret, had something of a national market for his product. New York's brewery bosses stayed out of the competition for nationwide markets which was increasingly divided up among a few of the large "shippers" who brewed in Milwaukee (Pabst, Miller, and Schlitz) and St. Louis (where the largest shipper was Anheuser Busch).[3] While in the 1870s New York's brewing industry seemed poised to capture a position of national prominence, the 1880s would show that the conservative marketing strategy of New York's brewers limited the industry to New York regional markets.

The relatively slow expansion of New York's brewing industry was accompanied and probably also caused by the fact that ownership patterns changed very little in the city's beer-making businesses. New York's breweries continued to be family enterprises, although limited partnerships (with two or three partners) also became frequent toward the end of the century. Only seven New York breweries were owned by shareholding companies in 1900. A group of British investors who bought a number of larger breweries in the midwestern states during the 1880s had little luck in New York. Despite tempting offers from investors, only two brewery owners sold their businesses. In an age when an increasing number of enterprises belonged to groups of shareholders who could provide the large capital investments needed for machinery, most New York breweries continued to be in the hands of German-American families who personally directed their business and remained involved in day-to-day decisions.[4]

But with all their personal involvement, group cohesion, and conservative consensus, New York's brewery bosses were not able to fend off incursions by the big shippers into their New York fiefdom. Once the technology was available to transport bottled beer in refrigerated railroad cars over long distances (by the mid-1880s), the brews from Milwaukee, St. Louis, and Rochester showed up in New York taprooms, too. Under the competitive pressure from outsiders, many publicans became less dependent on deliveries of the local brewery boss and the traditional bonds between saloonkeepers and brewers in New York City were loosened. During a price war (started by British-owned midwestern breweries that were trying to break into the national market), the price of a barrel of beer fell from the eight dollars New York brewers considered fair to four or five dollars in many of the most competitive markets.[5] New York brewery owners dreaded such competition. In order to keep what they considered "their" city out of the beer wars, they entered into a mutual agreement in 1885 which fixed a scale of prices. In extensive provisions the local brewery bosses tried to head off the various means of price cutting that had already become established in the brewing industry, such as rebates or loans to saloonkeepers, and the "stealing" of wholesale customers through other enticements. In contrast to other localities (where it was also attempted) this cartel program of self-regulation worked well in New York for a number of years. The New York brewery owners were thus spared the low prices and increasing monopolization by a few firms that characterized the beer market in other areas.[6]

Political pressures grew too as prohibitionist sentiment increased in the traditionally "wet" New York area. Blue laws curtailing drinking hours were popular weapons of the temperance movement which threatened sales, especially in Brooklyn, the "City of Churches." For a while, beer gardens and other public drinking establishments were ordered closed on Sundays by the excise board in Brooklyn, much to the dismay of the brewers and the German-American community at large. New Jersey also enacted some prohibitionist legislation. Brewery owners spent considerable resources combating the movement. They published books extolling the virtues of beer and helped organize antiprohibitionist demonstrations.[7] In New York City the brewery owners were quite successful in challenging the prohibitionists' advance, but the struggle also tied up time and money that the bosses might have employed elsewhere—for example, against labor, which began organizing again by the mid-1880s.

The Rebuilding of New York's Brewery Workers' Union, 1884–86

While the brewery bosses were fighting their own wars to protect their turf, the brewery workers made tenuous attempts at organizing as well. Amid the activism that characterized New York labor in 1884–86, a small band of about a dozen brewery workers met in early 1884 to found a new brewery workers' union. After the bitter experience of 1881 the brewery workers decided to organize in secret, a fact which hampered the spread of the organization considerably. By the beginning of 1885, the union still only had twenty-five members, and even though it joined the Knights of Labor, the organization was unable to prevent the dismissal of its president, Louis Herbrandt, from his job at Peter Doelger's brewery after his role in the revival of the union became known.[8]

It was not until the early spring of 1885 that the Central Labor Union of New York City took an interest in the brewery workers and began a systematic campaign to bring about their unionization. In 1884 the CLU had tried to organize a boycott against George Ehret, the city's largest brewer. But the campaign against Ehret's beer, which was initiated by the bricklayers' union because Ehret employed non-union bricklayers in his plant, failed completely, for almost none of Ehret's employees were unionized. The unsuccessful boycott brought the brewery workers to the attention of activists in the CLU and in late January the organization announced that "it had worked out a specific organizing plan for all brewery workers which looks very promising and whose realization will be undertaken in the coming days."[9] A specially appointed committee held well-attended mass meetings for the workers at specific breweries, at which up to two-thirds of those present joined the union (which was no longer secret) immediately.[10] The new campaign soon ran into resistance from brewery owners. The first one to fight the organization of his workers was Peter Doelger, owner of the brewery where the death of four workers had spurred the earlier unionization attempt. Doelger simply dismissed all workers who had joined the new union. The CLU immediately tried to fight back by putting a boycott on Doelger's beer, but had difficulty sustaining such an action since the majority of the city's skilled lager beer brewers were still not members of the union. Only four small breweries were completely unionized and could thus be recommended as producing "union beer."[11] Even the support from the Central Labor Union did not advance the organizing efforts of the brewery workers very far.

In this problematic situation help came from an unexpected corner: the "United Lager Beer Brewers of New York and Vicinity." Representatives of this local branch of the United States Brewers Association secretly approached union president Herbrandt in May of 1885. As union leader, Herbrandt later recalled, they asked him if the union was willing to enter into an agreement with the employers. "Well, I was at the time rather astonished to hear something like that from a brewer boss," observed Herbrandt drily later.[12] Given the employers' long-standing hostility to unionization, the union president hesitated to accept the offer. He thought his union too small to be a strong bargaining partner in contract negotiations. To his amazement, though, the employers' confident response was that "they would see to that," that is, they would help to increase the union's membership. Herbrandt finally agreed to cooperate with the bosses.[13]

Without referring to this understanding with the union, which remained secret for three years, the members of the United Lager Beer Brewers soon thereafter embarked on a vigorous membership campaign for the brewery workers' union, encouraging workers to join the organization with propaganda and pressure tactics. One worker later recalled that at his brewery, "several times circulars were posted up enjoining men to join the union." Since the workers were at first reluctant to do so, the owner decided that "on a certain Friday they had to join the union and whoever did not join the union would be dismissed."[14] In the case of Peter Doelger's brewery (where the union founder had worked until his dismissal), the owner's change of mind on union membership looked like a conversion experience to the amazed workers. Doelger himself rented a saloon for his workers' initial union meeting at which he was present. "It was an uplifting experience for me to see this millionaire before our committee and ask a workers' organization for mercy," reported a member of the union.[15] With such a concerted effort by the employers, twelve breweries in the New York area were organized in late 1885. By the end of March, the workers in fifty-six New York area lager beer breweries had joined the organization, which by then had over 1,500 members—90 percent of all skilled lager beer brewers in greater New York. In the eyes of the New York working class the unionization campaign of the Central Labor Union had reached a very successful conclusion.[16]

The arrangement of the brewery workers' union with the bosses was unique in nineteenth-century New York, especially because the union had started out as an organization opposed by the employers and continued to be anything but a company union. The brewery workers' organization, aware of the unprecedented (and possibly problematic) nature of the arrangement, kept it a secret. But the union's politics and history cannot be understood apart from this unusual arrangement. It saved the organization years of building up union consciousness among the workers and of constructing a durable organization. The journeymen brewers were spared the years of slow struggle and minimal growth which the cigar makers and others experienced in the 1870s and 1880s. But this easy success came at a high price. Workers who joined a union at their bosses' behest would view their organization differently from workers who had joined unions in order to resist their employers. The union was in danger of becoming just one more employer-dominated organization within the frame of paternalistic labor relations.

The first area in which the bosses' support for the union turned out to be detrimental in the long run was in recruitment of new members from outside the German-American work force. Because the union was in such a cozy alliance with the employers, unionists felt little need to reach out for allies in the labor movement. Internally the organization remained a union of German-American craftsmen; unskilled workers and non-German brewers did not join the union and were not asked to do so. Union business was always conducted in German, most union members did not speak English, and even union secretary Herbandt's English was only rudimentary.[17] The union also kept a low profile in the city's labor organizations. Some of the founding members of the union were socialists and members of the Socialist Labor party, and the union was affiliated with the Knights of Labor during its first year of existence, but the journeymen brewers played no significant role in either group.[18] Nor did the young organization take elaborate measures to build up a network of membership services. Prospective union members paid an initiation fee of two dollars and, to remain in good standing, low monthly dues of 35 cents. The money paid for the union's office on Rivington Street in the center of the German Lower East Side and for Herbandt's salary of $15.00 per week as well as for a part-time financial secretary. The office also served as a hiring hall for union members, a service intended to break the control of boardinghouse keepers over the job market for brewery workers. Apart from this labor exchange the union offered no services of any kind, such as life or sickness insurance or unemployment benefits. Such support systems were left to employers, who continued to be cast (and cast themselves) in the role of benevolent masters taking care of employees in time of need.[19]

If the union's benefit program remained modest when compared to other organized trades, its demands were ambitious by the standards of the brewing industry. In 1881 the union wanted to achieve shorter hours, a general improvement in working conditions, and higher wages. These demands were also central to the contract negotiations which the brewery workers' union started in March of 1886 with the employers—a year after the unionization campaign had begun in earnest. Once again the negotiations were secret, but this time the resulting contract was published in April. In it the union had gained very advantageous terms for its members, winning the closed shop in all USBA breweries (only the sons of brewery owners and the foremen were exempted). The contract also introduced a twelve-hour workday with regular breaks and fixed shifts. Sunday work, paid at twice the normal hourly rate, was limited to two hours. Wages ran from $10.00 to $18.00 a week, depending on the worker's rank. The contract also specified that "no worker who has been recommended by a boardinghouse-keeper or saloonkeeper will be hired." Instead, brewers found work through the union or by directly applying to the brewery itself. According to the contract, all brewery workers were to be promoted regularly from relatively low-skilled jobs (such as work in the wash house) to more highly qualified work in the brew-house or in the fermenting rooms. Promotions were to be decided on by a committee consisting of two elected workers and the brewmaster. In addition, the terms of regular apprenticeship were specified, including a final examination given by the brewery workers' union. One apprentice was to be allowed per twenty-five workers. Another important innovation introduced by the contract was a citywide arbitration panel which consisted of four brewery workers and four brewmasters; it had to mediate disputes in all breweries covered by the contract.[20]

The agreement of 1886 marked the first time a major New York industry was covered by a union contract. This achievement of the brewery workers' union should not obscure the fact that the contract reflected the split identity of the union and its members. On the one hand the union acted as a progressive force pushing the working conditions and wages up to the level of other skilled workers; on the other hand the brewery workers' union had assumed the position of a craftsmen's guild, guarding over the craft's continuity and the value of the brewers' skill. Especially the regulations covering apprenticeship resembled old-time guild laws.[21] But such a way of thinking could only be maintained by the union if the employers also accepted the implicit premise contained in the contract: that the brewery owners and their craftsmen-workers were equal partners in the preservation of craft virtues and that the trade union was the official trustee in this relationship. In 1886 most New York brewery owners were at least verbally ready to concede such a position to the union. They did so for a number of reasons. As Gilded Age capitalists they faced troubling times on many fronts and preferred to take in their workers as "partners" in keeping labor peace, at least as long as business was difficult. To the employers such an arrangement implied a certain control over the union, its growth and its demands. They might have hoped, for example, to keep socialists in check. But beyond this most brewery owners also had a past as brewery workmen themselves. Some of the men now called "princes" harbored feelings of craft solidarity with their workers and might have envisaged an organization in which workers and employers cooperated for the common good of the trade, and against the encroachments from the big outside shippers, overcoming the walls of class warfare which were so prominent in other trades.

The brewery workers, for their part, celebrated their success in New York as a permanent step in establishing the union's position as an arbiter over the brewers' lives. They had little awareness of how fortuitous were the circumstance that permitted their success. Despite their socialist sympathies, the leaders of the union lacked the distance and skepticism toward their employers that marked the attitudes of other socialist union leaders.

The brewery worker union's image of itself was an amalgam of industrial and craft unionism, socialist thought and traditional artisanal beliefs; such a mixture also pervaded the *Brauer-Zeitung*, the publication of the National Union of Brewers, started in 1886. In its inaugural issue Louis Herbrandt, by then head of the national union as well as its New York branch, stated the goals very simply: "the union proposes the advancement of the material and intellectual welfare of the brewers in this country through organization, through enlightenment in work and writing, through a reduction of working hours, an increase of wages and preference for practical and experienced brewers." But he also stated that the union was to try to "keep peace between employers and workers in order to maintain and secure the prosperity of our trade in a lasting way. Long live the craft in all phases of development!" he proclaimed at the conclusion of his programmatic article.[22] This very traditional-sounding credo would be challenged and modified in various ways during the following years from critical socialists and other more aggressive unionists inside and outside the union, as the brewery workers struggled to make use of their quick success and to find their place within the wide political spectrum of New York's labor movement. But for the time being they represented the dominant mood in the young union.

The marriage of old-world craft beliefs and activist unionism marked the flag dedication ceremony which the New York brewery workers' union held in the spring of 1887. The local had adopted a red flag, as the *Brauer Zeitung* pointed out proudly (and the brewery owners noticed with some misgivings). Stitched in the red silk was the squat figure of Gambrinus, legendary god of beer drinkers and beer makers from Roman times, with a large beer mug in his hands. He was surrounded by a garland of hops plants and inscriptions such as "Hops and Malt—May God Preserve" and "Victory through Struggle," a well-known union motto. The president of the local union interpreted the flag's mixture of traditional and progressive goals as follows: "With the extinction of the guilds, the brewers' flag also lost its significance and its bearers rested on their laurels for too long. . . . But now the time of enlightenment has come! The brewers guild, which had been asleep for so long, has woken up and is demanding its rights. The flag is unfurled anew and flutters ahead of the fighting troops just as in olden times, in its fight against the modern day robber barons."[23]

The Beginnings of a National Union and the New York Contract

Even before the successful conclusion of the contract negotiations, New York's journeymen brewers attracted attention for their organizing successes and were asked to lead an effort to unify all existing brewery workers' organizations in the country. At the invitation of the New Yorkers, delegates from groups in Philadelphia, Detroit, Newark, and Baltimore met in August 1886 in Baltimore to found a nationwide organization, the National Union of Brewery Workmen. A constitution was worked out and the leadership chosen. Louis Herbrandt, head of the New York union (which became Local 1 of the National Union), was elected president, and the headquarters of the group were established in New York City. Herbrandt, at the same time, became editor of the union's *Brauer Zeitung*, which appeared monthly starting in October 1886. The organization grew rapidly during its first two years and by early 1888 it had thirty-five local unions. The locals everywhere resembled the New York local in structure and membership: members were almost all German-speaking, and most were skilled brewers. Recognizing the growing importance of ancillary occupations for the industry, the brewery workers' union began in 1886 to organize groups of beer drivers and maltsers; in many places, firemen and brewery engineers joined the union as separate locals in 1887.[24]

The years 1886–88 were a time of political upheaval within New York's labor movement. Fortunately for the brewers, they coincided with a period of prosperity in the city's brewing industry. Because of the relatively generous wages fixed by the contract of 1886 (which was renewed in 1887), the brewery workers shared modestly in this prosperity, becoming the best-paid journeymen brewers in North America. The favorable conditions of the contract were unusual enough to attract hundreds of German immigrants to New York City's breweries after 1886. "Since the contract has been signed, New York has been swamped with brewery workers," Local 1 reported a bit worriedly. "Every steamer arriving from Germany has lately brought a great many colleagues who, drawn by high wages, have left the Fatherland to make their fortune."[25] This influx soon created problems for workers in established lager beer breweries, for the number of jobs for skilled brewers did not expand with the growing production volume of the late 1880s. Machinery and the subdivision of labor meant that the need for brewers well-versed in all departments decreased, while a growing number of journeymen brewers were employed in what were in fact semiskilled positions (such as bottlers, cellarmen, etc.) in just one department of the brewery. Such developments were hardly altered by the contract, and the pressure on skilled workers was increased by the arrival of newcomers willing to take these more lowly jobs at what to them were skilled men's wages.

Local 1 responded by implementing drastic protective measures. Beginning in March 1887, prospective candidates for union membership had to be nominated by union members and pay an initiation fee of $20.00. A month later the fee was raised to $50.00. In any case, no new members were accepted for the time being. Newly arrived workers were told to find work in the hinterlands. New York's breweries were effectively closed to the newcomers at a time when all New York lager beer brewers were organized and operated under closed-shop regulations.[26]

The closing of Local 1 to new members was a unique event in late-nineteenth-century New York. On the face of it, the move manifested the union's character as a conservative restrictive craft union. The closing of the union made its membership static, isolated from the labor market and from the most recent group of German immigrants. This step further limited the union's connection with the ever growing and changing German-American community in the city. Even though criticism in the labor press was muted, such a step put the brewery workers' union squarely at odds with the majority of the German-American labor movement which favored a more open form of unionism in keeping with socialist principles. By closing themselves off to newcomers, the brewery workers risked losing political and moral support from other German working-class immigrants, a group whose help might be crucial in future conflicts.

The closing off of the union had compensating effects, too, however: the moratorium gave it a chance to stabilize as a group and find a niche in the New York labor movement during a particularly dynamic time. Within the factions that became visible in the year of the Henry George campaign, the brewery workers could usually be found with the German-American socialists. To affirm this alliance the union also joined the United German Trades (Vereinigte Deutsche Gewerkschaften), the German-American umbrella organization which understood itself as a more political union group than the CLU, though not in opposition to it. After the failure of Henry George's bid for the mayoralty, the brewery workers' union became quite actively involved in the Progressive Labor party's electoral campaign of 1887. The PLP failed badly in the 1887 effort and the brewery workers did not become active in electoral politics again.[27]

These forays into the political arena highlighted some problems which continued to limit the union's effectiveness in the late 1880s. Unlike the cigar makers, whose union leaders remained acutely aware of the need to form coalitions with a variety of labor groups if they wanted to be heard in the political arena, the brewery workers limited themselves to alliances with German-American socialists without making contacts outside this circle. While this put them in the middle of much activism in 1886–87, in the end it had not served to widen the union's exposure to broader coalitions of workers and their organizations but, on the contrary, confirmed their relative isolation within one ethnic group and its associated political faction. In the case of the brewery workers, ethnicity had served to isolate the workers and their union in ways that would become detrimental to the movement of brewery workers in the long run.

At least as important, however, was the dichotomy within the union between the socialist principles its leadership officially espoused and the conservatism of its rules and its rank and file members. The employers as well as the union leadership considered the brewery workers' union a socialist group, although it is not clear how far this belief reached down to the ranks of the union members. From their actions during and after the year of the contract and their testimony before the New York State arbitration commission in 1888, the brewery workers continued to appear as a generally conservative group of workers, given to cautious action and belief in a cooperative relationship with their employers. The preservation of the craft and the craft status of workers was foremost in their minds, and if this could be achieved with the help of socialist activists, the union members were willing to go along, though they were not ready to become prominent and exposed disciples of socialism.

The leaders of the brewery workers' union were well aware that union members' enthusiasm for socialist politics might be limited and that the union needed more than the support of a small band of like-minded German radicals. On a national level the founding of the National Union of Brewers in August of 1886 and its subsequent affiliation with the American Federation of Labor in early 1887 helped the brewery workers' movement gain important allies outside New York City. Locally the alliance with the Knights of Labor proved to be of more immediate importance—mostly as a source of problems.[28]

Since 1884 the New York brewers had been members of the Knights of Labor (in District Assembly 49), and as in the case of the cigar makers, this did not cause any problems for a few years. But in 1886 another brewery workers' union emerged within District Assembly 49, consisting of Anglo-Irish brewers who worked in the diminishing number of the city's ale and porter breweries. This was the one part of the brewing industry which still had a heavily Anglo-Irish work force, but as more and more consumers switched to lager beer, ale and porter breweries had tried to shore up their fortunes by adding lager beer to their product line. To do so they hired German-born brewery workers to make the new product. Such developments did nothing to bring the English-speaking ale and porter brewers and the German lager beer brewers closer: on the contrary, a keen sense of competitiveness seems to have prevailed, especially on the Anglo-Irish side.[29] The two unions showed little interest in cooperating with each other and their common membership in the Knights and the CLU could not prevent a number of conflicts about the right to organize German lager beer workers in formerly Anglo-Irish ale and porter breweries. In the competition for new members the ale and porter brewers' union had the support of the district assembly, while the German union (which left the Knights in early 1887) managed to have the ale and porter union excluded from the CLU.[30] Other organizations of brewery workers, such as those of the engineers and firemen, the beer drivers, and the maltsers split along the same lines. The gradual parting of ways had parallels in other cities, too.[31] For the National Union of Brewery Workmen the break from the Knights cost it a local source of support, but at the national level its subsequent affiliation with the American Federation of Labor in early 1887 meant that the union remained with a growing and, over time, increasingly powerful national alliance of unions. The ale and porter union remained within the Knights of Labor and its importance diminished in the following years.[32]

But in the struggle to transform their organizations into unions capable of organizing an increasingly industrialized and mixed work force, both unions were losers. As both unions strictly limited themselves to organizing within their respective ethnic groups, the atmosphere of tribal warfare surrounding the conflict would continue. The head of the ale and porter union, an Irishman named O'Donell, was called a "German Eater" by the lager beer workers; they ascribed his union's hegemonic aspirations to the hatred of Germans supposedly common among the Irish. The German brewery workers, on the other hand, made virtually no attempt to give up their monolingual and culturally limited ways and did very little to integrate themselves with the majority of workers organized in English-speaking unions in the city.

This period was also a time of unprecedented turmoil within New York labor organizations, a time that saw the gradual decline of the Knights of Labor and the ascent of the American Federation of Labor; at the same time ethnically based rivalries between conservative Anglo-Irish unions and socialist Germans were also on the increase. As it turned out, the brewery workers were caught in the middle of these conflicts. Surrounded by increasingly heterogeneous union building during the late 1880s, with newly powerful political alliances breaking down provincial loyalties, the brewery workers refused to give up their ethnic distinctiveness and retained the social marginality that went with it. The foray into labor politics in 1886–87 only heightened the sense that ethnic bonds were of primary importance in preserving labor solidarity, at least locally. Ethnicity determined the basic structure of labor organization for the brewery workers, and despite an increasing interest and involvement in the political world around them, the contours of the community of workers around the brewery and its German-American world changed little.[33]

The Cancellation of the Contract and the Great Lockout

Though the brewery workers' union seemed to have found a comfortable niche in the stormy late 1880s, their cozy arrangement with the New York brewery bosses did not last for long. If the labor force was increasingly organized and conscious of the need for united action, so were the employers, who had weathered the worst business period by 1888 and were now ready to tackle what they considered an increasingly problematic arrangement with the union. Midwestern brewery bosses grew especially impatient. After the first New York contract, brewery workers elsewhere had begun to fight for improved wages and hours. Lager beer workers had succeeded in overcoming strong resistance and winning advantageous contracts in such cities as Milwaukee and St. Louis, where relations with the Knights of Labor were good and cohesion in the German-American community (the dominant ethnic group in both cities) was very strong.[34]

The aggressive actions of local unions in gaining better conditions usually had the backing of the leaders of the national union, which stood behind them even if it was not always enthusiastic about national strikes and boycotts. A typical conflict supported by the national union (first verbally, then financially) was the strike of the Milwaukee maltsers' union (an affiliate of the National Union of Brewery Workmen) which broke out in the fall of 1887. This originally obscure struggle, designed to raise the wages of maltsers in the malthouses to the level of maltsers' wages in breweries, turned gradually from a strike of malthouse workers to a national boycott of all Milwaukee beer.[35] The boycott, which the leadership of the national union undertook hesitantly, was regarded as a declaration of war by the brewery bosses nationwide, who decided in a series of meetings in February 1888 to make New York the testing ground for a new hard-line policy against the union in the entire country.[36] In a sense this was a humiliation of the New York brewery owners, who had initiated the policy of union recognition and who had, overall, profited from it. New York's brewers' interests were not identical with those of the big shippers elsewhere, who chafed under the conditions of the union contract, but ultimately the New Yorkers, too, acceded to the USBA strategy. Despite the differences within the industry, and despite years of cooperation between owners and workers in New York, even here the brewery owners ultimately had more in common with the fellow owners in the Midwest than with their own employees.

In mid-March of 1888 the union began, as it had the year before, to put out feelers toward the employers' organization about renewing their contract. They received no answer, despite repeated inquiries. This did not trouble the union's leadership, which expected smooth sailing. The union and its members were therefore flabbergasted when, on March 27, the New York members of the United States Brewers Association published a declaration unilaterally renouncing its partnership with the union.[37] "Because of a total lack of cooperation brewery owners in all larger cities of the United States have had to bow under pressure from despotic union rule. . . . We brewery owners of the country have therefore decided to end this imbalance and to return to independent control and leadership of our businesses." The declaration affirmed the workers' right to organize but denied unions the right to negotiate contracts with members of the USBA. The manifesto stated bluntly that "after the expiration of the contract now existing, no new agreements between the brewery proprietors and the brewery workmen shall be entered into."[38]

The cancellation of the partnership with the union came as a complete surprise for the local and the national union. For many days after the publication of the manifesto, the officials of Local 1 could not quite believe that the New York brewery bosses had abandoned their former partners. They told their fellow workers to "wait patiently" and tried to start negotiations with individual breweries about a new contract. This tactic had limited success. Four smaller breweries in the New York area renewed the contract.[39] Elsewhere the union encountered stonewalling tactics from all brewers. In their desperation the leaders of Local 1 called on the New York State Board of Mediation and Arbitration to help them. But before that organization could convene, the Central Labor Unions of New York, Brooklyn, and Newark turned to more aggressive tactics and declared a boycott (starting April 13) against all beer made by members of the United States Brewers Association.[40] The brewery bosses seem to have been waiting for such an action, for they promptly declared that "if the boycott was not lifted from a certain date, they would reorganize their workers." Since the CLU bodies showed no signs of dropping the boycott, the employers carried out their threat and locked out their workers on April 16 in fourteen breweries in greater New York. Brewery workers willing to sign a no-union pledge were accepted for reemployment a day later. But the majority struck with the union and remained on the street, locked out, as they saw it; striking, from the employers' standpoint.[41]

The following weeks would quickly show how well prepared the brewery bosses were for a prolonged conflict and how little the union was ready for such a struggle. As the workers soon found out, large quantities of beer had been brewed and delivered to customers in the weeks before the lockout. To maintain at least a minimum of running operations most breweries also began to employ unskilled workers in larger numbers than ever before—"Slovaks and Italian riff raff" was how the *Brauer Zeitung* perceived them.[42] Increasing mechanization made it possible for new unskilled immigrants to replace skilled workers in many breweries, a development the union contract had only temporarily delayed. To fill positions still requiring skilled labor, employers could recruit recent immigrant brewers who had been unable to find work because of the closed membership policy of Local 1. The new recruits were attracted by the high (union) wages which the employers continued to pay for the time being.[43] Skilled technical maintenance workers in the breweries (engineers, machinists, and firemen) were more difficult to replace, and employers adopted a more flexible stand toward this group, allowing them to remain members of the union if they were willing to come back to work. Since relatively few were unionized as part of the national union, and even those who were had yet to develop strong loyalties to the organization, they remained on their jobs. The brewmasters also stayed in the breweries, although the foremen were locked out together with their workers.[44]

But the union was confronted with a more deep-seated problem in maintaining a united front against the employers. After three years of amicable relations and a cooperative contract, the workers' (and the union's) sense of community was still fundamentally shaped by the commonalities of all brewers, workers *and* employers. The brewery workers' attempts to strengthen their ties to the organized labor movement in New York had not been overwhelmingly successful, and had not been enough to replace the bonds of trade and craft solidarity that still bound many journeymen to their place of employment. Seen another way, the identity of the brewery workers was also still shaped by their high degree of identification with the product they made as brewers. Their skill and knowledge in this regard, however, was becoming increasingly obsolete by the late 1880s and other skilled workers, from machinists to firemen, were becoming at least as important in the industrialized trade.[45] But even though the national union and the leaders of the local were promoters of an industrial model of organizing, the shop-floor solidarity with those workers who were not journeymen brewers (and who were more likely to be non-Germans as well) was not very strong. A union which in reality (if not in principle) still depended on the common historical and cultural bonds of its workers to the extent that the New York brewery workers did was not ready for organizing a diverse work force in a large-scale industrial conflict. And, most important, it was not prepared to confront their employers as adversarial capitalists.

The union was also unprepared in some practical matters for an extended conflict with employers. The brewery workers' union, unlike so many other craft unions, still had made no provisions for financial support of its members in cases of strike, unemployment, illness, or death. It had depended on the employers' sickness funds and individual bosses' compensation for death or disability on the job and was in no position to raise the funds needed to support the locked-out brewers. For financial support the brewers could only turn to brewery workers in other cities and the rest of the New York labor movement. But unlike the cigar makers in their 1877 strike, the brewery workers were unable to win enough community aid. Although a number of New York unions gave money and the Arbeiter Liedertafel (workers' singing society) offered benefit performances for the locked-out workers, the results were disappointing: only about $1,000 was donated during the first month of the lockout, and donations did not pick up much afterwards. The sources for financial aid for the workers were simply too shallow: although the New York brewing industry was of national importance, support for the workers was almost entirely limited to German-American labor organizations in New York City. Most of the money for support of the workers, $40,000 in all, had to be paid out of the reserves of the brewery workers' union itself.[46]

While the union was not able to turn community backing into financial largesse, its main efforts centered not on financial but on political support of the workers. The leaders of Local 1 considered the organization of an effective beer boycott their greatest priority. For them a consumers' boycott calling on the neighborhood and ethnic community was the cornerstone of a strategy of popular support for the workers' cause. Many unions and Vereine within the German-American community were familiar with boycotts, although a beer boycott in the balmy spring and summer season posed a difficult challenge to their cohesion and organizational resources. Since the union was locked out of virtually all lager beer breweries in New York, very little union beer was available to city drinkers (ale and porter breweries were included in the lockout). Thus the beer boycott amounted to something close to a call for total abstinence—a most difficult action to enforce. At least verbally the other unions and Vereine were quite energetic in their pursuit of the boycott. Some unions threatened a $10.00 fine for members caught drinking nonunion beer. Many unions and Vereine moved their meetings to locations with union beer.[47] On a larger level, District Assembly 49 of the Knights of Labor passed a resolution of solidarity with the brewery workers, endorsing the boycott, but the Knights showed no interest in the matter after that. Nor did the Anglo-Irish ale and porter union do anything to promote the boycott. The beer boycott turned out to be an affair of the German-American community.

Saloonkeepers became crucial allies in this difficult situation. Traditionally the saloonkeepers were closely connected to the brewery workers' community. Some of them were former brewery workers themselves, while others ran boardinghouses for journeymen brewers on the side. On the other hand, saloonkeepers were also particularly dependent on brewery owners, who not only supplied them with beer but also helped them with credits and supplied free fixtures. It was therefore almost impossible for saloonkeepers to boycott their suppliers who could (and did) remove all the bar fixtures and recall their debt overnight if they found one of their customers supported the boycott. Only saloonkeepers without debt could try to switch to the few union brewers and thus avoid the potentially disastrous consequences of a boycott by their working-class customers.[48] Caught between the two sides, saloonkeepers asked the union for help in organizing the delivery of union beer, but with limited success. Brewers from outside the city would not move in and risk the wrath of New York's brewery bosses. For the majority of saloonkeepers in New York, the boycott created an insoluble dilemma.[49]

By early May it was clear that the boycott was failing to have the desired effect. Unions and other working-class organizations just stopped taking it seriously, and compliance began to level off. After a few weeks, it was obvious that a consumers' boycott of beer was simply unenforceable in such a large, diverse, working-class metropolis as New York City, whose population had virtually no access to alternative sources of beer. A beer boycott was not comparable to a boycott of one or two retailers or workshops such as a bakery. The structure of the industry, its retailing practices, and its dominance of the local market made the brewery princes largely immune to consumer boycotts by the late 1880s. But the limited appeal of the union's cause was also rooted in the union's isolation from the New York labor movement during the previous years. As a belated entry into the world of organized labor and a consistent ally of the German-American socialist unions, the brewery workers' organization could not gain the wider support which might have existed for other unions.[50]

Solidarity was not only weak among other groups of organized labor; it was also a problem for members of the union itself. Employer pressure soon proved to be too much for the journeymen, and hundreds of brewery workers renounced their membership in the union and decided to return to work after the first few weeks of the lockout. After five weeks of struggle, the number of unionists shrank to about five hundred. This inner collapse made the brewery workers' campaign a lost cause by early summer.[51] Although the position of the brewery bosses was a powerful one not just locally but nationwide, and may not have been overcome in 1888 at any rate, the union's flaws—its lack of financial resources and its isolation—went back to its beginnings as an employer-sponsored organization. In the end, it proved unable to overcome its past and stand on its own as an independent labor representative. Its contractually enforced close cooperation with the bosses diluted the members' militance despite the leaders' aggressive rhetoric. Workers whose primary self-image was that of craftsmen who wanted to restore the cooperative world of an imagined past were too weak to contend with employers united against them.

The National Defeat of the Union and Its Aftermath

New York was not the only city in which brewery workers came under assault in the summer of 1888. Elsewhere, too, contracts gave way to conflict. The struggle took a different overtone in communities in which the union had been more militant and confrontational from the beginning and in which organized labor was more united in its support of the journeymen brewers. But almost nowhere could the union hold out against united brewery bosses. Immediately after the beginning of the New York conflict, the Chicago members of the United States Brewers Association forced their employees to sign a no-union pledge. Workers who refused to do so were dismissed. Employers took similar actions against the union in Buffalo, Cincinnati, and Milwaukee.[52] In July 1888, after the defeat of the union in many cities, the union leaders met at a special conference in Chicago to assess the situation. The national union turned out to be in a rather sorry position. Only twenty-six locals out of thirty-five had survived the struggle of the past months; membership had dropped from 5,000 to 1,800. The national treasury was empty and many unionists refused to pay their dues. In the hope of improving organizational cohesion and creating a less isolated leadership, the convention unseated president Herbrandt (who had suddenly left for Europe during the New York lockout) and revamped the leadership structure.[53] Despite the reorganization, union membership continued to drop, reaching a low of 1,300 in early 1890. Afterwards, the brewery workers' union had to start almost from scratch to rebuild its organization.[54]

It took the involvement of the growing American Federation of Labor to revive the almost defunct organization. Slowly the AFL and its affiliates, together with the brewery workers' union, began to rebuild the brewery workers' movement, choosing the large shippers—Anhaeuser Busch and Pabst—as their first targets in the 1890s. A nationwide boycott against these two firms took three years, but the outcome was a new contract between them and the brewery workers' union. Gradually the union won victories in other midwestern locations; by the end of the nineteenth century membership in the National Union of Brewery Workmen was once again on the rise.[55]

While the brewery workers nationally began to rebuild their organization in the 1890s, the New York workers remained out in the cold for over a decade. In late 1888 the union had a contract with only four breweries in the New York area and the formerly mighty Local 1 had shrunk to only about 125 members (from its former high of 1,800).[56]

At the same time the disintegration and severe internal discord in the New York labor movement further weakened local support for the union in the city. As the brewery workers' union became a pawn in the struggle between the American Federation of Labor and the Socialist Labor party (which was allied with radical members of the Knights of Labor), the union had no hope of mounting a serious effort against the power of the "pool brewers."[57] It was not until the mid-1890s, when the depression as well as the rise of the prohibition movement and the concurrent rise in the taxation of beer threatened the profits of the brewing industry, that the New York brewery workers found themselves in a better position. A more conciliatory line toward the union seemed again a promising course for the brewery owners by the end of the century. The union had to wait until 1902, however, to achieve a contract covering all lager beer breweries in New York City. Wages and working hours in it were comparable to the terms of the contract of 1887–88. Many other brewery workers' unions in the country had by then achieved much more advantageous arrangements with their employers. Never again would New York's brewery workers regain their dominant status within the union.[58]

The change of focus in the struggle of the brewery workers away from New York City to the national level was, of course, a fitting response to the nationalization of the industry in general. Since the days of the railroad strikes in the 1870s, the limited effectiveness of local labor activism had been evident especially in the more capital intensive and technologically advanced mass production industries. The formation of national labor organizations was in part a response to these developments. But by the mid-1890s the efficacy with which labor could respond to the national pressures from employers had increased vastly because more centralized and bureaucratized models of union organization had grown around the unions of the American Federation of Labor. Whereas a spontaneous outburst of local solidarity from the community had been sufficient to win in earlier years (such as in the brewery workers' strike of 1881), by the late 1880s similar conflicts could no longer be won on a local level, nor could these struggles be waged on anything but a highly coordinated basis on many levels at once.[59] The National Union of Brewery Workmen in close cooperation with the American Federation of Labor and its affiliates was able to wage such a struggle, targeting a few employers at a time, linking their struggle with a political effort to bring the shippers to the bargaining table and marshaling the solidarity of their affiliates nationwide in support of a national selective beer boycott. The removal of the center of union activism from the local community—especially in New York—was thus an adequate and largely successful effort to cope with the reorganization of the trade nationwide. Very gradually the National Union of Brewery Workmen grew into a centralized, industrial, and bureaucratic union which did not need to rely on local community activism to make headway on a national level. A standard workday of ten hours was adopted for all locals to follow in 1892 and a national policy of organizing allied trades such as machinists, firemen, and coopers was pursued vigorously, against the resistance of the AFL and its craft union affiliates. Other centrally mandated policies, such as a general retreat from the Knights of Labor or the recommendation to vote for the Socialist party, were not universally followed. But despite remaining differences between the locals, the brewery workers' union became more and more of a homogeneous national body by the turn of the century, and an effective ally of the American Federation of Labor before World War I.[60]

From Ethnic Craft to Industrial Union: The Brewery Workers in Comparative Perspective

The development of New York's brewery workers' union presents a remarkable contrast to that of the cigar makers and other German-American labor organizations, such as the furniture makers. The brewers' and the cigar makers' unions, while both originating in industries dominated by German immigrants and closely tied to their ethnic communities from the outset, illustrate different, often opposite, approaches to the meaning and use of ethnic ties in building the union, the organizational response to change in the industry, and the political role of the union within the American labor movement at large.

The differences between the cigar makers and the brewery workers were most evident in the almost opposite roles ethnicity and community played for workers and their unions in both industries. Compared to the relatively diverse cigar makers, the brewery workers, especially in New York, presented an extreme case of segregation by ethnicity. With over 70 percent of all New York lager beer brewers of German birth in the 1870s and 1880s, brewing was probably the most German of all occupations. Moreover, workers faced a group of employers who also were almost exclusively of German background and thus formed a community without parallel in any other industry in the city. As we have seen in previous parts of this study, being of German origin did not necessarily provide a close tie—although the southern German origin of many workers and employers probably cemented common cultural bonds to an unusual degree. But the combination of ethnic homogeneity and the way in which the brewing trade was organized—the long hours, the boardinghouse system, and a generally paternalistic system of labor relations—bound the brewery workers together while isolating them from other parts of German-American New York as well. Such a tight organization of the trade was absent among the cigar makers and other sweatshop trades in which Germans were numerous. The fluid structure of the sweatshop trades characterized by the dispersal of small shops throughout the community made contacts between workers and the rest of the New York working class inevitable. For brewery workers, casual day-to-day interaction with the outside world was difficult, however.

The organizing advantages for brewery workers, on the other hand, lay in their common traditions as craftsmen and immigrants. But it was not easy to translate this common past into a meaningful form of labor organization. In contrast to the cigar makers, garment makers, or furniture workers, the political heritage of most German-American brewery workers was not an emancipatory one. German brewery workers, especially those from the south, had been spectators in the labor movement in their home country until the mid-1890s. With a majority of German-American brewery workers inexperienced in labor politics, even the socialist leaders of the union had a difficult time in defining a clear political identity for the organization during the late 1880s and 1890s. This task was not made easier by the fact that after 1886 the German socialists and the Knights of Labor, with whom the brewery workers' union aligned itself in various ways, entered a period of unprecedented internal strife. Even for a union with a relatively firm political identity (such as the cigar makers) such infighting would pose problems, but for less politically seasoned organizations, such as the brewery workers (and the bakers), this could threaten the very survival of the organization.

The brewery workers' search for a political identity was made particularly difficult by the vast industrial changes in the trade in late nineteenth century on the one hand and the fractured political landscape of the labor movement on the other. Mechanization and the increasing specialization of labor diminished the role of craftsmen in an industry in which craft identity and craft pride continued to play an important role, as we have seen. The close cooperation with employers which the union chose as a way to organize (while maintaining the semblance of a craft status) could only be a temporary measure. When the employers unilaterally renounced this tactic, the union was rudderless.

What did, in the end, save the union was its firm stand as an industrial organization, its increasingly centralized structure, and its pragmatic alliance with the American Federation of Labor. In many ways a centralized and bureaucratized union structure spelled retreat from the local community of workers—just as it had for the cigar makers. But while for the CMIU a retreat from local communities meant a retreat from an important part of the industry (which remained local in character), for the brewery workers this was a forward-looking response to the changing circumstances of their trade. As the cigar makers' union thus became more and more a preserve of craft workers, the brewery workers' union was one of the more integrated industrialized craft unions within the American Federation of Labor in the Progressive Era.[61]

By the time of World War I, the brewery workers had found their niche within the structure of the American Federation of Labor. It had been a slow rapprochement, but by the second decade of the twentieth century, the brewery workers had been integrated into the mainstream of the North American labor movement. The remaining differences between the brewery workers and other labor organizations—a still audible socialist critique of the political accommodationism of the AFL and the industrial union structure—were integrated into the federation, which saw the power of its own craft unions diminish and the need for more industrial forms of organization and for more outspoken political resistance as well. That the AFL integrated such different approaches successfully is a testimony to the diversity and heterogeneity of the umbrella group.

9

The German Bakers of New York City: Ethnic Particularism in the Sweated Trades

The written history of organized labor is dominated by tales of struggles won under difficult circumstances. So far this study is no exception. In the organization of skilled workers the cigar makers were pioneers during the second half of the nineteenth century. For the brewery workers the road to effective union organization was much more difficult, but their success was obvious too by the early twentieth century. For the bakers, on the other hand, the road to unionization was thornier. Of the German-American trades discussed in this book, the bakers exemplify the failure to organize cohesively in the nineteenth-century city.[1] In this study, common themes of ethnic traditions and industrial change link different workers' communities. Ethnicity and changes in the workplace, we have argued, defined labor organizations in all trades under discussion here. But if the result was progress for the cigar makers and the brewers, the example of the bakers demonstrates that sometimes the circumstances of work and tradition were so adverse that they were almost impossible to overcome.

An important subtext of the discussion in the following chapter is that the period covered stretches from the early 1880s until the early twentieth century. For the bakers, the decisive attempts to form a lasting union did not start until the late 1880s and stretched well into the twentieth century. During this time, the New York labor movement was vastly different from, say, the 1870s and early 1880s, when the cigar makers experienced an important phase in their organization. The bakers' immature union was thrust into the midst of a fractious time with relatively well-defined adversarial parties.[2] By the 1890s, the bakers' cause was also taken up by progressive reformers from outside the union movement, making the bakers the only group under discussion here whose lot was influenced in important ways by reformers from the middle class. Only if we keep these additional considerations in mind can we make sense of the history of the bakers in New York City in the context of a growing and strong labor movement in New York City and the nation.

Next to the brewers—traditionalists in a changing trade—and the cigar makers—new workers in a new craft—the bakers represented traditional workers in a trade which was relatively little affected by technology during the period under discussion. Much of baking was still taking place in craft shops in late-nineteenth-century New York and the bakers were almost always skilled craft workers with years of European training. But the circumstances of work and life for the bakers were more closely related to the sweated trades so numerous in the metropolis than to those of traditional craftsmen.[3] Like workers in sweatshop trades, bakers worked in cellars under often abominable conditions, and for longer hours than even the brewers. Unlike garment makers and shoe workers, bakers suffered relatively little from seasonal irregularities, and they benefited from a steadily growing base of consumers for their highly perishable goods as the city's population grew. But with thousands of new bakers arriving every year, the trade remained impoverished. Like cigar making and garment making, baking was unregulated and spread out into numerous small workshops which fiercely competed against each other with low labor and capital investment costs.[4]

German bakers located their cellar bakeries almost everywhere in the city and were therefore often not part of a German neighborhood at all. Even though baking took place in neighborhoods, the cultural and social ties of the neighborhood did not necessarily include the German baker, who might toil in relative anonymity in heavily Irish or "American" surroundings during long nights in his cellar.[5] While baking was closely tied economically to the neighborhood where the bread was sold, the bakers themselves were not necessarily part of its social fabric, a fact that would limit the ability of the bakery workers to organize themselves on a local basis.

The majority of New York City's bakers in 1880 were German-born. Their sheer numbers made German bakers ubiquitous. In 1880 over 1,200 of them were living in Manhattan. The city's German bakers gave the entire trade their ethnic imprint, but they also formed a subgroup within the German community which occupied a central place in the daily life and neighborhoods of German New York. The address books of the 1880s list 150 bakeries on the German Lower East Side alone in 1880, the highest density of bakeshops in the city.[6]

Other German trades (especially food businesses) had the dual function of supplying their fellow German-Americans with familiar wares while also selling to the diverse population of many New York neighborhoods. Lager beer saloons, butchers, wine merchants, and confectioners offered things German to anyone seeking a taste of the Old World. But the bakers and confectioners from German-speaking Europe not only supplied much of the daily bread for the city's inhabitants but also were known for regional specialties. The German Swiss were renowned confectioners, as were the Alsatians, while Austrians made so-called Vienna bread. Alongside the central Europeans toiled their neighbors the Bohemians and the Jewish bakers, both known for rye bread, and the English pie makers. This sort of product specialization divided the labor market in the city's bakeries into more ethnic subgroups than in most other trades. Such specialization and subdivision persisted to a remarkable extent throughout the nineteenth century and would have profound consequences for the bakers' ability to organize themselves into unions.

The social and economic fragmentation of the bakers alone created very different circumstances for organizing than those for German-Americans in the breweries or the cigar shops. The difficulties of organizing bakers stand out even more sharply if we turn to traditions of the German bakers who arrived in late-nineteenth-century New York City to practice their trade.

European Traditions

Bread baking was the oldest of the three trades discussed in this book. Unlike brewing it was a truly guild-dominated craft in medieval times. Guilds cooperated with municipal authorities to enforce strict rules governing the training and licensing of bakers and the selling of bread. Prices and quality for bread and other bakery products were closely monitored as was the number of bakers allowed in each community. The bakers in many towns were counted among the wealthiest citizens.[7]

But the wealth of the craft did not survive the deterioration of the German economy in the late Middle Ages and went into a long decline amid the European wars of the sixteenth and seventeenth centuries. By the nineteenth century, Europe was flooded with mobile young men, especially Germans, desperate to eke out a living as journeymen bakers. As prices fell under the competitive pressure of too many small shops, German bakers became one of the most degraded groups of skilled workers in Europe in the mid- and late nineteenth century.[8] Karl Marx took the German bakers of London as an example of the inevitable degradation of workers under capitalism—even in trades where handwork still predominated. In a lengthy passage in *Capital* describing their starvation wages and working conditions Marx concluded that "no other trade preserved up to the present day a method so archaic, so . . . pre-christian as baking."[9]

The actual work process in most European bakeries during the late nineteenth century had changed little from earlier centuries. Few machines could be found in most bakeries. Ingredients were mixed in by hand; the kneading was also still a physically arduous task. Firewood had to be chopped to heat the oven and supplies had to be moved to and from storage rooms; the dough had to be rested and put in the oven; the baked bread had to be laid on racks for cooling and put into bread bins; the journeymen were also expected to deliver the bread to wholesale customers after their work in the bakeshop had ended. Cleaning up was also part of their job.[10] It was a trade with very long hours; competitive pressure in the nineteenth century lengthened the workday of German bakers to at least fourteen hours a day, seven days a week. The German socialist politician August Bebel found in his 1889 study *On the Situation of the Bakery Workers* (*Zur Lage der Arbeiter in den Bäckereien*) that bakers had the longest workday of any of the trades he studied in central Europe. Bebel also found that as a consequence of these inordinately long hours, most journeymen either lived directly with their employers (sleeping in a bed shared with another worker, or just on a flour sack in the bakery) or in a bakers' hostel kept by the *Innung* (a guildlike organization of the bakery masters). Masters supplied grossly inadequate meals that consisted mainly of bread and watery soups. Wages were meager: most journeymen made no more than about $2.00 a week plus room and board, while apprentices labored for less than 25 cents a week.[11]

Despite low wages and miserable working conditions the trade attracted plenty of apprentices during the nineteenth century. Laborers and small farmers were eager to have their sons learn a trade that required no apprenticeship fees. Since it paid a small stipend plus room and board, it seemed to promise a better life for their children than the alternative of day labor and agricultural jobs. In addition, apprentice bakers did not face the prolonged unemployment experienced by unskilled workers in industrializing Germany. During slack times journeymen could stay in the bakers' hostel on credit (which had to be paid back after work was found again through the *Innung* employment service). At the same time, the trade was known for the high mobility of its workers. Journeymen bakers traveled widely all over Europe in search of work and just to see something of the world. Some crossed Europe on foot, while others ventured farther, working on ships to see other continents. Like cigar makers in the New World, bakers in the Old World were known as travelers.[12] Unlike cigar makers and other skilled tradesmen who could choose to settle down in their work, however, few bakers stayed in the trade to middle age. The median age for Bavarian bakers in 1882 was only twenty-four years. Few bakers wanted to or could withstand the harsh living or working conditions they found everywhere in the trade. Moreover it was nearly impossible to support a family on a journeyman's wages; most journeymen bakers (and almost all the bakers in Bebel's study) were bachelors.[13]

It would have been difficult to organize any trade as impoverished as the bakers, with its mobile labor force and dispersal of the journeymen in countless small shops; the survival into the late nineteenth century of its traditional craft structure made any independent organization of journeymen especially cumbersome. Even though the medieval guilds had long since lost their power in Europe, the trade was not formally opened to all practitioners until the mid-nineteenth century in many German states. Only in 1869 did the trades law (*Gewerbeordnung*) of the North German Federation lift the last restrictions on crafts and ostensibly submit them completely to free market pressures. But even then, the old organization of bakery masters remained in place on a voluntary basis in most localities. While not sanctioned by the state, these so-called *Innungen* retained control over the workers in bakeries in many places. They maintained hostels for journeymen and an employment service as well. A certain uniformity of apprenticeship rules also survived because of the *Innungen*. These successors to the guilds held on to their power tenaciously, making the complete liberalization of trades little more than a fiction. Beginning in 1881, a succession of laws formally sanctioned the role of the *Innungen* in regulating apprenticeships and determining the qualifications of journeymen and masters.[14]

As the power of the *Innungen* never entirely ceased in most parts of Germany, and actually increased during the last decades of the nineteenth century, the German labor movement had to struggle to organize the journeymen bakers on an industrial basis. The socialist labor movement in Germany made several attempts to organize the bakery workers, but only began to make headway during the mid-1880s. Unionization remained difficult until bread factories became more widespread in the early twentieth century. Even so, the Dach-

verband deutscher Bäckergehülfen und verwandter Berufe (Organization of German Bakery Workers and Related Trades) only had about
660 members as late as 1895. The *Verband* members were almost entirely limited to bread factories and large bakeries; the thousands of
journeymen laboring in the small bakeries of Germany were too dependent on the *Innungen* and too closely supervised by their employers to be able to organize on a tradewide basis.[15]

Pressure for reform came less from the workers themselves than
from middle-class social reformers and legislators (some of them socialists) cooperating with the state to improve the conditions of the
bakers' trade. Such activism for protective legislation on behalf of the
working class was part of a movement for social reform in many industrializing nations, but in contrast to similar initiatives in the United
States, the German movement was to a certain extent preempted by
government action. Intent on forestalling the spread of socialism, Bismarck encouraged the passage of protective and workers' compensation legislation as early as the 1880s. Bismarck's successors imple-
mented a government decree in 1896 limiting the hours of work and
improving sanitary conditions in Germany's bakeshops. The law prohibited work before four A.M. and most Sunday work, and introduced
the thirteen-hour workday.[16] These measures only modestly improved
the wages and living conditions of most bakers. Their effect on the
self-organization of workers, however, became clear very soon: bakers participated very little in the German trade union movement, and
in few localities did the bakery workers' union achieve recognition
as a bargaining agent for the workers. On the contrary, reform legislation helped dissuade workers from organizing against the state and
the existing order in the baking trade.[17]

In many ways the situation of German bakers during the second
half of the nineteenth century was worse than that of the brewers
or cigar makers. Bakers were poorer and less secure in their work
than brewers. Few of them had the means or money to open their
own shop or move into high-end work, as cigar makers could. Nor
did circumstances favor the type of organization which was part of
the heritage of the cigar makers and many other German trades.
Bakers were less than marginal in the labor movement during the
late nineteenth century. Their tradition of organizing, as far as it
existed at all, was tied to the guilds; it emphasized dependencies
on employers and subservience to political authorities. Neither in
the Old World nor in the New did their way of life hold out much
promise of self-emancipation.

The Baking Trades in New York City

Bakers and the products of their trade were ubiquitous in nine-teenth-century Manhattan. While the baking trade could not match the breweries in architectural splendor or the garment industry in economic importance, few trades expressed the multiplicity of immi-grant traditions in Manhattan as well as the bakers. By the late nine-teenth century there was hardly a block in New York without a bak-ery, and the most densely settled neighborhoods had a cellar bakery every few houses. In 1855 there was one baker per 169 inhabitants.[18]

Immigrants ran the overwhelming majority of bakeries through-out the second half of the nineteenth century with Germans the dom-inant group.[19] The very high density of bakeshops and the takeover of the trade by immigrants in the second half of the nineteenth cen-tury contributed to the decline in economic status for the bakers in New York. Until the early nineteenth century the New York baking trade had been moderately prosperous. Limited immigration and municipal regulation of bread prices sheltered it from too much com-petition. But by the 1820s these barriers were crumbling. The regula-tion of bread prices ceased in 1825, and growing immigration of im-poverished journeymen bakers from central Europe soon lowered the economic status of the city's bakers even further, so that by the mid-nineteenth century many resembled their wretched colleagues in the Old World.[20] Especially in the city's working-class wards (where there was about one bakery for every twenty-five houses) bakeries were most often housed in cellars, with no separate retail store. Few bak-ery owners could afford the rent for a first-story shop or store. Cellar bakeries consisted of one room, usually eight feet high or less, with a dirt floor. The room could only be reached from the street by a steep staircase. Windows (usually just chutes) were about one foot above street level. Most of the one-room shops had no special place for the coal-fired oven, nor did they have running water. Often sewage pipes for the entire tenement ran through the same cellar space. Coal and other fuels were stored next to the bread; street dirt and vermin were unavoidable.[21] It was obvious to anybody who had seen New York's cellar bakeries that hygienic conditions in these workshops were ter-rible. Even the bakers themselves considered the New York baking trade "the dirtiest of trades, dirtier than in any other part of the world."[22]

The division of labor and hierarchies of the Old World persisted, with some modifications, in most New York bakeries. The journey-

Table 2. Bakers in New York and Brooklyn, 1870–1900.

	Manhattan			Brooklyn		
	Bakers	German (%)	Bakeries	Bakers	German (%)	Bakeries
1870	3,855	55.0	802	1,213	54.3	
1880	5,013	54.2	1,108	2,018	49.7	
1890	5,778	59.6	1,174	3,172	60.0	730
1900	12,060	—	1,281	4,083	—	735

Source: *Ninth, Tenth, Eleventh,* and *Twelfth Census of the United States, Census of Population; Wilson's Business Directory for New York City,* 1870–1900; *Lain and Healy's Brooklyn Directory,* 1890, 1900.

men, called "first," "second," and "third" hands respectively, worked under the supervision of the "bakery boss." Apprentices were rare.[23] Preparations began in the late afternoon. As in Europe most of the work took place at night and lasted until the early morning hours. When the baking was done, journeymen had to deliver bread to neighborhood grocery stores. Until the 1880s fifteen to sixteen hours were a regular night's work; from Friday to Saturday bakers worked up to twenty-three hours, while five to six hours were the rule from Saturday night to Sunday. Holidays did not exist. Continuing one of the worst old-world traditions, most bakers worked at least one hundred hours a week.[24]

In their net wages, German-American bakers were among the lowest-paid skilled workers in the city. According to a statistical report by the New York bakery workers' union, journeymen bakers earned an average of $8.20 a week in 1881. That is, most bakers were laboring for eight to ten cents an hour. Workers in large bakeries and foremen received $12 to $14.[25] Because unemployment was rare, bakers' yearly wages were higher than in some other trades, but higher earnings were offset by the exhausting nature of the work, which permitted few men to spend more than two decades in the trade without ruining their health. Most bakers (at least those who had not made the transition to operating their own small business) dropped out of the industry by the time they reached early middle age. The bakery workers' union found in 1881 that bakers were on the average twen-

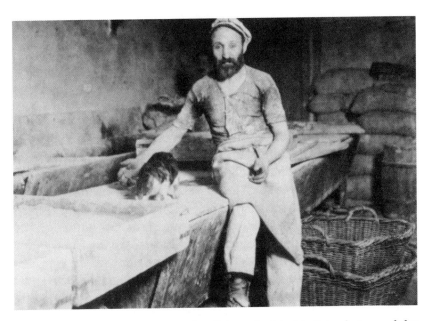

A baker in a cellar bakery, 1910. Conditions depicted in this photograph by Lewis Hine were similar to those under which bakers labored in the 1880s and 1890s.

ty-eight or twenty-nine years old and had about ten years' experience in the trade.[26] Bakers had notoriously bad health. A physical examination of nine hundred bakers in 1909 showed that 57 percent had serious diseases (mainly respiratory ills, stomach problems, and skin ailments). To judge from the patent medicines and doctors' services widely advertised in the trade press, frequent diseases of bakers also included rheumatism, venereal diseases, and alcoholism. Chronic overwork and the special stress of night work probably contributed to the high suicide rate among German bakers.[27]

As in Europe the working hours and the small scale of most bakery businesses meant that bakers had to live at or very near their workshop. Bakery owners usually lived in the tenement in which the workshop was located, although the poorest of them camped out in the bakery itself. Journeymen and other helpers either slept in the cellar (on flour sacks or in the dough vat) or boarded with their employer in his apartment.[28] A sizable minority of young bakery workers lived in bakers' boardinghouses, especially if they worked in larger establishments. The boardinghouses for the journeymen bakers differed from the brewers' boardinghouses in that they were usually not affiliated with one employer exclusively, but run by self-appointed entrepreneurs—some of them bakers, others saloonkeepers. Acting as a contractor, the boardinghouse keeper often ran an informal employment service for his clients too and provided credit for temporarily unemployed bakers. As useful as this system was for the new immigrant who needed help in orienting himself and finding work, it was also open to abuse. In a system that duplicated features of European *Innungen*, boardinghouse keepers had exclusive contracts with some employers, and workers would be required to make use of the boardinghouse keeper's services if they wanted to have access to credit in times of unemployment. The system of bakers' lodging and recruitment resembled the arrangement that brewery workers encountered in which the "free" market system of the New World permitted the most oppressive features of the old corporate order to survive.[29]

The social consequences of these miserable living and working conditions for the journeymen bakers were severe. As in Germany, low wages and long hours condemned most to bachelorhood and life as a boarder. Weekly earnings of $8.20 did not feed even a small family in New York City during the 1880s, and only 36 percent of the journeymen bakers counted by the union in 1881 had families.[30] The fact that journeymen bakers were not only poor but too poor to marry was not lost on these immigrants. It was considered one of the greatest indignities they had to suffer, something that reminded them of the poverty they had hoped to leave behind. The hope of earning a family wage loomed large behind the efforts of the journeymen bakers' union during the last decades of the nineteenth century.

For many immigrant bakers the only hope for an improved standard of living was to set up one's own shop. The freewheeling capitalism of North American cities treated all small entrepreneurs alike in this respect. The contrast to Germany was striking: the trade was open to anyone with the money and energy to set up shop for himself. In contrast to Germany, no system of *Innungen* discriminated against journeymen without a "master's" qualifications. Rents and overhead costs for cellar bakeries were low, and there was little money needed for capital investment. But since the status of the independent bakers was unprotected, the competition among them, especially in Manhattan's low-rent district, was fierce. Hours were no shorter for the "boss baker" than for his employees. The work was just as demanding. Like other sweatshop operators, the owners of small bakeries led a precarious existence, always in danger of slipping back into the ranks of the employed journeymen and in many ways no different from their employees at all.[31] Some things set them apart, of course. For one thing, independent bakers were more often able to have families, not so much because they earned more but because they could organize their shop to stretch their income. Their older children could be "apprentices"; "boss" bakers' families usually rented an apartment in the tenement above the bakery where they took their employees in as boarders. This was one of the few ways the baker's wife could earn income; most had small children (a census sample of 118 German-American bakers and confectioners from the 1880 census showed 3.6 children living with each family on the average) and housekeeping was even more demanding in tenements in which husbands slept during the day after a lengthy night shift.[32]

The bakers (like most other working people in the city) are anonymous in the available historical sources, but reconstruction of households from census records permits a glimpse into the family economy of sample bakeshops. Two families living on the same block of the Lower East Side illustrate the rather narrow options most independent bakers faced when they tried to set up shop on their own. The Guenzer family on Orchard Street was a typical case of a small independent baker trying to get by on the Lower East Side. The six-member family lived in what must have been a small tenement apartment on Orchard Street, in the middle of a largely German area. They shared the house with fourteen other families, and their bakery was probably located in the cellar of the tenement. Joseph Guenzer came from Württemberg and his wife was Austrian-born. Both were thirty-nine years old, and the oldest of their four children was nine-year-old Fanny (her age indicates that they had married quite late, as was typical for journeymen bakers). Annie, the youngest, was only two, giving the mother plenty of work in the crowded home. A boarder, Charles Schäfer, an immigrant from Bavaria, also worked in the trade, perhaps with Guenzer. Schäfer was unmarried at age twenty-seven. The Guenzers' home life must have been very crowded, with father and boarder sleeping during the day, the rest of the family at night.[33]

If a family had slightly older children or other family members working with them, their economic situation was somewhat better. The Schmidt family a few houses down from the Guenzers at 105 Orchard Street was a good example of this. The Schmidts shared their house with only one other family. Florian Schmidt, the forty-four-year-old head of the household, worked together with his fifty-eight-year-old brother Anton and a thirty-year-old baker who boarded with them. Florian's wife, Anna, had a large household to care for: in addition to the two boarders she had five children between five months and fifteen years old. But at least the oldest son was still able to go to school at age fifteen (or so the census taker was told), a sign that the family was, if not prosperous, at least economically secure. Other bakers' children were drafted to work as "apprentices" in their fathers' shops at age fourteen. In fact, almost no young Germans who lived with their families worked as bakers unless their fathers were also bakers, suggesting that (as in the case of the cigar makers) only those who had no choice entered their fathers' craft.[34]

The New York baking trade was not unique in many of the conditions it presented to the late-nineteenth-century observer. But the combination of factors that characterized it were extreme. Like other sweated trades in the metropolis, baking retained many elements of craft work and involved only a minimum of mechanization. Nevertheless the status of bakers, like that of the tailors and shoemakers, had badly deteriorated since the early nineteenth century. The physical and mental degradation that went along with the long hours and the arduous work resembled that of many other industrializing trades. What made it harder to remedy, however, was that the bakers' exploitation and degradation was firmly entrenched in premodern European social and economic patterns. As a result of the continuing poverty of the trade, conditions differed little in New York and the journeymen bakers had very little power to shape their own lives. The formation of a cohesive trade union movement would be difficult under these circumstances.

Late Beginnings: The Building of an Ethnic Union

Given the fragmented nature of the workers' community in the bakers' trade, any organization would have to shoulder the double burden of uniting the workers across ethnic divides and of fighting for the improvement of working conditions. Obviously the organization of New York's German bakers (who provided the majority of workers in the trade by the mid-nineteenth century) was of paramount importance and had to precede any truly multi-ethnic organization. But unless the bakers' organizations wanted to stay on the level of ethnic brotherhoods with little chance to transform working conditions, the inclusion of all workers was also vital.

Before the Civil War, New York's baking trades had had a lively history of organizing. Bakers' societies, some English- and some German-speaking, could be found among the groups organizing within the frame of republican working men in the 1840s and early 1850s. In 1834, the "Bakers' Trade Union Society" became a member of the

General Trades Union. As members of this organization the journeymen bakers had their first strike for lesser hours and against Sunday work.[35] German bakers were also part of a union in the 1840s, the Operative Bakers Society. Bakers who emigrated from Germany after the 1848 revolution could sometimes be found among the sympathizers of Theodor Weitling and other German radicals. Neither the radical groups nor any of the unions survived the 1850s and the Civil War; by the late 1870s the bakery trade was one of the few industries without any form of union organization in the city.[36] A few groups organized bakers into mutual benefit societies, and the bakers' Bäckergesangverein Eurenia (Eurenia Glee Club) entertained at festivities of labor organizations, but these groups, although they may have been remnants of earlier, more political organizations, were not involved in the politics of labor in any way. By the time hundreds of newly arrived German bakers looked for work and settled into the city's bakeshops during the 1870s and 1880s, the history of involvement in the city's labor movement by the bakers was a faded memory.[37]

Nobody expected much of a renewed attempt to organize the city's bakers in 1880; at least the union press barely mentioned an initiative of the socialist union activist George Block, who hoped to create a new bakers' organization in the spring of that year. Block was at the time a reporter for the *New Yorker Volkszeitung*. A recent German immigrant of the 1870s who had supported himself as a pocketbook maker in Philadelphia and New York sweatshops, he had once briefly worked as an unskilled "hand" in Shults's bread factory in New York's Williamsburg before becoming a journalist. His credentials as a socialist activist (he was a member of the Socialist Labor party) were more solid than his background in the bakery trade. With this unconventional background, Block did not approach the task of organizing the bakers in order to preserve a specific craft identity or tradition; rather he saw the city's bakeries as sweatshops, exploitative and degrading.[38]

His organizing had immediate success in the spring of 1880. At a public gathering for German-American bakery workers he launched the "Journeymen Bakers Union of New York and Vicinity" on April 12, 1880, and within a few weeks the union consisted of five sections and about six hundred bakers.[39] While the membership at the beginning was exclusively German-speaking, other groups of bakers joined the union within its first year. In mid-1881 an English-speaking section was founded (which remained small, with about fifty members), and a few weeks later Yiddish-speaking bakers and Bohemians formed sections as well. A year after it was founded, about three thousand bakers were members of the new union in metropolitan New York.[40] With its ethnic sections the bakery workers' union reflected the divisions of the trade: German members, subdivided by city neighborhoods, were dominant, while other ethnic sections were only loosely connected with the Germans. Scattered records indicate that mostly employees of large bakeries became organized. Large workshops such as Shults's or Fleischmann's Vienna Model Bakery on Lower Broadway, as well as the bakers' hostels where employees of the larger shops lived, best lent themselves to union efforts. Journeymen who worked at shops like Jacob Guenzer's were much more difficult to reach. They were too isolated from each other and too directly dependent on their bosses to organize even though they were most in need of organization, earning as they did the lowest wages and working the longest hours.[41] Like the trade itself, the labor organization was not centralized; indeed, its leadership was rotating, and as far as the labor press was concerned, anonymous. Limited by its members' poverty, the union required low dues and offered no financial benefit program.[42]

Improving the working and living conditions of the poorest workers was the union's most important goal. Its demands reflected the needs of the overworked, underpaid journeymen. A six-day work week and a shorter working day as well as "sufficient wages for the entire family" were the core demands voiced again and again at union meetings. In speeches and articles in the labor press, the union opposed the custom of having journeymen board with their employers as well as mandatory residence in boardinghouses for employees of large bakeries.[43] In order to break the power of the boardinghouse keepers, the union also started its own hiring hall at its offices. Soon fifty to eighty union members a week were able to find work with the help of this bureau, and the employment service became one of the organization's main attractions for prospective members.[44] To buttress its demands for more humane working conditions and hours the union undertook a statistical survey of its members' wages and working hours, which it published in 1881. Block himself put together this study in both a German and an English version entitled *Slavery in the Baker Shops*, which publicized the working and living conditions in the trade.

During the union's first year, however, these activities were not accompanied by any strikes or demonstrations. Obviously Block and his allies wanted to do a maximum of organizing and propagandizing for the bakers' cause before they would take any spectacular action against the employers.[45] But as the organizing efforts of the new union grew increasingly successful during 1880, they ran into resistance from the owners of larger bakeries. Employer pressure in turn pushed the union toward greater militance. By April 1881, the union's leaders declared—against the advice of George Block, who thought such actions premature—that May 2 would be the day on which the organized bakers of New York and Brooklyn would strike for a twelve-hour day.[46]

Hundreds of bakers convened on the appointed day in the temporary headquarters of the union, the Lower East Side's Irving Hall on East Fourteenth Street. From there they marched in their white shirts and caps, accompanied by American flags and a marching band, in a morning parade through the Lower East Side. After their return to the hall they were ready to have their employers sign an agreement stipulating the following conditions: (1) twelve hours of work a day; (2) six days of work a week; and (3) abolition of the boarding system.[47]

Over 220 bakery bosses, almost all of them owners of small bakeries, were ready to reemploy their workers under the new conditions immediately. Hundreds of workers returned to work a day later after celebrating their victory with suitable quantities of beer and much merriment.[48] But while many employers had obviously been moved by the competitive situation in their business to give in to the union, others, especially the owners of large bakeshops, were not convinced. They held out against the workers, and soon a considerable number of union members returned to work under the old conditions. Employers who had initially agreed to the union's demands rescinded their promises once they saw their colleagues' successful resistance. Although a small band of faithful unionists remained on strike and kept alive a bread boycott throughout the summer, this first large-scale strike effectively failed after about a week. As a result the union suffered a severe loss of members from late May on, from which it was unable to recover. A year after its spectacular May action the union had shrunk to thirty-five members in New York and Brooklyn, and a few months later the German bakers' union had ceased to exist.[49]

At a time when many New York trades experienced their first sustained successes since the depression of the 1870s, the bakery workers had failed to build a durable organization. As in other sweated trades, impoverishment and isolation made it difficult for them to maintain their independence. Their experience resembled a similar failure of the first union of lager beer brewers in the city a year later.

Even though brewing and baking were at different stages in their industrial and technical development, the similarity in tactics and failures of their early union organizations is striking. Both trades were deeply rooted—both culturally and socially—in central European paternalism. Their circumstances in New York City still resembled what they had hoped to leave behind, especially the interminable hours and boarding with employers. The latter often created a sense of familial dependency on their bosses that made it difficult to mobilize against the "boss bakers" as an alien class. The isolation of the brewers' and bakers' work setting was twofold: the paternalistic shop was exclusively German, and it even cut them off from other German workers. Because they were separated from many parts of the German-American labor movement, the leaders of both unions could not benefit enough from the skills or solidarity of more successful unions to sustain their movements in the early 1880s. Yet even if the bakers had been fully integrated into the movement of German-American workers, they would not have been able to change the conditions of the German workers in the trade, for in contrast to the brewers, the German bakers of New York just barely formed a majority. Ethnic subdivision of production and consumption deepened the workers' isolation and increased the potential for exploitation of bakers from all ethnic backgrounds. For sustained success the German bakers would have had to cooperate closely with English-speaking and other immigrant bakers; this alone would have precluded the use as strikebreakers of one ethnic group against another. It was never easy to build a union in the late nineteenth century, but the case of the German bakers in the early 1880s shows overwhelming odds against their success.

Ethnic Separation and the Struggle for One Union

Like the brewery workers' union, the German bakers' movement lay largely dormant between 1882 and 1885. During these important years, the cigar makers' union went through a period of internal dissent but ultimately consolidated as an organization. The Central Labor Union grew powerful and unified enough to mount the Henry George campaign in 1886. With the rise of the CMIU and a number of other unions within the CLU also came a rise of modified craft unionism which would make up the core of the American Federation of Labor. For contemporary observers the rise of the Knights of Labor was the most visible and impressive development within organized labor. In other words, these were years when a number of im-

portant labor organizations in the city would grow beyond their original ethnic and craft confines, into national, quasi-industrial unions
which were united by a common political agenda. Only by overcoming their traditional boundaries of culture and work specialization
were they able to face the increasingly unified employers and the challenge of technological change later during the 1880s and 1890s.

Unions such as the brewery workers and the bakers were absent
from the list of labor groups which organized in a durable way during the early 1880s. When these latecomers did gather into unions in
the mid-1880s or after, they were able to take advantage of the relatively advanced level of labor organization in New York City by having CLU organizers and the support of other unions. But no outside
help could build a unified political consensus and a clear union identity. This they had to do themselves during the late 1880s, a much
stormier time of change than the earlier years in which other unions
had undergone a similar process. The bakery workers were in a particularly difficult situation as latecomers. As we will see, they faced
the task of building a political agenda and common organizational
principles at a time of unprecedented factionalism and infighting in
the New York labor movement. This would prove to be an enormous
hurdle on the way to a durable trade union.

The first group to revive the bakers' movement on a small scale
after the debacle of 1881 was the English-speaking bakers in 1882.
But—as if to underline their separate traditions and position—they
did so with different tactics than the German bakers. A relatively
small group in the baking trade, English-speaking bakers organized
into two main unions, the "Progressive Bakers Club" and the "Long
Island Protective Association." Both groups affiliated with District
Assembly 49 of the Knights of Labor (in which they kept a low profile, however). A group of German factory bakers from Brooklyn also
joined the Knights as the "Bakers Advance Association" in May 1884.[50]

Like the earlier union of 1881, the Knights-affiliated bakers fought
primarily for shorter hours and higher pay, but their organizing strategies and their priorities differed in important ways from the earlier
bakers' union. English-speaking bakers were in a relatively privileged
position. Few of them worked in cellar bakeries, and most earned
better wages than their German counterparts, working in medium-
sized specialty shops. Conscious of their position as a relatively privileged minority, the English factory bakers were more interested in
improving their position within the trade than in organizing the entire industry. They set out to win the ten-hour day (as opposed to the
twelve-hour day desired by the German bakers) and attempted to

prohibit Sunday work altogether. Even though they were factory workers, they behaved like a true craft union and set about reaching their goals through lobbying and other forms of pressure politics. They asked state assemblymen and municipal agencies to consider the ten-hour day for bread factories; the English bakers in Brooklyn even tried to bring a lawsuit to abolish Sunday baking by invoking the city's rather strict Blue Laws before the courts. None of these campaigns had much immediate success, though they may have helped to stem a deterioration in working conditions in the bread factories.[51]

New York and Brooklyn English-speaking bakers were also active in the newly founded Central Labor Unions of their respective cities, though they never gained much influence there or within the Knights of Labor.[52] Despite their organizing abilities, the English-speaking bakers' unions remained small groups which lacked the informal backing of a network of ethnic and neighborhood supporters. English-speaking and German-American bakers would have to pool their strength in order to launch a durable union movement.

It took until early 1885 for the Germans to launch a second bakers' union. This time circumstances were more auspicious than four years earlier. As in the case of the brewers, the Central Labor Union, now three years old, was able to back the new movement, which began, once more, under the leadership of George Block, with mass meetings in January of that year.[53] "The reorganization has surpassed our highest expectation," wrote the *New Yorker Volkszeitung*, reporting also that three sections were formed, all for German-speaking bakers.[54] The organizing success of the new union was based on entirely different principles from that of the English-speaking bakers and addressed a different group of workers. The German bakers' organization envisioned itself as a mass organization encompassing the entire trade, and including workers of all skill and pay levels on an equal basis. This was a tall order given the dismal experiences of the past. In order to build a lasting organization, George Block and his supporters had to sustain a campaign of information and education before promoting activist unionism. The establishment of a firm organization had priority over winning higher wages and other demands at individual shops. Not everyone involved in this effort agreed with Block's basic ideas or understood their implications. The establishment of a *Bäckerzeitung* (nominally independent from the union) was at first criticized by many unionists as a superfluous luxury, but the weekly, filled with informative articles on the trade and entertaining anecdotes and stories as well as advertisements, proved to be a potent recruiting tool for the union.[55] By mid-August Block counted seven hundred members. "For the past three years the English-speaking bakers in New York have taken the leading part, but now the Germans are stronger and are taking the lead," remarked *John Swinton's Paper* admiringly.[56]

After its initial organizing successes among the German-born bakers who worked in small and medium-sized shops, the union also tried to reach out to other immigrant bakers, notably Yiddish-speaking and Bohemian workers who labored under conditions similar to those of the Germans. These two groups were organized into separate locals by 1886–87. Locals of pie bakers and confectioners (both German-speaking) were also started.[57] But English-speaking bakers, who were in the vanguard of organizing in the early 1880s and whose activism had received attention at a period during which the German bakers had virtually no organization, were entirely ignored by the new union.

While ethnic separatism eventually handicapped the growth of both unions, the German union could at first afford such exclusion, for it took a community-centered approach within the immigrant quarters where most of the non-English speakers worked. When trying to organize the workers of a small bakery, the union would send out emissaries and, after speaking with the journeymen about the purpose of the union, asked them to join in the organization. In some cases the unionists were not admitted to the shop by the suspicious bosses, or were thrown out; in other instances the employer would threaten to fire workers if they joined the organization. If the journeymen refused to join the union or remained indifferent to the unionists' entreaties, the union would place a boycott on the shop until the workers had joined. This tactic worked especially well in the German neighborhoods of the city, where the bonds created by daily living and shared language and customs were particularly strong. In many German neighborhood bakeries the mere threat of a boycott persuaded many employers to give in to the union.[58]

To counter stiffer resistance, the unionists developed techniques of neighborhood organization in which shoppers and neighbors of all ethnic backgrounds were mobilized, as befitted a trade in which workers were at times from a different ethnic background from the consumers. The most publicized of these actions was the 1886 boycott of Mrs. Gray's bakery on Hudson Street in Lower Manhattan, an area then inhabited mostly by Irish immigrants. Mrs. Gray, the proprietor, was Irish, but her four bakers were German-born; she forbade them to join the Journeymen Bakers National Union. Even though they were not German, most of her customers bought their bread elsewhere

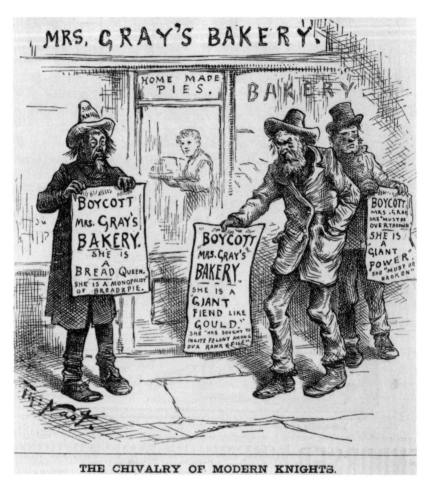

THE CHIVALRY OF MODERN KNIGHTS.

An anti–Knights of Labor cartoon, referring to the bakers' boycott of Mrs. Gray's bakery in Manhattan in 1886. From *Harpers Magazine,* May 1, 1886.

when the bakers' union declared a boycott of her bakery. The action received unprecedented publicity in the city's press, which portrayed Mrs. Gray as a struggling widow trying to fend off the united forces of the New York labor movement. These stories induced middle-class patrons to venture down to Hudson Street from their uptown quarters to buy her bread. The better-off sent their servants or gave cash. Despite this support, Mrs. Gray, who depended on neighborhood business, gave in and permitted her four employees to join the bakery workers' union.[59]

In the Gray boycott and other similar actions, the union clearly succeeded in enlisting working-class customers across ethnic lines in their cause and fending off the employer and her middle-class supporters. Other unions such as the brewers used the same tactic successfully with businesses dependent on working-class neighborhoods. The German bakers made this their main approach to organizing in their first two years.[60]

At the same time New York's bakers were going through an unprecedented period of political and organizational activity, during the mid-1880s, elsewhere, too, bakers were organizing. In the fall of 1885 newly formed bakers' groups from Boston to San Francisco contacted George Block after the *Bäcker Zeitung* had published a call to organize a national union. In January of 1886, delegates representing fourteen different bakers' organizations from all over the country met in Pittsburgh to found a national bakers' union. The meeting passed by-laws and laid the groundwork for the Journeymen Bakers National Union of the United States (JBNU).[61] Unlike its official English name, the German title National Verband der Deutschen Bäcker der Vereinigten Staaten (National Association of German Bakers of the United States) did not hide the fact that the new union consisted exclusively of German-speaking groups. The New York German bakers' organization became Local 1 of the new national union, and New York also became its headquarters. New York City and Brooklyn had four more locals by 1886.[62] The German bakers of the city seemed poised for a central role in the movement to organize their long-neglected trade.[63]

With 1,500 members and a large proportion of the bread production in union hands, the New York locals of the Journeymen Bakers National Union could finally try to achieve their long-sought goals of shorter hours, higher wages, and the abolition of compulsory room and board with employers. The union again opted for a decentralized, shop-centered approach, which involved only a few groups of workers at any given time. This was in marked contrast to the tactic of the 1881 strike and fit well with its neighborhood-based boycott tactic. In most cases the organized bakers won their demands, sometimes after a brief strike and boycott.[64] To assert its power in a more lasting way, the union also introduced a union label which was directly affixed to the bread made by union members. By the summer of 1886 the union contended that half of all bread in New York and Brooklyn was baked and labeled by union members.[65] Under these circumstances wages, working hours, and working conditions had improved markedly for the bakers of the city. "The bakers may be mentioned as a striking instance of specific reforms effected. They have been successful in obtaining great reconstruction. Their hours ranging from fourteen to the whole of twenty-four have been reduced from ten to fourteen," reported the Commissioner of Labor for the State of New York in 1886.[66] The statistical researches of the bakery union buttressed this statement. They also showed that wages had increased to $9.50 for second and up to $14.00 for first hands. Except for "second-hand cockroach bosses," as the unionists called them, employers no longer forced their workers to board with them.[67]

By late 1887 the organization of the German bakers had reached considerable power in the city's baking trade. It had improved working conditions for the majority of those organized, and its efforts had been successful beyond the confines of the city's German community. The union was becoming a force to be reckoned with in the New York labor movement. It looked as if the pragmatic approach of George Block and his fellow unionists, building a union on relatively autonomous ethnic locals and shop-oriented action, was successful for this highly divided trade. But organizational coordination of a widely diverse membership would not be sufficient given the political and organizational pressures on New York unions in 1886–87. For the bakers to maintain their position would require a greater degree of political unity and centralization. Amidst the turmoil of the post–Henry George years, this was a difficult task for the young union.

In New York City the problems of continuing disunity played themselves out in three areas of conflict: the struggle for a shorter workday, the rivalry between the Journeymen Bakers National Union and the Knights of Labor, and the conflict about the role and influence of socialists within the union.

From its first days as a union in 1881, the struggle for a shorter workday was a dominant theme for the bakers' organization. But even after years of organizing the question of what exactly should be the desired length of a workday for union bakers was still unresolved. The English-speaking bakers, organized in the KOL, achieved the twelve-hour day in the early 1880s. By the mid-1880s they were ready to campaign for a ten-hour day. Led by John Kelly of Brooklyn, they complained bitterly about the Germans, who with their never-ending supply of "green" immigrants and their endorsement of the seventy-two hour week seemed to further exploitative conditions in the trade.[68] From the viewpoint of the German bakers, most of whom still worked about fifteen hours, twelve hours seemed to be a goal within reach of the organized bakers. Since Germans dominated the trade overall, they reasoned, it was important to organize as many of them as possible first and struggle for attainable goals for all, rather than fight for better conditions for a small "elite" as the English-speaking bakers proposed.[69]

These tensions played themselves out on a larger scale in the rivalry between the Knights of Labor—which encompassed the English-speaking bakers—and the Germans' JBNU, though some German-speakers also formed Knights' groups. Like the cigar makers in the same era, the Knights of Labor had strong hegemonic aspirations within the New York City labor movement in the mid- and late 1880s. Knights' leaders actively supported dual unionism and the leaders of District Assembly 49 frequently expressed open hostility to the organizing strategies of the German-American bakers. Because of these tensions, some Knights-affiliated bakers' groups in the city had not joined the Journeymen Bakers National Union as locals in 1886.[70] Some of the German bakers' locals tried to straddle the developing rift by affiliating with the Knights and the JBNU at the same time, although this seemed to intensify the potential for conflict.[71] Especially in Brooklyn, where District Assembly 49 retained a following among the bakers long after the Knights' decline had set in in Manhattan, the situation remained tense and conflict-ridden for the organized bakers until after the turn of the century.[72] Over time the Journeymen Bakers National Union remained the dominant organization, in part because it succeeded in integrating English-speaking bakers into its organizing structure. In contrast to the brewery workers' union, which never succeeded in breaking out of its ethnic mold, the JBNU was able to organize the English-speaking minority. As Local 80 of New York City they became an important stabilizing factor in the national union in later years.[73]

If the struggle with the Knights and the English-speaking bakers cost the union much energy, the internecine strife among German-American socialists was even more destructive. George Block, the founder of the JBNU, was a member of the Socialist Labor party and saw to it that the bakers union sided with the socialists in the electoral campaigns of 1886 and 1887.[74] But Block also was careful to keep the union's socialist support low-key. Any strident proselytizing for the SLP would have alienated many of the union's more conservative members. By 1888 the union's national secretary had become one of the important critics of the party, urging a close alliance with the union movement at large rather than an emphasis on ideological purity and election campaigns.[75] Block became suspect to a small group of bakers loyal to the SLP. They disaffiliated with the national union for a time to start a more radical "Progressive Bakers Union" in 1887–88.[76] But Block was also considered an intruder by conservative bakers elsewhere who were suspicious of his socialism and his lack of credentials as a baker.[77] Together these factors led to Block's retreat from the office of union secretary in 1887 and his dismissal as editor of the *Deutsch-Amerikanische Bäcker Zeitung* at the national convention of the JBNU in 1889.[78] The dismissal dismayed Block's many admirers. "Who is the Brutus?" wrote Michael McGrath, whose English-speaking Local 80 found the socialist infighting baffling.[79] Block's successor as head of the union, August Delabar, was also an SLP member, a position which would cause problems for the bakers amid the infighting between the Central Labor Union, the Central Labor Federation, and the American Federation of Labor in the early 1890s. The editorship of the *Bäcker-Zeitung* and eventually the leadership of the union next fell to Henry Weissmann, a San Francisco baker with anarchist sympathies, whose unrelenting hostility to the socialists caused even more problems.[80]

The internal factionalization and leadership crisis paralyzed the bakers' movement in the city at a crucial moment. As we saw in the preceding chapters, other unions, too, faced internal ideological divisions and had their leadership challenged. But in the case of the bakers these problems were particularly difficult to overcome. More than most trades, baking was still very factionalized, and the union's many locals in New York City continued to represent different ethnic and trade constituencies. The economic and ethnic subdivisions had taken on political labels by the late 1880s. A politically unified movement was very difficult to build on top of these divisions. Even unions with a firmer organizational and membership base than the bakers (such as the cigar makers and the furniture makers) or internally homogeneous membership (such as the printers) found it difficult to achieve political unity during the infighting of the late 1880s. The bakery workers' union, still unsure of its membership, inexperienced in labor politics, and without powerful labor allies, was vulnerable on many fronts. But the decisive challenge would come from the employers who in 1889 faced challenges of their own as bread-baking entered the first phase of industrialization and mechanization.

The Pool Bakers and the Defeat of the Union

Paralleling the changes already observed in the city's cigar and beer-brewing industries, baking also developed into a more industrialized trade during these and subsequent years. The most visible of these changes was the growth of bread factories and cracker and pie bakeries which produced for the wholesale trade on a larger scale.

The introduction of mechanical kneading and mixing machines, affordable only to entrepreneurs with some capital, made a larger operation more remunerative. Altogether about a dozen larger firms with between five and a hundred employees operated in the New York area by the mid-1880s, most of them situated in Brooklyn.[81] From there the bread was delivered to all parts of greater New York.

The owners of the large bakeries were a new class of entrepreneurs. Unlike the brewery princes, who successfully invoked a long European tradition and who formed a socially and culturally homogeneous group, bakery owners were a mixed collection of English, American, Swiss, Austrian, and German descent.[82] Unlike the old-fashioned bakery boss who labored with his journeymen in the basement and shared an apartment with them in the tenement upstairs, they were businessmen with little interest in the craft ambitions which their lesser competitors and their employees might still value.

The workers in bread factories had to submit to a strict factory discipline, and their working hours were also very long, but altogether the hours of factory hands were shorter than those of the cellar bakers, their employment was year round, and—on a yearly basis—they were better paid. Factory bakers also did not live at their place of employment nor were they tied to the neighborhood around the bread factory. In other words, the position of factory bakers resembled that of other factory workers (for example in the cigar industry) rather than that of retail bakers who resembled sweatshop workers.[83]

By the summer of 1889, with the bakery workers' union barely holding on to its membership and the New York labor movement showing no signs of gaining unity, the employers of factory bakers took the initiative to fight the union in a centralized fashion. In a chain of events reminiscent of the conflict that had broken the brewery workers' union a year before, the owners of the large bakeries of the city formed the innocuously named "Bakers Association of New York and Vicinity" in the summer of 1889. The employees of these bread manufacturers were to a large extent organized as members of the JBNU and provided the mainstay of a number of locals, especially Local 34 in Brooklyn and Local 1. For the fourteen members of the employers' group (who represented virtually the entire factory sector of the New York baking trade) this was a challenge. Unlike an earlier association of "Master Bakers" which had tried to reach an agreement with the union in a coordinated fashion during the mid-1880s, the factory owners (or "Pool Bakers," as the union would call them) had only one goal: to break the union's hold on their employees.[84]

An opportunity for united action against the union came soon.

In July 1889, the foreman at Rockwell's bakery (one of the big fourteen) slapped a young journeyman; the union representatives asked for the foreman's dismissal, a demand rejected by the owner of the bakery. In response, Rockwell's unionized employees went out on strike. The answer of the bakery owners' association seemed well-prepared. All fourteen employers required their employees to sign a new list of rules effectively prohibiting union membership. The five hundred union members who refused to give in to this demand found themselves locked out of all fourteen "pool bakeries" at the end of August.[85]

In 1886 and 1888, the cigar and brewery owners respectively had used the same tactics against their striking workers. The cigar workers had been well organized in a trade still dominated by skilled workers who could not easily be replaced and had won their test of strength. The brewery workers, on the other hand, had not been strong enough to withstand their powerful employers. The bakers had even fewer strengths than the brewers. Seriously weakened by internal quarreling, and without many allies in the factionalized New York labor movement, the union had to contend with a large supply of unorganized workers willing to take the place of the locked-out union bakers. It was easy for the employers to find nonunion workers, and the lockout hardly affected production in the fourteen pool bakeries. The tactics of the employers broke the union's hold in the bread factories within a few weeks.[86]

Despite their defeat, the bakery workers continued their struggle by organizing a citywide boycott of pool bread. This was no small task. Since the bread was only sold wholesale, grocers in the entire metropolitan area had to be induced to abandon their usual suppliers. If they refused to do so, they were placed under boycott by their neighborhood customers.[87] Housewives, renters, grocers, and members of the Socialist Labor party canvassed their neighborhoods to enlist support for the bakers' cause. But since they were recruited mostly from the German-American community, their activity was limited to largely German neighborhoods, an insufficient area, given the large market of the wholesale bakeries. Like the brewery workers, the bakers were not able to break out of the confines of ethnicity when it came to organizing support, yet their trade had expanded beyond the ethnically specific markets. Even if the neighborhood grocers were willing to switch their bread suppliers, no alternative suppliers were available. A boycott of wholesale bread therefore proved to be as impossible as a boycott of all the large New York breweries a year earlier. The bakery workers' strength, their neighborhood connection, could do little to oppose industrial production and distribution.[88]

As the cigar makers' union had shown, ample union finances could sustain a union in times of conflict even in an industry where neighborhood boycotts were not feasible. But the bakers' union had shallow financial reserves. Its membership fees and assessments had always been low, and even though the leaders of the JBNU were in favor of regular benefits, the union did not offer them until the early 1890s.[89] In the summer of 1889, the union had to rely on hastily imposed special assessments to offer some support to the locked-out workers, but few locals elsewhere in the country were willing or able to pay such extra assessments.[90] Two hastily started cooperative bakeshops provided little relief for anyone except twenty bakers who worked there.[91]

By the end of October the union conceded defeat—in an indirect way—by lifting the boycott of "pool bread." Instead it called for a selective boycott of the products of the Fleischmann bakery, which also manufactured widely sold baker's yeast. But by then the JBNU had lost its influence on the New York labor movement, and the Fleischmann boycott, too, remained largely ineffective.[92]

The lost fight with the pool bakers threw the JBNU into its most severe crisis since 1881. Local 1, which at the beginning of 1889 had had over one thousand members, shrank to fewer than thirty by the end of the year.[93] The Bohemian and English locals whose members were not directly involved in the lockout (because they rarely worked in the pool bakeries) were less affected, but since they had always been on the political periphery of the union, their stability had little effect on the overall situation. In effect the JBNU had lost its most important constituency in the greater New York area: workers in large bakeries.[94]

The disastrous lockout could not have come at a worse moment for the New York bakers, for the New York City labor movement was already torn apart by political infighting. In the struggles between the Central Labor Union, the Central Labor Federation, and the New York Federation of Labor, August Delabar, head of the local bakers and secretary of the JBNU, generally sided with the pro-AFL forces and thus turned against the socialists, whom many of his politically active members favored.[95] This increased the hostility among the remaining members of Local 1, many of whom left the JBNU, partly in order to join a rival socialist union (the Independent Bakers of New York), partly to reaffiliate with the Knights, and partly to stay away from unions altogether. Delabar resigned from office in 1893 only to be replaced by leaders who proved even less able to reunify the union.[96] The infighting paralyzed any effective labor movement within the New York baking trade for the next dozen years; moreover, since New York had always had such a central role in the JBNU's affairs, it rendered the national union's leadership ineffective, too. Not until after the turn of the century did New York's bakers recover from these internecine struggles.[97]

The lockout by the pool bakers and the resulting problems for the union show striking parallels with the brewers' struggle a year earlier. But while the brewery workers were able to recover from their nationwide defeats within a decade, no such development can be observed for the bakers. Just as the industry remained largely localized, so the unions were also still quite local in character and were unable to mount a national offensive, as the brewery workers did in the 1890s and thereafter. In contrast to the cigar makers, who like the bakers were faced with a localized industry which exploited cheap immigrant labor, the bakery workers were not able to rely on a core of skilled workers to pursue the union cause. Conditions in the industry changed very little in the 1890s, especially in immigrant cities like New York, and the changes that did take place resulted from health and safety concerns of middle-class reformers.

Changing the Trade without the Workers: The Progressive Movement and the Bakers of New York City

While leaders and followers fought out their differences, the community around them changed, as did the trade's organization and economy. After an all-time high of 3,445 German bakers had toiled in the city's bakeshops in 1890, their numbers steadily declined in subsequent years. Bakers from southern and eastern Europe increasingly replaced them. Germans and their Anglo-Irish colleagues retained their jobs, however, in the larger bread factories and the specialized bakeshops and confectioneries. The baking trades shared the pattern of the garment trades: as new immigrant groups arrived in the city eager for any type of work, the sweatshops accommodated them as readily as earlier generations of Germans, Bohemians, Irish, and English. The structures of the baking trade and the organization of the work force changed very little; newcomers had no choice but to accept the prevailing conditions. In the absence of an effective labor organization, conditions overall may have worsened in the 1890s after the gains of the late 1880s. The number of cellar bakeries did not decrease; even though they used an ever wider array of machinery, efficient bread factories could barely compete with the "cockroach bosses" in the city's downtown wards. One example of the difficulties middling bosses and large bakeries faced was the bankruptcy of Hersemann's, one of the original wholesale bakeries in Brooklyn, in 1895.[98]

As sweatshop exploitation began to grip a new generation of bakers, little effort was made by any of the bakery workers' unions to reach out to the new workers. An Italian union formed briefly in New York, without, however, having a lasting impact on the conditions in this newly emerging segment of the trade. French, Swedish, and most eastern European bakers remained entirely without union representation. The twenty-fifth anniversary issue of the bakery workers' union journal listed in detail the accomplishments and struggles of New York locals over the past decades, but other than Germans, only the Jewish and the Bohemian bakers—organized since the late 1880s—were even so much as mentioned.[99]

Instead of organizing the new generation of sweatshop bakers, the union leaders became involved in a campaign to improve the conditions in the cellar bakeries through legislation. This movement resembled the anti-tenement movement in some respects, although—occurring more than a decade later—it relied on a much better defined coalition of progressive reformers and politicians. Just as in the case of the tenement cigar laws, the bakeshop campaign had its origins in a newspaper article published in the *New York Press* in 1894 which described the abominable conditions in the city's cellar bakeries from the perspective of the tenement reformer and journalist Edward Marshall. JBNU president Weissmann supported the ensuing campaign for a law regulating the conditions in the city's bakeries and added the longstanding union demand for a ten-hour day as part of the reform law. The measure also prohibited sleeping in the bakeshop and set minimal hygiene standards for the workplace. As in the cigar makers' case, the workers in the cellar bakeries themselves contributed little to the passage of the law, which was signed by the governor of New York State in May 1895.[100] Thus baking became one of the few trades subject to legally sanctioned supervision by health and other public authorities in New York State. Enforcement of the law was entrusted to a team of state inspectors (among them John Hanlon, a former baker and member of Local 80) who knew what to look for and documented abuses in their reports. But their resources were stretched thin, and their sanctions, warnings, and fines did not count for much in an industry whose small owners could simply close shop and relocate without too much trouble. Because of the law, however, the baking trade became a well-documented industry, its dark cellars exposed by the camera of such photographers as Lewis Hine and the crisp prose of many an observer.[101] The law did in fact improve working conditions, especially in the larger bakeries. But the most substantial part, limiting the workday to ten hours, was difficult to enforce, and the ten-hour provision eventually helped to invalidate the law in 1905 after a Utica bakery owner, John Lochner, went to court.[102]

While protective legislation never had enough of an impact on the New York industry to change its basic structure, the gradual mechanization of the trade had a lasting effect. With at least temporary enforcement of shorter hours, and the desire for "ethnic" neighborhood bakeries waning among the more upwardly mobile middle and working classes, the neighborhood bakeries began to disappear around the turn of the century. Elsewhere in the country, bread factories with their kneading, dough-separating, and forming machinery had became important providers of daily bread by the turn of the century; in New York this trend slowly took hold in the baking trade as well. While the vast majority of bakers in the city had worked in establishments with five or fewer employers in the 1880s, the New York State factory inspector found over 60 percent of all bakers working in establishments with fifty or more employees in 1912. Bread factories with their increasingly sophisticated and accurate machinery provided a very different workplace from the cellar bakeries. There the work environment was comparatively comfortable and clean, and working hours were more easily regulated than in the small retail bakeries, since bakers could be employed in shifts.

The needs and priorities of workers in bread factories were also different from their colleagues in the smaller shops. Workers in bread factories were better paid. They supported mechanization but their level of skill usually declined. By the second decade of the twentieth century, a significant number of women and very young workers had also entered the trade; these were workers without traditional allegiance to the goals the union fought for—maintenance of craft skill and a "family wage." They provided promise and a new challenge to the unionization efforts of the JBNU at the same time. Essentially, though, the industrialization of the trade, not unlike the development in the cigar industry a decade and a half earlier, spelled the end of the community-based ethnic unionism of the bakery workers in New York City.[103]

The history of the bakery workers and their organizations in New York illustrates how ethnic community could fail to sustain economic and political organizing. This failure is a striking example of the ambiguous nature of tradition in union formation and community activism. Journeymen bakers had a rich legacy of craftsmanship, but the history of a self-governed guild trade had long deteriorated, and by the late nineteenth century only the most oppressive aspects of paternalistic labor relations had survived, punctuated by occasional outbursts of journeymen activism. Building up a class-conscious union within American capitalism was doubly difficult: social control of bosses over journeymen was considerable; at the same time many journeymen identified with their employers, for they themselves hoped to become "bosses." The inherited traditions that shaped the political expectations of journeymen bakers in the New World were self-defeating.

While tradition weighed heavily on both groups, the bakers faced even greater obstacles to organization than did brewers. Up to the 1880s bakers and brewers worked under similarly oppressive conditions; thereafter the baking trade remained in its pre-industrial phase and did not make the transition to mechanized mass production which brewing underwent in the late nineteenth century. Isolation of workers from their colleagues and close dependency on their bosses beset them decades longer.

Subdivision into ethnic branches was another important feature of the baking trade which made it extremely difficult to build a viable union movement. Not only were the German bakers strongly rooted in their own ethnic community, they had to contend with a sizable minority of bakers from other ethnic groups. Colleagues who spoke neither German nor English were especially difficult to organize because, in contrast to the cigar makers, the bakers had few "American" members who would serve as mediators to the world beyond an immigrant trade. As a result, the German-American bakers were faced with the task of not only organizing their own ethnic community, but also building bridges to other ethnic minorities and the English-speaking labor movement at the same time. This task proved too much for the representatives of the impoverished baking trade.

The bakery workers' attempts at building a strong union were unsuccessful during the nineteenth century not just compared to the more visible unions like the cigar makers' but also by almost any other measure: in New York and the rest of the nation the union had little power in any branch of the trade and within any ethnic group after twenty years of almost continuous existence. Unlike the brewers, who were able to maintain a cohesive union organization outside (though not always within) New York City, the bakery workers' national organization was in disarray during much of the late nineteenth century.

Political unity was hard to come by under these circumstances. Unlike the brewers or the cigar makers the bakers never reached a stage where they were even close to formulating their own political program. Unable to transcend ethnicity as their primary organizing structure, their leaders got caught up in the infighting among unions and labor organizations of the late 1880s and 1890s.

When mechanization did come to the trade, it enabled the bakery workers to organize more easily under factory conditions than in the pre-industrial cellar workshop. Mechanization and the reform legislation of the progressive era, two changes from "above" on which the community of workers had little impact, were the forces that improved the working life of the bakers enough to enable them to build a viable union during the first decades of the twentieth century. But the political and social basis for such a union would have to be quite different from the early days of the JBNU. It was the centralized business union that survived this change and proved effective as a negotiating voice for the largely industrialized union bakers during the coming decades.

Conclusion: German Immigrants and American Labor

On February 21, 1903, the *New Yorker Volkszeitung* celebrated its silver anniversary with a special edition recapitulating the history of Germans in the socialist labor movement of New York City. It was a proud occasion for the paper, which reached a readership of at least 20,000 every day and which was influential far beyond the relatively small circle of German socialists in New York City. Article after article pointed out the paper's humble beginnings and exhorted its readers to stay involved and engaged, since the first twenty-five years were only the beginning of the long struggle for socialism in the New World. "We have to heave the world from its hinges and put it in ruins, in order to build a better new world. What are twenty-five years for such a giant undertaking?" declared the leading editorial.[1] Indeed the editorialists had another decade of vigorous activism to look forward to, before the crisis of World War I dealt a succession of blows to North American socialists. But the German-American socialist movement and indeed the German-American labor movement in general had already reached its apex by the turn of the century and would steadily decline in the second quarter-century of the *New Yorker Volkszeitung.* The number of immigrants from Germany had decreased since the late 1880s; new recruits for German-American unions were not plentiful. "Today's immigrants from German lands are for the most part no longer the party stalwarts of the seventies and eighties," declared the *Volkszeitung,* adding "even if they are socialists, they did not experience the struggles of those days, and they therefore have only a vague idea of the idealism and readiness for sacrifice that the older ones had."[2] The tone of confident knowledge that vast hurdles still had to be overcome and nostalgia for the old days of difficult struggle but unprecedented enthusiasm within a growing movement of German-American unionists captured the mood of many old-timers around the turn of the century.

But as members of newer immigrant groups and U.S.-born men and women became the bearers of socialist unionism, nostalgia for the old days was not the only legacy left by German-Americans in the labor movement. As leaders and members of many unions, from the large cigar makers to the small German-American Typographia, German-American unionists had shaped the American labor movement in its formative period. Most visible was their presence as socialists within the North American labor movement at large. Even though by the turn of the century the German-American socialist presence was numerically not very large, this group of experienced unionists was an important counterweight to the increasingly conservative policies of the mainstream AFL. Less visible but at least as important were the many German-American unionists whose faithful adherence to the bureaucratic centralism of the American Federation of Labor also sprang from their experiences within German-American unions. A third characteristic shared by many German-American unionists, socialists as well as more mainstream unionists, was the adherence to craft tradition within an industrial setting. In this study I have attempted to describe and analyze the German origins and the American history of all three strains of union development: socialist unionism, craft traditionalism, and bureaucratic "business" unionism. We have not only examined three trades and their respective labor organizations but have also tried to see them as embedded in the social community of German-Americans and the political culture of labor politics in New York.

At the outset we positioned German-American unionists within the social and economic landscape of the city. German immigrants were a significant proportion of the working-class population at large and were organized within an unusually wide spectrum of social and political Vereine. The picture that emerged of the German-American community at large in New York was one of unprecedented diversity and a rich organizational culture that represented virtually all political wings and many different subcultures and classes. It is problematic to speak of *one* German-American community in this case, since unifying characteristics or actions were few. Even among working-class Germans, community was not something naturally transplanted or emergent. Instead Germans in New York chose to join and build communities based not just on the specific cultures and backgrounds they came from within German-speaking Europe but also on shared social lives and political goals that emerged in the New World.

One of the central arguments of this book is that German unions played a vital role in the building of community for German immigrants in North America. More than other forms of community organization, such as churches or regional groups, trade unions were in the best position to build community in a new and rapidly changing industrial society. A number of related questions were explored in this context and provided a more detailed view of this thesis: why were unions so well suited to the development and integration of the German-American working class into North American society and politics? What was the effect of the central role for trade unions on the community as a whole? And did unions carry that community-building role into the American trade union movement at large?

German immigrants of the late nineteenth century came from an industrial economy with a rich tradition of organizing craftsmen and workers that predated industrialization. By the late nineteenth century German unions combined craft consciousness with a close involvement in socialist politics as well. For German immigrants the combination of socialism and craft unionism was therefore not a contradiction. Indeed, it proved an attractive and integrative way of organizing for German immigrants in the United States as well. In the absence of a viable socialist party, which would absorb many of the political energies of German labor activists in Germany, the trade unions played an even more central role for the Germans in New York City than they had in the Old World. Aware of their multifaceted role as community builders, political organizers, and economic pressure groups, German-American unions faced enormous hurdles in representing their communities in so many ways. I have tried to examine the socialist labor tradition within the German-American labor movement in a new light by looking at how German immigrant unionists had to change their organizing tactics and political priorities in response to American circumstances.

The cigar makers' union exemplifies the gradual shift from socialism to what came to be known as "American" political and organizing tactics. New York's CMIU was a union with a strong socialist tradition, in part because many of its German immigrant members had been socialists before they came to the U.S. That cigar making was a craft with a strong socialist tradition in central Europe distinguished it from the other trades discussed in this book. But under the specific pressures of life in Gilded Age New York, socialist traditions were only partially helpful in the cigar makers' attempt to organize a growing number of workers. In the end, community building among the cigar makers had to be based on a wider variety of strategies than the socialists had to offer. Their grass roots approach and openness toward less-skilled workers was important in integrating an increasingly diverse labor force into the framework of organized labor, but their lack of economic and administrative stability and their propensity to get involved in arcane political causes were damaging.

Thus the cigar makers also turned to the tactics of what would later be termed business unionism to build a stable, solvent organization which would protect the status and pay of its members. In fact, under the leadership of Samuel Gompers and Adolph Strasser the cigar makers' union became the originator of what is often called business unionism; this study shows, however, that there were many more facets to Gompers's and even Strasser's thinking. Even though the socialist unionists resisted many of the principles associated with business unionism, thousands of German-American members of the union willingly supported the program of high dues, relatively ample benefits, and pragmatism on larger political issues. After all, the traditional approach to labor organizations as mutual benefit associations with a relatively bureaucratized administrative structure also had roots in the German labor movement which many immigrant cigar makers had known.

With its emphasis on protecting the jobs of male journeymen cigar makers against the incursions of women and semiskilled workers the CMIU also appealed to German traditions of craft organizing. Even though the craft traditions of the trade were to some extent invented, the CMIU succeeded as one of the most successful craft unions of the 1880s and 1890s. It marks the CMIU's special success that its "invented" European traditions were maintained under the banner of "American" principles of labor organization. This put the cigar makers and their largely German-American members squarely in the middle of mainstream unionism by the mid-1880s. While relying on "foreign" traditions and immigrant members in some important ways, the union had staked out a territory at the center of American political movements, which the American Federation of Labor would define and occupy in succeeding decades. On the other hand, the cigar makers largely forsook the role of community builders within the confines of the German-American community. By the end of the period under discussion, the CMIU had largely pulled out of the German community in New York in pursuit of national goals.

Traditions could work in contradictory and opposite ways during the formative period of American labor organizing, as German-American workers exemplified. If the cigar makers showed that both craft orientation and socialism were traditional ways of organizing for German-Americans and were not mutually exclusive, as has often been assumed, the German lager beer brewers in the United States were an even more striking example of a group of craftsmen with deep roots in the Old World who considered themselves at the same time to be socialists. Brewery workers organized in the mid-1880s in response to the rapid industrialization of their trade, which threatened their position as skilled workers. The New York City contracts of 1886 and 1887 affirmed the role of the union as an arbiter of craft qualifications which would continue to regulate access to the trade; in some ways the New York City brewery workers' union functioned almost like a guild during the years this contract was in force, and it played a more "traditional" role than brewery workers' organizations in Germany.

But the focus on craft unionism and the success in upholding tradition also had its pitfalls when it came to surviving in the rough world of industrializing America. Employers, while often voicing their devotion to traditional methods of production and (with an eye to the consumer) quality of product, were not interested in a traditional system of employee relations if that seemed to hamper their flexibility and profits. The "brewery princes" abandoned craft solidarity with their employees as soon as possible and fought the union as a hostile organization of socialists.

With ethnically circumscribed ideas about craft identity and socialism paramount, the union of brewery workers had a difficult time mobilizing support from outside against their employers. The community-building aspects of their creed were insufficient in the late 1880s to fight large-scale industrial enterprises. What did serve the brewery workers well during this crisis were the structures and priorities of a business union. A nationally coordinated, centrally administered effort to end the lockout of the union nationwide ultimately brought the union back to power. In the course of this shift in activism, the communitywide appeal of the old-style German-American organization was somewhat lost in favor of collaboration with the American Federation of Labor and its allies, but this was a price that the brewery workers saw as necessary in order to win representation for their union. What they got in turn, the support and voice of the American Federation of Labor, was more important to their survival as a craft union in an industrial setting. Within this national umbrella organization of labor, the brewery workers' voice was never as distinct as it had been on the local level in cities like New York; but in its attempt to link the principles of socialism with those of craft consciousness in a centralized union structure, the brewery workers' union resembled the mainstream of the German-American labor movement in many ways.

If adherence to tradition was problematic for the brewery workers, the organized bakers of New York City had an even more difficult task in defining their sense of tradition in positive terms and harnessing tradition in the service of an independent union movement. For the impoverished bakery workers, craft status was almost inevitably tied to sweatshop labor. On the other hand socialism had shallow roots, too, in this barely politicized community. While its leaders aligned themselves with various factions of socialists during the 1880s, this preference did not percolate deep into the rank and file of the union itself. In the end, business unionism won out in the bakery workers' union as well. This was a much delayed consolidation of political direction which illustrates with renewed clarity the pioneering role of the cigar makers and, to some extent, even the brewery workers in American labor's shift to centralized and bureaucratized organization.

The unions discussed in this book started out embodying a community of workers with shared social and cultural characteristics. It was their goal to translate this solidarity based on real or invented traditions into a common political program for the future and to create a political community around such a shared program. But the process of centralization and bureaucratization which went along with these efforts to gain greater political appeal and cohesion usually meant that the original focus of unions on the community of workers, neighbors, and fellow immigrants was left behind. The ultimate goal, a transition from a socially defined to a more politically defined *community* of unionists, remained elusive for North American trade unions.

The problems unions faced when trying to build a political program based on traditional social communities are nowhere more clearly illustrated than in the Henry George campaign of 1886. At the time of the campaign, New York's workers, German and non-German alike, had organized for decades, but little political cohesion had emerged from these attempts. If it had not been for the sudden emergence of a strong protest coalition and the availability of a widely recognized candidate, the Central Labor Union might not have entered the race at all. Even so, the interethnic coalition of labor behind the Henry George campaign was unable to formulate a cohesive political program which could reflect the diversity of this community. Instead, the formulation of a political platform was largely left to the single tax movement, which only had a very narrow base among New York's urban working class. The enthusiasm and cohesion of various ethnic and trade union constituencies carried the movement to an impressive vote on election day, but afterwards this coalition was as far from forming a political labor party as it had been in early 1886. Neither the single taxers nor the socialists, the two largest and most cohesive political groups within the Henry George campaign, were able afterwards to build a lasting movement. The Henry George campaign was not the only time American labor tried to mount a political party amid an electoral campaign, but it exemplified the failure of organized labor to bridge the gap between ethnic communities and political organizations of a large and diverse working class.[3]

Failure to translate their political aspirations into a broad political program binding together an ethnically diverse working class defined the unions' relationship to the political system of this country. Some observers, especially Europeans and German-American socialists, saw the reasons for this failure within the corrupt political culture that had developed because of the weak regulatory powers of the state. As the German social scientist August Sartorius von Waltershausen observed in 1890:

> The North American labor movement . . . differs profoundly from the continental European one in which Socialism and Social Democracy celebrated their first triumphs. The most obvious cause for this difference is the complete difference in political life [*Staatsleben*], power of the state [*Staatsmacht*] and the political consciousness of the people [*politisches Volksbewusstsein*]. The American constitution . . . offers the laboring population of the country the possibility to affect the social policies of their country in peaceful ways through its elected representatives. . . . But the wage laborers . . . are unable to do much with such pure democracy. They come almost exclusively from industry and live in cities. In these cities politics is in the hands of the party with the most money and the most unscrupulous persons. This can never be a young developing labor party.[4]

Waltershausen and other contemporary critics were impressed and appalled at the same time by the crass machine politics and the direct influence of money over electoral and policy outcomes in American political life. This sentiment was shared by the North American socialists and many other labor activists. At the same time, however, these critics overlooked the elasticity and responsiveness of American machine politics, a responsiveness which was embedded into the American political party system at large. In central Europe, working-class activists, excluded in many formal ways from political participation, created a political party movement out of a community of resistance. For the American working class the exclusion from mainstream politics was never as legalistic or systemic as in European countries and resistance to political powerlessness was correspondingly more ad hoc. In fact, as the years after the Henry George campaign demonstrated, the mainstream parties could be and indeed were attractive to labor activists, including many German-Americans, who often found a home within those party organizations. Integration into mainstream parties seemed a more promising route to many German-American unionists than continued separation from electoral politics. In most cases the Democratic and Republican parties succeeded in binding the loyalties of working-class voters just enough to blunt the efforts at independent political party activism on the part of trade unions. But neither the Democrats nor the Republicans would ever become the builders of community which the trade unions had been in their earlier phase.

Were there alternatives to these divisions of party politics, trade union bureaucracy, and community mindedness? The socialists and their voters certainly thought so. They continued to operate under the assumption that the working class of this country would realize how systematically excluded from the political process it really was and wake up to the possibilities of the Socialist party. Like their counterparts in Europe, the socialists promised an integrated cultural, social, and political world in which the divisions of community and organization did not exist. But the price of this adherence to a German model of political action was that the German-American socialists' vision remained both frozen and ethnically exclusive.

For most German-American workers the Socialist party would not play a central political role. Other than sporadic involvement in electoral campaigns, German-American workers in most places, but especially in New York, tried to find within trade unions the kind of political home that a socialist party would have provided in central Europe. This was a tall order for the North American labor movement to fill. Facing often contradictory demands, Gompers and his colleagues in the AFL were aware that forging a cohesive labor organization was difficult enough in itself and that the range of political activism had to be limited if unifying American workers into one organization was the goal.

Even though they were often unhappy with the limited political agenda of the AFL leadership and its antisocialist stand on many issues, most German-American unionists acknowledged the limited range of possibilities for the AFL leadership by the turn of the century. Most of them recognized that it could not be the role of the AFL to build up an alternative political organization. Some of them remained loyal to the Socialist Labor party as well as to their union, but many more found a home solely within the AFL. Thus the unions within the AFL could always count more socialists among their followers than the SLP would ever attract as voters.

"Why is there no socialism in America?"[5] For German workers Sombart's famous question was falsely posed. The answer did not necessarily involve failed ideals, as Sombart thought, but adaptation and transformation of traditions. Socialism was a flexible compound, not a fixed dogma that could only be realized within the parameters of a socialist party. In the United States, collective organizing, pressure politics, and labor reform—all parts of a socialist program which remained important in the New World—could most effectively be practiced within labor unions of skilled workers. It was in casting aside essentialist ideas of socialism and in using their traditions flexibly and creatively that German-Americans of the 1870s and 1880s shaped the American labor movement at a decisive moment in its history.

Notes

Abbreviations

AB	American Brewer	NYAZ	New Yorker Arbeiter
ASt	Arbeiter Stimme		Zeitung
AZ	Arbeiter Zeitung	NYStZ	New Yorker Staats-Zeitung
BZ	Brauer Zeitung	NYVZ	New Yorker Volkszeitung
CMOJ	Cigar Makers Official	SD	Social Democrat
	Journal	USTJ	United States Tobacco
DABZ	Deutsch-Amerikanische		Journal
	Bäckerzeitung	WA	Workingman's Advocate
LS	Labor Standard	WB	Western Brewer

Introduction

1. See for example both volumes of Albert B. Faust, *The German Element in the United States;* Carl Wittke, *Refugees of Revolution;* other studies by Wittke are *Against the Current: The Life of Karl Heinzen* (Chicago, 1945) and *The Utopian Communist* (Baton Rouge, 1950); see also A. E. Zucker, ed., *The Forty-Eighters.*

2. The studies of Frederick Luebke are an exception to this rule: *Immigrants and Politics: The Germans of Nebraska, 1880–1900* (Lincoln, Nebr., 1969) and *German Voters and the Election of Lincoln* (Lincoln, Nebr., 1972).

3. Frederick Luebke, *Bonds of Loyalty: German-Americans and World War I* (DeKalb, Ill., 1974); Phyllis Keller, *States of Belonging: Hugo Münsterberg, George Sylvester Viereck, Hermann Hagedorn, and the German-American Crisis of World War I* (Cambridge, Mass., 1979); Sander Diamond, *The Nazi Movement in the United States, 1924–1941* (Ithaca, 1974). German-Jewish refugees of the Nazi era were almost never seen by historians as "Germans," that is, connected by history or culture to German immigrants. See my M.A. thesis, "*Aufbau-Reconstruction* and the Assimilation of German Jewish Immigrants" (University of Massachusetts, 1975).

4. Kathleen Conzen, *Immigrant Milwaukee;* see, among others, Nora Faires, "Occupational Patterns of German Americans in Nineteenth Century Cities";

and Alan N. Burstein, "Immigrants and Residential Mobility." These studies were influenced by Thernstrom's paradigms of social and occupational mobility, as were some German studies, most prominently Reinhard Doerries's *Iren und Deutsche in der neuen Welt*.

5. Walter Kamphoefner, *The Westfalians;* Stanley Nadel, *Little Germany*.

6. Some of the more prominent studies are: Virginia Yans McLaughlin, *Family and Community: Italian Immigrants in Buffalo, 1880–1930* (Ithaca, 1977); Donna Gabaccia, *From Sicily to Elizabeth Street: Housing and Social Change among Italian Immigrants, 1880–1930* (Albany, 1984); John Bodnar, *Immigration and Industrialization: Ethnicity in an American Milltown, 1870–1940* (Pittsburgh, 1977); Daniel Walkowitz, *Worker City, Company Town: Iron and Cotton-Worker Protest in Troy and Cohoes, New York, 1855–84* (Urbana, 1978); Gary Gerstle, *Working Class Americanism: The Labor Politics in a Textile City, 1914–1960* (New York, 1989). For a more complete list of monographs on immigrant communities see John Bodnar, *The Transplanted: A History of Immigrants in Urban America* (Bloomington, 1985), 267–85.

7. This argument is made most concisely by Hartmut Keil and John B. Jentz in their articles and introduction to *German Workers in Industrial Chicago*.

8. Bruce Levine, *The Spirit of 1848*.

9. Among the major articles and publications are: *German Workers in Industrial Chicago*, with numerous articles on aspects of working-class life in the city; see also the collection of articles on the Chicago Projekt in *Amerikastudien/American Studies*, 29, no. 2 (1984), and in Hartmut Keil and John B. Jentz, eds., *German Workers in Chicago*. See also Keil's *German Workers' Culture in the United States* as well as his "Einwandererviertel und Amerikanische Gesellschaft"; and essays by Bruce Levine ("In the Heat of Two Revolutions: The Forging of German-American Radicalism") and Hartmut Keil ("German Working Class Radicalism from the 1870s to World War I") in Dirk Hoerder, ed., *Struggle a Hard Battle*. See further Hoerder's *Glimpses of the German-American Radical Press*.

10. Even though the close involvement of German immigrants in the origins of the industrial labor movement has always been given at least a nod of recognition, and sometimes extensive institutional treatment, traditional labor histories such as those by Commons and Foner have not dealt with working-class communities of Germans. The newer social histories, on the other hand, show little interest in the formal history of union organizations.

11. Among the older studies useful for my purposes were Hermann Schlueter's *Die Anfänge der deutschen Arbeiterbewegung in Amerika;* Norman Ware's extensive treatment of New York labor politics in *The Labour Movement in the United States*, esp. 258–79; and the differently pitched survey by Robert Ernst, *Immigrant Life in New York City*. Among the important newer studies on working-class New York are Sean Wilentz's *Chants Democratic*, a serious attempt to write a Thompsonian account of New York City's working class in the antebellum era; and Richard Stott's *Workers in the Metropolis*. Christine Stansell's *City of Women: Sex and Class in New York, 1789–1860* (New York, 1986) and Amy Bridges's *City in the Republic* were helpful as well. For

the Civil War era see Nadel, *Little Germany,* and Iver Bernstein, *The New York City Draft Riots.*

12. Among the notable late-nineteenth-century studies are Moses Rischin's *Promised City: New York's Jews, 1870–1914* (Cambridge, Mass., 1962) and Gabaccia's *From Sicily to Elizabeth Street,* although both are also mostly internally focused histories of one immigrant group. Among the useful political treatments of labor and city politics are Irvin Yellowitz, *Labor and the Progressive Movement in New York State;* Howard L. Hurwitz, *Theodore Roosevelt and Labor in New York State;* and, most useful, David Hammack's *Power and Society.*

Chapter 1
New York's German Immigrants

1. Theodore E. Steinway, *People and Pianos.*

2. Ibid., 11, 15; Walter Moeller to Henry Z. Steinway, Jan. 6, 1987, and Henry Z. Steinway to Walter Moeller, Jan. 15, 1987, Steinway family archives, New York City.

3. Steinway, *People and Pianos,* 14; Anna Suderode to Fritz Becker, 1935, Steinway family archives.

4. Carl Friedrich Theodor (C. F. T.) Steinway to his family, Dec. 26, 1857; C. F. T. Steinway to William Steinway, 1865; C. F. T. Steinway to his mother, n.d. (probably mid-1850s)—all in Steinway family archives.

5. For a survey of economic conditions in Germany on the eve of the 1848 revolution see Theodore Hamerow, *Restoration, Revolution, Reaction,* 3–85; and Hans Ulrich Wehler, *Deutsche Gesellschaftsgeschichte,* vol. 2, 25–139, 641–51. The recent research on the decline and change of crafts in nineteenth-century central Europe is vast; for a survey of the many monographic studies see Ulrich Engelhard, ed., *Handwerker in der Industrialisierung: Lage, Kultur und Politik vom späten 18. bis ins frühe 20. Jahrhundert,* and the more specific treatments by Helmut Sedaitis, *Liberalismus und Handwerk in Südwestdeutschland,* 119–39; and Karl Heinrich Kaufhold, "Grundzüge des handwerklichen Lebensstandards in Deutschland im 19. Jahrhundert," 146–49, 159–62. A brief but useful survey is Jürgen Kocka, *Lohnarbeit und Klassenbildung,* 96–110.

6. For a recent summary of the scholarship on workers and 1848 in English, see Levine, *Spirit of 1848,* 35–46. Levine's analysis pays little attention to the failure of the revolution in Germany.

7. Wehler, *Deutsche Gesellschaftsgeschichte,* vol. 2, 759–79; Hamerow, *Restoration,* 228–32, 242–50; and Kocka, *Lohnarbeit und Klassenbildung,* 167–79. See also the succinct summary by Bruce Levine in "Immigrants, Class and Politics," 121–26.

8. Mack Walker, *Germany and the Emigration,* and Wolfgang Köllmann and Peter Marschalck, "German Emigration to the United States." Wolfgang von Hippel, *Auswanderung aus Südwestdeutschland,* 148–280 passim; Kamphoefner, *Westfalians,* 12–68; and Levine, *Spirit of 1848,* 15–19, 30–34.

9. C. F. T. Steinway to his mother, no date (probably mid-1850s); C. F. T. Steinway to his parents and siblings, no date (early 1850s) and Dec. 25, 1854;

C. F. T. Steinway to his family, Wolfenbüttel, no date (early 1850s)—in Steinway family archives.

10. See letters cited in n. 9 and Walter Moeller to Henry Z. Steinway, Jan. 5, 1987, Steinway family archives.

11. The size of the German immigrant population was taken from data provided in the New York State censuses of 1845 and 1855, cited in Ernst, *Immigrant Life in New York City*, appendix 2, 188, 192–94, and the federal population censuses of 1860, 1870, 1880, and 1890; on emigration from Germany see Köllmann and Marschalck, "German Emigration to the United States," 499–554; on the growth of the German community since the early 1870s, see also *NYVZ*, July 4, 1879; and the brief survey in Nadel, *Little Germany*, 22–23.

12. Ernst, *Immigrant Life in New York City*, 198; Nadel, *Little Germany*, 23–24, 37–39.

13. On the Forty-eighters in New York and in the U.S. in general, see Charlotte Brancaforte, ed., *German Forty-Eighters in the United States*, esp. articles by Stanley Nadel and Bruce Levine; Zucker, *Forty-Eighters*, esp. 269–357; Wittke, *Refugees of Revolution*; Ernst, *Immigrant Life in New York City*, 119–20; Nadel, *Little Germany*, 18; and Levine, *Spirit of 1848*, 15–19, 57–61.

14. Nadel, *Little Germany*, 58. Single German women immigrants were almost unheard of, unlike single Irishwomen, who came in relatively large numbers during those years. See Carol Gronemann, "She Works as a Man, She Earns as a Child."

15. Nadel, *Little Germany*, 51–58; Köllmann and Marschalck, "German Emigration to the United States," 536.

16. Nadel, *Little Germany*, 29–31; LaVern Ripley, *The German-Americans* (Boston, 1976), 24; Anton Eickhoff, *In der neuen Heimath*, 131–55; *Charter and By-Laws of the German Society*, 1808; Ernst, *Immigrant Life in New York City*, 139, 89–113; the structure of property ownership and the names of the property owners can be gleaned from the municipal tax assessment books for the Eleventh and Seventeenth wards, Municipal Archives of the City of New York.

17. Steinway, *People and Pianos*, 11; Charles Steinway to C. F. T. Steinway, n.d. (probably fall 1852), Steinway family archives.

18. This sort of chain migration furthered the concentration of Germans in certain skilled trades, especially in the garment industry, woodworking, and cigar making. Similar effects of chain migration have usually been observed for more rural migrant communities prior to the 1890s; see, for example, John Gjerde's *From Peasants to Farmers: The Migration from Balestrand, Norway to the Upper Midwest* (Cambridge, Eng., 1985), 128–34, 137–66; and Kamphoefner, *Westfalians*, 70–105, 170–200. Kamphoefner also discusses the effects of immigrant concentration on general social mobility, pointing out that immigrants who lived in areas of high concentration with fellow *Landsleute* had lower upward mobility rates than those who formed a "minority" in the new home. In an urban context this points to the depressing effects on wages of the large number of Germans in certain trades.

19. On the degradation of traditional crafts in New York City during the

1830s and 1840s see Wilentz, *Chants Democratic*, 107–42; and Nadel, *Little Germany*, 68–74.

20. Charles Steinway to C. F. T. Steinway, n.d. (probably fall 1850), Steinway family archives; Ernst, *Immigrant Life in New York City*, chaps. 6, 7, 8; Wilentz, *Chants Democratic*, 385–86.

21. On the standard and cost of living in industrial Germany see my article, "'For Whom Are All the Good Things in Life?' German-American Housewives Discuss Their Budgets," 145–60.

22. A brief general survey of German immigration to the U.S. in the late nineteenth century can be found in Köllmann and Marschalck, "German Emigration to the United States," 536–41.

23. This constituted an increase of over 200 percent between 1870 and 1900; the city's population at large increased by over 360 percent from over 942,000 to 3,437,000 due to the incorporation of Brooklyn and Queens in 1898.

24. Köllmann and Marschalck, "German Emigration to the United States," 531–36; also *Statistisches Jahrbuch für das Deutsche Reich*, 1880, 19, and for comparative purposes, *Statistisches Jahrbuch für das Deutsche Reich*, 1901, 13–14. For data on the proportion of Germans in New York City see United States Census Bureau, *Ninth, Tenth, Eleventh*, and *Twelfth Census of the United States, Census of Population*; Nadel estimates that by 1880 second-generation Germans made up the majority of German-Americans in New York and that together the two generations supplied at least 30 percent of New York City's population in 1870 and 1880 (*Little Germany*, 41–42).

25. The Greys of the 1880s had been eyed suspiciously as "Greens" when they first arrived by the old-timers ("Greys") of the 1840s, feared for their shiftlessness, radicalism, and rabble-rousing propensities; see, for example, Faust, *German Element in the United States*, vol. 1, 588–91.

26. On intergenerational conflict within the German community see Wittke, *Refugees of Revolution*, 60, 73; Ernst, *Immigrant Life in New York City*, 177–78; *NYVZ*, May 30 and May 19, 1880, and Jan. 4, 1882.

27. "Monatsbericht der Deutschen Gesellschaft" in *NYVZ*, June 6, 1878; also Oct. 10 and Dec. 5, 1878, and Jan. 4, 1882. For proportional shift of German immigrants from southwest to northeast, see the table, "Auswanderer über Deutsche Häfen," in *Statistisches Jahrbuch für das Deutsche Reich*, 1880, 1883–1900; see also Nadel, *Little Germany*, 35–47.

28. *NYVZ*, Jan. 4, 1882; Nadel maintains that there was regional clustering of Germans from certain provinces (especially "Prussia," "Austria," and "Hanover") in the Tenth, Eleventh and Thirteenth wards of the Lower East Side and a stronger clustering in the outlying areas of Brooklyn (*Little Germany*, 37–40, 48–50).

29. Nadel, *Little Germany*, 171–73.

30. Hermann Mosenthal, *Geschichte des Vereins deutscher Liederkranz von New York*.

31. Alfred Kolb, *Als Arbeiter in Amerika*, 30; also *NYVZ*, June 9, 1880; Aug. 27, 1881.

32. Steinway, *People and Pianos*, 34–35; Charles Steinway to C. F. T. Stein-

way, Dec. 19, 1863. On the background of wealthy upper-class Germans in New York City during the Gilded Age, see Theodor Lemke, *Geschichte des Deutschthums in New York.*

33. Out of a random sample of 610 first- and second-generation German-American wage earners in New York's Lower East Side in 1880, 508 lived with their family. Even of the 102 single workers in the sample, 88 had joined a German family as lodgers; only 16 lived in boardinghouses or with non-Germans. My sample was derived from the microfilm Tenth Census of the United States, Population Schedules for New York County, Tenth Ward, New York, 1880. See also Nadel, *Little Germany,* 49–54.

34. My descriptions are based on a study of the manuscript censuses, guidebooks, and maps such as *New York Bädeker, The Sun's Guide to New York, King's Handbook of New York City, Deutscher Wegweiser durch New York und Umgegend.* For other descriptions of the neighborhood see Nadel, *Little Germany,* 58–71; and Richard Liebermann, "The New York City Neighborhoods—A Closer Investigation of the Ghetto," unpublished paper in the author's possession, 6–7.

35. Samuel Gompers, *Seventy Years of Life and Labor,* vol. 1, 24.

36. United States Industrial Commisssion, *Report,* vol. 1, 480; Ernst, *Immigrant Life in New York City,* 38–40; Lawrence Veiller, "A Statistical Study of New York's Tenement Houses," 201–2; and Lawrence Veiller and Robert DeForest, *Tenement House Problem,* vol. 2, appendix 9: "Tenement House Rentals." See also *NYVZ,* Oct. 31, 1881, to Nov. 5, 1881—a series on tenement cigar manufacturing.

37. Tenth Census of the United States, Population Schedules for New York County, Tenth Ward, enumeration district 205, 36–54.

38. Gompers, *Seventy Years,* vol. 1, 493.

39. Stuart Kaufman et al., eds., *The Samuel Gompers Papers,* vol. 1, 17; Nadel, *Little Germany,* 58–59, 66–67; Veiller and DeForest, *Tenement House Problem,* vol. 1, 202–3.

40. Veiller and DeForest, *Tenement House Problem,* vol. 2, appendix 9; Liebermann, "New York City Neighborhoods," map 1, 6–7.

41. Gompers, *Seventy Years,* vol. 1, 33–34.

42. For a list of businesses on the Lower East Side see *Wilson's Business Directory of New York City* during the 1880s. For a more extensive description and maps indicating the locations of businesses on the Lower East Side see my Ph.D. dissertation, "Gewerkschaft und Gemeinschaft: drei deutsche Gewerkschaften in New York City, 1870–1900" (University of Munich, 1983), 36–38.

43. *Wilson's Business Directory for 1880; Sun's Guide to New York,* 88; Thomsen and Detlevs's *Deutscher Wegweiser durch New York und Umgegend.*

44. For a typical uptown block with German settlement see, for example, Tenth Census of the United States, Population Schedules for New York County, enumeration district 598, 1–8; for uptown businesses, see *Murphy's Business Directory for 1888;* cf. *Sun's Guide to New York; Guide to Greater New York,* ed. George Walker (Boston, 1900); and *New York Bädeker.*

45. Friedrich Ratzel, *Sketches of Urban and Cultural Life in North America*, 23.

46. The census classifications are difficult to translate into modern terms. For the purposes of this study the following classifications have been termed "professional": clergymen, dentists, journalists, lawyers, musicians, teachers, physicians, and those working in banking, brokerage, and insurance; the following jobs have been termed "low white collar": clerks, traders and dealers, salesmen, saloonkeepers, bookkeepers, boardinghouse keepers, hotel and restaurant keepers, manufacturers, commercial travelers, and peddlers; the following are termed "unskilled": laborers, teamsters, domestic servants, lumbermen, and factory operatives.

47. A survey of New York's economy during the late nineteenth century remains to be written; a short account is contained in *Eleventh Census of the United States, Report on Manufacturing Industries*, 392–406; see also Jesse Pope, *The Clothing Industry in New York. Tenth Census of the United States*, vol. 1, 892.

48. *Tenth Census of the United States*, vol. 1, 892—the figure is likely to be much higher than 10 percent but large categories such as grocers or food peddlers are not enumerated separately in the printed census by ethnic group.

49. See chapters 7 and 8 below.

50. On bakers see chapter 9 below; on butchers and bakers see *NYVZ*, Dec. 4, 5, 1890; Ernst, *Immigrant Life in New York City*, 88; Wilentz, *Chants Democratic*, 137–40; *Wilson's Business Directory for New York City*, 1880; *Tenth Census of the United States*, vol. 1, 892.

51. Nadel, *Little Germany*, 133; Ernst, *Immigrant Life in New York City*, 86–87; *Wilson's Business Directory for New York City* named hundreds of grocery stores whose proprietors had German surnames in its 1880 edition.

52. Ernst, *Immigrant Life in New York City*, 90–91; *Wilson's Business Directory for New York City*; *Tenth Census of the United States*, vol. 1, 892; on the role of saloonkeepers in later labor conflicts see chapter 8.

53. See chapter 3 below for a history of the cigar industry in New York City.

54. Wilentz, *Chants Democratic*, 119–24; Ernst, *Immigrant Life in New York City*, 175–78; Pope, *Clothing Industry*, 27, 45–46, 52–53, 58–59; *Wilson's Business Directory for New York City*, 1880; *NYVZ*, June 23, 1879; Apr. 25, 1880; on women clothing workers see *NYVZ*, Mar. 29, Sept. 6, and Nov. 4, 1879; Jan. 21 and May 21, 1880; Feb. 1, 1882.

55. For the location of garment-making shops see *Wilson's Business Directory for New York City*.

56. Wilentz, *Chants Democratic*, 124–27; Ernst, *Immigrant Life in New York City*, 78–79; *NYVZ*, May 31, June 1, and June 3, 1890.

57. Very little is known about New York's important furniture industry. For the early period see Wilentz, *Chants Democratic*, 117–29; and Ernst, *Immigrant Life in New York City*, 80–81; for the later period see Peter Strickland, "Schindler, Roller and Co.," *Nineteenth Century*, 6 (Fall 1980): 39–43; *NYVZ*, Feb. 21, 1902; *ASt*, Dec. 3, 1876; and the forthcoming catalogue entry on the Herter Brothers in Katherine Howe and Catherine Hoover Voorsanger, eds., *Herter Brothers: Furniture Makers of the Gilded Age*.

58. On the increasing number of very poor unskilled workers among German immigrants see *NYVZ*, Feb. 26, 1881; *NYVZ*, June 9, 1880.

59. Nadel found that 17–20 percent of German women in the 1870 census indicated that they did wage work, but he estimates their actual percentage at about 35–40 percent (*Little Germany*, 151–52). My own research from the census sample cited in note 33 indicates that out of 432 German families only seventeen sent any women to work.

60. Pope, *Clothing Industry*, 14–30; *NYVZ*, July 3, 1879; Mar. 8, 28, 1881; *USTJ*, June 26, 1885. A tabulation of wages earned by German working-class families can be found in Schneider, "'For Whom Are All the Good Things in Life?'" 148; for data on the cost of living among working-class New Yorkers see also *NYVZ*, Aug. 2, 1880.

61. Gompers, *Seventy Years*, vol. 1, 24.

62. Nadel, *Little Germany*, 156–63; German families were noted for their strictness in enforcing this pattern with their children; see Louise Borland Moore, *Wage Earners Budgets* (New York, 1907), 89–92.

63. Gompers, *Seventy Years*, vol. 1, 155–56.

64. See note 59.

65. According to the census sample from the Tenth Census of the United States, Population Schedules for New York County (see note 33), about half of the 432 German families had only one wage earner, and 7 percent of them were headed by a woman. The German labor press occasionally reported stories on German women who resorted to abortionists because they felt unable to rear children on their own. Others were forced to work as prostitutes (often they had first been seduced as domestic servants) because they were unable to earn an adequate living otherwise; see *NYVZ*, Nov. 16, 1880; Dec. 7, 1890.

66. Deutsche Gesellschaft der Stadt New York, *Jahresbericht*, 1872–80, passim; on Germans in insane asylums see *NYVZ*, Jan. 10, 1882; on suicides, *NYVZ*, Jan. 2, 1890; on Wards Island, see *NYVZ*, Jan. 24, 27, Feb. 11, 14, 1881.

Chapter 2
Politics and Culture of German New York

1. Geoff Eley and David Blackbourn, *The Peculiarities of German History*, 196–97; Ingo Tornow, *Das Münchner Vereinswesen in der ersten Hälfte des 19. Jahrhunderts*; Thomas Nipperdey, "Verein als soziale Struktur im späten 18. und frühen 19. Jahrhundert"; Wolfgang Hardtwig, "Strukturmerkmale und Entwicklungstendenzen des Vereinswesens in Deutschland 1789–1848."

2. Nipperdey, "Verein als soziale Struktur"; Hardtwig, "Strukturmerkmale und Entwicklungstendenzen," 45–50; Dieter Langewiesche, "Vereins und Parteienbildung, 1848–49."

3. Hardtwig, "Strukturmerkmale und Entwicklungstendenzen," 19–39; Klaus Tenfelde, "Die Entfaltung des Vereinswesens während der industriellen Revolution in Deutschland," 69–71, 103–9; Alfons Hueber, "Vereinsrecht im Deutschland des 19. Jahrhunderts," 115–32.

4. Nipperdey, "Verein als soziale Struktur," 29–42; on connections between working-class Vereine and political parties see also Klaus Tenfelde, "Vereinskultur im Ruhrgebiet," 22–33.

5. For listings of Vereine in mid-nineteenth-century New York City see Bretting, *Soziale Probleme Deutscher Einwanderer in New York City,* 201–4; for the late nineteenth century, see Bernhard Meyborg, *Geschichte des plattdütschen Volksfest-Vereen von New York und Umgegend;* and *New Yorker Vereins-Kalender für das Jahr 1884;* an excellent analysis of the role of Vereine and their festivities for German-Americans is Kathleen Conzen, "Ethnicity as Festive Culture."

6. On Church-State relations between 1871 and 1914 see Ernst Rudolf Huber, *Deutsche Verfassungsgeschichte seit 1789,* vol. 4, 645–874 passim; for a concise, critical survey on the position of state and church in Germany up to 1848 see also Wehler, *Deutsche Gesellschaftsgeschichte,* vol. 2, 59–77; or Thomas Nipperdey, *Deutsche Geschichte,* 403–51.

7. Nadel, *Little Germany,* 92–95; and Jay Dolan, *The Immigrant Church,* 22, 84–85, 182. Dolan has a higher figure for active German Catholics in the late 1860s; my estimates were based on the number of German Catholic parishes, the size of the churches, and the enrollment in parochial schools provided in John Gilmary Shea, *The Catholic Churches of New York City,* 123, 189, 356–58, 366, 413, 455, 462–63, 536–37; see also Florence Cohalan, *A Popular History of the Archdiocese of New York,* 156.

8. Dolan, *Immigrant Church,* 77, 79–81; Nadel, *Little Germany,* 92–95; Bernstein, *New York City Draft Riots,* 113–14; for a national assessment of the Catholic church in 1848 see also Levine, *Spirit of 1848,* 94–95.

9. Dolan, *Immigrant Church,* 70–85, 89–98; Nadel, *Little Germany,* 94–95; Coleman Barry, *The Catholic Church and German-Americans,* 186; Karl Arndt and May Olsson, *German-American Newspapers and Periodicals,* 335–411, which counts at least twelve Catholic newspapers and periodicals edited in New York City in 1880; for voluntary associations see also *Sadlier's Catholic Directory,* 104; Shea, *Catholic Churches of New York City,* 189, 356–58, 413, 462, 536; John Talbot Smith, *The Catholic Church in New York,* vol. 1, 326–27; *Handbook of Benevolent Institutions of New York; King's Handbook of New York City,* 448–449.

10. *Sun's Guide to New York,* 272.

11. George U. Wenner, *The Lutherans of New York,* 35–37, 41, 48; Nadel, *Little Germany,* 95–97; *NYVZ,* June 27 and Aug. 20, 1880.

12. On the effects of the Enlightenment on German Jewish self-organization see Stephen Lowenstein, *Frankfurt on the Hudson* (Detroit, 1989), 29–36.

13. Nadel, *Little Germany,* 99–103; Mosenthal, *Geschichte des Vereins deutscher Liederkranz von New York,* 143–61; *Sun's Guide to New York,* 254, 257, 274–75; Arthur Goren, *New York Jews and the Quest for Community,* 17; *Handbook of the Benevolent Institutions of New York;* Hammack, *Power and Society,* 65–68; *King's Handbook of New York City,* 400–402.

14. Nadel, *Little Germany,* 110–11, 116–17; *NYVZ,* Aug. 25, 26, 27, 1878; Aug. 27, 1879; Meyborg, *Geschichte des plattdütschen Volksfest-Vereen.*

15. Nadel, *Little Germany,* 111–12.

16. On the changing character of the Deutsche Gesellschaft see *Charter and*

By-Laws of the German Society (includes membership list), for the years 1808, 1849, 1852, and 1863.

17. Nadel, *Little Germany*, 115–16; Arndt and Olsson, *German-American Newspapers*, 335–411; *Sun's Guide to New York*, 108; see also pp. 82 and 201 on the organizations of cigar store owners and master bakers respectively.

18. Nadel, *Little Germany*, 121; *NYVZ*, Feb. 21, 1903, 36, 39, 47, 59–60. Researchers of the Chicago Project have discussed the efforts at creating an "alternative culture" in the socialist Vereinswelt. See Christine Heiss, "German Radicals in Industrial America," and Klaus Ensslen and Heinz Ickstadt, "German Working Class Culture in Chicago"; see also the essays by Ensslen and Ickstadt in Keil, *German Workers' Culture in the United States*, for similar research; for social democratic culture in Germany see Vernon Lidke, *Alternative Culture*.

19. Levine, *Spirit of 1848*, 84–94; Ernst, *Immigrant Life in New York City*, 112–21.

20. Nadel, *Little Germany*, 118–19, 122–23; Levine, *Spirit of 1848*, 105.

21. Nadel, *Little Germany*, 118–19, 124–30; Levine, *Spirit of 1848*, 117–19, 124–25, 136–38, 140–45; Ernst, *Immigrant Life in New York City*, 112–21; Wittke, *Refugees of Revolution*, 43–54; Schlueter, *Anfänge der deutschen Arbeiterbewegung*, 17, 49–50, 69–70, 86–95.

22. A focus on the abolitionist movement defined the politically active German immigrant working class in the decade before the Civil War, according to Levine's *Spirit of 1848;* see esp. 160–69. Levine's rich study goes far in filling a void in existing scholarship, which commonly either focused on the 1830s and 1840s or on the post–Civil War era. See also Nadel, *Little Germany*, 121.

23. Howard Quint, *The Forging of American Socialism*, 9; Philip S. Foner and Brewster Chamberlin, eds., *Friedrich A. Sorge's Labor Movement in the United States*, 153–55; Schlueter, *Anfänge der deutschen Arbeiterbewegung*, 128–74; Nadel, *Little Germany*, 141–42.

24. Paul Buhle, *Marxism in the United States*, 32–38; Quint, *Forging of American Socialism*, 8–10.

25. Philip Foner, *History of the Labor Movement in the United States*, vol. 1, 448; Foner and Chamberlin, *Friedrich A. Sorge's Labor Movement*, 159–60; Herbert Gutman, "The Tompkins Square Riot in New York City on Jan. 13, 1874"; Stuart Kaufman, *Samuel Gompers and the Origins of the American Federation of Labor*, 48–50; Gompers, *Seventy Years*, vol. 1, 59–62, 82–94.

26. Foner and Chamberlin, *Friedrich A. Sorge's Labor Movement*, 162; Foner, *History of the Labor Movement*, vol. 1, 450–51; Quint, *Forging of American Socialism*, 13–14.

27. Hammack, *Power and Society*, 124. The all-time highs for the SLP in New York City were reached in the late 1870s, when it garnered 2000 votes (in 1877) and 4000 votes (in 1878). John R. Commons, *History of Labour in the United States*, vol. 2, 282; see also ibid., 288; Quint, *Forging of American Socialism*, 16, 18, 23–25; on other socialist election campaigns see *NYVZ*, especially in the first week of November in 1885, 1886, 1887, and 1889; for socialists and immigrants from Germany, see Keil, *German Workers' Culture*, 6–8, 13–17.

28. See note 18; for a good survey of the culture of the German-American socialists see also Hartmut Keil and Heinz Ickstadt, "Elemente einer deutschen Arbeiterkultur in Chicago zwischen 1880 und 1890." See also Keil and Jentz, *German Workers in Chicago.*

29. Levine gives a detailed account of the political allegiance of German immigrants during this period (*Spirit of 1848,* chaps. 6–9 passim). See also Luebke, *Ethnic Voters and the Election of Lincoln* (see Introduction n. 2 above).

30. Interestingly, Havemeyer and Gunther had little connection with their ethnic communities, which may have explained their lack of success. Though, in 1874, Oswald Ottendorfer, editor of the *New Yorker Staats-Zeitung* and a leading figure in the German-American business class and kingmaker of the previous election, himself also failed to gain significant access to the German-American working-class vote. Trying to rescue the reform Democrat coalition he had helped build a year earlier (with Havemeyer as a candidate) he put himself up for mayor but he lost resoundingly in the mayoral contest of 1873 (see Nadel, *Little Germany,* 150–52, and Bernstein, *New York City Draft Riots,* 222–24).

31. For German support of reform candidates during the 1870s see Frederick Leubuscher, *William Frederick Havemeyer,* 148, 151–52; and Howard Gosnell, *Boss Platt and His New York Machine,* 126. On the 1880s see Hammack, *Power and Society,* 125–27. My own voting analysis is based on votes as published in the *New York Herald* for the elections in 1879, 1880, 1882, 1884, 1886, 1887, 1888, 1890, and 1892, after election day in early November; see also Martin Shefter, "The Electoral Foundations of the Political Machine," 273, 280, 282.

32. Nadel, *Little Germany,* 133–36; Carl Degler, "Labor in the Economy and Politics of New York City," 284–309 passim; Edward Spann, *The New Metropolis,* 396; Levine, *Spirit of 1848,* 240, 242, 246; and Bernstein, *New York City Draft Riots,* 185–86.

33. This observation is based on my own voting analysis of the heavily German assembly districts 10, 12, 14, and 24 of Manhattan for the elections of 1879, 1880, 1882, 1884, 1886, and 1888.

34. Hammack, *Power and Society,* 140–53; for German upper–class opinions see the *New Yorker Staats-Zeitung,* which was consistently supportive of reform Democrats.

35. Hammack, *Power and Society,* 140–53; Shefter, "Electoral Foundations," 290–92.

36. Tenfelde, "Entfaltung des Vereinswesens," 24–25.

37. A useful if somewhat cursory history of German trade unions in English is John A. Moses, *Trade Unionism in Germany;* see also the assessments by Klaus Tenfelde, Dieter Schönhoven, and Dirk Müller in *Trade Unionism in Britain and Germany 1880–1914,* ed. Wolfgang Mommsen and Gerhard Husung (London, 1985).

38. Wilentz, *Chants Democratic,* 373, 375–77, 385–86. *Republik der Arbeiter,* Apr. and Aug. 1850; Nadel, *Little Germany,* 126–28; Levine, *Spirit of 1848,* 116–22, 126–45 passim.

39. *Die Reform,* Apr. 24, June 7, 1853; *NYStZ,* Apr. 2, 9, 1853; Sept. 23, 24, 26, 27, Dec. 3, 1859; *Der Arbeiter,* Mar. 27, 1858; Nadel, *Little Germany,* 129–30.

40. *NYAZ,* Sept. 3, 1864; Sept. 15–Dec. 29, 1864, passim, esp. Sept. 30, Oct. 21, 28.

41. *NYAZ,* Oct. 21, 28, 1864; June 12, 1865; *NYStZ,* Oct. 2, 1865.

42. The first edition of the *Arbeiter Union* is dated June 13, 1868. On the Franco-Prussian war and internal conflict see *Arbeiter Union,* July 21 through late Aug. 1870. The split occurred between the antiwar, internationalist socialists and pro-German socialists among German workers. Once again it was a question of European politics which had inflamed passions among Germans in New York, not a problem relating to the American political scene. The demise of the Arbeiter Union coincided with the decline of the National Labor Union.

43. *NYStZ,* June 30 and July 15, 1872; Mar. 28, Apr. 25, 1873. Nadel, *Little Germany,* 138–41, 143; Kaufman, *Samuel Gompers,* 43–54.

44. *AZ,* Nov. 1, 11, 1873. Some arriving German immigrants, on seeing the dismal prospects in the New World, reportedly asked to be taken back to Europe in exchange for ship labor (*NYStZ,* Nov. 13, 1873; see also *AZ,* Sept. 5, 1874).

45. *AZ,* Nov. 1, 1873; Foner and Chamberlin, *Friedrich A. Sorge's Labor Movement,* chaps. 6 and 7; one exception was the German-American printers who drew strength and support from their membership in the International Typographical Union.

46. See chapter 3.

47. *NYVZ,* Nov. 16, 1878; Apr. 5, June 21, 1879; *LS,* Apr. 7, 21, 28, 1877; for cooperatives see *AZ,* Nov. 1, 1873, to late 1874; see also Foner and Chamberlin, *Friedrich A. Sorge's Labor Movement,* 120-21.

48. Foner and Chamberlin, *Friedrich A. Sorge's Labor Movement,* 154, 159–61, 199–206; and Hermann Schlueter, "Die Anfänge der deutschen Arbeiterbewegung und ihre Presse," *NYVZ,* Feb. 21, 1903.

49. Shevitch was supposedly an aristocrat born in the Baltics. He returned to Riga in 1891 with his wife.

50. On the history of the *Volkszeitung* see *NYVZ,* Feb. 21, 1903, esp. 15–16, 20; Dirk Hoerder, Renate Kiesewetter, and Thomas Weber, eds., *Glimpses of the German-American Radical Press,* 9–13; see also Buhle, *Marxism in the United States,* 28–29; and Kaufman et al., eds., *Gompers Papers,* vol. 2, 465.

51. Jonas and Shevitch, despite their criticism of the SLP, ran on the Socialist ticket in local and statewide elections in 1878 and 1887. In 1889 the so-called *Volkszeitung* faction even ousted the leadership of the SLP and installed its own pro-union representative as leaders of the party; see Quint, *Forging of American Socialism,* 25–26, 56–59; Hoerder, Kiesewetter, and Weber, eds., *Glimpses of the German-American Radical Press,* 11.

Chapter 3
New York's Cigar Makers and Their Trade

1. *Ninth Census of the United States,* vol. 1, 793; *Tenth Census of the United States,* vol. 1, 892.

2. Walter Frisch, *Die Organisationsbestrebungen der Arbeiter in der deutschen Tabakindustrie*, 10–14.

3. Ibid.; H. Witteler, *Das Deutsche Zigarrengewerbe*, 111–12; August Zimmermann, "Die Tabakindustrie," 12, 14–16; Franziska Naber, "Die wirtschaftlichen und sozialen Verhältnisse der Zigarrenarbeiter," 19–20, 44.

4. Frisch, *Organisationsbestrebungen*, 7–30 passim. There are almost no references to the large number of Jewish workers in the industry; the few exceptions are Frisch, ibid., 12, and Naber, "Zigarrenarbeiter" (the latter study shows the influence of Nazi anti-Semitism).

5. Frisch, *Organisationsbestrebungen*, 14.

6. Ludwig Heyde, *Die volkswirtschaftliche Bedeutung der technischen Entwicklung in der Zigarren und Zigarettenindustrie*, 144–51; "Die soziale Lage der Zigarrenarbeiter im Grossherzogtum Baden," 39–50, 90–103; Zimmermann, "Tabakindustrie," 18–19; Frisch, *Organisationsbestrebungen*, 31–32; Harald Hitz and Hugo Huber, *Geschichte der Österreichischen Tabakregie*, 174–80.

7. Frisch, *Organisationsbestrebungen*, 15–27.

8. Hitz and Huber, *Geschichte der Tabakregie*, 174–80; Frisch, *Organisationsbestrebungen*, 15–16, 18, 24–25.

9. Kaufman et al., eds., *Gompers Papers*, vol. 1, 4; *CMOJ*, Mar. 1876.

10. Frisch, *Organisationsbestrebungen*, 31–32; Naber, "Zigarrenarbeiter," 28–33; Zimmermann, "Tabakindustrie," 14–19.

11. Frisch, *Organisationsbestrebungen*, 31–88 passim.

12. For settlement patterns see *Ninth Census of the United States*, vol. 1, and *Tenth Census of the United States*, vol. 1.

13. Victor Clark, *History of Manufactures in the United States*, vol. 2, 50; Edith Abbott, *Women in Industry*, 188, 190; *USTJ*, Sept. 11, 1878; Nov. 9, 1881; July 20, 1889.

14. Gompers, *Seventy Years*, vol. 1, 43; *USTJ*, Sept. 11, 1881.

15. *USTJ*, Sept. 11, 1881.

16. Gompers, *Seventy Years*, vol. 1, 34–35, 44, 68–69; *USTJ*, Nov. 9, 1881; July 20, 1889.

17. Abbott, *Women in Industry*, 193–94; Gompers, *Seventy Years*, vol. 1, chaps. 2–4 passim; unfortunately we have no accounts about life in the early cigar shops except from Gompers's memoirs; for the manufacturers perspective see *USTJ*, July 20, 1889.

18. *Ninth Census of the United States*, vol. 1, 793; Abbott, *Women in Industry*, 195; *USTJ*, Nov. 9, 1878, Sept. 11, 1881.

19. Dorothee Schneider, "Gewerkschaft und Gemeinschaft," 60–62.

20. Gompers, *Seventy Years*, vol. 1, 44.

21. Ibid., 34–35, 44, 68–69; *USTJ*, July 20, 1889.

22. United States Department of Labor, *Eleventh Special Report of the Commissioner of Labor*, 557; George McNeill, *The Labor Movement, the Problem of Today*, 597.

23. McNeill, *Labor Movement*, 597.

24. See chapter 2.

25. Gompers, *Seventy Years*, vol. 1, 87.

26. A good description of the cigar–making process can be found in Abbott, *Women in Industry*, chap. 9, and in Willis N. Baer, *The Economic Development of the Cigar Industry*, 81–83. See also *AZ*, Feb. 14, 1874; Meyer Jacobstein, *The Tobacco Industry in the United States*, 82–84, 90; and Gompers, *Seventy Years*, vol. 1, 47.

27. Abbott, *Women in Industry*, chap. 9.

28. United States Commissioner of the Internal Revenue, *Annual Report* for 1863–79 (the data cover the fiscal years, e.g., July 1862–June 1863); this report contains data on the cigars manufactured and sold in each revenue district (New York City had two) and, after 1872, the number of licensed factories in each district.

29. Gompers, *Seventy Years*, vol. 1, 89–90, 106–7; *CMOJ*, 1876–78 passim; *USTJ*, Feb. 2, 1878; *Sun*, Jan. 13, 1878.

30. Abbott, *Women in Industry*, 196–97; Jacob Riis, *How the Other Half Lives*, 136–47; *NYVZ*, Nov. 7, 1881.

31. *NYVZ*, Nov. 7, 1881.

32. Frisch, *Organisationsbestrebungen*, 12–13, 31–32; "Die soziale Lage der Zigarrenarbeiter," 21; Erich Jaffe, "Hausindustrie und Fabrikbetrieb in der Deutschen Zigarrenfabrikation," 288–99.

33. *Ninth Census of the United States*, vol. 1; *Tenth Census of the United States*, vol. 1.

34. These and the following data on families were all taken from the microfilm Tenth Census of the United States, Population Schedules for New York County, for the Eleventh, Thirteenth, and Seventeenth wards. These wards, encompassing much of the Lower East Side and part of the Upper East Side, were examined in their entirety.

35. Ibid.

36. *Twelfth Census of the United States*, vol. 1, 792; see also Schneider, "Gewerkschaft und Gemeinschaft," 201.

37. Tenth Census of the United States, Population Schedules for New York County.

38. Ibid.

39. Thomas Capek, *The Czechs (Bohemians) in New York*, 23–25; Emily Greene Balch, "Slav Emigration—Its Source," 591–601.

40. Capek, *Czechs*, 23–25, 50; *USTJ*, Apr. 20, 1889.

41. Capek, *Czechs*, 23–25.

42. Ibid.; *SD*, Feb. 17, 1875.

43. This information is quite evident from Tenth Census of the United States, Population Schedules for New York County.

44. In the census sample cited above, 170 of the 270 married Bohemian cigar makers were married to other cigar makers.

45. Tenth Census of the United States, Population Schedules for New York County.

46. Abbott, *Women in Industry*, 199. Abbott even maintains that Bohemian women preceded Bohemian men in emigrating and working in the North American cigar industry. According to her, Bohemian women in Chicago were

known to have emigrated in groups without family or male kin, finding work as cigar makers in urban industries. Many of them set up all-female households in groups in order to save money, which was then used to finance the emigration of the rest of the family to America. Contemporary census data for New York, however, do not provide any evidence that this kind of planned female migration occurred in this city; for a list of Bohemian "Ladies' Sickness Societies" see Cigar Makers' Central Organization, *Financial Report*.

47. Capek, *Czechs*, 25–26.

48. Gompers, *Seventy Years*, vol. 1, 63–88; *Workmens Advocate*, Jan. 10, May 2, and Oct. 24, 1874; *Iron Moulders Journal*, Nov. 1873; *Arbeiter Union*, Jan. 13, 1870.

49. Kaufman, *Samuel Gompers*, 22–44; Gompers, *Seventy Years*, vol. 1, 33–34; *SD*, Jan. 3, 1875.

50. *SD*, Jan. 24, 1875.

51. Ibid.

52. *SD*, Dec. 27, 1874; Jan. 24 and Dec. 17, 1875; *Sun*, Feb. 6, 1875.

53. *SD*, June 10, 1874; Jan. 3, 24, Mar. 14, and Dec. 17, 1875; *New York Tribune*, June 17, 1874.

54. *Sun*, Feb. 6, 1874; *AZ*, Feb. 14, 1874; *SD*, Jan. 24, 1875.

55. The CMIU changed some of its admission criteria and administrators in preparation for this unification. At the 1875 CMIU convention in Paterson, New Jersey, the union officially opened its ranks to bunchbreakers and rollers (mold workers), unified its leadership structure, and took steps to edit its own union newspaper. Moreover, Adolph Strasser, who held a membership in Local 90 as well as in the United Cigar Makers, was elected second vice president of the CMIU (McNeill, *Labor Movement*, 601–3).

56. Ibid.; *SD*, Sept. 26, Oct. 24, 31, 1875; *ASt*, Dec. 5, 1875.

57. *SD*, Oct. 24, 1875.

58. Ibid.

59. *SD*, Oct. 22, 1876; *LS*, June 19, 1877.

60. *SD*, Oct. 25, 1875. The constitution theoretically permitted so-called language groupings (*Sprachgruppen*) once the union had grown to at least five hundred members, but this rule effectively prohibited the formation of ethnic groups.

61. *SD*, Oct. 24, 1875. Strasser was a German-speaking Hungarian Jew. There were rumors that he came from a well-to-do-family, and it seems that he had little if any connection to the still small eastern European Jewish community. Gompers was of Dutch Jewish descent, but had been born in London. His mother tongue was English, but he claimed to have learned German well in his youth from his German colleagues in New York. Gompers had, partly through fraternal organizations, partly through his extended family, some connection with the small Dutch Jewish community in the city (Gompers, *Seventy Years*, vol. 1, 109; Kaufman et al., eds., *Gompers Papers*, vol. 1, 504).

62. Gompers, *Seventy Years*, vol. 1, 126; *SD*, Dec. 12, 1875; Mar. 12, 1876.

63. Gompers, *Seventy Years*, vol. 1, 144–45; *CMOJ*, Mar., June, Oct., and Dec. 1876; Feb. 1877; *SD*, Sept. 26, 1875.

64. Gompers, *Seventy Years,* vol. 1, 116–17; *CMOJ,* Apr. and Sept. 1876; *SD,* Oct. 24, 1875; Mar. 12 and Oct. 22, 1876; *LS,* Apr. 7, 1877. Membership fees remained a steep 25 cents a week; in return the local offered life insurance and accident and sick pay. The payment of unemployment funds was attempted but not realized until 1880.

Chapter 4
The Great Strike of 1877

1. Philip Foner, *The Great Labor Uprising of 1877,* 115–24; *New York Herald,* July 23, 24, 26, 27, 1877; *New York Tribune,* July 24, 25, 26, 27, 1877.

2. *New York World,* July 26, 1877; *Sun,* July 24, 25, 26, 1877.

3. *New York World,* July 25, 27, 1877; *Sun,* July 27, 1877.

4. *LS,* Aug. 28, 1877; *Sun,* Dec. 22, 1877; Gompers, *Seventy Years,* vol. 1, 143.

5. *LS,* Sept. 9, 1876; Sept. 23, 1877; *Sun,* Oct. 11, 1877; Gompers, *Seventy Years,* vol. 1, 147.

6. *LS,* Aug. 28, 1877; *SD,* Sept. 26, 1875; *WA,* Oct. 11, 1873; *ASt,* Oct. 10, 1875; Gompers, *Seventy Years,* vol. 1, 117.

7. Gompers, *Seventy Years,* vol. 1, 147–48.

8. *CMOJ,* Oct. 10, 1877.

9. *New York Times,* Oct. 15, 16, 1877; *New York Herald,* Oct. 15, 1877; *NYStZ,* Oct. 17, 1877.

10. *LS,* Sept. 30, Oct. 21, 1877; *NYStZ,* Oct. 16, 1877; *New York Herald,* Oct. 18, 1877; *Sun,* Oct. 18, 1877; *CMOJ,* Nov. 19, 1877.

11. *New York Times,* Oct. 15, 18, 1877; *New York Herald,* Oct. 16, 1877; *USTJ,* Oct. 16, 1877; *Sun,* Oct. 18, 1877; *CMOJ,* Nov. 10, 1877.

12. *New York Times,* Oct. 18, 24, 1877; *Sun,* Oct. 20, 22, 23, 24, 1877; *New York Herald,* Oct. 18, 24, 25, 1877; *New York Tribune,* Oct. 23, 27, 1877; *NYStZ,* Oct. 16, Nov. 12, 1877; *USTJ,* Nov. 27, 1877.

13. *LS,* Aug. 28, 1877; *Sun,* Sept. 6, 1877; *NYStZ,* Oct. 20, 1877.

14. *New York Tribune,* Oct. 17, 1877; *CMOJ,* Nov. 10, 1877.

15. *New York Herald,* Oct. 16, 17, 18, 19, 1877; *New York Tribune,* Oct. 17, 1877; *Sun,* Oct. 19, 1877; *New York Times,* Oct. 16, 1877.

16. *USTJ,* Dec. 4, 1877.

17. *New York Tribune,* Oct. 17, 1877; *NYStZ,* Oct. 17, 1877.

18. *Sun,* Oct. 25, 1877.

19. *Sun,* Oct. 21, 1877; *New York Herald,* Oct. 21, 24, 1877; *New York Times,* Oct. 23, 1877; *CMOJ,* Dec. 10, 1877.

20. *New York Herald,* Oct. 18, 29, 1877; Cigar Makers' Central Organization, *Financial Report.*

21. Cigar Makers' Central Organization, *Financial Report; New York Herald,* Dec. 18, 19, 28, 30, 1877; *CMOJ,* Nov. 10, Dec. 10, 24, 1877; *LS,* Dec. 23, 1877.

22. Cigar Makers' Central Organization, *Financial Report; New York Herald,* Oct. 24, 31, 1877; *Sun,* Oct. 25, 1877.

23. *Sun,* Nov. 14, 1877.

24. The *NYStZ*, by far the largest German newspaper in the city, took a more conservative stand on the strike than most English-language papers. The *Staats-Zeitung* supported the strikers hesitatingly and only for about the first month of the conflict. The paper was openly anti-union in all its articles. Neither the *Staats-Zeitung* nor the *Volkszeitung* nor the *Cigar Makers' Official Journal* report much support from the German Vereine. The *Financial Report* of the Cigar Makers' Central Organization also shows the same fact. I am under the impression that this pattern was to become increasingly frequent in coming years, when the vast network of German Vereine withheld its support from many strikes involving German-speaking workers. See also *NYStZ*, Oct. 18, 20, 23, Nov. 11, Dec. 3, 1877; *Sun*, Oct. 21, 1877; *New York Herald*, Oct. 30, 1877; Gompers, *Seventy Years*, vol. 1, 154.

25. *Sun*, Oct. 22, 26, 27, 1877; *New York Herald*, Oct. 17, 23, 24, 26, 28, 1877; *NYStZ*, Oct. 22, 23, 24, 25, 26, 31, 1877. "Dives" is a nineteenth-century expression for a rich person.

26. *New York Times*, Oct. 16, 1877; *New York Herald*, Oct. 17, 1877; *New York Tribune*, Oct. 20, 1877; the manufacturers' organization seems to have existed before, albeit not in the same form. Among the large firms who were not NMA members were Straiton and Storm (seven hundred workers), Brown and Earle (two hundred workers), and the tenement factories of George Bence, Mendel Brothers, and Schwartzkopf.

27. *NYStZ*, Oct. 20, 29, 1877; *Sun*, Oct. 20, 27, 1877; *New York Herald*, Oct. 18, 24, 27, Nov. 11, 1877; *New York Tribune*, Oct. 24, 1877; *New York Times*, Oct. 23, 1877; *CMOJ*, Nov. 10, 1877.

28. *Sun*, Oct. 21, 22, 1877; *New York Herald*, Oct. 21, 25, 29, Nov. 2, 1877; *USTJ*, Oct. 23, Nov. 6, 1877; *NYStZ*, Oct. 22, Nov. 2, 23, 1877. Among the members of the Cigar Manufacturers and Storekeepers Association was Oscar Hammerstein, editor of the *United States Tobacco Journal*.

29. *New York Herald*, Oct. 19, 26, 27, Nov. 11, 15, 16, 17, 1877; *Sun*, Oct. 18, 19, Nov. 6, 13, 14, 1877; *New York Tribune*, Oct. 19, 20, 1877; *NYStZ*, Nov. 26, Dec. 6, 23, 1877; *Labor Standard*, Nov. 18, 1877.

30. *New York Tribune*, Nov. 2, 13, 15, 1877; *New York Times*, Nov. 13, 15, 1877; *Sun*, Nov. 17, 23, 26, 1877; *New York Herald*, Nov. 11, 13, 20, 22, 1877.

31. *USTJ*, Nov. 13, 1877; *Sun*, Nov. 19, 26, 1877; *NYStZ*, Nov. 20, 1877; *New York Herald*, Nov. 25, Dec. 11, 1877; *New York Tribune*, Nov. 27, 1877; *CMOJ*, Dec. 24, 1877.

32. *Sun*, Nov. 19, 26, 1877; *NYStZ*, Nov. 26, 27, 1877; *New York Herald*, Nov. 25, 26, Dec. 1, 1877; *New York Tribune*, Nov. 16, 23, 26, 1877; *USTJ*, Dec. 12, 20, 1877.

33. *New York Herald*, Oct. 18, Nov. 9, 15, 16, 27, Dec. 18, 1877; *New York Tribune*, Oct. 18, Nov. 12, 16, 1877; *Sun*, Nov. 10, 17, 1877; *NYStZ*, Nov. 15, 27, Dec. 4, 1877.

34. *New York Herald*, Oct. 19, 27, Nov. 6, 8, 1877; *Sun*, Oct. 23, 24, 30, Nov. 3, 4, 6, 1877; *NYStZ*, Nov. 3, 1877.

35. *New York Herald*, Nov. 2, 6, 8, 11, 13, 27, 28, Dec. 1, 1877; *Sun*, Nov. 3, 6, 9, 21, Dec. 22, 1877; *NYStZ*, Nov. 6, 13, 1877; *USTJ*, Dec. 4, 1877; *ASt*, Dec. 9, 1877; *New York Tribune*, Dec. 15, 1877; *LS*, Dec. 23, 1877.

36. *New York Herald*, Oct. 31, Nov. 8, 9, 1877; *NYStZ*, Nov. 3, 1877; *New York Tribune*, Nov. 1, 3, Dec. 1, 1877; *Sun*, Nov. 3, 1877; *USTJ*, Nov. 6, 1877; *New York Times*, Nov. 11, 1877; *CMOJ*, Dec. 10, 1877.

37. *New York Tribune*, Nov. 12, 21, 1877; *New York Herald*, Nov. 13, 15, 16, 20, 22, 24, Dec. 5, 6, 1877; *Sun*, Dec. 22, 1877.

38. *New York Herald*, Nov. 20, 1877.

39. *New York Herald*, Dec. 13, 1877; *New York Herald*, Jan. 7, 1878.

40. *Sun*, Nov. 16, 1877; *NYStZ*, Dec. 7, 1877.

41. *Sun*, Nov. 16, 1877; *New York Herald*, Dec. 7, 1877.

42. *CMOJ*, Dec. 10, 1877.

43. *Sun*, Dec. 7, 1877; *NYStZ*, Dec. 7, 1877; *New York Tribune*, Dec. 7, 1877; *New York Herald*, Dec. 8, 1877.

44. Gompers, *Seventy Years*, vol. 1, 152; *New York Herald*, Dec. 7, 8, 9, 23, 1877; *New York Tribune*, Dec. 6, 1877; *NYStZ*, Dec. 9, 1877; *ASt*, Dec. 16, 1877; *LS*, Dec. 16, 1877; *Sun*, Jan. 12, 1878.

45. *New York Herald*, Dec. 7, 1877; *New York Tribune*, Dec. 7, 1877; *USTJ*, Dec. 11, 1877; *CMOJ*, Dec. 24, 1877; *Sun*, Jan 12, 1878.

46. *New York Herald*, Dec. 11, 14, 20, 22, 1877; *NYStZ*, Dec. 29, 1877; *ASt*, Jan. 13, 1878.

47. *New York Herald*, Dec. 8, 18, 1877; *NYStZ*, Dec. 16, 1877; *USTJ*, Dec. 18, 1877; *ASt*, Jan. 1, 20, 1878; *CMOJ*, Jan. 10, 1878.

48. *New York Herald*, Nov. 22, 1877; *Sun*, Jan. 6, 1878; *New York Herald*, Jan. 6, 10, 16, 1878; *New York Tribune*, Jan. 9, 25, 1878; *LS*, Jan. 13, 1878; *USTJ*, Jan. 26, 1878.

49. *NYVZ*, Jan. 28, 29, 31, Feb. 9, 1878.

50. *NYVZ*, Feb. 7, 9, 14, 18, 25, 1878; *CMOJ*, Nov. 1878.

51. *CMOJ*, Jan. 10, 1878; *New York Tribune*, Jan. 18, 1878; *Sun*, Jan. 20, Feb. 4, 1878; *NYVZ*, Feb. 4, 11, 14, Apr. 9, 17, 1878.

52. *CMOJ*, Feb. 10, 1878.

Chapter 5
Cigar Makers and Trade Unions

1. The cigar makers' union first reported that the New York trade was brisk in late 1879. The upsurge continued throughout the fall of that year, and from Aug. 1879 until Jan. 1880 cigar makers enjoyed full employment almost continuously. The rhythm of long-lasting seasonal highs (followed by a cyclical slack season during the winter) was repeated during the following years, becoming irregular after 1884 and dropping after 1887, as the industry entered its permanent decline in New York. Overall figures from the Commissioner of Internal Revenue for 1879 show an increase in cigar production of over 42 percent more than 1877, the bottom year of the depression; see also *USTJ*, Aug. 30, Nov. 1, 1879; *CMOJ*, Apr. through Nov. 1880 and Oct. 1878. The *CMOJ* published monthly reports about the state of the trade for all cities with CMIU locals; see also *CMOJ* for the summer months of 1881 and 1882 respectively.

2. See United States Commissioner of the Internal Revenue, *Annual Report*, for data on factories and production; for labor force data on the early 1880s see *USTJ*, Nov. 1, 1879; *NYVZ*, Feb. 21, Mar. 17, 1880. The 1880 census counted 13,920 cigar makers among New York's inhabitants, but this figure seems too low in light of the sources cited above.

3. *USTJ*, Oct. 22, 1881; also Apr. 13, 1878; May 1, 1880; Jan. 8, 1881.

4. *USTJ*, Oct. 22, 1881.

5. See note 76.

6. Data for 1877 are taken from information published in the *CMOJ* during the 1877 strike, especially in the editions of Nov. and Dec. 1877; for 1881 see *United States Tobacco Journal*, "Directory of Cigar Manufactures"; for 1888, *USTJ*, Apr. 14, 1888.

7. Glenn Westfall, "Don Vincente Ybor y Martínez, the Man and His Empire"; *USTJ*, Oct. 21, 1878; Oct. 22, Nov. 20, 1881.

8. *USTJ*, Apr. 14, 1888; *CMOJ*, July 1889; see also Schneider, "Gewerkschaft und Gemeinschaft," 137. On the industry in Pennsylvania and its origins see Patricia Cooper, *Once a Cigar Maker*, 163–65.

9. *USTJ*, Apr. 22, 1882.

10. Capek, *Czechs*, 25–26.

11. My name analysis of the manuscript census showed that many "Germans" seem to have been Polish Jews who were enumerated as Germans by the census takers since western Poland was part of the kingdom of Prussia during much of the nineteenth century (see chapter 3, note 34, for a description of the sample).

12. *USTJ*, Mar. 4, 1884.

13. *NYVZ*, July 3, 1882.

14. *USTJ*, Aug. 18, 1888; *NYVZ*, Aug. 16, 1888.

15. *NYVZ*, Aug. 16, 1888.

16. Ibid. and *USTJ*, Aug. 18, 1888.

17. United States Industrial Commission, *Report*, vol. 15, 470; Capek, *Czechs*, 22–23.

18. The *New Yorker Volkszeitung* printed a lot of news on cigar makers' strikes, particularly during the following periods: Sept.–Nov. 1879; Apr. 16–24 and May of 1880, Apr., June, and Aug. 1881; for an example of how the strikes were organized see reports on the walkout at Kerbs and Spiess in *NYVZ*, Dec. 24, 1880–Jan. 18, 1881.

19. According to the *CMOJ* almost thirty new members signed up each month with Local 144 during the summer and fall of 1880, but most of these new recruits dropped out after three months or less; see *CMOJ*, Oct.–Dec. 1880, and monthly from there on, and *NYVZ*, June 19, 1880.

20. *NYVZ*, Feb. 14, 1881.

21. *NYVZ*, Nov. 23, 1881. For the first time, the elite cigar packers, who had been organized separately, agreed to join the CMIU as a separate local. The cigar packers had been an organized group for some time but had stayed aloof from the union up to then (*NYVZ*, Mar. 28, Apr. 10, Sept. 26, Oct. 13, 14, 1879; *CMOJ*, June 1878).

22. *NYVZ*, Feb. 23, Mar. 31, 1881; *CMOJ*, Apr. 1880; Apr. and July 1881; Feb. 1882; Apr. 1883. The success can be gleaned from the lists of new members which the *CMOJ* published regularly from 1880 on. Whereas none of the fifty-one new members of Local 144 had an identifiably Czech name in January of 1881, 13 percent of the new members had Czech surnames a year later, and by the fall of 1883 the majority of new names were Czech, while the number of members with English (or Anglicized) names dramatically dropped off during the same period.

23. Reasons other than demographics played an important role in this decision to reintroduce ethnic unionism into the CMIU in a controlled way. See pages 102–3; *CMOJ*, Oct. and Nov. 1882; June and Sept. 1883; Dec. 1884; Apr. 1885; *NYVZ*, Sept. 27, Nov. 22, 1882.

24. Gompers, *Seventy Years*, vol. 1, 147–48; see also *CMOJ*, Dec. 1881; Jan. 1882; *NYVZ*, Dec. 15, 1881; Jan. 10, 16, 1883; *USTJ*, Oct. 22, 1881.

25. *NYVZ*, Oct. 28, 1878.

26. Gompers, *Seventy Years*, vol. 1, 184–85; *NYVZ*, Jan. 24, Feb. 12, 22, 1879; *USTJ*, Feb. 22, June 30, 1879; *CMOJ*, Mar. and June 1879; Gompers, *Seventy Years*, vol. 1, 185.

27. *NYVZ*, June 2, 23, Nov. 19, 1879; *NYVZ*, Feb. 21, 28, Apr. 2, 3, 4, 5, 1880; *CMOJ*, July 1879; Mar.–Aug. 1880; Dec. 1881; Mar. 1882; *USTJ*, July 5, 1879; Apr. 3, 1880; July 16, Oct. 1, 15, Nov. 19, 1881.

28. *NYVZ*, Oct. 31–Nov. 4, 6, 7, 11, 12, 14, Dec. 12, 15, 1881; Gompers, *Seventy Years*, vol. 1, 192–93.

29. Gompers recalled in his memoirs, "In the closing hours of the legislature, a member from Buffalo called for consideration of the bill. . . . The clerk looked in the file where the official copy should have been, but the space was empty. The search continued, but meanwhile the legislative situation altered, so that no action could be had." He attributed this "theft" to the connivings of the Senate Speaker, "Bald Eagle" Husted (*Seventy Years*, vol. 1, 192–93).

30. The beginning of regular involvement of organized labor in the passage of reform legislation has usually been put into the Progressive Era. For a survey of labor activism in the legislative arena in New York City and state, see Yellowitz, *Labor and the Progressive Movement*, esp. chap. 5, 88–127; for other descriptions of labor lobbying in the legislative arena see Robert Asher, "Failure and Fullfillment: Agitation for Employers Liability Legislation and the Origins of Workmen's Compensation in New York State 1876–1910," *Labor History*, 24 (1983): 198–222; and Roger W. Walker, "The AFL and Child Labor Legislation: An Exercise in Frustration," *Labor History*, 11 (1970): 321–440.

31. *ASt*, May 12, 18, 1878.

32. Gompers, *Seventy Years*, vol. 1, 190–92; *NYVZ*, Nov. 11, 19, 1879; Jan. 2, 9, 16, Feb. 9, Mar. 16, 1880; Nov. 2, 1881.

33. *NYVZ*, May 22, 25, July 19, 21, 26, 1881; Jan. 16, Feb. 21, Apr. 18, 1882.

34. *NYVZ*, July 26, 1880; May 18, Aug. 28, Sept. 14, Nov. 5, 7, 1881; Jan. 7, 9, Feb. 2, 1882.

35. *NYVZ*, Jan. 9, 11, 16, Feb. 21, Mar. 16, 24, Apr. 1, 4, 1882; *CMOJ*, Feb. 1882; Gompers, *Seventy Years*, vol. 1, 199–200.

36. *NYVZ*, Mar. 24, 1882. In addition to the candidates named below the socialists also backed a Czech cigar maker named Novak. The CMIU slate of candidates backed by the union's established leaders consisted of Meyer Dampf, an experienced trade unionist; John Bloete, like Dampf, a friend of Gompers; a cigar maker named Rosenberg; and George Hallahan, one of the few English-speaking members involved in the conflict.

37. Samuel Schimkowitz, a German immigrant, was elected president; George Walter, a longtime socialist activist and immigrant from Hamburg, became treasurer; and Vincent Woytisek, a Bohemian cigar maker, became vice president. The only nonsocialist elected was George Hallahan as secretary (*NYVZ*, Apr. 8, 1882).

38. CMIU president Strasser claimed that Samuel Schimkowitz, the socialist, could not hold office because he had a manufacturer's license, an accusation Schimkowitz refuted. Nevertheless, the CMIU executive backed Strasser, ruled the election results to be invalid, and put candidates of its own choice into office (*NYVZ*, Apr. 8, see also May 6, 1882; *CMOJ*, May and June 1882).

39. *NYVZ*, Apr. 14, 15, June 8, 24, 1882.

40. *NYVZ*, July 14, 17, 1882.

41. *Progress*, Aug. 1882; Sept., Oct., and Nov. 1882; May 1883; *NYVZ*, July 24, 25, Aug. 18, 1882.

42. In response to the emergence of the CMPU, the CMIU modified its leadership structure somewhat in 1883. The new constitution passed at the CMIU's Toronto annual meeting that year lowered membership dues and reorganized the leadership so that union president Strasser was now to be assisted by no fewer than six vice presidents, who came from different parts of the country and would make important decisions collectively. If any local disagreed with this collegial board on a major issue, it could demand a vote by all locals. Although cumbersome, this procedure was in fact used frequently in the coming years. On the local level the CMIU met the progressive challenge by chartering two new locals, one (No. 141) Bohemian, the other (No. 13) a German group. Two new locals were also chartered in Brooklyn. Nevertheless the large "American" Local 144 continued to dominate the CMIU in New York (*CMOJ*, Sept. 1883; see also *NYVZ*, Apr. 27, July 25, 27, 30, Aug. 7, 15, Oct. 3, Nov. 22, 1882; *CMOJ*, Oct. and Nov. 1882; June, Sept., Oct., Nov. 1883; Dec. 1884; Apr. 1885; *Progress*, Aug. and Oct. 1882).

43. *CMOJ*, Sept. 1883; "President's Biennial Report," *CMOJ*, Sept. 1885; also *CMOJ*, Sept. and Dec. 1883; Oct. 1884; June and Nov. 1886.

44. *CMOJ*, Mar. 1886.

45. The best brief summary of the importance and role of the Federation of Trade and Labor Unions can be found in Kaufman et al., eds., *Gompers Papers*, vol. 1, 275-77.

46. Within a year it had taken root in other East Coast and midwest cities from Boston to Massillion, Ohio (*NYVZ*, July 25, 27, 30, 1882; Aug. 7, 15, 1882; *Progress*, Aug. and Oct. 1882).

47. *Progress*, Oct. and Nov. 1882; June 1883; *NYVZ*, Sept. 8, 11, Nov. 29, 1882; Jan. 5, 8, 11, 12, 15, 18, 20, Nov. 29, 1883; *CMOJ*, Aug. and Sept. 1883.

48. *NYVZ,* July 24, 1882.

49. *Progress,* Aug. 1882.

50. *USTJ,* Dec. 21, 1882.

51. For descriptions of cultural activities among progressive cigar makers see *Progress,* Sept., Oct., and Dec. 1882; *NYVZ,* Aug. 23, 25, 1884.

52. *NYVZ,* Apr. 3, July 17, 24, 31, Aug. 7, Sept. 18, 24, 1882; Oct. 19, 20, 22, Nov. 4, 7, 1883; *John Swinton's Paper,* Oct. 14, 26, 1883.

53. As the labor movement in the city continued to grow at a rapid pace in the mid-1880s, such diverse trades as the carpenters and other building trades and, after 1885, the musicians, bakers, brewers, and many others experienced a period of so-called dual unionism caused by ethnic and political fissures. On building trades' rivalries see *John Swinton's Paper,* Sept. 14, 22, 1884; for later union rivalries (musicians, bakers) see *John Swinton's Paper,* Feb. 21, June 13, 20, Dec. 12, 1886; *NYVZ,* Sept. 4, 1882; Oct. 19, 1885.

54. *Progress,* Oct. 1882; Feb. 1883; *The People,* Sept. 1891; Ware, *Labour Movement,* 265–69; Kaufman, *Samuel Gompers,* 36–37; Commons, *History of Labour,* vol. 2, 399–401. Members of the CMIU also joined the Knights in New York; against the protest of D.A. 49, they received a charter from the leadership of the Knights in order to counteract the effectiveness of the CMPU's alliance. But with D.A. 49 in ascendance during a national power struggle over the next two years, the CMIU could not counteract what strength the CMPU derived from their pact with the district assembly (Ware, ibid.).

55. Despite its name the organization at that point was not national nor did it include most manufacturers. Only some of the largest shop operators joined it (*CMOJ,* Feb. and July 1879; *USTJ,* May 15, 1880; *NYVZ,* Feb. 17, 1881).

56. *USTJ,* Apr. 4, 1885. The NCMA joined forces with the New York Leaf Tobacco Board of Trade in 1885.

57. The progressive union also pursued an anti-tenement campaign, but much less vigorously and consistently than the CMIU. It mainly addressed itself to the working conditions and low wages of the tenement workers and encouraged them in numerous mass meetings to organize themselves. No legislative efforts were made by the CMPU (*NYVZ,* Jan. 16, 1883; *Progress,* Oct. 26, 1883; *NYVZ,* Nov. 18, 1882; Jan. 6, 1886).

58. For a more detailed description of the second phase of the anti-tenement campaign see Schneider, "Gewerkschaft und Gemeinschaft," 172–74; also *NYVZ,* Dec. 10, 21, 1882; *CMOJ,* Mar. and Apr. 1883; *USTJ,* July 7, Oct. 27, 1882; Mar. 17, Aug. 28, Dec. 15, 1883; Jan. 6, Oct. 6, 1886; Gompers, *Seventy Years,* vol. 1, 191–93; *Progress,* June and Oct. 1883; Jan. 1884.

59. *NYVZ,* Dec. 21, 24, 1887; June 16, 23, 30, 1888; Jacobstein, *Tobacco Industry,* 91.

60. *CMOJ,* Oct. 1884; Gompers, *Seventy Years,* vol. 1, 193–94; *USTJ,* Sept. 8, 22, 29, Oct. 6, 1883.

61. *Progress,* Aug. 1883; *CMOJ,* Aug. 1883; *USTJ,* May 5, 1883; *NYVZ,* July 17–21, 27, 1883.

62. *NYVZ,* July 18, 1883.

63. *NYVZ,* July 18, 19, 20, 21, 25, 29, Aug. 3–5, 18, 24–26, 31, 1883; *Progress,* Aug. 1, 28, 1883.

64. *Progress*, Mar. 25, Apr. 22, 25, May 27, 1884; *CMOJ*, Mar. 1884. Even though the boycott was ineffective and declared void in New York, the officials of the national Knights continued to place Straiton and Storm's cigars on their list. Their failure to remove the boycott officially had delayed effects in New England in 1885. When the firm found out that the numerous Knights in New England still boycotted its cigars, it reached an agreement permitting the CMIU to organize its workers (*USTJ*, Nov. 28, 1885; *John Swinton's Paper*, Dec. 6, 1885).

65. *NYVZ*, Aug. 25, 1884; see also *NYVZ*, July 20, 1885.

66. *CMOJ*, Oct. 1885; Jan., Apr., May, 1886; *John Swinton's Paper*, Nov. 8, Dec. 13, 1885.

67. *USTJ*, Oct. 17, 24, 31, 1885; *NYVZ*, Jan. 3, 17, 19, 20, 23, 27, 28, 1886.

68. *NYVZ*, Jan. 7, 9, 12–16, 1886; *USTJ*, Jan. 16, 1886.

69. *NYVZ*, Jan. 17, 19, 20, 23, 27, 28, 1886; *USTJ*, Jan. 16, 1886; Ware, *Labour Movement*, 103–12.

70. *NYVZ*, Jan. 26, 1886.

71. *NYVZ*, Jan. 22, 23, 26, 28, 1886; *USTJ*, Jan. 30, 1886.

72. Though 102 wage groups received a slight raise, in seventy-five classes of work cigar makers would have their pay reduced compared to the previous year. As it happened, the pay cuts were mostly aimed at the most skilled cigar makers, who were only scantily represented in the CMPU. For the majority of low-paid members of the CMPU the new contract brought a slight increase in wages.

73. *NYVZ*, Jan. 15, 20, 21, 23, 31, Feb. 8, 12, 13, 1886; *USTJ*, Jan. 9, 30, Feb. 6, 13, 1886.

74. *NYVZ*, Feb. 8, 9, 14, 24, 25, 1886; *John Swinton's Paper*, Feb. 28, 1886.

75. Ware gives a blow-by-blow account of this complicated conflict (*Labour Movement*, 272–79); see also Schneider, "Gewerkschaft und Gemeinschaft," 197–98; and *NYVZ*, Apr. 24, 29, July 26, 1886.

76. The cigar-bunching machine had been developed by the firm of Lewyn and Mortin, a New York cigar manufacturer, during the previous year, and was in use in a number of firms by the spring of 1886. The hand-cranked machine made cigar bunches mechanically and thus eliminated the need for bunchmakers. One machine operator (usually a woman) replaced five to six bunchmakers. By mid-1886 four to five thousand bunchmakers (again, mostly women) had lost their jobs to the machine. The CMIU did not permit the use of bunch-making machines in its shops, and the members of the CMPU were also opposed to its use despite the agreement made on their behalf by the Knights. In exchange for the Knights' permission to use the machines, the manufacturers had made a one-time payment to the District Assembly 49. This arrangement increased tensions between the Knights and the progressives considerably during the summer (*NYVZ*, July 29, 30, Aug. 1, 1886).

77. *CMOJ*, Aug. 1886; *NYVZ*, July 30, Aug. 1, 3, 8, 1886; *John Swinton's Paper*, Aug. 1, 15, 1886; *NYVZ*, Aug. 1, 3–6, 8, 9, 1886; *USTJ*, Aug. 7, 1886.

78. *NYVZ*, July 29, Aug. 1, 3, 8, 1886; *USTJ*, Aug. 7, 1886.

79. On a national level, however, the CMIU leadership had become very

involved in the conflict between the Knights and the cigar makers' unions which was taking a toll on the union elsewhere as well. Strasser and Gompers even addressed the Knights' general assembly in Cleveland and pleaded the cause of independent trade unionism there (*NYVZ*, May 26, June 2, 1886; see also Kaufman et al., eds., *Gompers Papers*, vol. 1, 395–96, 399–409).

80. *John Swinton's Paper*, Aug. 1, 8, 1886; *NYVZ*, Aug. 2, 4, 5, 7, 11, 12, 1886.

81. *USTJ*, Aug. 14, 1886; *John Swinton's Paper*, Aug. 15, 1886; *NYVZ*, Aug. 11, 12, 13, 14, 18, 25, 28, Sept. 10, 1886.

82. *NYVZ*, July 27, 1886.

83. *NYVZ*, Aug. 14, 15, 17, 1886; *John Swinton's Paper*, Aug. 15, 1886; *USTJ*, Aug. 21, 1886.

84. *CMOJ*, Sept. 1886.

85. *CMOJ*, Apr., Aug. 1888; Oct. 1889.

86. *CMOJ*, Nov. 1887; Oct. 1889.

87. *CMOJ*, Sept. 1889; Apr. 1890; Sept. 1912, 18; for a survey of union locals see also the last pages of the *CMOJ*, especially in 1899–1900.

88. For changes affecting the New York industry see *CMOJ*, Sept. 1887; *USTJ*, Aug. 8, 1888; United States Department of Labor, *Eleventh Special Report of the Commissioner*, 581–82. On the cigar industry around the turn of the century see Willis N. Baer, *The Cigar Industry in the United States* (New York, 1933), 99–106; Jacobstein, *Tobacco Industry*, 90–91; Abbott, *Women in Industry*, 194–97; for a study of the largely rural Pennsylvania cigar industry in the early twentieth century, see Cooper, *Once a Cigar Maker*.

89. See regular reports by the CMIU's organizer, e.g., *CMOJ*, June and Oct. 1887; also United States Department of Labor, *Eleventh Special Report of the Commissioner*, 357–58, 368–71.

90. *CMOJ*, Apr., June, July, and Aug. 1888; Sept. 1889; *NYVZ*, Sept. 22, 1889.

91. There are numerous accounts of the eight-hour movement, which was nationwide. For New York City in particular, see Gompers, *Seventy Years*, vol. 1, 289–94; *NYVZ*, Sept. 7, 14, Nov. 10, 14, Dec. 4, 14, 1885; Feb. 28 and 15, Mar. 30 and daily from Apr. 13 through May 7, as well as June 20, 1886; *John Swinton's Paper*, Feb. 4, Mar. 14, 23, and weekly through Apr. and early May 1886; Kaufman et al., eds., *Gompers Papers*, vol. 1, 275–78.

92. On the Henry George campaign the New York labor press such as *John Swinton's Paper* and the *New Yorker Volkszeitung* had reports in almost every issue from late Sept. through Nov. 7; for earlier reports see also *NYVZ*, Aug. 1, 8, 15, 17, 20, 27, 1886; and Gompers, *Seventy Years*, vol. 1, 311–26; see also chapter 6.

Chapter 6
Working-Class Politics and the Henry George Campaign of 1886

1. The literature on the Henry George mayoral campaign is large. The most detailed account is Louis F. Post and Frederick Leubuscher, *An Account of the George-Hewitt Campaign;* other, more analytical treatments can be found in Alexander Speek, "The Single Tax and the Labor Movement"; Hurwitz, *The-*

odore Roosevelt and Labor; Thomas Condon, "The Politics of Reform and the New York City Election of 1886"; Charles A. Barker, *Henry George,* 453–81; Hammack, *Power and Society,* 172–76 and 112–15; Commons, *History of Labour,* vol. 2, 446–54.

2. Speek, "Single Tax," 26; *John Swinton's Paper,* July 4, 1886.

3. Eric Foner, "Class, Ethnicity and Radicalism in the Gilded Age."

4. Speek, "Single Tax," 69–70; Commons, *History of Labour,* vol. 2, 449–50.

5. Speek, "Single Tax," 41–42; Ware, *Labour Movement,* 111–15.

6. Two other labor groups, the Amalgamated Trade and Labor Union and the German unions' United German Trade Unions (Vereinigte Deutsche Gewerkschaften), existed parallel to the CLU, at least in its early years. Overtures by Samuel Gompers and Adolph Strasser to join the Amalgamated Trade and Labor Union were rather brusquely rebuffed by the Central Labor Union. The German unions who were members of the United German Trades encouraged their members to join the CLU (*NYVZ,* Jan. 31, Feb. 6, 27, Mar. 11, 13, 18, Apr. 17, 1882).

7. *NYVZ,* July 17, 1882, also June 26, July 24, 1882.

8. *NYVZ,* Aug. 7, 21, Oct. 23, 30, 1882; Oct. 19, 20, 22, Nov. 4, 7, 1883; *John Swinton's Paper,* Oct. 14, 1883.

9. The German brewery workers and bakers were both organized with the active support of the Central Labor Union, see chapters 7 and 9 respectively; for other strikes and unions supported by the CLU see Speek, "Single Tax," 29–31, and the numerous reports in the *New Yorker Volkszeitung* and *John Swinton's Paper* between 1884 and 1886.

10. Speek, "Single Tax," 29; *John Swinton's Paper,* Aug. 10, Sept. 7, 1884; Jan. 21, Feb. 7, June 6, 13, 1886.

11. *John Swinton's Paper,* Nov. 24, 1884; June 6, 13, 20, 1886; *NYVZ,* Mar. 13, 1886.

12. *NYVZ,* July 16, 1885; among the more prominent unions which resigned were the furniture workers' Local 7 and Robert Blissert representing the Journeymen Tailors' Union; see *NYVZ,* July 10, 1882; Jan. 26, June 29, July 16, 23, Oct. 26, Nov. 2, 1885; *John Swinton's Paper,* Oct. 26, Nov. 9, 24, 30, Dec. 7, 13, 1884.

13. *John Swinton's Paper,* Dec. 21, 1884.

14. Speek, "Single Tax," 31–32; Commons, *History of Labour,* vol. 2, 375–85; *John Swinton's Paper,* Mar. 21, Apr. 25, May 2, 9, 16, 30, 1886; *NYVZ,* Sept. 7, Nov. 9, 16, Dec. 4, 1885, Jan. 24, Feb. 15, Mar. 30, Apr. 13, 18, 25, 29, 30, May 1, 2, 3, 4, 7, 10, 11, 20, June 1, 1886.

15. United States Industrial Commission, *Report,* vol. 2, 623, quoted in Commons, *History of Labour,* vol. 2, 386.

16. Commons, *History of Labour,* vol. 2, 444–45; *NYVZ,* Mar. 10, July 5, 8, 1886; *John Swinton's Paper,* July 11, 1886.

17. *NYVZ,* June 23, 30, 1886; *John Swinton's Paper,* July 11, 1886; Commons, *History of Labour,* vol. 2, 445; Speek, "Single Tax," 58–61.

18. *NYVZ,* July 5, 8, 1886.

19. Commons, *History of Labour,* vol. 2, 446; Speek, "Single Tax," 62–63;

NYVZ, July 16, 25, 1886; *John Swinton's Paper*, July 25, 1886; Post and Leubuscher, *George–Hewitt Campaign*, 5–6.

20. *NYVZ*, Aug. 6, 1886.

21. Ibid.; *John Swinton's Paper*, Aug. 8, 1886; Post and Leubuscher, *George-Hewitt Campaign*, 6–7; Speek, "Single Tax," 63–64. John Morrison, a Knights of Labor machinist and critic of District Assembly 49, was elected to chair the meeting, winning over James Archibald, who was more closely identified with the Knights locally, and George Block, a German-American socialist. The most articulate opponents of political action were the members of Local 6 of the typographical union, a powerful craft union in the city who argued that "it will require much money and a knowledge of practical politics to make even a decent showing at the polls" (*John Swinton's Paper*, Aug. 1, 1886).

22. Post and Leubuscher, *George-Hewitt Campaign*, 6–11; Speek, "Single Tax," 65–66; *NYVZ*, Aug. 20, 27, 1886; *John Swinton's Paper*, Sept. 5, 1886.

23. *NYVZ*, Aug. 27, 1886; *John Swinton's Paper*, Sept. 5, 1886.

24. *NYVZ*, Aug. 27, Sept. 12, 1886; Speek, "Single Tax," 64–65.

25. *John Swinton's Paper*, Sept. 5, 12, 1886.

26. *John Swinton's Paper*, Sept. 12, 1886.

27. *NYVZ*, Sept. 25, 1886.

28. *NYVZ*, July 12, 15, 16, 25, 1886; *John Swinton's Paper*, July 25, Aug. 1, 1886.

29. *NYVZ*, July 25, 1886; Hurwitz, *Theodore Roosevelt and Labor*, 116–17.

30. *NYVZ*, Oct. 14, 1886.

31. *NYStZ*, Sept. 28, Oct. 5, 6, 15, 1886.

32. *NYVZ*, Oct. 31, 1886.

33. One prominent black leader of the Knights, Frank Farell, was also prominent in the campaign organization; Speek, "Single Tax," 63–64; *NYVZ*, Aug. 6, 20, 27, 1886.

34. Speek, "Single Tax," 66–71; Post and Leubuscher, *George–Hewitt Campaign*, 13–16; *NYVZ*, Sept. 23, 1886; *NYStZ*, Sept. 24, 25, 1886; *John Swinton's Paper*, Sept. 26, 1886.

35. Speek, "Single Tax," 70; Hurwitz, *Theodore Roosevelt and Labor*, 116–17; *NYVZ*, Oct. 1, 1886.

36. The organizers of the campaign took some pains to define broadly the meaning of working class. They held a campaign rally for "a large class of working men . . . who belonged to no labor organization, and whom the vulgar do not classify as working-men. These were physicians, clergymen, lawyers, teachers and working employers." Among the middle-class supporters was Daniel DeLeon, at that time an obscure lecturer at Columbia University (Post and Leubuscher, *George-Hewitt Campaign*, 15–16, 128–49; *NYVZ*, Sept. 19, 1886; Speek, "Single Tax," 84–86).

37. *NYStZ*, Sept. 26, 1886.

38. The Gilded Age prose of the *Staats-Zeitung* is worth quoting in the original: "die Mayorswahl hat so aussergewöhnliche Prinzipienfragen angeregt, dass eine intelligente Beurteilung derselben höhere Anforderungen an das

Denkvermögen der Wähler stellt, als es sonst bei ähnlichen Gelegenheiten der Fall zu sein pflegt. Es ist deshalb naturgemäss, dass diejenigen Elemente der Bürgerschaft, welchen ein selbständiges politisches Handeln zu eigen ist, eine leitende, wenn nicht ausschlaggebende Rolle spielen werden. Wir hoffen stark, dass die deutschen Bürger, deren Unabhängigkeit in der Politik ja gemeiniglich auf die Fähigkeit des selbständigen politischen Denkens zurückgeführt wird, ihr Renomee auch diesmal aufrecht erhalten und sich nicht durch eine leider zum grossen Teil von Deutschen geleiteten Hurrahkampagne zu einer unsinnigen und gefährlichen Experimentalpolitik hinreissen lassen" (*NYStZ*, Oct. 20, 1886).

39. Speek, "Single Tax," 75–81; Hurwitz, *Theodore Roosevelt and Labor*, 119; Hammack, *Power and Society*, 130–39; Condon, "Politics of Reform," 374–75; *NYStZ*, Sept. 22, 25, 30, Oct. 1, 2, 1886.

40. Hammack, *Power and Society*, 135; *NYStZ*, Oct. 2, 5, 6, 1886; Speek, "Single Tax," 76–79.

41. *NYStZ*, Oct. 7, 8, 9, 13, 14, 15; Condon, "Politics of Reform," 376–84; Hammack, *Power and Society*, 135–37.

42. *NYStZ*, Oct. 15, 1886; see also Post and Leubuscher, *George-Hewitt Campaign*, 31–43.

43. Post and Leubuscher, *George-Hewitt Campaign*, 43–44; Speek, "Single Tax," 79–80; Hurwitz, *Theodore Roosevelt and Labor*, 119–22; *NYStZ*, Oct. 16, 18, 21, 1886.

44. *NYVZ* and *NYStZ*, Nov. 3, 1886; Post and Leubuscher, *George-Hewitt Campaign*, 153–70.

45. Condon, "Politics of Reform," 390–91; *NYVZ*, Nov. 3, 1886.

46. Hammack, *Power and Society*, 137; Shefter, "Electoral Foundations of the Political Machine," 282–83.

47. The election reports of the *New Yorker Staats-Zeitung* underline the presence of German-Americans on the committees of the Democratic and Republican parties in 1886 (*NYStZ*, Oct. 11, 16, 19, 24, 26, 28, 1886).

48. *NYVZ*, Nov. 4, 14, 30, 1886; *John Swinton's Paper*, Nov. 21, 1886.

49. *NYVZ*, Aug. 8, 19, 1887.

50. *NYVZ*, Aug. 22, 29, Sept. 9, 29, Oct. 24, Nov. 7, 8, 1887; *Chicago Vorbote*, Nov. 11, 1887.

51. *NYVZ*, Aug. 20, Sept. 3, 17, Oct. 1, Nov. 10, 12, 1888; Sept. 16, 1889; *WA*, Aug. 25, Sept. 1, 13, 15, Nov. 17, 1888; see also Hammack, *Power and Society*, 177–78.

52. *NYVZ*, Sept. 23, 1889; Sept. 16, 1890; Foner, *History of the Labor Movement*, 514–16.

53. The split occurred when members of the brewery workers' union found that some CLU leaders (and known members of the KOL) had been bribed by brewery owners to induce the CLU to lift the beer boycott. The Central Labor Federation promptly affiliated directly with the American Federation of Labor. The CLF reunited with the CLU temporarily in December of the same year, but split off once more in late spring of 1890. The affiliation with the AFL was sought in order to counteract the influence of the

Knights of Labor in the CLU (Gompers, *Seventy Years*, vol. 1, 384–88; *NYVZ*, Jan. 3, 28, Feb. 4, 7, 11, 12, 18, 24, 28, 1889).

54. The situation was aggravated for the bakers, because while Locals 1, 7, and 93 joined the CLF, the rest of the journeymen bakers' locals remained in the CLU; see *WA*, Nov. 2, 16, 24, 1889; June 28, July 5, 1890; and *DABZ*, June 5, 1890. The conflict between the central labor organizations of New York City has been described extensively in the literature; the most detailed and accurate account can be found in the introductions and documents of Kaufman et al., eds., *Gompers Papers*, vol. 2, 191–92; documents 193, 195, 206–7, 358–59, 367–71, 386–408.

Chapter 7
New York's Brewery Workers and Their Union

1. John Paul Arnold, *History of the Brewing Industry*; United States Brewers Association (USBA), *One Hundred Years of Brewing*; and George Ehret, *Twenty-Five Years of Brewing* are books that promote this image; workers, too, made references to beer as a special commodity, see *NYVZ*, Feb. 20, 1885.

2. Emil Struve, *Die Entwicklung des bayerischen Braugewerbes*, 9, 20–21; Erich Borkenhagen, *Hundert Jahre Deutscher Brauerbund*, 13–14; USBA, *One Hundred Years of Brewing*, 100–101.

3. Karl Friedrich Wernet, *Wettbewerbs- und Absatzverhältnisse des Handwerks in historischer Sicht*, vol. 1, 231–34, 238–39.

4. Struve, *Entwicklung*, 31–32, 50–52, 54–57, 60; Borkenhagen, *Hundert Jahre*, 13.

5. *Statistisches Jahrbuch für das Deutsche Reich*, 1880, 1, 49; and *Statistisches Jahrbuch für das Deutsche Reich*, 1881, 133; Struve, *Entwicklung*, 133.

6. Struve, *Entwicklung*, 24, 70; *Statistisches Jahrbuch für das Deutsche Reich*, 1880, 49; *Statistisches Jahrbuch für das Deutsche Reich*, 1885, 15, 44–45; Borkenhagen, *Hundert Jahre*, 34.

7. Arnold, *History of the Brewing Industry*, 33–57 passim; Günter Schmölders, *Die Brauindustrie in den Vereinigten Staaten*, 32; USBA, *One Hundred Years of Brewing*, 207–8, 254, 539; Ehret, *Twenty-Five Years of Brewing*, 45–47; Stanley Baron, *Brewed in America*, 184–90.

8. *Dogget's New York Business Directory for 1848* and *Wilson's Business Directory of New York City*, 1868; see also USBA, *One Hundred Years of Brewing*, 253.

9. The United States Commissioner of the Internal Revenue's *Annual Report* for 1864 records the output of breweries by state and revenue district. Manhattan consisted of Districts 2 and 3 in New York State. For data on specific breweries see also Frederick Salem, *Beer, Its History and Its Economic Value*, appendix 1.

10. This was not allowed in Germany where a sixteenth-century purity law forbade the mixing of unmalted grains into the wort; see note 2.

11. USBA, *One Hundred Years of Brewing*, 77, 80–82, 87, 90–91; see also Ehret, *Twenty-Five Years of Brewing*, 58–82.

12. USBA, *One Hundred Years of Brewing,* 121–31; Ehret, *Twenty-Five Years of Brewing,* 83–95.

13. The gap between large and small breweries can be observed by studying the detailed *Annual Report* of the United States Commissioner of the Internal Revenue, which indicates the output and number of breweries in each revenue district and comparing these data with Frederick Salem's data on production per brewery in 1878 and 1879 in Manhattan and Brooklyn. It is obvious that the number of middling breweries shrank especially in the late 1870s, while some brewers had to go out of business or join the larger mechanized breweries. See Salem, *Beer, Its History,* appendix 1.

14. USBA, *One Hundred Years,* 139, 141–42.

15. *WB,* Jan. 1880, with numerous illustrations of New York breweries in addition to Fallert's and Philip Ebeling's.

16. *NYVZ,* Feb. 18, 1881.

17. Kolb, *Als Arbeiter in Amerika,* 39–47; Gompers, *Seventy Years,* vol. 1, 24.

18. A good general description by a middle-class observer can be found in Kolb, *Als Arbeiter in Amerika,* 39–41, 318.

19. *NYVZ,* Jan. 8, Feb. 18, Feb. 25, 1881; Feb. 25, 1888; Kolb, *Als Arbeiter in Amerika,* 40–41.

20. Southern Germans were also dominant among the brewery owners: ten out of eighteen whose birthplace we know were southerners. It is also likely that most of the southern brewery workers were Catholics; some of the brewery owners were known as pious Catholics, although the industry also had Protestant and Jewish owners. This information is taken from biographical data published on a number of New York brewery owners in the USBA's *One Hundred Years of Brewing,* 213, 230, 232, 246–47, 255–56, 260, 268, 275, 364, 370, 378, 380, 457; also in *AB,* 1890, 377; 1889, 112, 329; see also Will Anderson, *The Breweries of Brooklyn,* 22.

21. Kolb, *Als Arbeiter in Amerika,* 51; Hermann Schlueter, *The Brewery Industry and the Brewery Workers Movement in America,* 92–93. The analysis of the province of origin of German immigrant brewers was derived from a sample of 244 German-born brewers culled from the population schedules of the 1880 census for Manhattan's Eleventh, Tenth, Twelfth, and Nineteenth wards.

22. Tenth Census of the United States, Population Schedules for New York County; Schlueter, *Brewery Industry,* 93; *NYVZ,* Feb. 18, 1881; only the baking trades had similar arrangements, though not for as many workers, see chapter 9.

23. *NYVZ,* Feb. 18, 1881; Tenth Census of the United States, Population Schedules for New York County; the difference between brewers and cigar makers was that the cigar makers worked in their residences as well (see chapter 3).

24. The demographic data are based on an analysis of the Tenth Census of the United States, Population Schedules for New York County, especially those of the Nineteenth Ward of Manhattan.

25. Schlueter, *Brewery Industry,* 93; *NYVZ,* Jan. 8, Feb. 18, June 3, 1881.

26. New breweries continued to be founded up to World War I, the over-

whelming majority of them by groups of businessmen which we would call venture capitalists today, who hired an experienced foreman from another brewery to run the business. See USBA, *One Hundred Years of Brewing*, 254–55.

27. In larger establishments, the brewmasters were in charge of all day-to-day operations, while the owner limited his responsibility to the marketing of his product; on foremen see *NYVZ*, Feb. 8, 9, 10, 1882; Dec. 26, 1884; *WB*, Feb. 15, 1885.

28. Schlueter, *Brewery Industry*, 90-93; *NYVZ*, July 19, 1881; *WB*, Feb. 2, 1881.

29. Verband der Brauerei und Mühlenarbeiter, *Geschichte der Brauereiarbeiterbewegung*, 73–87.

30. Schlueter, *Brewery Industry*, 68–69; *NYVZ*, Jan. 4, Sept. 8, 9, 1879; Jan. 18, 19, Dec. 23, 1880; Jan. 10, 1881.

31. *AB*, Oct. 1881, 692; *NYVZ*, Dec. 8, 1881.

32. Schlueter, *Brewery Industry*, 98–99, 107; International Union of United Brewery, Flour, Cereal, Soft Drink, and Distillery Workers of America, *Seventy-Five Years of a Great Union*, 13.

33. *NYVZ*, Jan. 7, 8, 9, 1881.

34. *NYVZ*, Feb. 8, 9, 10, 1881.

35. Ibid.

36. Ibid.

37. *NYVZ*, Feb. 18, 1881.

38. *NYVZ*, Jan. 10, Feb. 6, 18, 25, 1881.

39. *NYVZ*, Feb. 24, 25, 7, 1881.

40. *NYVZ*, Mar. 5, 7, 1881.

41. Block was the most important German-American union organizer in New York during the 1880s. Born in 1848 in Bohemia, he came to the U.S. in 1870. Working as a pocketbook maker and a journalist Block, a member of the SLP, was a reporter for the *New Yorker Volkszeitung* in the early 1880s. By the mid-1880s he had helped found the New York Central Labor Union and in 1886 became secretary of the Journeymen Bakers' National Union. See Kaufman et al., eds., *Gompers Papers*, vol. 1, 475; see also pp. 189–90, 194–95, 199–200.

42. *NYVZ*, Mar. 5, 7, 14, 1881.

43. *NYVZ*, Apr. 11, 14, 25, 1881.

44. *NYVZ*, Mar. 7, 18, 19, 23, 1881; Apr. 7, 1881.

45. *NYVZ*, Mar. 16, 17, 18, 19, 20, 21, 23, Apr. 11, 18, May 19, 24, 1881.

46. *NYVZ*, Apr. 31, 1881.

47. For the origins of the USBA see its *Souvenir of the 25th Convention*, 1–3; USBA, *One Hundred Years of Brewing*, 537–74; see also *AB*, 1868–82.

48. *NYVZ*, Mar. 16, 18, 19–21, Apr. 5, 1881. To counter the union's effectiveness, the organ of the United States Brewers Association advocated that the brewery owners improve working conditions on their own. Acknowledging that reform was needed, the *American Brewer* called on the employers to create a working environment "which would meet all humanitarian needs" (*AB*, Apr. 1881, 197).

49. *NYVZ*, June 2, 1881.

50. *NYVZ*, June 7, 1881.

51. *NYVZ*, June 5, 6, 8, 1881.

52. *NYVZ*, June 6, 8, 1881.

53. *NYVZ*, June 8–12, 15, 16, 24, 1881.

54. There had been almost no strikes in the German brewing industry prior to 1880; see Verband der Brauerei und Mühlenarbeiter, *Geschichte der Brauereiarbeiterbewegung*, 75–76.

55. *NYVZ*, June 10, 12, 14, 16, 28, 1881.

56. Most of these groups were part of the German-American labor movement, although the Irish Land League and a few English-speaking organizations also joined in (*NYVZ*, June 10, 12, 16, 17, 18, 1881; *WB*, June 12, 1881).

57. *NYVZ*, June 4, 11, 12, 15, 16, 1881.

58. *NYVZ*, June 28, 1881; *AB*, July 1881; *WB*, July 1881.

59. *NYVZ*, July 7, 14, 1881; Schlueter, *Brewery Industry*, 106–7.

60. *NYVZ*, Oct. 19, Nov. 15, Dec. 7, 1881.

Chapter 8
The New Organization of Brewery Workers

1. *NYVZ*, Dec. 13, 16, 23, 26, 1884.

2. Between 1880 and 1900 the nation's beer production tripled, although growth slowed considerably after 1893. The persistent economic stagnation of the 1890s and the growing strength of the prohibition movement were mostly responsible for this drop. The data for the statistical survey can be found in United States Commissioner of the Internal Revenue, *Annual Report*, vols. 13–34 (1880–1900), table A.

3. It is important to keep in mind that the metropolitan brewing industry had had a head start in terms of productivity since most of its breweries were already relatively efficient in 1880. The average New York brewery still made twice as much beer as the average North American brewery at the turn of the century. See United States Commissioner of the Internal Revenue, *Annual Report*, vols. 13–34 (1880–1900), and *The Brewers Handbook* produced by the H. S. Rich Company.

4. Only seven New York breweries were owned by partnerships in 1900, most of them by two or three partners. English investors who bought up many midwestern breweries found only two New York breweries for sale during the 1890s. Those two were the only ones which belonged to outside investors before World War I (USBA, *One Hundred Years of Brewing*, 448–57; Baron, *Brewed in America*, 265, 270; Donald Bull and Manfred Friedrich, *Register of United States Breweries*, vol. 1).

5. Baron, *Brewed in America*, 267–68; Thomas Cochran, *The Pabst Brewing Company*, 102–28; Arnold, *History of the Brewing Industry*, 80–81.

6. *BZ*, Apr. 28, 1888; Baron, *Brewed in America*, 270–71. Elsewhere, however, and especially on a national level, such agreements turned out to be unenforceable. "The lack of cohesion among the brewers of the leading cit-

ies is a great loss for the trade. Petty jealousies, local quarrels, foolish cut-throat competition has time and again jeopardized great interests," complained the *American Brewer*. Attempts by the United States Brewers Association to make its members sign a pledge of solidarity against unions in 1886, stating that "we shall not take advantage of the misfortunes of any competing brewer whose business is suffering by reason of a strike, boycott or lockout," had only limited effect since only a bare majority signed this so-called St. Louis declaration (*WB*, Jan. 15, 1887; Schlueter, *Brewery Industry*, 144–45).

7. *NYVZ*, Sept. 9, 1879; Aug. 18, 1880; Dec. 22, 1881.

8. Schlueter, *Brewery Industry*, 114–15.

9. *NYVZ*, Jan. 26, 1885.

10. *NYVZ*, Dec. 16, 17, 24, 1884; Jan. 12, 26, 1885.

11. *NYVZ*, Mar. 9, 11, 16, 20–24, 30, Apr. 13, 20, May 4, 9, June 18, July 13, 20, 1885; Schlueter, *Brewery Industry*, 116.

12. New York State Board of Mediation and Arbitration, *First Annual Report* (New York, 1886), 37.

13. Ibid., 37–38.

14. Ibid., 122.

15. *NYVZ*, Oct. 12, 1885.

16. New York State Board of Mediation and Arbitration, *First Annual Report*, 122; *NYVZ*, Apr. 20, May 4, 18, July 13, Oct. 2, 9, 12, 1885.

17. Ale and porter brewers (most of whom were English and Irish immigrants at that time) had their own local assembly within the Knights of Labor; German-American maltsers who worked in breweries were welcome in the brewery workers' union (*BZ*, Oct. 2, 1886).

18. New York State Board of Mediation and Arbitration, *First Annual Report*, 51, 62, 67, 107; *NYVZ*, Mar. 2, 15, 1886; on the role of socialism in the National Brewery Workers' Union see J. M. H. Laslett, "Marxist Socialism and the Brewery Workers of the Midwest." In my opinion Laslett underestimates the conservatism of the brewery workers' rank and file membership.

19. New York State Board of Mediation and Arbitration, *First Annual Report*, 51, 62, 86, 107, 132; *NYVZ*, Mar. 2, 15, 1886.

20. *WB*, May 1886; *BZ*, Oct. 2, 1886, published the contract. The mediation panel was indeed called to mediate a number of times, up to 1888, usually in cases where the workers were fighting against what they considered to be unjustified dismissals. The union usually won in the mediated disputes; see e.g., "An Appeal Issued by the American Federation of Labor to Affiliated Unions and the Working People of America," New York, May 10, 1888, rpt. in Kaufman et al., eds., *Gompers Papers*, vol. 2, 112–15.

21. Indeed the New York provisions went further than traditional guild laws in most European localities, where guilds in the brewing craft had never been entirely autonomous. See Schneider, "Gewerkschaft und Gemeinschaft," 205–6.

22. *BZ*, Oct. 2, 1886.

23. *BZ*, July 30, Aug. 13, 1887.

24. Schlueter, *Brewery Industry*, 120–30, 135.

25. *BZ*, Apr. 23, 1887; *NYVZ*, June 27, 1887.

26. *BZ*, Feb. 12, Apr. 23, June 25, 1887; *NYVZ*, June 27, 1887.

27. During the election campaign the brewery workers had started a special Progressive Labor Club for brewery workers which claimed to attract many members. In the *Brauer Zeitung* as well as in many public meetings the leaders of Local 1 showed up as active supporters of the Socialist Labor party as well (*BZ*, Apr. 30, Oct. 9, 22, 29, Nov. 5, Dec. 9, 1887; see also chapter 6).

28. Schlueter, *Brewery Industry*, 129–31.

29. *BZ*, May 7, 1887; Schlueter, *Brewery Industry*, 198–99.

30. *BZ*, Jan. 1, May 7, June 6, July 16, 1887; *NYVZ*, June 13, 10, 1887.

31. *BZ*, Feb. 19, Mar. 5, 1887; *NYVZ*, Feb. 14, 1887; Schlueter indicates that some locals stayed with the KOL (*Brewery Industry*, 136).

32. *BZ*, May 30, June 6, July 16, Dec. 3, 1887; Schlueter, *Brewery Industry*, 198.

33. *BZ*, May 2, 30, July 16, 18, Dec. 3, 1887.

34. *WB*, May 15, 1886; Schlueter, *Brewery Industry*, 121, 124, 149–50; Cochran, *Pabst Brewing Company*, 283–85; *BZ*, Dec. 31, 1887.

35. Schlueter, *Brewery Industry*, 149–50; Cochran, *Pabst Brewing Company*, 283–85; *BZ*, Dec. 31, 1887; New York State Board of Mediation and Arbitration, *First Annual Report*, 82–83, 178–79.

36. Schlueter, *Brewery Industry*, 144, 147; Cochran, *Pabst Brewing Company*, 385.

37. *NYVZ*, Mar. 31, Apr. 7, 1888; New York State Board of Mediation and Arbitration, *First Annual Report*, 22–28; Schlueter, *Brewery Industry*, 151–52.

38. *AB*, Apr. 1888, 97.

39. These businesses, Eppig's, Bechtel's, and Knickerbocker's breweries in Brooklyn, and the Union Hill Brewery in New Jersey, were not members of the local arm of the USBA, although they belonged to the national organization; see New York State Board of Mediation and Arbitration, *First Annual Report*, 47, 162–63; *BZ*, Apr. 2, 7, 1888; *NYVZ*, Apr. 7, 1888.

40. *NYVZ*, Apr. 14, 28, May 5, 1888; *BZ*, Apr. 14, May 9, 1888.

41. New York State Board of Mediation and Arbitration, *First Annual Report*, 165; *BZ*, Apr. 21, 1888; *NYVZ*, Apr. 21, 1888.

42. *BZ*, Apr. 21, 1888.

43. Ibid.; *NYVZ*, Apr. 28, 1888.

44. *NYVZ*, Apr. 28, 1888.

45. The increasing importance of a machinist's skill and the decreased need for skilled craft workers can be observed in other Gilded Age industries as well; see for example John Jentz's discussion of cabinetmakers and machinists in "Skilled Workers and Industrialization," in *German Workers in Industrial Chicago*, 78–82.

46. *BZ*, June 9, 1888; *NYVZ*, May 5, June 16, 1888; Schlueter, *Brewery Industry*, 157.

47. *NYVZ*, Apr. 15, May 25, June 16, 1888.

48. *NYVZ*, Apr. 14, 21, 28, July 7, 1888.

49. *BZ*, May 12, 19, June 30, 1888; *NYVZ*, Apr. 21, 1888; *WB*, May 5, 1888.

50. *BZ*, May 26, June 2, 16, 23, 1888.

51. *BZ*, Apr. 21, 1888; *WB*, May 5, 1888; *NYVZ*, June 2, July 14, 21, 28, 1888.

52. Schlueter, *Brewery Industry*, 168–70; *BZ*, May 12, 1888.

53. Schlueter, *Brewery Industry*, 168; *BZ*, June 2, 9, 16, 23, 1888; *NYVZ*, May 26, June 9, 16, July 7, 28, 1888.

54. Schlueter, *Brewery Industry*, 171–77.

55. Schneider, "Gewerkschaft und Gemeinschaft," 294–96.

56. Two other locals made up of firemen and beer drivers added another 150 workers to the union rolls (Schlueter, *Brewery Industry*, 149; *NYVZ*, Sept. 1, Dec. 22, 1888; *BZ*, Aug. 11, 25, 1888).

57. For a more detailed description of the role of the brewery workers in the conflict among New York's central labor organizations see chapter 6, n. 53. The CLU actually split over the lack of support for the brewery unions' cause in 1889 (Schneider, "Gewerkschaft und Gemeinschaft," 297–99; Laslett, "Marxist Socialism," 18–21). The peculiar problems of the socialist unions in New York City within the New York labor movement and the AFL seriously weakened the influence of the socialists on the brewery workers of the city, whereas elsewhere, such as in the cities of the Midwest, socialist sympathies and local alliances continued to flourish into the early twentieth century among the brewery workers, as Laslett has demonstrated.

58. Schlueter, *Brewery Industry*, 183–204; United States Commissioner of the Internal Revenue, *Annual Report*, 1898, table A, for declining beer production after 1897.

59. Locally conceived labor conflicts became national concerns for the labor movement with increasing frequency during the 1890s. Best known among these conflicts are the Pullman strike and the Homestead strike. On the national involvement of the AFL in those conflicts see Kaufman et al., eds., *Gompers Papers*, vol. 3, 186–95, 206–10, 217–19, 231–34, 236–40, 249–50, 521–42, 548–49, 554–84, 587–88.

60. Laslett, "Marxist Socialism," 28–34; Schlueter, *Brewery Industry*, 181, 183–86.

61. Laslett, "Marxist Socialism," 13–14.

Chapter 9
The German Bakers of New York City

1. The secondary literature on the history of the baking trade in the United States is very sparse. Among the few treatments are John B. Jentz, "Bread and Labor"; see also Stuart Kaufman, *A Vision of Unity*; both studies paint the portrait of a rather successful movement, outside New York City.

2. See chapter 6.

3. For a comparative view on sweatshop trades in New York City see the excellent survey of Sean Wilentz in *Chants Democratic*, 119–29, 134–42; and Richard Stott in *Workers in the Metropolis*, 38–42, 55–58, 63–67; for Germans and their role in the sweatshop economy see Nadel, *Little Germany*, 68–72.

4. Strictly speaking, baking was not a sweatshop trade, since formal sub-

contracting was not part of its structure. However, the majority of New York bakeries did not sell their wares directly to their customers but produced bread for grocery stores, acting in fact as subcontractors to food retailers.

5. For the relatively even distribution of bakers in different neighborhoods, see Stott, *Workers in the Metropolis*, 196.

6. Tenth Census of the United States, vol. 1, 892.

7. Wernet, *Wettbewerbs- und Absatzverhältnisse*, vol. 1, 45–46, 67–88.

8. Walter Badke, *Zur Entwicklung des deutschen Bäckergewerbes*, 88–89, 90–91, 94–95, 110–11; Johann Schwarz, *Das Handwerk der Bäcker in München*, 135.

9. Karl Marx, *Capital*, vol. 1, ed. Friedrich Engels, (London, 1906), 273.

10. For a description of the actual work processes in a bakery see Philipp Arnold, *Das Münchner Bäckergewerbe*, 28; August Bebel, *Zur Lage der Arbeiter in den Bäckereien*, 22–168 passim.

11. Bebel, *Zur Lage der Arbeiter*; see also O. Allmann, *Geschichte der deutschen Bäcker- und Konditorenbewegung*, vol. 1, 155, 339–42.

12. See for example the sketch of Charles Iffland, in Kaufman, *Vision of Unity*, 4.

13. Arnold, *Das Münchner Bäckergewerbe*, 67–68, 75; Bebel, *Zur Lage der Arbeiter*, 22–168 passim; Allmann, *Geschichte der deutschen Bäcker- und Konditorenbewegung*, vol. 1, 80–82; Schwarz, *Das Handwerk der Bäcker in München*, 67.

14. Schwarz, *Das Handwerk der Bäcker in München*, 61–74; Friedrich Wolle, *Siebenhundert Jahre Bäckerhandwerk zu Erfurt*, 78–93; Arnold, *Das Münchner Bäckergewerbe*, 6–13. For a survey on craft legislation see also Huber, *Deutsche Verfassungsgeschichte seit 1789*, vol. 3, 1010–14. A viable competition outside the *Innung* craft shop system that dominated in Germany during the late nineteenth and well into the twentieth century was possible for large bread factories which emerged in the early twentieth century as machinery became more widely available and cost-effective for bakeries to use; see Arnold, *Das Münchner Bäckergewerbe*, 21–26, 30–32; Allmann, *Geschichte der deutschen Bäcker- und Konditorenbewegung*, vol. 1, 385–89.

15. Allmann, *Geschichte der deutschen Bäcker- und Konditorenbewegung*, vol. 1, 12–15, 26–27, 74, 133, 250–399 passim; Schwarz, *Das Handwerk der Bäcker in München*, 51–53; Arnold, *Das Münchner Bäckergewerbe*, 79–81.

16. Allmann, *Geschichte der deutschen Bäcker- und Konditorenbewegung*, vol. 1, 143, 144–55, 238–40, 256–57, 315, 334–39, 349; Wernet, *Wettbewerbs- und Absatzverhältnisse*, vol. 1, 95–96; Wolle, *Siebenhundert Jahre Bäckerhandwerk zu Erfurt*, 93; Paul Hirschfeld, *Die freien Gewerkschaften in Deutschland*, 110–11; Walter Troeltsch and Paul Hirschfeld, *Die deutschen sozialdemokratischen Gewerkschaften*, 104–5.

17. Wolle, *Siebenhundert Jahre Bäckerhandwerk zu Erfurt*, 93; Schwarz, *Das Handwerk der Bäcker in München*, 76–84; Allmann, *Geschichte der deutschen Bäcker- und Konditorenbewegung*, vol. 1, 143, 315–34.

18. Ernst, *Immigrant Life in New York City*, 214.

19. The data for the number of bakers and their ethnic origin are derived from the Census of Population, those of the number of bakeries from the Cen-

sus of Manufactures. Since these two parts of the census relied on different methods of collecting data and classifying them, the figures are not strictly comparable.

20. Ernst, *Immigrant Life in New York City*, 191, 213–14; Wilentz, *Chants Democratic*, 43, 139–40; Howard B. Rock, "The Perils of Laissez-Faire."

21. State of New York, *Preliminary Report of the Factory Investigation Commission*, vol. 1, 209; vol. 2, 311, 315, 354, 672, 741.

22. Ibid., vol. 2, 212–17, 312–14; *NYVZ*, Apr. 27, 1881.

23. State of New York, *Preliminary Report*, vol. 1, 208; vol. 2, 323.

24. Bakers Journeymen Union of New York, Brooklyn and Vicinity, *Slavery in the Baker Shops*.

25. Ibid., 5–6.

26. Ibid., 7.

27. State of New York, *Preliminary Report*, vol. 1, 81, 227–29; vol. 2, 686–90; *DABZ*, 1886–92, passim, see esp. 3, 4.; for suicides see, for example, *NYVZ*, Mar. 21, 27, 1879; *John Swinton's Paper*, Aug. 31, 1884.

28. State of New York, *Preliminary Report*, vol. 1, 218; vol. 2, 324; Bakers Journeymen Union of New York, Brooklyn and Vicinity, *Slavery in the Baker Shops*, 5.

29. *NYVZ*, Sept. 20, Nov. 22, 1880; May 7, 1881; Bakers Journeymen Union of New York, Brooklyn and Vicinity, *Slavery in the Baker Shops*, 5.

30. Bakers Journeymen Union of New York, Brooklyn and Vicinity, *Slavery in the Baker Shops*, 6.

31. Ibid., 13–14; *John Swinton's Paper*, July 26, Nov. 16, 1887; *DABZ*, Nov. 16, 1887.

32. The census sample was taken from the Tenth Census of the United States, Population Schedules for New York County, for the Tenth, Eleventh, and Seventeenth wards; on bakers' wives and families see also *DABZ*, Nov. 3, 1886; Nov. 16, 23, 1887.

33. Tenth Census of the United States, Population Schedules for New York County, enumeration district 205, reel 72.

34. Ibid.

35. Wilentz, *Chants Democratic*, 223, 232; Ernst, *Immigrant Life in New York City*, 108–9.

36. Ernst, *Immigrant Life in New York City*, 109, 255, n. 33; *New York Daily News*, July 25, 1864; *NYVZ*, Sept. 13, 1880; *Bakers Journal*, Jan. 11, 1911.

37. *NYVZ*, May 17, 31, Sept. 13, Nov. 8, 1880; Kaufman, *Vision of Unity*, 4.

38. Kaufman, *Vision of Unity*, 1. Block would also later play an important role in the founding of the brewery workers' union; see chapter 7, n. 41.

39. Kaufman, *Vision of Unity*, 1–2; *NYVZ*, Mar. 14, Apr. 12, 26, May 3, 17, 31, 1880.

40. *NYVZ*, Apr. 4, 16, 24, Sept. 14, 1881.

41. *NYVZ*, May 17, Sept. 13, 1880; Apr. 15, 27, May 4, 1881.

42. *NYVZ*, Apr. 26, May 3, 31, 1880.

43. *NYVZ*, Mar. 7, Apr. 12, May 12, Aug. 18, 1881; Bakers Journeymen Union of New York, Brooklyn and Vicinity, *Slavery in the Baker Shops*.

44. *NYVZ*, Apr. 11, Aug. 9, 16, 25, 1881.

45. Bakers Journeymen Union of New York, Brooklyn and Vicinity, *Slavery in the Baker Shops*.

46. *NYVZ*, Apr. 23, 24, 1881.

47. *NYVZ*, May 2, 3, 1881.

48. *New York Evening Post*, May 4, 1881; *Sun*, May 5, 1881; *NYVZ*, May 3, 4, 1881; Kaufman, *Vision of Unity*, 3.

49. George Block, *A Concise History of the Bakers Union of New York and Vicinity*; *NYVZ*, May 3, 5, 6, 9–14, June 6, Aug. 18, Sept. 3, Oct. 17, 1881; Jan. 23, Feb. 6, July 5, 1882.

50. Jonathan Garlock, ed., *A Guide to the Local Assemblies of the Knights of Labor*, 314, 322; *John Swinton's Paper*, Apr. 5, 1885; *NYVZ*, June 20, 21, July 2, 1881; *Journal of the Knights of Labor*, 4, no. 5 (1884).

51. *Sun*, June 18, July 9, 11, 1883; *John Swinton's Paper*, Nov. 18, 1883; Nov. 18, 1884; Jan. 11, 22, 25, 1885; Apr. 11, 1886; *WA*, Oct. 4, 1885; *NYVZ*, Nov. 1, 1885.

52. *John Swinton's Paper*, Feb. 2, Mar. 15, 18, Apr. 5, Aug. 10, 1884; *NYVZ*, Jan. 11, Feb. 22, Mar. 15, Apr. 5, 1885; *John Swinton's Paper*, Nov. 18, 1884.

53. *NYVZ*, Jan. 20, 21, 1885.

54. *NYVZ*, Jan. 24, Apr. 5, May 3, 1885.

55. In its three pages of text (one page was filled with advertisements) readers were informed about politics, the labor movement, and scientific advances in all fields. The paper also published serialized novels and short stories. The *Bäcker Zeitung* was not cheap at five cents an issue and Block, as its editor, made few concessions to the specialized interests of its readers (recipes and hints for the bakers' workshop were rare) (Block, *Concise History*, 4; *NYVZ*, Feb. 23, May 10, 1885; *DABZ*, May 2, 1885 to Dec. 1889 passim; *Bakers Journal*, Jan. 11, 1911).

56. *John Swinton's Paper*, Aug. 16, 1885.

57. *DABZ*, May 12, 19, 1886; *Bakers Journal*, Jan. 14, 1911, 43; *NYVZ*, Apr. 5, 19, 1886.

58. *DABZ*, Sept. 28, 1887; New York State Bureau of the Statistics of Labor, *Fourth Annual Report*, 738; *NYVZ*, Mar. 4, July 25, 1886; *WA*, Oct. 10, Dec. 26, 1886. A similar type of action was reported as early as 1881; see *NYVZ*, Apr. 16, 1881; Kaufman, *Vision of Unity*, 8–10.

59. New York State Bureau of the Statistics of Labor, *Fourth Annual Report*, 748–50; Michael Gordon, "The Labor Boycott in New York City," 213–19; *NYVZ*, Apr. 25, 1886.

60. *John Swinton's Paper*, Sept. 26, 1886; *WA*, Dec. 12, 1886; New York State Bureau of the Statistics of Labor, *Fourth Annual Report*, 486–88; Kaufman, *Vision of Unity*, 13–16.

61. Kaufman, *Vision of Unity*, 5–7.

62. The four other locals in greater New York were Local 13 (New York Vienna Bakers), Local 22 (Bohemian Bakers of New York), Local 31 (Jewish Bakers of New York), and Local 34 (Brooklyn). The latter consisted of Section 1 (members of the Knights of Labor Atlantic Association), Section 2 (Ger-

man-speakers), and Section 3 (members of the Knights of Labor Advance Association) (*DABZ*, June 9, 1886).

63. Kaufman, *Vision of Unity*, 7, 11; *DABZ*, May 5, 1886; *NYVZ*, May 10, 1886.

64. *DABZ*, July 6, 1887; New York State Bureau of the Statistics of Labor, *Fourth Annual Report*, 420–21, 625.

65. *Boycotter*, June 19, 1886; *John Swinton's Paper*, July 4, 1886.

66. New York State Bureau of the Statistics of Labor, *Fourth Annual Report*, 659.

67. *DABZ*, Sept. 21, Nov. 30, Dec. 7, 1887.

68. *NYVZ*, Apr. 11, 1886.

69. The national union set twelve hours as the standard for which the union should fight nationwide (*DABZ*, Jan. 14, 1886).

70. *NYVZ*, Apr. 11, 1886; *John Swinton's Paper*, May 23, 1886; *Bakers Journal*, Jan. 14, 1911, 37.

71. The JBNU united its own Brooklyn local (No. 7) with two Knights of Labor affiliates (the Bakers Advance Association and the Atlantic Association of Bakers) into a new local (No. 34) in 1887; see *Bakers Journal*, Jan. 14, 1911, 8; *NYVZ*, Mar. 1, 22, 29, Apr. 5, 11, 12, 1886; *DABZ*, Sept. 26, Nov. 24, Dec. 1, 1886; Jan. 5, 12, 28, Feb. 16, 1887; July 25, 1888; *Boycotter*, May 22, 1886; *CMOJ*, Sept. 1886.

72. *Bakers Journal*, Jan. 14, 1911, 38–40; see also Schneider, "Gewerkschaft und Gemeinschaft," 347–49.

73. Kaufman, *Vision of Unity*, 15–16; *Bakers Journal*, Jan. 14, 1911, 38.

74. *DABZ*, May 11, 1887.

75. Kaufman, *Vision of Unity*, 25; *DABZ*, Dec. 28, 1887; Mar. 20, 1888; *WA*, Dec. 8, 1888; *Der Socialist*, Nov. 14, 1888.

76. *DABZ*, Mar. 20, 1889.

77. *Bakers Journal*, Jan. 14, 1911, 32–33.

78. *DABZ*, Feb. 29, Mar. 14, 1888; Mar. 20, 1889; *Bakers Journal*, Jan. 14, 1911.

79. *Bakers Journal*, June 4, 1889; see also *DABZ*, Mar. 20, 1889.

80. Kaufman, *Vision of Unity*, 26–29; *Bakers Journal*, Mar. 20, 1889; Jan. 14, 1911, 33; *DABZ*, June 4, 1889.

81. *Bakers Journal*, July 6, Aug. 24, 1889; Jan. 14, 1911, 38. It is difficult to identify bread factories from business directories or published census records. One indication of the increase in larger businesses is the growing list of bakeries with more than one address, presumably chains of retail establishments. In 1884 the *New York Mercantile Union Business Directory* listed fifteen establishments which either had more than one address or were known to be large bakeries (from other reports). In 1890 forty-two such larger bakeries were listed in *Trows Business Directory for New York City*, and in 1900 there were forty-four in *Trows Business Directory* for that year.

82. The diverse origins of some of the big bakery owners can only be traced through the census; in this case the federal census of 1880 was used. In it the Fleischmann family is listed as coming from Saxony, with one of the younger brothers already having been born in New York; only Louis Fleisch-

mann called himself a baker, his brothers called themselves distillers. John Shults, owner of a large factory employing over ninety bakers at the time, was from Germany. Hersemann, later owner of a big shop, was the New York–born son of German parents; Henry Cushman, another big "bakery boss," was born in Ireland. See Tenth Census of the United States, Population Schedules for New York County, vol. 34, enumeration district 139; vol. 54, enumeration district 283; vol. 55, enumeration district 337; and vol. 31, enumeration district 73. See also *Sun*, May 4, 1881.

83. Kaufman, *Vision of Unity*, 3–6; *John Swinton's Paper*, Aug. 12, 1884; Apr. 19, July 26, 1885.

84. *John Swinton's Paper*, Sept. 6, 1885; May 23, 1886; *DABZ*, May 12, 18, June 30, Aug. 10, 1886; *NYVZ*, May 10, June 2, 16, Apr. 30, 1887; *Bakers Journal*, May 25, 1887; *Union*, Apr. 30, 1886.

85. *NYVZ*, Aug. 21, 1889; *Bakers Journal*, Aug. 24, 1889; Jan. 14, 1911; New York State Bureau of the Statistics of Labor, *Seventh Annual Report*, 637, 638.

86. *Bakers Journal*, Aug. 31, 1889; Jan. 14, 1911; *NYVZ*, Aug. 23, 1889.

87. *NYVZ*, Aug. 26, 29, 30, 31, 1889; Sept. 11, Oct. 2, 1889; *Bakers Journal*, Aug. 21, Sept. 14, 21, 1889; *Paterson Labor Standard*, Nov. 2, 1889; *Bakers Journal*, Sept. 14, 1889.

88. *NYVZ*, Aug. 25, 26, 29, 30, 31, Sept. 4, 7, 9, 10, 24, 1889; *Bakers Journal*, Sept. 14, Oct. 19, 1889.

89. Kaufman, *Vision of Unity*, 26.

90. *NYVZ*, Sept. 11, Oct. 2, 1889; *Bakers Journal*, Aug. 21, Sept. 14, 21, 1889; *Paterson Labor Standard*, Nov. 2, 1889.

91. *NYVZ*, Sept. 16, 19, 22, 1889; *Bakers Journal*, Sept. 23, 1889, Jan. 14, 1911.

92. *NYVZ*, Sept. 14, 30, 1889.

93. *Bakers Journal*, Jan. 14, 1911.

94. Ibid.

95. August Delabar, national secretary of the JBNU, was a member of the Socialist Labor party and had expected to play an important role in the Central Labor Federation. When the SLP nominated (and the CLF endorsed) the socialist Lucien Sanial as a representative of both the SLP and the CLF to the congress of the Second International in Brussels instead of Delabar, the union secretary could not forgive them and decided to cast his lot with Samuel Gompers. Delabar was excluded from the party but found an ally in the union in Henry Weissmann, editor of the *Bäcker Zeitung*. The two men joined some other allies of Gompers in founding the New York Federation of Labor (*Bakers Journal*, Jan. 14, 1911, 38, 40, 56).

96. *The People*, Sept. 13, 20, Nov. 1, Dec. 6, 1891; Jan. 3, 10, Oct. 23, 1892; *NYVZ*, Oct. 26, 1891; *Bakers Journal*, Apr. 4, 11, 1891; Jan. 5, Apr. 23, May 7, 1892; *Der Sozialist*, Aug. 29, 1891.

97. Kaufman, *Vision of Unity*, 26–33, 34–43; *Bakers Journal*, Jan. 14, 1911, 32–34, 38–39.

98. New York State Bureau of the Statistics of Labor, *Twelfth Annual Report*, vol. 2; *Bakers Journal*, Mar. 30, 1895; *NYVZ*, Feb. 18, 1892; *The People*, Nov. 20, 1892.

99. *The People,* Aug. 4, 1895; New York State Department of Labor, *Seventeenth Annual Report,* vol. 3, 171–75; Factory Inspectors of the State of New York, *Tenth Annual Report,* 41–44; George M. Price, "Report on Bakeries and Bakers in New York City," in State of New York, *Preliminary Report of the Factory Investigation Commission,* vol. 1, appendix 3, passim (contains photos).

100. Paul Kens, *Judicial Power and Reform Politics,* 44–59; *Bakers Journal,* Apr. 6, 1895; Kaufman, *Vision of Unity,* 34–38.

101. Kens, *Judicial Power,* 79–80; Price, "Report on Bakeries and Bakers in New York City"; Factory Inspectors of the State of New York, *Tenth Annual Report;* New York State Bureau of the Statistics of Labor, *Tenth Annual Report,* part 2, 441–46.

102. Kens, *Judicial Power,* 115–27; the case was argued for the defendant by (among others) Henry Weissmann, the former head of the JBNU, who had helped bring the law about.

103. New York State Department of Labor, *Seventeenth Annual Report on Factory Inspection,* part 3, 40; Kaufman, *Vision of Unity,* 45–51; Hazel Kyrk, *The American Baking Industry,* 56–61.

Conclusion

1. *New Yorker Volkszeitung, Jubiläums Beilage,* Feb. 21, 1903, 1; rpt. in Hoerder, Kiesewetter, and Weber, eds., *Glimpses of the German-American Radical Press,* 42–43.

2. Ibid.; for an assessment of the differences between older and newer German immigrants in Chicago, see Hartmut Keil, "Chicago's German Working Class in 1900," in Keil and Jentz, eds., *German Workers in Industrial Chicago,* 19–36.

3. During the first decades of the twentieth century, the cities of Milwaukee, Wisconsin; Butte, Montana; and Schenectady, New York, had socialist mayors while about sixty socialists served in various state legislatures. Victor Berger of Milwaukee and Meyer London of New York City served in Congress as members of the Socialist party of America. See Ira Kipnis, *The American Socialist Movement, 1897–1912* (New York, 1952), 358–64.

4. August Sartorius von Waltershausen, *Der moderne Socialismus in den Vereinigten Staaten von Amerika* (Berlin, 1890), 410; Waltershausen's analysis predates Sombart's by more than a decade and a half and takes into account the complexities of American labor politics in a much more differentiated manner than Sombart.

5. Werner Sombart, *Why Is There No Socialism in America?* (1906; rpt., White Plains, 1976).

Bibliography

Census Material and Statistical Reports

Census of the State of New York. 1845.

Census of the State of New York. 1855.

Charter and By-Laws of the German Society with a List of Members. New York, 1808, 1849, 1852, 1863.

Municipal Tax Assessment Books. New York County, 11th and 17th Wards. Municipal Archives of the City of New York.

State of New York. *Preliminary Report of the Factory Investigation Commission.* Vols. 1 and 2. Albany, 1912.

Statistisches Jahrbuch für das Deutsche Reich. Berlin, 1880, 1881, 1883–1901.

United States Census Bureau. *Eighth Census of the United States.* Washington, D.C., 1860.

———. *Eleventh Census of the United States. Census of Population.* Washington, D.C., 1890.

———. *Eleventh Census of the United States. Report on Manufacturing Industries.* Vol. 6. Washington, D.C., 1895.

———. *Ninth Census of the United States. Census of Population.* Washington, D.C., 1870.

———. *Tenth Census of the United States. Census of Population.* Washington, D.C., 1880.

———. *Tenth Census of the United States, Population Schedules for New York County.* Microfilm.

———. *Twelfth Census of the United States. Census of Population.* Washington, D.C., 1902.

Annual and Special Reports

Cigar Makers' Central Organization. *Financial Report.* New York, 1878.

Deutsche Gesellschaft der Stadt New York. *Jahresbericht.* New York, 1848, 1872–80.

Factory Inspectors of the State of New York. *Tenth Annual Report.* Albany, 1896.

New York State Board of Mediation and Arbitration. *First Annual Report*. New York, 1886.

New York State Bureau of the Statistics of Labor. *Annual Report for the Year 1895*. Vol. 2. Albany, 1896.

———. *Fifth Annual Report*. Albany, 1888.

———. *Fourth Annual Report for the Year 1886*. Albany, 1887.

———. *Seventh Annual Report*. Albany, 1890.

———. *Tenth Annual Report*. Albany, 1893.

———. *Twelfth Annual Report*. Albany, 1896.

New York State Department of Labor. *Seventeenth Annual Report on Factory Inspection*. Part 3. Albany, 1903.

Price, George M. "Report on Bakeries and Bakers in New York City." In State of New York, *Preliminary Report of the Factory Investigation Commission*. Albany, 1912.

"Die soziale Lage der Zigarrenarbeiter im Grossherzogtum Baden." *Beilage zum Jahresbericht des grossherzoglich badischen Fabrikinspektors für das Jahr 1889*. Karlsruhe, 1889.

United States Commissioner of the Internal Revenue. *Annual Report*. Washington, D.C., 1863–1900.

United States Department of Labor. *Eleventh Special Report of the Commissioner of Labor, Regulation and Restriction of Output*. Washington, D.C., 1904.

United States Industrial Commission. *Report*. Vols. 1, 2, 15. Washington, D.C., 1903.

United States Tobacco Journal. "Directory of Cigar Manufactures." New York, 1881.

Newspapers

American Brewer. New York, 1868–82, 1889–90.

Arbeiter, Der. New York, 1858.

Arbeiter Stimme. New York, 1875, 1876, 1878.

Arbeiter Union. New York, 1868, 1870.

Arbeiter Zeitung. New York, 1873–74.

Bakers Journal. 1887, 1889, 1891–92, 1895, 1911.

Boycotter. New York, 1886.

Brauer Zeitung. New York, 1886–88.

Chicago Vorbote. 1887.

Cigar Makers Official Journal. New York, 1875–90; Chicago, 1899–1900.

Deutsch-Amerikanische Bäckerzeitung. New York, 1885–92.

Iron Moulders Journal. Cincinnati, 1873.

John Swinton's Paper. New York, 1883–87.

Journal of the Knights of Labor. Philadelphia, 1884.

Labor Standard. New Haven, Conn., 1876–77.

Neue Arbeiter-Zeitung. New York, 1875.

New York Daily News. 1864.

New Yorker Staats-Zeitung (NYStZ). 1853, 1859, 1864–65, 1872–73, 1876–77, 1878, 1886.
New Yorker Volkszeitung (NYVZ). 1877–94, 1903.
New York Evening Post. 1881.
New York Herald. 1877, 1892.
New York Times. 1877.
New York Tribune. 1877.
New York World. 1877, 1886.
Paterson Labor Standard. 1889.
People, The. New York, 1892, 1895.
Progress. New York, 1882–84.
Reform, Die. New York, Apr. 24, June 7, 1853.
Republik der Arbeiter. New York, 1850.
Social Democrat. New York, 1874–76.
Sozialist, Der. New York, 1891.
Sun, The. New York, 1877.
United States Tobacco Journal. New York, 1877–90.
Western Brewer. Chicago, 1880–81, 1886–87.
Workingman's Advocate. New York, 1885–89.
Workmens Advocate. New Haven, Conn., 1873–74.

Guidebooks and Handbooks

Arndt, Karl, and May Olsson. *German-American Newspapers and Periodicals.* Heidelberg, 1956.
The Brewers Handbook: A Supplement to the Western Brewer. Chicago, 1888–1900, annually.
Bull, Donald, and Manfred Friedrich. *Register of United States Breweries.* Trumbull, Conn., 1976.
Deutscher Wegweiser durch New York und Umgegend. Edited by Thomsen and Detlevs. New York, 1884.
Dogget's New York Business Directory for 1848: Guide to Greater New York. Boston, 1847.
Handbook of Benevolent Institutions of New York. New York, 1877.
King's Handbook of New York City. Edited by Moses King. Boston, 1892.
Lain and Healy's Brooklyn Directory. Brooklyn, 1890, 1900.
Murphy's Business Directory for 1888. New York, 1887.
New York Bädeker. Edited by H. Mischke and R. P. Francis. New York, 1880.
New York Mercantile Union Business Directory. New York, 1850–51.
New Yorker Vereins-Kalender für das Jahr 1884. Edited by H. A. Dittrich. New York, 1883.
Sadlier's Catholic Directory. New York, 1885.
Sun's Guide to New York. Jersey City, 1892.
Trow's Business Directory for New York City. New York, 1857, 1890, 1900.
Wilson's Directory for New York City. New York, 1880–90.

Books and Articles

Abbott, Edith. *Women in Industry.* New York, 1910.

Allmann, O. *Geschichte der deutschen Bäcker- und Konditorenbewegung.* 2 vols. Hamburg, 1910.

Anderson, Will. *The Breweries of Brooklyn.* Groton Falls, 1976.

Arnold, John Paul. *History of the Brewing Industry and Brewing Science in America.* Chicago, 1933.

Arnold, Philipp. *Das Münchner Bäckergewerbe, eine wirtschaftliche, technische und soziale Studie.* Stuttgart, 1895.

Badke, Walter. *Zur Entwicklung des deutschen Bäckergewerbes.* Jena, 1906.

Baer, Willis N. *The Economic Development of the Cigar Industry in the United States.* Lancaster, 1931.

Bakers Journeymen Union of New York, Brooklyn and Vicinity. *Slavery in the Baker Shops—a pamphlet on the condition of journeymen bakers for information and instruction of employers and employees in that trade.* N.d.

Balch, Emily Greene. "Slav Emigration—Its Source." *Charities and Commons,* 15 (1906): 591–601.

Barker, Charles A. *Henry George.* Oxford, 1955.

Baron, Stanley. *Brewed in America: A History of Beer and Ale in the United States.* Boston, 1962.

Barry, Coleman. *The Catholic Church and German-Americans.* Washington, D.C., 1953.

Bebel, August. *Zur Lage der Arbeiter in den Bäckereien.* Stuttgart, 1895.

Bernstein, Iver. *The New York City Draft Riots: Their Significance in American Society and Politics in the Age of the Civil War.* New York, 1990.

Block, George. *A Concise History of the Bakers Union of New York and Vicinity.* New York, n.d.

Borkenhagen, Erich. *Hundert Jahre Deutscher Brauerbund.* Bonn, 1971.

Brancaforte, Charlotte, ed. *The German Forty-Eighters in the United States.* New York, 1989.

Bretting, Agnes. *Soziale Probleme Deutscher Einwanderer in New York City: 1800–1860.* Wiesbaden, 1981.

Bridges, Amy. *A City in the Republic: Antebellum New York and the Origins of Machine Politics.* New York, 1984.

Buhle, Paul. *Marxism in the United States: Remapping the History of the American Left.* London, 1987.

Burstein, Alan N. "Immigrants and Residential Mobility: The Irish and Germans in Philadelphia, 1850–1880." In *Philadelphia: Work, Space, Family and Group Experience in the Nineteenth Century,* edited by Theodore Hershberg. New York, 1981.

Capek, Thomas. *The Czechs (Bohemians) in New York.* New York, 1924.

Clark, Victor. *History of Manufactures in the United States.* Vol. 2. New York, 1929.

Cochran, Thomas. *The Pabst Brewing Company.* New York, 1948.

Cohalan, Florence. *A Popular History of the Archdiocese of New York.* Yonkers, 1983.

Commons, John R. et al. *History of Labour in the United States*. Vol. 2. New York, 1918.

Condon, Thomas. "The Politics of Reform and the New York City Election of 1886." *New York Historical Society Quarterly*, 44 (Fall 1960): 363–93.

Conzen, Kathleen. "Ethnicity as Festive Culture: Nineteenth Century German America on Parade." In *The Invention of Ethnicity*, edited by Werner Sollors. New York, 1989.

———. *Immigrant Milwaukee: Accommodation and Community in a Frontier City*. Cambridge, Mass., 1976.

Cooper, Patricia. *Once a Cigar Maker: Men, Women, and Work Culture in American Cigar Factories, 1900–1919*. Urbana, 1987.

Degler, Carl. "Labor in the Economy and Politics of New York City." Ph.D. Dissertation, Columbia University, 1952.

Doerries, Reinhard. *Iren und Deutsche in der neuen Welt: Akkulturationsprozesse in der amerikanischen Gesellschaft im späten neunzehnten Jahrhundert*. Wiesbaden, 1986.

Dolan, Jay. *The Immigrant Church: New York's Irish and German Catholics*. Baltimore, 1975.

Dubofsky, Melvyn. *When Workers Organize: New York City in the Progressive Era*. Amherst, 1968.

Ehret, George. *Twenty-Five Years of Brewing*. New York, 1891.

Eickhoff, Anton. *In der neuen Heimath*. New York, 1884.

Eley, Geoff, and David Blackbourn. *The Peculiarities of German History*. Cambridge, Eng., 1984.

Engelhard, Ulrich, ed. *Handwerker in der Industrialisierung: Lage, Kultur und Politik vom späten 18. bis ins frühe 20. Jahrhundert*. Stuttgart, 1984.

Ensslen, Klaus, and Heinz Ickstadt. "German Working Class Culture in Chicago: Continuity and Change in the Decade from 1900 to 1910." In *German Workers in Industrial Chicago*, edited by Hartmut Keil and John B. Jentz. DeKalb, Ill., 1983.

Ernst, Robert. *Immigrant Life in New York City, 1825–1863*. New York, 1948.

Faires, Nora. "Occupational Patterns of German Americans in Nineteenth Century Cities." In *German Workers in Industrial Chicago*, edited by Hartmut Keil and John B. Jentz. DeKalb, Ill., 1983.

Faust, Albert B. *The German Element in the United States*. Vol. 1. New York, 1904.

Foner, Eric. "Class, Ethnicity and Radicalism in the Gilded Age: The Land League and Irish America." *Marxist Perspectives*, 1 (Summer 1978): 6–45.

Foner, Philip. *The Great Labor Uprising of 1877*. New York, 1977.

———. *History of the Labor Movement in the United States*. 2 vols. New York, 1947, 1955.

Foner, Philip, and Brewster Chamberlin, eds. *Friedrich A. Sorge's Labor Movement in the United States*. Westport, Conn., 1977.

Frisch, Walter. *Die Organisationsbestrebungen der Arbeiter in der deutschen Tabakindustrie*. Leipzig, 1904.

Garlock, Jonathan, ed. *A Guide to the Local Assemblies of the Knights of Labor*. Westport, Conn., 1982.

Gompers, Samuel. *Seventy Years of Life and Labor.* Vol. 1. New York, 1925.

Gordon, Michael. "The Labor Boycott in New York City." *Labor History,* 16 (Summer, 1975): 184–229.

Goren, Arthur. *New York Jews and the Quest for Community: The Kehillah Experiment, 1908–1922.* New York, 1970.

Gosnell, Howard. *Boss Platt and His New York Machine: A Study of the Political Leadership of Thomas C. Platt, Theodore Roosevelt and Others.* Chicago, 1924.

Gronemann, Carol. "She Works as a Man, She Earns as a Child." In *Class, Sex and the Woman Worker,* edited by Bruce Laurie and Milton Cantor. Westport, Conn., 1977.

Gutman, Herbert. "The Tompkins Square Riot in New York City on January 13, 1874: A Reexamination of Its Causes and Its Aftermath." *Labor History,* 6 (1965): 44–83.

Hamerow, Theodore. *Restoration, Revolution, Reaction: Economics and Politics in Germany, 1815–1871.* Princeton, 1958.

Hammack, David. *Power and Society: Greater New York at the Turn of the Century.* New York, 1982.

Hardtwig, Wolfgang. "Strukturmerkmale und Entwicklungstendenzen des Vereinswesens in Deutschland 1789–1848." *Historische Zeitschrift,* n.s., supp. 9:11–50. Munich, 1984.

Heiss, Christine. "German Radicals in Industrial America: The Lehr and Wehrverein in Gilded Age Chicago." In *German Workers in Industrial Chicago,* edited by Hartmut Keil and John B. Jentz. DeKalb, Ill., 1983.

Heyde, Ludwig. *Die volkswirtschaftliche Bedeutung der technischen Entwicklung in der Zigarren und Zigarettenindustrie.* Stuttgart, 1910.

Hippel, Wolfgang von. *Auswanderung aus Südwestdeutschland: Studien zur Württembergischen Auswanderung und Auswanderungspolitik im 18. und 19. Jahrhundert.* Stuttgart, 1984.

Hirschfeld, Paul. *Die freien Gewerkschaften in Deutschland—ihre Verbreitung und Entwicklung, 1896–1906.* Jena, 1908.

Hitz, Harald, and Hugo Huber. *Geschichte der Österreichischen Tabakregie, 1784–1935.* Vienna, 1975.

Hoerder, Dirk, Renate Kiesewetter, and Thomas Weber, eds. *Glimpses of the German-American Radical Press.* Bremen, 1985.

Huber, Ernst Rudolf. *Deutsche Verfassungsgeschichte seit 1789.* Vols. 3 and 4. Stuttgart, 1969.

Hueber, Alfons. "Vereinsrecht im Deutschland des 19. Jahrhunderts." *Historische Zeitschrift,* n.s., supp. 9:113–33. Munich, 1984.

Hurwitz, Howard. *Theodore Roosevelt and Labor in New York State, 1880–1900.* New York, 1943.

International Union of United Brewery Flour, Cereal, Soft Drink, and Distillery Workers of America. *Seventy-Five Years of a Great Union.* Cinncinati, n.d.

Jacobstein, Meyer. *The Tobacco Industry in the United States.* New York, 1907.

Jaffe, Erich. "Hausindustrie und Fabrikbetrieb in der Deutschen Zigarrenfabrikation." *Hausindustrie und Heimarbeit in Deutschland und Österreich.* Schriften des Vereins für Sozialpolitik, no. 86, vol. 3. Leipzig, 1899.

Jentz, John B. "Bread and Labor: Chicago's German Bakers Organize." *Chicago History*, 12 (Summer 1983): 24–35.

———. "Skilled Workers and Industrialization." In *German Workers in Industrial Chicago*, edited by Hartmut Keil and John B. Jentz. DeKalb, Ill., 1983.

Kamphoefner, Walter. *The Westfalians: From Germany to Missouri*. Princeton, 1987.

Kaufhold, Karl Heinrich. "Grundzüge des handwerklichen Lebensstandards in Deutschland im 19. Jahrhundert." In *Arbeiter im Industrialisierungsprozess, Herkunft, Lag, Verhalten*, edited by Werner Conze and Ulrich Engelhard. Stuttgart, 1979.

Kaufman, Stuart. *Samuel Gompers and the Origins of the American Federation of Labor*. Westport, Conn., 1974.

———. *A Vision of Unity: A History of the Bakery and Confectionery Workers International Union*. Kensington, Md., 1986.

Kaufman, Stuart et al., eds. *The Samuel Gompers Papers*. Vols. 1–3. Urbana, 1985, 1987, 1989.

Keil, Hartmut. "Einwandererviertel und Amerikanische Gesellschaft." *Archiv für Sozialgeschichte*, 24 (1984): 47–89.

———. "German Working Class Radicalism from the 1870s to World War I." In *Struggle a Hard Battle: Essays on Working Class Immigrants*, edited by Dirk Hoerder. DeKalb, Ill., 1986.

———, ed. *German Workers' Culture in the United States, 1850 to 1920*. Washington, D.C., 1988.

Keil, Hartmut, and Heinz Ickstadt. "Elemente einer deutschen Arbeiterkultur in Chicago zwischen 1880 und 1890." *Geschichte und Gesellschaft*, 5, no. 1 (1979): 103–24.

Keil, Hartmut, and John B. Jentz, eds. *German Workers in Chicago: A Documentary History of Working-Class Culture from 1850 to World War I*. Urbana, 1988.

———. *German Workers in Industrial Chicago, 1850–1910: A Comparative Perspective*. DeKalb, Ill., 1983.

Kens, Paul. *Judicial Power and Reform Politics: The Anatomy of Lochner vs. New York*. Lawrence, Kans., 1990.

Kocka, Jürgen. *Lohnarbeit und Klassenbildung: Arbeit und Arbeiterbewegung in Deutschland, 1815–1875*. Berlin, 1983.

Kolb, Alfred. *Als Arbeiter in Amerika: unter Deutsch-Amerikanischen Großstadt Proletariern*. Berlin, 1904.

Köllmann, Wolfgang, and Peter Marschalck. "German Emigration to the United States." Translated by Thomas C. Childers, in *Perspectives in American History*, vol. 7. Boston, 1973.

Kyrk, Hazel. *The American Baking Industry, 1849–1923*. Stanford, 1929.

Langewiesche, Dieter. "Vereins und Parteienbildung, 1848/49." *Historische Zeitschrift*, n.s., supp. 9:51–53. Munich, 1984.

Laslett, J. M. H. "Marxist Socialism and the Brewery Workers of the Midwest." In J. M. H. Laslett, *Labor and the Left*. New York, 1972.

Lemke, Theodor. *Geschichte des Deutschthums in New York*. New York, 1890.

Leubuscher, Frederick. *William Frederick Havemeyer: A Political Biography*. New York, 1965.

Levine, Bruce. "Immigrants, Class and Politics: German-American Working People and the Fight against Slavery." In *The German Forty-Eighters in the United States*, edited by Charlotte Brancaforte. New York, 1989.

———. "In the Heat of Two Revolutions: The Forging of German-American Radicalism." In *Struggle a Hard Battle: Essays on Working Class Immigrants*, edited by Dirk Hoerder. DeKalb, Ill., 1986.

———. *The Spirit of 1848: German Immigrants, Labor Conflict, and the Coming of the Civil War*. Urbana, 1992.

Lidke, Vernon. *Alternative Culture: Socialist Labor in Imperial Germany*. Oxford, 1985.

Mandel, Bernard. *Samuel Gompers: A Biography*. Yellow Springs, Ohio, 1963.

McNeill, George. *The Labor Movement, the Problem of Today*. Boston, 1888.

Meyborg, Bernhard. *Geschichte des plattdütschen Volksfest-Vereen von New York und Umgegend nebst Adressbuch*. New York, 1892.

Moore, Louise Borland. *Wage Earners Budgets*. New York, 1907.

Mosenthal, Hermann. *Geschichte des Vereins deutscher Liederkranz von New York*. New York, 1897.

Moses, John A. *Trade Unionism in Germany from Bismarck to Hitler*. Vol. 1. Totowa, N.J., 1986.

Naber, Franziska. "Die wirtschaftlichen und sozialen Verhältnisse der Zigarrenarbeiter im Amtsbezirk Wiesloch." Ph.D. Dissertation, University of Heidelberg, 1943.

Nadel, Stanley. *Little Germany: Ethnicity, Religion, and Class in New York City, 1845–80*. Urbana, 1990.

Nipperdey, Thomas. *Deutsche Geschichte, 1800–1866*. Munich, 1983.

———. "Verein als soziale Struktur im späten 18. und frühen 19. Jahrhundert." In *Geschichtswissenschaft und Vereinswesen im 19. Jahrhundert*, edited by Hartmut Boockman et al. Göttingen, 1972.

Pope, Jesse. *The Clothing Industry in New York*. Columbia, Mo., 1906.

Post, Louis F., and Frederick Leubuscher. *An Account of the George-Hewitt Campaign in the New York Municipal Election of 1886*. New York, 1887.

Quint, Howard. *The Forging of American Socialism*. New York, 1953.

Ratzel, Friedrich. *Sketches of Urban and Cultural Life in North America*. Edited and translated by Stuart Stehlin. New Brunswick, 1988.

Riis, Jacob. *How the Other Half Lives*. New York, 1903.

Rock, Howard B. "The Perils of Laissez-Faire: The Aftermath of the New York Bakers Strike of 1801." *Labor History*, 17 (1976): 372–87.

Salem, Frederick. *Beer, Its History and Its Economic Value as a National Beverage*. New York, 1880.

Schlueter, Hermann. *Die Anfänge der deutschen Arbeiterbewegung in Amerika*. Stuttgart, 1907.

———. *The Brewery Industry and the Brewery Workers Movement in America*. Cincinnati, 1910.

Schmölders, Günter. *Die Brauindustrie in den Vereinigten Staaten von der Kolonialzeit bis zur Gegenwart*. Berlin, 1932.

Schneider, Dorothee. "'For Whom Are All the Good Things in Life?' German-

American Housewives Discuss Their Budgets." In *German Workers in Industrial Chicago,* edited by Hartmut Keil and John B. Jentz. DeKalb, Ill., 1983.

———. "Gewerkschaft und Gemeinschaft: drei deutsche Gewerkschaften in New York City, 1870–1900." Ph.D. Dissertation, University of Munich, 1983.

Schwarz, Johann. *Das Handwerk der Bäcker in München.* Munich, 1899.

Sedaitis, Helmut. *Liberalismus und Handwerk in Südwestdeutschland.* Stuttgart, 1979.

Shea, John Gilmary. *The Catholic Churches of New York City.* New York, 1878.

Shefter, Martin. "The Electoral Foundations of the Political Machine." In *The History of American Electoral Behavior,* edited by Joel Silbey, Allan Bogue, and William Flanigan. Princeton, 1978.

Smith, John Talbot. *The Catholic Church in New York.* Vol. 1. New York, 1909.

Spann, Edward. *The New Metropolis: New York City, 1840–1857.* New York, 1980.

Speek, Alexander. "The Single Tax and the Labor Movement." *Bulletin of the University of Wisconsin,* 8, no. 3 (1917).

Steinway, Theodore E. *People and Pianos: A Century of Service to Music.* New York, 1953.

Stott, Richard. *Workers in the Metropolis: Class, Ethnicity and Youth in Antebellum New York City.* Ithaca, 1990.

Struve, Emil. *Die Entwicklung des bayerischen Braugewerbes im 19. Jahrhundert.* Leipzig, 1893.

Tenfelde, Klaus. "Die Entfaltung des Vereinswesens während der industriellen Revolution in Deutschland." *Historische Zeitschrift,* n.s., supp. 9:56–111. Munich, 1984.

———. "Vereinskultur im Ruhrgebiet." *Duisburger Forschungen,* 33 (1985): 22–33.

Tornow, Ingo. *Das Münchner Vereinswesen in der ersten Hälfte des 19. Jahrhunderts.* Schriftenreihe des Stadtarchivs München. Heft 75. Munich, 1977.

Troeltsch, Walter, and Paul Hirschfeld. *Die deutschen sozialdemokratischen Gewerkschaften.* Berlin, 1905.

United States Brewers Association. *One Hundred Years of Brewing, A Supplement to the Western Brewer.* Chicago, 1903.

———. *Souvenir of the 25th Convention of the United States Brewers Association,* held at New York City. New York, 1885.

Veiller, Lawrence. "A Statistical Study of New York's Tenement Houses." In Lawrence Veiller and Robert DeForest, *The Tenement House Problem.* Vol. 1. New York, 1910.

———. "Tenement House Rentals." In Lawrence Veiller and Robert DeForest, *The Tenement House Problem.* Vol. 2. New York, 1910.

Verband der Brauerei und Mühlenarbeiter und verwandter Berufsgenossen. *Geschichte der Brauereiarbeiterbewegung,* edited by Eduard Backert. Berlin, 1916.

Walker, Mack. *Germany and the Emigration, 1816–1885.* Cambridge, Mass., 1964.

Ware, Norman. *The Labour Movement in the United States, 1860–1920: A Study in Democracy.* New York, 1929.

Wehler, Hans Ulrich. *Deutsche Gesellschaftsgeschichte.* Vol. 2. Munich, 1988.

Wenner, George U. *The Lutherans of New York, 1648–1918.* New York, 1918.

Wernet, Karl Friedrich. *Wettbewerbs- und Absatzverhältnisse des Handwerks in historischer Sicht.* Vol. 1. Berlin, 1967.

Westfall, Glenn. "Don Vincente Ybor y Martínez, the Man and His Empire." Ph.D. Dissertation, University of Florida, 1978.

Wilentz, Sean. *Chants Democratic: New York City and the Rise of the American Working Class, 1789–1850.* New York, 1984.

Witteler, H. *Das Deutsche Zigarrengewerbe—Entwicklungen, Bedingungen und Tendenzen.* Stuttgart, 1932.

Wittke, Carl. *Refugees of Revolution: The German Forty Eighters in America.* Philadelphia, 1952.

Wolle, Friedrich. *Siebenhundert Jahre Bäckerhandwerk zu Erfurt.* Erfurt, 1928.

Yellowitz, Irvin. *Labor and the Progressive Movement in New York State, 1897–1916.* Ithaca, 1965.

Zimmermann, August. "Die Tabakindustrie—unter besonderer Berücksichtigung badischen Materials." In *Über den Standort der Industrien,* pt. 2, vol. 8, edited by Alfred Weber. Tübingen, 1931.

Zucker, A. E., ed. *The Forty-Eighters: Refugees of the German Revolution of 1848.* New York, 1950.

Index

Books in the Series The Working Class in American History

Solidarity and Fragmentation: Working People and Class
Consciousness in Detroit, 1875-1900
Richard Oestreicher

Counter Cultures: Saleswomen, Managers, and Customers
in American Department Stores, 1890-1940
Susan Porter Benson

The New England Working Class and the New Labor History
Edited by Herbert G. Gutman and Donald H. Bell

Labor Leaders in America
Edited by Melvyn Dubofsky and Warren Van Tine

Barons of Labor: The San Francisco Building Trades and
Union Power in the Progressive Era
Michael Kazin

Gender at Work: The Dynamics of Job Segregation by Sex
during World War II
Ruth Milkman

Once a Cigar Maker: Men, Women, and Work Culture
in American Cigar Factories, 1900-1919
Patricia A. Cooper

A Generation of Boomers: The Pattern of Railroad Labor
Conflict in Nineteenth-Century America
Shelton Stromquist

Work and Community in the Jungle: Chicago's Packinghouse
Workers, 1894-1922
James R. Barrett

Workers, Managers, and Welfare Capitalism: The Shoeworkers
and Tanners of Endicott Johnson, 1890-1950
Gerald Zahavi

Men, Women, and Work: Class, Gender, and Protest in the
New England Shoe Industry, 1780-1910
Mary Blewett

Workers on the Waterfront: Seamen, Longshoremen,
and Unionism in the 1930s
Bruce Nelson

German Workers in Chicago: A Documentary History of Working-Class
Culture from 1850 to World War I
Edited by Hartmut Keil and John B. Jentz

On the Line: Essays in the History of Auto Work
Edited by Nelson Lichtenstein and Stephen Meyer III

Upheaval in the Quiet Zone: A History of Hospital
Workers' Union, Local 1199
Leon Fink and Brian Greenberg

Labor's Flaming Youth: Telephone Operators and
Worker Militancy, 1878-1923
Stephen H. Norwood

Another Civil War: Labor, Capital, and the State
in the Anthracite Regions of Pennsylvania, 1840-68
Grace Palladino

Coal, Class, and Color: Blacks in Southern West Virginia, 1915-32
Joe William Trotter, Jr.

For Democracy, Workers, and God: Labor Song-Poems
and Labor Protest, 1865-95
Clark D. Halker

Dishing It Out: Waitresses and Their Unions in the Twentieth Century
Dorothy Sue Cobble

The Spirit of 1848: German Immigrants, Labor Conflict,
and the Coming of the Civil War
Bruce Levine

Working Women of Collar City: Gender, Class, and Community
in Troy, 1864-86
Carole Turbin

Southern Labor and Black Civil Rights: Organizing Memphis Workers
Michael K. Honey

Radicals of the Worst Sort: Laboring Women
in Lawrence, Massachusetts, 1860-1912
Ardis Cameron

Producers, Proletarians, and Politicians: Workers and Party Politics
in Evansville and New Albany, Indiana, 1850-87
Lawrence M. Lipin

Trade Unions and Community: The German Working Class
in New York City, 1870-1900
Dorothee Schneider